FRIENDS
&
RIVALS

Also by Giles Radice

Socialism in the Recession (with Lisanne Radice)
Labour's Path to Power: The New Revisionism
Offshore: Britain and the European Idea
'Southern Discomfort' (Fabian Pamphlet series)
The New Germans
What Needs to Change (ed.)

FRIENDS
&
RIVALS

Giles Radice

run your life with pace and let your character shine through!

Giles

LITTLE, BROWN

A *Little, Brown* Book

First published in Great Britain in 2002
by Little, Brown
Reprinted 2003

A CIP catalogue record for this book
is available from the British Library.

ISBN 0 316 85547 2

Typeset in Goudy by M Rules
Printed and bound in Great Britain
by Clays Ltd, St Ives plc

Little, Brown
An imprint of
Time Warner Books UK
Brettenham House
Lancaster Place
London WC2E 7EN

www.TimeWarnerBooks.co.uk

Contents

For Lisanne

Acknowledgements

The idea of writing a comparative biography of Tony Crosland, Roy Jenkins and Denis Healey first came to me during a conversation with Brian Lapping in the summer of 1996. He suggested that a book on Labour intellectuals, including Crossman and Crosland, would be interesting. I replied that I would prefer to write about the three big politicians who had most influenced my political life, Crosland, Jenkins and Healey. I was not able to start the work until the winter of 1998 and I finished it early in 2002.

I would like to thank Brian Lapping, Lord Lipsey, Lisanne Radice and Lord Roper for commenting on drafts of the book. I am grateful to Denis Healey and Roy Jenkins for answering my questions so patiently. Susan Crosland kindly agreed to a lengthy interview about her husband: I also talked to both Edna Healey and Dame Jennifer Jenkins, who was very helpful.

I was fortunate to be able to interview a number of people; these included Michael Barnes, Lord Barnett, Tony Benn, Hugh Brace, Lord Callaghan, the late William Camp, Lord Croham, Gavyn Davies, Olga Davenport, the late Edmund Dell, the late Donald Dewar, Lord Hattersley, Sir Edward Heath, Richard Heller, Sir Nicholas Henderson, John Horam MP, Lord Jones, Gerald Kaufman MP, William Keegan, Maurice Kogan, Alan Lee Williams, Dick Leonard, Lord Lester, Ian Little, Bryan Magee, David Marquand, Lord Maclennan, Sir Michael

Palliser, Sir Hayden Phillips, the late Sir Leo Pliatzky, Christopher Price, Lord Rodgers of Quarry Bank, Madron Seligman, Alan Watkins, Phillip Whitehead, and Baroness Williams of Crosby.

I am grateful to Andrew Blick for his research work at the Public Record Office and his help in checking sources. The House of Commons and the House of Lords libraries were as efficient as always. I should also like to thank Alan Samson, Catherine Hill and Linda Silverman of Little, Brown for their help, as well as Sue Martin for her index. Once again, I owe a debt of gratitude to Denyse Morrell for her invaluable work on the word processor and for her sympathy, patience and good humour.

Finally, I should add that I take sole responsibility for the opinions expressed in this book.

Introduction

Crosland, Jenkins and Healey were my political heroes. Tony Crosland's book *The Future of Socialism* helped shape my approach to politics. I was attracted by his intellectual glamour, by the insouciance with which he sported his brightly coloured braces, and his romantic attachment to Grimsby, the east-coast fishing port that he represented in Parliament. Roy Jenkins had an aristocratic drawl and an inability to pronounce his 'r's but he was the best parliamentary speaker of his generation, able to sway the Commons by a combination of skilfully deployed argument and Celtic passion. I was captivated by his charm, admired his elegant style and was impressed by his political courage and his European commitment. With his bushy eyebrows and florid complexion, Denis Healey was earthier than either Jenkins or Crosland and had a reputation for being a bit of a bruiser. But he possessed an enormous zest for life and one of the finest brains in British public life, which enabled him to master the complexities of defence and economic policy. I campaigned and voted for Jenkins in the 1976 leadership election and acted as a campaign manager for Healey in both his unsuccessful 1980 leadership election and his narrowly victorious 1981 deputy leadership election.

The three men were Oxford contemporaries. They shared the experience of war, became Labour MPs within four years of each other, and were all supporters of Hugh Gaitskell, the Labour leader from 1955 to

1963. When Labour came to power in 1964 under Harold Wilson, their careers took off.

In conventional terms, they were all highly successful politicians. In Harold Wilson's first government, Crosland was an innovative Education Secretary. He later became President of the Board of Trade, Secretary of State at the Department of Environment, and, in 1976, Foreign Secretary. He died in office in February 1977. Healey was a notable Defence Secretary from 1964–70, long-serving Chancellor of the Exchequer from 1974–79, and Deputy Leader of the Labour Party from 1980–83. Jenkins is rightly praised as Home Secretary from 1965–67 (he was also Home Secretary again from 1974–76); he was a successful Chancellor of the Exchequer from 1967–70, Deputy Leader of the Labour Party from 1970–72, the first British President of the European Commission from 1977–81 and then, in an extraordinary reincarnation, Leader of the Social Democratic Party (SDP) from 1982–83. All three, especially Jenkins and Healey, were talked about as likely leaders of the Labour Party and potential Prime Ministers.

They were not, however, merely conventional ministers. They were among the most intellectually able politicians since the war. All got Firsts at Oxford. Crosland was Labour's leading revisionist intellectual, whose *Future of Socialism*, published in 1956, influenced a whole political generation. For a professional politician, Jenkins' literary output was phenomenal. His biographies of Dilke and Asquith remain standard works, while his later lives of Gladstone and Churchill have quickly become bestsellers. As International Secretary of the Labour Party from 1945–52, Healey probably knew as much about foreign affairs as anybody in the United Kingdom. In the 1950s and '60s, he made himself the foremost defence intellectual in the country. He has written movingly about his delight in music, art, poetry and photography, and his autobiography was widely praised. The three had what Edna Healey, Denis's wife, called 'hinterland'.

They were 'larger than life' characters. Healey described Crosland as being a very 'dashing' army officer during the war and, after his death, as 'the most attractive character in the cabinet'.[1] Jenkins called him 'the most exciting friend of my life'.[2] Especially before he married his second wife, Susan, Tony could also be sensationally rude and arrogant to both sexes, ruining a party by his behaviour.

Jenkins said about Healey 'he has long carried light ideological baggage on a heavy gun carriage'.[3] Both Crosland and Jenkins complained about Healey's 'one-upmanship'. It is true that Healey is an inveterate name dropper, though he had almost always met or read the book of the person whose name he is dropping.

Healey said that Jenkins' performance as a minister was 'bloody good',[4] but argued that Jenkins saw politics 'as the interplay of personalities seeking preferment' and 'always wanted to be top'.[5] Roy had the capacity to inspire his colleagues and friends and was, by far, the best House of Commons performer of the three. He can, however, be somewhat grand in manner, one of nature's Whigs. Healey described him as having 'the sleek pomposity of Mr Podsnap'.[6]

They liked the good things of life. Jenkins was celebrated for preferring fine claret: 'Let's leave the vintages to Roy,' Crosland is supposed to have said. But Tony drank wine, whisky and brandy, while Denis liked large gin and tonics, claret and brandy. All three could and did dominate a room; and one almost invariably felt better for seeing or listening to them. In their different ways, all three were 'life enhancers'.

In another crucial sense, they were more than conventional politicians. After the death of their mentor, Hugh Gaitskell, they became the leading revisionists of the Labour Party, the 'modernisers' of the 1960s. They believed that Labour had to break with its old nationalising tradition, adopt a less class-ridden approach, and revise its policies in line with changing conditions. Crosland was the theoretician, whose writings tried to show how a modified capitalism could be combined with a commitment to greater equality; as Education Secretary, he was the main architect of comprehensive education. Jenkins was the liberalising Home Secretary and the leader of the Labour 'Europeans' who believed that Labour's destiny lay in Europe. Healey was the reforming Defence Secretary, who did much to develop a rational defence policy suitable for a medium-sized power and, in the 1970s, was the first Labour Chancellor to steer the British economy in the world of global markets.

Yet, despite the eminence of these men and the distinguished contribution which they made both to the Labour Party and to politics more generally, somehow their combined overall achievement was less than might have been expected. Though Jenkins and Healey came close, none of the three became either leader of the party or Prime

Minister: Roy Jenkins believed he had the intellectual capacity to be Prime Minister, though Crosland was cleverer and Healey more of a political operator.[7] And though they remained committed to their revisionist social democratic approach, by the beginning of the 1980s the Labour Party seemed out of touch and left behind, too dominated by the unions and too extremist for the voters. The creation of the breakaway Social Democratic Party, the absurdities of the Foot leadership, and Labour's catastrophic defeat in 1983 were, to a considerable extent, marks of the failure of Labour's revisionists.

It would be wrong to attribute all the blame to them. There were other factors which made it difficult for a modernising Labour leader to be successful in the 1960s and '70s, including a strong left, powerful trade unions and credible 'consensus' leaders from the centre of the party, like Wilson and Callaghan, better able to unite the warring party factions.

However, rivalry between these three big politicians clearly played a part in the failure of revisionism, as Jenkins and Healey both admitted. Speaking about Crosland, Jenkins said, 'Had he and I been able to work together as smoothly as did Gaitskell and Jay or Gaitskell and Gordon Walker a decade before it might have made a decisive difference to the balance of power within the Labour Party and hence to the politics of the early 1980s.'[8] Healey wrote about Jenkins: 'With hindsight, I regret that, though we often worked closely together, an element of mutual jealousy prevented us from co-operating more effectively.'[9]

I learnt at first hand of the destructive nature of their political rivalry during the 1976 leadership election, following Harold Wilson's resignation as Prime Minister. It was reasonably clear that, given the balance of forces inside the Parliamentary Labour Party (the body which then chose the leader), Wilson's successor would come from the centre right. The key issue of the first ballot was, therefore, which candidate from this side of the party would take on the main candidate of the left, Michael Foot, in the second or third ballot. Everybody knew that Jim Callaghan, the Foreign Secretary and Harold Wilson's favourite to succeed him, would put his hat in the ring. The question for the revisionists was whether someone else from the centre right, someone, in our view, more imaginative, cleverer and more inspiring could beat him (though Callaghan proved a good Prime Minister).

It was certain that Roy Jenkins, the Home Secretary and former Chancellor who had resigned from the deputy leadership over the referendum and the European issue four years before, would stand. However Denis Healey, the Chancellor of the Exchequer, and Tony Crosland, the Environment Secretary, also decided to run. Even I, a rookie Labour MP, could see that, with the three most prominent standard bearers of the revisionist tendency inside the Labour Party competing for the same pool of voters, none of them had a hope of winning.

Though I was soon deeply immersed in the election campaign, I could not help, perhaps naïvely, wondering, as I was approached by emissaries from the rival camps, how it had come about that the three men, who, at least on paper, still had much in common, could not get together and sort things between them. I also noted that the combined Jenkins-Healey-Crosland first-round vote added up to nineteen more than Callaghan's total. It was my 1976 experience which prompted me to write to Gordon Brown to congratulate him when, in the 1994 leadership election, he had the good sense to stand down in favour of Tony Blair.

This book is, above all, a comparative biography of three of the most brilliant and charismatic British politicians of the last half century and of the times in which they lived. It is also a study of the ups and downs of their mutual rivalry and the damaging effect which it had both on their own careers and the fate of the Labour Party – and so of Britain – in the 1970s and early '80s. It is a remarkable, often exhilarating story, though, at times, a depressing and even tragic one.

1

Provenance

Healey, Crosland and Jenkins were born in a three-year span between 1917 and 1920; Denis Winston Healey, at Mottingham in Kent, on 30 August 1917; Charles Anthony Raven Crosland, at St Leonards-on-Sea in Sussex, on 29 August 1918; and Roy Harris Jenkins, at Abersychan in Monmouthshire, on 11 November 1920.

They grew up into a world in which many of the certainties and landmarks of the early twentieth century had been destroyed by the Great War of 1914–18. The empires of Austria–Hungary and of the Ottomans had collapsed, but the new settlement for central and eastern Europe and the Balkans, agreed at Versailles and based mainly on national self-determination, was precarious. Germany had been defeated by the two Western European powers, Britain and France, but only with help from the other side of the Atlantic. For the moment Germany was down but most Germans did not accept that Versailles was a just agreement; the Russian Revolution had created great uncertainty on Europe's eastern borders; while the United States Congress quickly disowned the Treaty of Versailles and US membership of the League of Nations, even though both had only been achieved thanks to the inspiration of the American President, Woodrow Wilson. Post-First World War Europe was politically, economically and socially unstable.

In this uncertain world, Britain, one of the victor powers, still ruled over an empire which covered a quarter of the globe. But British imperial rule was already being challenged, especially in India. At home, instead of the land fit for heroes promised by the British war leader, Lloyd George, at the Khaki election of 1918, the twenties and early thirties saw economic stagnation, persistently high unemployment and chronic labour unrest, culminating in the General Strike of 1926. Although the Conservatives dominated the politics of the interwar period, the Labour Party formed its first minority government in 1924 and its second in 1929; but the failure of the MacDonald administration to deal with unemployment and its collapse in 1931 dashed the hopes of Labour supporters.

In divided interwar Britain where class remained so important, the Crosland household was highest up the social scale. Tony's father, J. B. Crosland, was a senior civil servant who concluded his career as number two at the War Office, while Tony's mother, Jessie, was a Raven, an intellectually distinguished family, in which, unusually for Victorian England, daughters as well as sons were educated. Jessie had been a lecturer at Westfield College and wrote extensively on French medieval literature.

The Croslands were comfortably off. They lived first in a semi-detached Golders Green house with a big garden (including a tennis court) and, in 1929, when Tony was eleven, they moved to a larger house, 46 Sheldon Avenue, Highgate, an even leafier suburb. They employed nannies and three servants, including a cook, and took family holidays in the Isle of Wight or in the Highlands. Tony, the apple of his parents' eyes, contracted tuberculosis when he was four and was sent to a Swiss sanatorium where he recovered and learnt to speak French. When he was eleven he went to Highgate, first to the junior school, then, as a senior Foundation scholar and weekly boarder, to the senior establishment, a minor public school whose reputation had been enhanced by its formidable headmaster Dr J. A. C. Johnston.

But the Croslands were by no means a conventional professional middle-class family. What was unusual about Tony's parents was that both sides of the family had been, for several generations, members of the Plymouth Brethren, a rigidly non-conformist Protestant sect. The distinctive feature of the religious approach of the Brethren was their rejection of formal organisation or priesthood and their puritan lifestyle. J. B. Crosland and Jessie Raven had met through the

Exclusive Brethren, the most restrictive branch of the sect, and Tony
was strictly brought up in their austere and narrow faith. What that
meant is well described in Susan Crosland's biography of her husband.

> The Exclusive Brethren had a creed but it was difficult for an
> outsider to gather what it was. They didn't have rules. There
> were pressures, things one didn't do – these shibboleths. They
> didn't do that, they did do this. They didn't go to the opera;
> they did go to concerts. They had some way of making the two
> consistent when they weren't. Ritual was shunned. Pleasure for
> its own sake was eschewed. Love for another human being
> must not overwhelm, total surrender to the physical and
> natural beauties of life could shut out the spirit. When a
> beloved died, grief was curtailed. One should rejoice that the
> creature wrenched away was now with Jesus.[1]

Sundays were taken up with prayer meetings and religious instruc-
tion. The reading of newspapers was forbidden, as was the eating of
ice-cream. Between meetings, members of the Exclusive Brethren
were invited to tea at Sheldon Avenue and Tony helped hand round
bread and butter. After 8 p.m., there was some relaxation and Tony
was allowed to come downstairs in his dressing-gown. Even during the
rest of the week, the restrictions continued. The Croslands did not go
to the theatre, or ballet. No radio was allowed in the house. Drink in
moderation was permitted but no smoking.

As Tony grew into his teens, he began to question the tenets of his
parents. J. B. Crosland was a Liberal and discussed politics at home
with his wife, his two daughters, and Tony. Yet the Brethren were not
allowed to vote. 'What's the point in discussing politics if you then
don't vote?' Tony asked his elder sister. At Highgate, Tony was a bit of
a rebel, on occasions leading others astray, according to his friend, Alan
Neale. He was beaten by his housemaster. He wanted to join the
Officers' Training Corps at Highgate. But his father, even though he was
at the War Office, forbade it. Tony loyally accepted his father's decision
but not the pacifism behind it. Though he continued to accompany his
parents to Sunday meetings, he was drifting away; instead of partici-
pating, he sat in the back of the hall with other older boys.

His father's early death at sixty in 1935 when Tony was seventeen was a devastating personal blow. J. B. Crosland was tall and immaculately dressed, and had been a crucial figure in the 1921 settlement conference for the Middle East. For egalitarian and Exclusive Brethren reasons he had turned down a knighthood. He had been the dominating figure in the Crosland household.

The loss of his father, however, helped shape Tony Crosland's life-long commitment to left-of-centre politics and ideas. A year earlier, when he was sixteen he had already joined the Labour Party, then in the wilderness. His loyalty to Labour was strengthened by a visit to South Wales where he met unemployed miners. Now, alone in his room, he devoured the monthly volumes of the Left Book Club (founded by Victor Gollancz with a political stance close to the Communist Party) and listened to the radio that he had smuggled into the house, to his mother's fury. Tony had agreed, following his father's death, to become a day pupil in order to be with his mother, but he overrode her protests about the radio.

At Highgate, he was an outstanding pupil, becoming a confident performer in the sixth form debating society and winning the school mile in style, as well as writing some provocative essays for his teachers. One of these was entitled 'Bread for the Masses, Cake for the Few', while in another he wrote, 'We may be certain that it is the duty of each of us to be eccentric in thought, and not to conform weakly to the ideas of age, class and country. Non-conformity must be regarded as a virtue, as a proof of a bold and independent spirit.'[2] In 1937, he won, at the second attempt, an open scholarship in classics to his father's old college, Trinity College, Oxford.

The good-looking nineteen-year-old, who went to Oxford in the autumn term of 1937, was already, to a considerable extent, his own person. He had broken away from his parents' strongly held religious beliefs and their politics. But the egalitarianism and independence of the Brethren, the work ethic and involvement in public affairs of his father, and the concern for scholarship of his mother, were all to be important ingredients in his make-up. His upbringing had also given him a sense of reserve, the feeling of being apart, which came from once having been a member of the Brethren. Despite his own and others' (especially his second wife, Susan's) best efforts, Tony Crosland was never completely able to escape it.

*

Denis Healey was born into a different world. His father's father was a Yorkshire tailor who had emigrated from Enniskillen in Northern Ireland and lived in a two-roomed terraced house in Todmorden. His mother's father was a signalman and stationmaster at Newham on Severn in Gloucestershire.

Denis's father, Will, was one of four able sons. Through evening classes, Will Healey won an engineering scholarship to Leeds University, no mean achievement; and then, after five hard years' apprenticeship as a fitter and turner, qualified as an engineer. His first job was in Gloucester where at the outbreak of the First World War he met Denis's mother, Winnie, an intelligent and beautiful young school-teacher, at the local tennis club. After Will proposed, Winnie showed her strength of character by insisting, to the horror of her mother, that the couple go away to the Isle of Man for a trial period. The trial was a success. They married and then moved to Woolwich, where Will got a job at the Arsenal.

Denis's earliest memories were of the temporary housing estate put up to house Woolwich Arsenal workers during the war. The houses were made of creosoted weatherboard outside and distempered asbestos inside. Denis looked back with fondness to 'the hollyhocks by the fence, a tiny square of lawn where I could sit at a wooden table and draw with coloured chalks, and a forest of artichokes where I hunted tigers with my friend Robin'.[3]

In 1922, when Denis was five, his father left Woolwich and was appointed Principal of Keighley Technical School at the respectable salary of £600 a year. The Healeys moved to Yorkshire, first to a nineteenth-century terraced house at 11 Holker Street in Keighley and then, when Denis was eight, to a semi-detached house, Kirkside, 49 Granby Street in the village of Riddlesden on the outskirts of Keighley. This was at the edge of Ilkley Moor, which, at weekends, the Healeys loved to explore. Later when Denis was given a bicycle, he went further afield, discovering, to his lasting delight, the Yorkshire Dales, especially Airedale and Wharfedale, which he described as his 'land of lost content'.

The driving force in Denis's early life was his mother. Denis's father, who worked most nights at the Technical College, saw little of his son who found him distracted and bad tempered. It was his mother who supervised his homework, encouraged him to read widely and fostered his growing interest in the arts. She had a thirst for learning (every year she took Workers' Educational Association classes in literature and current affairs) and was determined that her clever son should make the most of Bradford Grammar School to which Denis had won a scholarship in 1925 when he was eight.

Bradford Grammar School had a high academic reputation and its brightest pupils were expected to win scholarships (mainly in classics) to Oxford or Cambridge, and then join the civil service. Denis was good at Latin and Greek but even better at English, in which he was always top of the class. By his teens, he was reading voraciously; at the age of thirteen he devoured twenty-four books in one term. He read G. K. Chesterton, the Brontës (who had lived at Haworth, not far from Denis's home) and the great Russian novelists – Dostoyevsky, Tolstoy and Turgenev. When he was sixteen and in the sixth form, he was taught English and current affairs by a young teacher who at Cambridge had recently studied under F. R. Leavis. He introduced Denis not only to the new criticism of the Leavisites but also to the new wave of writers and poets – D. H. Lawrence, E. M. Forster, Virginia Woolf, W. B. Yeats, W. H. Auden, Stephen Spender, Louis MacNeice and Cecil Day-Lewis. Healey's (and his mother's) special favourite was Virginia Woolf; he won a school prize for an essay on her novel *To the Lighthouse*. Although he had friends at school, the young Healey was already something of a loner, who was happy to spend much of his time reading books.

As well as the delights of literature, Denis also acquired a passion for painting, music, film and the theatre. He spent his pocket money on postcards of Monet and Van Gogh from the church bookshop; he went to every performance of the Hallé Orchestra's subscription concerts at Bradford's St George's Hall; and he was so inspired by seeing Eisenstein's *The General Line* at Bradford Theatre's Film Club that as soon as he got home, he wrote out a complete 'scenario' of it. In contrast to the Croslands, the Healeys had only one seaside holiday during the whole of Denis's childhood. However, every year the family accompanied Denis's father to London where he attended the annual Principals' conference. They would spend the mornings in museums and galleries, and go in the afternoon and evening to the theatre (a pleasure forbidden to Tony Crosland).

On one memorable weekend, Denis saw Lunt and Fontanne in

Reunion in Vienna, Noël Coward and Yvonne Printemps in *Conversation Piece*, Edmund Gween in *Laburnum Grove*, Elizabeth Bergner in *Escape Me Never*, Charles Laughton and Flora Robson in *Macbeth* and Angela Baddeley in *Richard of Bordeaux*. His characteristically sweeping claim to have seen on these expeditions to London 'all the leading actors of the thirties' is no exaggeration.[4]

Until he went to Oxford, Denis Healey was not much interested in politics. As a nine-year-old, he noticed the General Strike mainly because he had to cycle to school and because the most popular master, who had been an officer during the war, defended the strikers. Later, he made a speech in the school debating society against Nazism, though he also resigned from the Officers' Training Corps on the pacifist grounds which Tony Crosland so resolutely opposed. At nineteen Denis won an exhibition in classics at Balliol College, Oxford in 1936 (he had chosen Balliol rather than Queen's because of its high intellectual reputation). He was clearly very bright with exceptionally wide interests and self-confidence for his age but it seemed far more likely that he would end up as an English lecturer or art historian, or even a civil servant, than become a politician.

In some ways, Roy Jenkins had the most secure and protected upbringing of the three. Unlike Tony and Denis, he was an only child. This is not to imply that the Croslands or the Healeys neglected their children. On the contrary, Tony, who had two sisters (one older, the other younger than him), was, until adolescence, very close to his family, while Denis was the elder of the two Healey boys and very much his mother's pride and joy. But as an only child (an earlier son was stillborn), Roy was the focus of attention of both parents who, from Roy Jenkins' own account, seem to have been exceptionally attentive and caring.

Roy's father, Arthur, was a Welsh miner who had a distinguished public career. He became a Monmouthshire county councillor in 1919 and a Welsh Miners' Federation official in 1921; he served during the 1920s as a member of the National Executive Committee of the Labour Party; and he was elected Member of Parliament for Pontypool in 1935. In 1937 he was appointed parliamentary private secretary to Clement Attlee, the Leader of the Labour Party. He was thus a considerable local and, to some extent, national politician. Unlike his son, he was not very ambitious but he was a man of enormous charm, with the rare ability to light up a room with the strength of his personality. Edward Heath described how he used to take Roy's undergraduate friends out to lunch at Oxford, while he became very much a mentor for Roy's friend Tony Crosland.[5] When Arthur Jenkins died in 1946, the streets were lined with mourners for most of the three quarters of a mile from the Jenkins' house to St James' Church in the centre of Pontypool. For Roy, he was 'an almost perfect father, devoted, mind awakening and enjoyable to be with'.[6]

Roy's mother, Hattie, also became a public figure in her own right. She was the daughter of the manager of the local Bessemer steel works and thus came from a background several steps up the valley's social hierarchy from that of her husband. But her mother's early death and, twelve years later, that of her father, forced her to fend for herself from the age of seventeen until she married Arthur in 1911. In the 1930s she also became an active local personality both as an MP's wife and as chairman of the local magistrates court and of Pontypool Girls School. Hugh Brace, Roy's schoolboy friend, said that she had great style. He remembered a striking black cape, which she often used to wear.[7]

According to Leo Abse, one of Arthur Jenkins' successors as MP for Pontypool, Hattie Jenkins was a snobbish woman who had an unfortunate influence on her son.[8] Roy Jenkins, however, made a strong defence of his mother in his autobiography. He accepted that most of her close friends were wives of the local professional middle class – the doctors, dentists, schoolteachers, and bank managers of Pontypool – but pointed out how that fitted in with his parents' way of life as he grew up, especially after Arthur became MP in 1935. He argued that, if his own taste for 'grandees of a liberal outlook' owed anything to his parents, it came from his father who felt as much at ease meeting the local gentry (provided that they were public-spirited) as he did those from his own background.[9]

Roy was born in a polychrome brick, six-roomed terrace house just outside Abersychan, a few miles up the valley from Pontypool, on Armistice Day in 1920. In 1925, the Jenkins moved to a slightly bigger house nearby which had a sizeable back garden, running down to the railway embankment. Here Roy had a swing on which he spent many hours working out measurements of time and distance in his head, a practice which he continued throughout his life. He always knew exactly how far it was and how long it took from one place to another, as well as the precise details of relevant railway timetables.

When Roy was six, during the six months' miners' lockout which continued after the 1926 General Strike, Roy's father was convicted of illicit assembly and sentenced to nine months' imprisonment at Monmouth assizes. Arthur Jenkins, who had certainly been involved in organising a mass picket and also in speaking to it, always maintained that his role had been a pacifying one and that the police had been unjustified in launching a baton charge against the pickets. However, despite the support as character witness at the trial of a former Conservative chairman of the County Council, Arthur was sent to jail. Widespread protest followed. The leader of the South Wales coalowners wrote a letter, praising Jenkins' moderation and fairmindedness, to Thomas Jones, Deputy Cabinet Secretary, and Jenkins was released after only three months as an act of executive clemency by the acting Home Secretary, Lord Birkenhead. The harshness with which he had been treated and his dignified bearing during the trial won him respect across the political spectrum. When the Labour MP for Pontypool retired from Parliament in 1935, it was inevitable that Arthur Jenkins should be his successor.

For years, his father's imprisonment was kept secret from Roy, to his subsequent regret. When Arthur Jenkins was put in jail, Roy and his mother were taken to Newport to stay with a well-off Labour county councillor. Roy was told that his father was in Germany inspecting mines. He only found out when he was twelve and then from chance remarks from others.

Soon after Arthur Jenkins was released, he was, in fact, sent to Germany by the Liberal newspaper *The Daily News*. Roy and his mother went to London to see him off. It was on this occasion that, when his father expressed uncertainty how to get from Russell Square to the Zoo, Roy said 'Easy, Daddy. Take a taxi' – hardly the typical reply of a boy from the Welsh valleys. But the point was that Roy was not a typical boy from the Welsh valleys but a kind of local prince. His father was a trade union official and a well-known and highly respected county councillor, who was clearly destined to become an MP. Both parents had lofty ambitions for their only child.

At eight, Roy was third on the scholarship list for admission to a secondary or grammar school. Perhaps unfortunately, he went to the nearest school at Abersychan rather than the more prestigious West Monmouth School. Here, he was an adequate rather than an outstanding student. Unlike Tony Crosland and Denis Healey, he was never a serious candidate for an Oxford scholarship. However, his father, who had himself been a student at Ruskin College from 1908 to 1909 and loved Oxford, was determined that Roy should go there. After Roy had managed only moderate Higher Certificate results in 1937, Arthur Jenkins removed him from Abersychan and sent him for six months to University College, Cardiff. More to the point, he paid for Roy to be privately tutored by a young female assistant lecturer, Dorothy Marshall, in how to write Oxford-style essays. This tuition was probably crucial in securing Roy's entry to Balliol, then the only Oxford men's college with a competitive entry for commoners. It may also have helped lay the foundations for Jenkins' celebrated prose style and a highly successful literary career, though his friend, Hugh Brace, noted his ability at school to express himself both verbally and on paper.

Roy's education was, in any case, more than just academic. The Jenkins family seldom took seaside holidays. Travelling more extensively than either the Croslands or Healeys, Roy and his mother accompanied Arthur Jenkins on his journeys as a trade union official and Labour notable round Wales, as well as going further afield to conferences in Oxford or London or to the Labour and TUC annual conferences, often in Arthur's small car which he had bought in 1929. In 1929, Roy also went abroad for the first time, accompanying his father to a Socialist International meeting in Brussels.

When Arthur Jenkins became Labour MP for Pontypool in 1935, the Jenkins moved to a substantial white house, Greenlands, at the edge of Pontypool, where they loved entertaining guests. When such prominent Labour figures as Clement Attlee, Herbert Morrison, Hugh Dalton and Ellen Wilkinson came to South Wales, they stayed with Arthur Jenkins. Roy was especially impressed by Dick Crossman, then an iconoclastic young Oxford don. From the age of fifteen onwards, instead of going to the theatre like Denis Healey or reading in his study like Tony Crosland, Roy came to London and became a House of Commons 'groupie', listening to innumerable debates and hearing speeches by the leading politicians of the time – Lloyd George,

Baldwin, MacDonald, Austen and Neville Chamberlain, Simon, Samuel, Lansbury and Maxton.

Like Tony Crosland and, to some extent, Denis Healey, Roy's development inevitably took him away from his original social background. In Roy's case (like Denis Healey's but unlike Tony Crosland's), it was with the enthusiastic support of his parents who wanted their son to have the chances which had been denied them. And it was Roy, with all the contacts which flowed from his father being a prominent MP, who seemed the most likely of the three to become a politician. However, Oxford and war were to politicise all of them.

2

Oxford on the Eve

The Oxford generation on the eve of the Second World War has been described by Denis Healey as 'perhaps the most political generation in Oxford's history'. He also observed that their politics 'was overwhelmingly of the left'.[1] In the summer term of 1939, out of an undergraduate population of under four-and-a-half thousand, a third were members of the Labour Club.

This interest and involvement in politics, especially left-wing politics, was hardly surprising. The international situation was menacing. Winston Churchill called these years 'the gathering storm'. In October 1935, Italy's Fascist dictator, Benito Mussolini, had invaded Abyssinia, a member of the League of Nations. Yet the half-hearted response of the League – the partial imposition of sanctions – not only failed to stop Mussolini; it undermined the League of Nations and belief in collective security. Then the next year in Spain, General Franco led a right-wing uprising against the democratically elected Republican government; the tragic and bloody civil war which followed, with Germany and Italy on the side of the insurgents and, a little later, the Soviet Union on the side of the government, caught the imagination of the left who deplored the 'non-intervention' policy of Britain and France.

By far the greatest threat to the peace of Europe, however, was from Adolf Hitler, who had come to power in Germany in 1933. In March

1936, he sent German troops into the demilitarised Rhineland without meeting any resistance from Britain or France; in March 1938 he forced Austria into union with Germany; and, in the summer and autumn of 1938, Hitler threatened Czechoslovakia. The Chamberlain government in Britain and weak French administrations tried to appease Hitler. The British Labour Opposition was all for collective security but without being willing wholeheartedly to support rearmament.

For many on the left, only the Communists seemed to be prepared to offer serious resistance to Hitler, and their advocacy of a 'popular front' against him appeared, at least superficially, to provide a means of uniting the forces of resistance. Left-wing intellectuals, ignoring or brushing aside the extermination of the Kulaks, Stalin's purges, and the Moscow show trials, also believed that state central planning could provide a more effective economic system than a crisis-torn capitalism which, in the 1930s, had led to the great Depression and mass unemployment across the industrialised world. In 1935 the Webbs published their *Soviet Communism: a New Civilisation?*; in the second edition, published in 1937, they removed the question mark from the title.

In the summers before they went up to Oxford, Healey, Crosland and Jenkins each visited the continent. These and subsequent European trips just before the start of the Second World War formed an important part of their education. In 1936, between leaving Bradford Grammar School and going to Balliol, Denis Healey cycled across a large slice of northern Europe to see Reinhardt's production of Goethe's *Faust* at the Salzburg Festival. The whole holiday, including the boat fare across the North Sea, cost him only £5.

In Germany, Healey visited art galleries in Frankfurt and Munich and his diary devoted more pages to art than politics. But, with his ear for languages, he was able to talk to people of his own age whom he met on the road or in youth hostels. Most enthusiastically supported Hitler. Ominously, he saw collection boxes for the Luftwaffe in the shape of wooden bombs in every village square. In the summer of 1937, Tony Crosland also went to Germany to see the castles of the Black Forest; he drove there in a second-hand MG, a gift from his mother, which he called the Red Menace. Like Healey, he became convinced by his trip that war was imminent.

In 1938 Roy Jenkins took a holiday in France before going up to

Balliol. He went with his father to Paris and then stayed on alone for a month in a pension off the Boulevard de Port Royal on the Left Bank to learn French. His room had a view of the eastern sky, which, during that summer of repeated threats to Czechoslovakia by Hitler, Roy could not help reminding himself was the direction of the German border. He wrote later about his mood in Paris: 'I do not remember feeling apprehensive about the approach of Oxford. What I did feel apprehensive about was the approach of war'.[2]

In the 1930s, very few eighteen-year-olds received a higher education at all.[3] By 1938–39, the total number of undergraduate students was only just over 50,000,[4] a miniscule proportion of the age cohort. Oxford and Cambridge were much smaller than they are now; at the end of the 1930s, Oxford had four-and-a-half thousand undergraduates, a quarter of the number sixty years later. Oxbridge was also overwhelmingly the preserve of males from private schools (the so-called 'public schools'): out of every thousand children at a state elementary school, only four managed to reach a university; less than one in a thousand reached Oxford or Cambridge.[5]

Before the state or county scholarships introduced after the war, the key to getting to Oxford (or Cambridge) was the size of one's parents' or friends' bank balance. Few colleges even had an entrance exam. Provided they passed the modest matriculation qualification and satisfied the college dons in an interview, most young men from public schools who wanted to go to Oxford and could pay for it, got there. Woodrow Wyatt has described how in June 1936 the then Provost of Worcester asked him to write a twenty-minute essay on 'Hyde Park' as an indication of his 'intellectual attainment'. After reading the essay, the Provost looked up and said, 'I think that will do very well. So we'll see you in October.'[6]

Even more than now, Oxford was a collection of colleges; one's Oxford experience depended to a considerable extent on one's college. Denis Healey and Roy Jenkins were fortunate to be at Balliol. Balliol was a meritocracy, where clever young men from different backgrounds learnt from each other as much as from their tutors. Founded in 1292, it owed its modern reputation to Benjamin Jowett, Master from 1870 to 1895, who had seen the college's role as preparing able undergraduates for top-level civil service jobs. A. D. (Sandy) Lindsay,

Master from 1924 to 1949, the first avowedly Socialist head of an Oxford college who had worked for many years for the Working Mens' Education Association, developed the Jowett tradition.

At Balliol, clever ex-grammar school boys like Denis Healey, Roy Jenkins and Edward Heath rubbed shoulders with intelligent old Etonians such as Julian Amery (later a Conservative minister), Maurice Macmillan (also to be a Conservative minister), Nigel Nicolson (son of the writer, Harold Nicolson), Hugh Fraser (son of Lord Lovat), and George Howard (heir to Castle Howard) and socially concerned old Rugbeians like Freddie Temple and Murray Maclehose (later to be Governor of Hong Kong). In addition, there was a significant leavening of Rhodes Scholars from North America, the old Dominions and Germany, as well as students from India and Africa.

When Denis Healey first arrived at Balliol as a scholarship boy from a northern grammar school, he admitted to being uncharacterically nervous. 'The sound of confident public-school voices in the quad sometimes gave me an inferiority complex,' he wrote,[7] and, to begin with, he sought his friends from American, Commonwealth or Scottish undergraduates who were outside the English class system. He soon discovered that his interests in the arts and later politics bridged all barriers. As Edward Heath remarked about the college in the 1930s, 'what little snobbery there was tended to be intellectual rather than social',[8] and, intellectually, Denis Healey, as his fellow undergraduates quickly recognised, more than measured up.

Healey got a Double First in Mods (an exam after five terms which required a thorough knowledge of classical Greek and Latin literature) and in Greats (an exam at the end of the fourth year which concentrated on ancient history and philosophy, and on later philosophers up to Kant). Already intent on acquiring a 'hinterland', he also pursued an awesomely wide range of other intellectual and artistic interests. In his first year, he read sixteenth- and seventeenth-century poetry in the Balliol College library; he wrote essays on T. S. Eliot's *Murder in the Cathedral* and *Burnt Norton*; and he was encouraged to explore Kierkegaard, Berdyaev and Shestov by the Master of Balliol. In addition, he helped set up the New Oxford Art Society. The Art Society held exhibitions of Picasso's current work and of Surrealist paintings and drawings, including Magritte's controversial *Le viol* which had to be covered with a velvet curtain in case it shocked Oxford women.

One of the lecturers attracted to Oxford by the Society was Anthony Blunt who talked to Healey and his friends about Poussin rather than spying. Healey even found time to become, first, Secretary of the Junior Common Room when Heath was president and then, in his turn, President. One of his successors was Roy Jenkins.

Roy came up to Balliol in 1938, two years after Denis Healey. As a son of a well-known Labour MP, he was perhaps more self-confident than Healey had been. He had already acquired an upper-class drawl, and it is said that, in the Balliol Senior Common Room, Jenkins was referred to as 'nature's old Etonian'. Even so, there is little doubt that he, like Healey, benefited from the anti-establishment, meritocratic spirit of Balliol. In the Oxford of the 1930s, even Roy Jenkins might have been out of place at socially prestigious colleges like Christ Church or Magdalen and certainly less stimulated by one of the smaller colleges.

Balliol, which supplied a third of the Oxford Union's inter-war presidents, gave him a fast track at the celebrated debating nursery of so many budding politicians. It was his Balliol colleague, Hugh Fraser, (President of the Union in the summer term of 1939) who ensured that Roy was given a 'paper' speech (fifteen minutes to open a debate) in the spring of 1939. Balliol, the Union, and the Labour Club between them also provided Roy with most of his first circle of friends, many of whom went on to distinguished careers; Ronald McIntosh, the Director General of the National Economic Development Council, Madron Seligman, Tory Member of the European Parliament, Anthony Elliott, a diplomat who was tragically drowned, David Ginsburg, the Labour MP, and Mark Bonham Carter, the Liberal politician, came from Balliol; Leo Pliatzky, the Treasury knight, Peter Benenson, the founder of Amnesty, Nicko Henderson, the distinguished ambassador to both Paris and Washington, and Tony Crosland were from other colleges.

It was at Oxford that Roy discovered that he had a special talent for making and keeping friends. Though he devoted much of the time which could have been spent on academic studies to Oxford politics, Roy Jenkins was already a 'socialiser', greatly enjoying talking, drinking and eating with his close friends. In the holidays, he invited his friends to stay with his parents at Pontypool, visits which everybody, including Roy's parents, enjoyed. It was a tribute to Roy's social self-confidence,

the charisma of his Labour MP father and the charm of his mother
that these visits were so successful. The Jenkins' house at Pontypool
was sufficiently different for upper middle-class boys from London or
the Home Counties to be intrigued; 'it was almost like being taken to
visit a Druse stronghold in the Lebanon',[9] as Roy Jenkins later colour-
fully described it.

Tony came up to Trinity, his father's old college, as a classical scholar
in the autumn term of 1937. Whereas Balliol was clearly the right college for both Roy and Denis, Trinity was not an obvious choice for
Tony, with his growing enthusiasm for left-wing politics and ideas.
Although next door to Balliol, Trinity was very different. Balliol's
architecture was mostly nineteenth and early twentieth century, while
Trinity was mainly eighteenth century. In contrast to Balliol's meritocratic, cosmopolitan ethos, Trinity was public school and 'county',
the college for upper-class 'hearties'. Crosland's Trinity contemporary,
Richard Hillary, later a Battle of Britain ace, wrote in his *The Last
Enemy*, of Trinity undergraduates that 'we were cliquey, extremely
limited in our horizon, quite conscious of the fact and in no way dis-
satisfied with it'.[10] Characteristic Trinity behaviour was, after a good
dinner, to assemble outside Balliol and shout, in a tasteless reference to
Balliol's African and Indian undergraduates, 'bring out your white
man'.

Tony Crosland's response to Trinity was, together with a few chosen
friends, to form his own clique, most of them scholars or from grammar
schools. His second in Mods in 1939 may have been a disappointment
to his tutors: but as far as Tony was concerned it reflected his boredom
with classics rather than a lack of intellectual ability. His first in
politics, philosophy and economics (PPE) after the war showed what
he could do. His real interest was in politics and economics and, in
the summer of 1939, he switched to PPE. One of his closest friends
was Philip Williams, an ex-grammar school student, who was reading
history at Trinity and already knew much about the Labour
Movement. Crosland and Williams discussed political ideas, especially
those of British socialist theoreticians such as John Strachey, G. D. H.
Cole and Douglas Jay. They also studied Marx, who influenced
Crosland greatly. Both Denis Healey and Roy Jenkins later agreed
that, at least until 1940, Tony Crosland regarded the class struggle as

central to politics and described himself as a Marxist, though without joining the Communist Party. Tony himself remembered a decade later how he and others would troop off to the Labour Club 'pausing only to spit through the Trinity gate as we went past. We lived in a world of pamphlets, meetings, marches, demonstrations – and very exhilarating it was. Marxism had the same appeal to young people as Christianity.'[11]

By the time Crosland and Jenkins became friends, Crosland was already a prominent Oxford figure. Intellectually and socially self-assured, he was able to dominate a room or a meeting. With his matinée idol good looks and long camel-hair coat, he also cut a dashing figure, especially when driving his red MG. During his trip to the Black Forest in the summer of 1937, he had had his first brief romance with an American girl. But in his autobiography, Woodrow Wyatt wrote that, at Oxford, his homosexual side was 'in the ascendant', a claim which is confirmed by a number of his contemporaries.[12] Although there were four women's colleges, the University did its best to discourage heterosexual activity. Women were not allowed in men's colleges after six and men were not permitted in some of the women's colleges without a chaperone. Homosexuality at Oxford was described by A. J. P. Taylor as normal;[13] even if that is an exaggeration, Evelyn Waugh's novels demonstrate that for would-be intellectuals homosexuality was fashionable.

Roy Jenkins described, in a memoir written on Crosland's death in 1977, how Tony came to his rooms at Oxford in the autumn of 1939 'probably on some minor point of Labour Club business, and having settled it, remained uncertainly on the threshold, talking, but neither sitting down or departing for nearly two hours. His character was more ambivalent than I had thought, but also more engaging.'[14] Their meeting was the start of a friendship which persisted 'on an intense but fluctuating basis for nearly four decades'. Jenkins later called Crosland 'the most exciting friend of my life'. There is no doubt that their relationship at Oxford was extremely close, as close, according to Denis Healey, as the Heavenly Twins, Castor and Pollux. After their first meeting, Roy saw Tony nearly every day during term time until Crosland left Oxford for the army in the summer of 1940. For almost a year, they were continuously in each other's company, either at the Oxford Union or at the Labour Club, with Tony, on Roy's admission, very much the senior partner. According to contemporaries, Tony Crosland adopted a patronising air towards Roy Jenkins, which Roy seemed prepared to accept.

Roy Jenkins wrote to Tony Crosland, on 22 March 1940, in reply to a letter from Tony complaining that a previous letter from Roy was 'hardly worth reading' and that he (Tony) was now extremely uncertain about coming to Pontypool. Roy replied: 'I should not have thought of writing at that stage had I not been continually terrified by the thought that the great but temperamental Tony, the complex character, the difficult boy, would suddenly erect a facade of sulkiness and for some obscure but significant reason refuse to communicate with me for the rest of the vacation, thereby infusing his whole being with a feeling of intense satisfaction. I should in fact be bitterly disappointed if you did not arrive next week, but you need not feel that you have to carry out the task of amusing me for ten days or so. Finally, I hope that you will not be so foolish as to misunderstand this paragraph. I want you to come very much.'[15]

This letter illustrates the intimacy of their relationship, the subservient role of Jenkins at this stage, and the temperamental strain in Crosland's character. In fact, Crosland's visit to Pontypool in the spring of 1940 was a great success. Tony got on so well with both of Roy's parents that he became a regular visitor even when Roy was not there. Crosland struck up a correspondence with both Hattie and Arthur Jenkins; he seemed to have regarded Arthur as a kind of father figure, certainly someone older to turn to for political advice.

Denis Healey knew Tony and Roy at Oxford but far less well than they knew each other. Denis was two years Roy's senior at Balliol, and Tony was at a different college, though Denis found the offhand brilliance of Crosland, whom he saw at Labour Club meetings, 'most engaging'.[16] Denis differed from the other two in that, in the summer of 1937, he joined the Communist Party (CP).

Until the war, the distinction between Oxford Labourites and Communists was not all that great. Members of the CP had been admitted to the Labour Club since 1935 and many members of the Labour Club, who, like Crosland, did not take the final step of joining the Party, still considered themselves Marxists and fellow travellers and agreed with many of the Party's positions. Denis took his membership of the CP seriously, though his Marxism came more from reading

Left Book Club works than from a study of Marx. He became the 'culture boss' of the Party at Oxford, writing the art criticism for *Oxford Forward* and, in 1939, he was the successful Communist candidate for the chairmanship of the Labour Club. He is remembered by Oxford contemporaries as wearing a belted mackintosh which they thought gave him something of the air of a genuine Russian commissar. According to them, he already possessed much of the confidence in his own views which later was to be so characteristic.

Healey, Crosland and Jenkins all played an active part in the Oxford by-election of 27 October 1938, the apotheosis of pre-war left-wing political Oxford.[17] The by-election, caused by the death of the sitting member for Oxford, became virtually a referendum on the Munich agreement of 30 September, which took the Sudetenland from Czechoslovakia and incorporated it into Hitler's Germany. Most people were relieved that war had been avoided but a significant minority, including many Oxford dons and undergraduates, were appalled by the dismemberment of Czechoslovakia and the feebleness of British foreign policy.

On 10 October, Roy Harrod, the Christ Church economist, wrote to the *Oxford Mail*, appealing to the Labour and Liberal candidates in the forthcoming by-election to stand down in favour of an independent anti-Munich candidate. Two young Labour dons and future Labour Cabinet ministers, Richard Crossman and Frank Pakenham, had already approached their chosen candidate, Sandy Lindsay, Master of Balliol.

Then, on 13 October, Edward Heath, speaking at the Oxford Union, proposed the motion 'that this House disapproves of the policy of Peace without Honour'. Deriding the Munich Agreement as the 'peace which passeth all understanding', he accused Chamberlain of 'turning all four cheeks to Hitler at once'. He was supported by Christopher Mayhew, former President of the Union and an Oxford star who described Chamberlain's policy as being '*reculer pour mieux reculer*'. The motion was carried by 320 votes to 266. Roy Jenkins, who was attending his first debate, voted for Edward Heath's victorious motion. It was clear that there was a head of steam building up across the political spectrum, including some dissident Conservatives like Heath, behind the idea of turning the Oxford by-election into a referendum on Munich.

The problem for the anti-Munich campaigners was how to per-suade the Labour and Liberal candidates to make way for Lindsay. The key figure was the Labour candidate, the Christ Church history don and future Labour Cabinet Minister, Patrick Gordon Walker, who was reluctant to stand down, partly on personal grounds (he had come second in the 1935 general election) but partly because he believed that 'popular fronts' were against the long-term interests of the Labour Party.

The crucial meeting was an informal Labour Party gathering called to prepare for the election. Pro-Lindsay students flooded it and carried a motion by 109 to 30 asking Gordon Walker to stand down. Both Healey and Crosland backed the effort by left-wing and Communist undergraduates to pack the meeting. According to Denis Healey, who was present, many of the participants were Liberals or Communists and some even came from outside Oxford. With some justice, Gordon Walker saw the meeting 'as an attempt to overbear me by a sort of organised hooliganism'.[18]

On 15 October, Gordon Walker was forced to stand down. Healey and Jenkins, together with leading Balliol undergraduates such as Heath and students from other colleges like Crosland, worked for Lindsay against the official Conservative candidate, Quintin Hogg, a fellow of All Souls' and fervent supporter of the Munich Agreement. Roy Jenkins remembered canvassing in the Woodstock Road 'with fallen leaves swirling around the "gabled Gothic houses"'.[19]

Harold Macmillan, then Conservative MP for Stockton, coura-geously came down to support Lindsay and was amused to see the Conservative posters defaced with the words 'Love me, Love my Hogg'.[20] The slogan of Lindsay's supporters was 'Hitler wants Hogg'. Hogg supporters accused Lindsay of having received telegrams of sup-port from Stalin. After a short, tumultuous campaign, which not only stirred the University but also captured national attention, Lindsay reduced a 6645 Tory majority to one of 3434, a swing of 3.9 per cent against the Chamberlain government.

From then onwards the approach of war overshadowed Oxford life. In March 1939 Hitler occupied Prague, showing Chamberlain's appeasement strategy to be a total failure. On 31 March, the British and French governments reversed policy and gave Poland a guarantee against aggression, though there was little directly they could do to keep Hitler out. Throughout the summer, they tried to negotiate an alliance with Russia; the talks broke down on the refusal of the Poles to allow the Red Army on to Polish territory. On 23 August Ribbentrop and Molotov signed the Nazi-Soviet pact, thus clearing the way for Hitler's invasion of Poland on 1 September. On 3 September, Britain and France declared war on Germany.

In the summer of 1939, Denis Healey was given a scholarship from Balliol to visit Greece.[21] Travelling from Brindisi to the Piraeus in the hold of a small steamer, he immediately fell in love with the landscape, art and people, though he was not impressed either by middle-class Athenians whom he found 'corrupt, self-seeking and shallow' or by the inhabitants of the British School of Archaeology, whose company he described as 'a trifle too spicy'. After exploring the islands, he was arrested as a Nazi while taking photographs at Eleusis, opposite the Greek naval base at Salamis; apparently his shorts led some school-boys to think he was German. He was soon released.

Returning home, Denis was working in his bedroom at his Keighley home on Kant's views on the transcendental synthetic unity of appre-ciation when his mother burst into his room, crying, 'Put away your books! War has been declared.'[22] As a Communist, Denis was under Party orders to support the Nazi-Soviet pact, but he immediately vol-unteered for the army. He was accepted for the Royal Artillery, only to be told at the end of November to go back to Oxford to finish his degree.

For the first two weeks of the summer vacation of 1939, Roy Jenkins went on the Balliol Players' tour of southern England, in a production in English of Aristophanes' *Birds*. Roy then went to France, where he was taken on as a courier by the Paris office of the Workers' Travel Association to escort parties of British visitors across the city. He met Denis Healey on his way back from Greece at a Paris railway station; Denis immediately offered him tips on how to get round Paris. Roy, having been there all summer, was irritated by this characteristic piece of one-upmanship. It was an early example of Healey and Jenkins rub-bing each other up the wrong way. In the later half of August, Roy Jenkins went with Ronald McIntosh to stay in a villa near Toulon. But the news about the Nazi-Soviet pact put an abrupt end to their seaside holiday and they hastened back to Britain.

*

For the first few months of the war, nothing much happened – it was the time of the so-called 'phoney war' when Britain and France remained on the defensive, waiting for Germany to attack. Both Denis Healey and Tony Crosland spent another year at Oxford before being called up, while Roy Jenkins stayed on at Balliol until the summer of 1941 and then had to wait until February 1942 before he finally received the summons to join the army.

The war did, however, lead to a significant shift in Oxford left-wing politics, one in which Crosland and Jenkins played a decisive role. The Nazi-Soviet pact had shocked many Communists but, during the last months of 1939, Crosland, still a committed Marxist, continued to defend the Soviet Union, even after the dismemberment of Poland by Hitler and Stalin. During a Union debate in November, he even claimed, in a speech which the *Oxford Magazine* judged to be his best so far, that the Soviet Union had made the pact in self-defence, after the Poles had refused to allow Russian troops on to their soil.

It was the Red Army's invasion of Finland which changed Crosland's mind. Although in January 1940 he helped organise a Labour Club demonstration against a meeting called in favour of aid to Finland under the absurd banner of 'Hands off Russia', he, like Jenkins, was finding the Communist line increasingly implausible. While the Communist faction on the Labour Club executive had been anti-Nazi, it had been relatively easy to coexist. But now that the Communists were claiming that the war against Hitler was 'imperialist' and that the Red Army was fighting to 'liberate' the Finnish people from a reactionary government, it became intolerable. Together with Roy Jenkins, who was Balliol College Labour Club representative, and another executive member, a mature trade union student called Ian Durham, Crosland decided to split the club and form a breakaway organisation, which would both be in favour of the war against Hitler and closely linked to the Labour Party.

Acting with boldness and resolve, the three dissident executive members made their plans during the Easter vacation and immediately on their return to Oxford at the end of April 1940 set up the new organisation, the Democratic Socialist Club, of which Crosland became the first Chairman, Durham the Secretary, and Jenkins the Treasurer. It quickly attracted over four hundred members, many more than the existing Labour Club which now became a shadow of its former self.

Denis Healey, like Iris Murdoch, opposed the split, remaining loyal to the Communist-dominated rump. He came to regret his inaction which, he later wrote, derived 'more from inertia and indifference than from conviction'.[23] He was, he explained, working hard for his Greats examination; he could also have added that the dissident group was led by his juniors who had never been in the Communist Party, while, as an immediate Communist past president of the Labour Club, he had some residual loyalty to those who had supported him. On his own admission, it was not until the fall of France in June 1940 that he finally broke with the Communist Party.

As Denis Healey sat down in June for the first of twenty-four papers in his Greats examination, German motorcyclists entered Abbeville, just across the Channel. It was difficult to concentrate when France was collapsing but Healey showed his staying power by getting his First. After leaving Oxford, he invited Edna Edmunds, a graduate of St Hugh's who was taking a teaching course at Keighley Girls' Grammar School, to stay at his parents' home, and they fell in love. At the end of the summer he was ordered to report to the Royal Artillery Field Training Unit in Uniacke Barracks outside Harrogate, just after his twenty-third birthday.

Tony Crosland, too, left Oxford for the army at the end of the summer of 1940, though without finishing his degree. Walking down Piccadilly at the end of June, with Britain now fighting alone, he noticed two soldiers with a black flash on the back of their tunics. According to Susan Crosland's account, his eagerness to wear the black flash was his sole reason for joining the Royal Welsh Fusiliers, which he did a few weeks later, a month before his twenty-second birthday. He told his mother, however, that he wanted to have a base in the west, as Arthur Jenkins knew many people in the area and 'this might be useful at a later stage',[24] a remark which suggests that Tony was already thinking about the possibility of a political career.

Roy Jenkins, younger than Denis by three years and Tony Crosland by two, stayed at Oxford. The gloomy course of the war did not blunt the keenness of his ambitions. As he frankly remarked in his autobiography, 'I have often been shocked, looking back, to think that I was almost as cast down by defeat for the presidency of the Oxford Union as by the fall of France. And in June 1941 my desire to get a good schools result was not diminished by the German attack on Russia.'[25] The war had, in fact, opened up his Oxford political prospects. In the Easter (Hilary) term of 1940 he had become Secretary of the Union, with Crosland as Treasurer; and in February he was elected Librarian, when Crosland was defeated for the presidency. Although Jenkins was beaten for the presidency of the Union twice in 1940, the first time in the summer narrowly and then in the autumn term more comfortably, at the end of 1940 he succeeded Crosland and Durham as Chairman of the Democratic Socialist Club. Drawing on his father's contacts, he managed to put together an impressive list of speakers to address the club, including Dalton and Attlee. In 1940–41, Jenkins was also elected President of Balliol Junior Common Room.

However, Roy Jenkins' most impressive Oxford achievement was undoubtedly getting a First. He was not a scholar like Crosland nor an exhibitioner like Healey; he had devoted almost all his time to politics or socialising; and although he did his weekly essays for his PPE tutors conscientiously, he had failed to attend a single lecture in his second or third year. One of the reasons for his success lay in his ability to work in a sustained way, eight hours a day seven days a week for nearly three months, in revising for his exams. Another reason was the similarity of approach and subject between his Oxford political life and the current affairs-orientated PPE degree. The officers of the Democratic Socialist Club were accustomed to address group meetings on such questions as 'Why did the Weimar Republic fail?' or 'Can Keynes cure unemployment?'. Roy had also developed a mastery of prose style. During a tutorial, one of his tutors said, 'I am not sure how much you know but you write it in a fine style.'

In Jenkins' view, he learnt more from his fellow undergraduates, especially Crosland, than from his tutors. There was, however, one exception amongst the dons; the Hungarian economist, Thomas Balogh, who had just become a fellow at Balliol, made a qualitative difference to his economics marks (though his most impressive papers were in political history). Balogh was apparently so amazed that Roy had been awarded a First that he had to have a brandy to recover from his surprise. Roy Jenkins attributed his success both in schools and in his other Oxford activities partly to meeting his future wife, Jennifer Morris, daughter of the Town Clerk of Westminster, at a Fabian summer school in August 1940. Falling in love with Jennifer gave him 'a singularly well-timed injection of confidence and optimism', which spilt over into other facets of his life.[26]

Crosland, Healey, and Jenkins got much out of Oxford. If Crosland's degree in Classical Mods was a disappointment, he had the best claim of the three to be called an Oxford 'figure'. Edmund Dell, who was on the Labour Club executive with Crosland, said that he was 'outstanding'.[27] Edna Healey, who was herself a Labour Club member, told Henry and Nancy Kissinger that, of the three, she expected Tony to be the one who would go to the top of politics.[28] He had polished his speaking at the Union; he had played the leading role in setting up the Democratic Socialist Club; and he was already showing the passionate interest in political ideas which was to be such an important facet of his political career. In a remarkably mature and prescient memorandum he wrote in January 1940 on the Labour Party and the war, he was critical of Marxist analysis as being too simplistic and argued that the Labour Party should be a classless party with an appeal transcending its working-class base.[29] The revisionist thinker was beginning to emerge from the Marxist chrysalis.

Oxford was also important for Denis Healey. He had excelled academically. He had been able to pursue his wide artistic and cultural interests, what he later called his 'hinterland'. For a relatively poor undergraduate, he had also been able to travel extensively in Europe. Above all, he had become involved in Oxford politics. Although he deliberately kept away from the Oxford Union, he was the Communist-backed chairman of the Labour Club in the summer of 1939. As an ex-grammar school boy, Denis Healey was apprehensive when he first went up to Oxford. But he left Balliol with considerable confidence in his own views and abilities.

At Oxford, Roy Jenkins was the least flamboyant of the three. His contemporaries describe him as diffident in manner. He was content to play second fiddle to his close friend, the more self-confident Crosland. Yet it was at Oxford that Roy first showed the steel of his ambition. He became Chairman of the Democratic Socialist Club, President of the Balliol Junior Common Room, and was only narrowly defeated for the presidency of the Oxford Union. Above all, against expectations he got a First. He also learnt to think for himself.

Although many members of the Labour Club, including both Healey and Crosland, called themselves Marxists, Roy's heroes were Roosevelt and Keynes. He left Oxford with both an absorbing interest in and growing knowledge of public affairs, as well as a keen ambition to become a Labour Member of Parliament.

3

Wartime

War marked off the generation of Crosland, Healey and Jenkins from the ones which followed. Tony Crosland and Denis Healey both saw active service, mainly in Italy, while Roy Jenkins, after two years of soldiering in the United Kingdom, spent the rest of the war helping to decode German ciphers at Bletchley Park. Healey admitted to having enjoyed his five years in the army: 'It was a life very different from anything I had known or expected. Long periods of boredom were broken by short bursts of excitement.'[1] Crosland was more ambivalent: 'My personality is dual: one wants a VC, the other a quiet cultural life,' he noted in his diary.[2] Jenkins wrote in his autobiography: 'I half enjoyed my two years of field soldiering, even though I fired no shots in anger,'[3] while 'Bletchley exhausted the mind, and to some extent, with the difficulty of adjustment to a frequent change of shift, the body.'[4]

As Healey and Crosland began their basic army training in the late summer of 1940, the battle for national survival was being fought and won in the skies over Britain. In August and September, a mere 2500 young British, Commonwealth, Polish, and Czech pilots preserved Britain from German invasion, thoroughly justifying Churchill's proud words in his 20 August speech to the Commons: 'Never in the field of human conflict was so much owed by so many to so few.'

But, if the Battle of Britain had rendered impossible a German cross-Channel invasion and thus prevented Hitler knocking Britain out of the war (which had seemed quite possible after Dunkirk and the fall of France), the imbalance of land forces between Britain and Germany made a serious British military attack on the mainland of Europe quite out of the question. So, by the end of 1940, there was a strategic stalemate.[5] As Churchill always understood, without Russian support, the Allies could not launch a major assault on the continent; and, without American participation, there would be no second front or Allied victory. And throughout 1940, Russia was Hitler's ally, while the US was neutral. So it looked likely to be several years before new recruits, like Healey and Crosland, would see active service.

After the uncertainties of his last year at Oxford, Denis Healey positively welcomed the regimentation of army life at Uniacke Barracks outside Harrogate. None of the other recruits, mostly drawn from the industrial towns of Yorkshire and Tyneside, talked about politics and few even mentioned the war. In his new enthusiasm for the army, he claimed to be as proud of being asked to lead the physical training class as he had been of getting a Double First. Unfortunately, at a routine medical he was diagnosed as suffering from a rupture and, to his dismay, had to have an immediate operation. His only consolation was being able to read André Malraux's classic novel *La Condition Humaine* in hospital.

After sick leave, he was sent at the end of 1940 to the Artillery depot at Woolwich, near his birthplace, to await a posting. Woolwich was badly damaged by the Luftwaffe's bombing campaign. Most nights, he heard the blare of sirens warning of air raids and the boom of the heavy anti-aircraft guns made the walls of the barracks tremble. Healey was impressed not only by the warm comradeship of his fellow soldiers, many of whom had fought at Dunkirk, but also by their ingenuity in breaking out of barracks at night to see their girlfriends. During the blitz, each night might be one's last.

At the beginning of 1941, Denis was sent to Swindon station as a railway checker. His job was to count service personnel getting on and off trains, an impossible task which he eventually got round by guessing the numbers. He encountered Roy Jenkins there on his way to Pontypool to see his parents. Jenkins remembered receiving friendly advice from Healey on the right time and platform for his train which, like their meeting in Paris before the war, irritated Roy. Occasionally,

Denis spent weekends in the Cotswolds with his girlfriend, Edna Edmunds.

Then, after a few months at Swindon, he attended an Officers' Selection Centre at Scarborough and was commissioned on the General List. He was posted to Derby to learn about Movement Control (the crucial work of organising a modern army's movement of forces by land, sea and air). Healey spent the rest of 1941 and the first half of 1942 as Rail Traffic Officer in Hull, Halifax, York, Leeds and Sheffield, which he found very tedious. He staved off boredom by trying to learn Russian and rummaging for treasures in second-hand bookshops. Finally, in the summer of 1942, he volunteered for combined operations training in Scotland, to learn how to become a Military Landing Officer in a Beach Group, a far more exciting job, though (as the disastrous Allied raid on Dieppe in August 1942 showed) much more hazardous.

To Tony Crosland, the army came as much more of a culture shock. In August 1940, he wrote to Philip Williams from the Royal Welsh Fusiliers' training camp at Northwich in Cheshire:

> Army life is getting more bearable gradually. At first I was too miserable for words and often literally on the verge of tears – the worst thing being the utter loneliness engendered by the impression of Cockneys en masse, loud-voiced, coarse, perpetually swearing, etc. But I gradually discovered that taken singly they are amazingly pleasant and really generous, though very stupid. I am treated very definitely as an intellectual from a different world, which helps matters, and altogether I get along with them far better that I ever thought I could. I am gradually ferreting out the relative intelligentsia of the place and spend the weekend with them. Everybody hates army life, and frankly morale is non-existent.[6]

In contrast to Healey, Crosland found army discipline irksome, especially standing about waiting for the next thing to happen and saluting officers whom he found stupid and class-conscious. He was confined to barracks for seven days for calling a corporal 'Comrade' during the first exercise in handling a Bren gun. However, despite concerns about his left-wing political views, he passed the interview for officer training. At the officer training centre at Barmouth, Crosland enjoyed the luxury of a comfortable bed in a seaside boarding house but he complained to Philip Williams about 'the appalling atmosphere of earnest-mindedness that prevades the place . . . I need hardly say that I do not fit very happily into this Sunday School atmosphere, and I am officially disapproved of . . . I made a thoroughly bad start by omitting to move my pipe from my mouth during a mock bayonet charge'.[7]

Despite his critical attitude to officer training, in the spring of 1942 Tony Crosland was commissioned and sent to the Royal Welsh Fusiliers' depot at Wrexham, where he went on a two-month signals course. Once again, he ran up against authority, this time by challenging the right of the officers' mess to charge the wartime subalterns, who were living in a dingy annex, the same rate as the senior professional officers, who enjoyed the full magnificence of the regimental mess. He was promptly posted on home defence duties with the 10th Battalion on the South Coast.

A more constructive response to the irritation and tedium of army life was Tony Crosland's remarkable correspondence with Philip Williams, which Tony suggested they should keep ('we owe a duty to our biographers'). In these letters, which were sometimes many pages long, Crosland and Williams analysed not only wartime events but also political, social and economic developments.[8] Crosland strongly defended the Labour Party for entering the wartime coalition; in his view, the powerful positions of Ernest Bevin and Herbert Morrison in the government fully justified the party's strategy. His reply to the call of Communists for greater radicalism was to point to the apolitical attitudes of the working-class London and Welsh soldiers whom he met in the army. When Hitler invaded Russia in June 1941, Crosland warned against euphoria on the left. He wrote that many failed to distinguish between the short-term need for an alliance with Russia and the danger of a speedy Red Army victory which would result in Soviet domination of mainland Europe.

As Crosland read more widely, he became more critical of Marxism. In February 1941 he said that he was 'bang in the middle of the steady process of intellectual flux that started when my faith in the Communist Party and 100 per cent Marxism was shattered, and continued when my belief in the Left intellectuals and 85 per cent

Marxism was shattered. Where I shall end Heaven knows – I am still moving.' By the late summer of 1941, Tony was convinced that there was little to learn from Marx and Engels, except for a view of history as a dynamic process revolving around class change. Crosland already saw himself not only as a future parliamentarian but as also a major revisionist theoretician. He confidently and presciently wrote to Williams: 'I am engaged on a great revision of Marxism and will certainly emerge as the modern Bernstein,' a reference to the famous German Social Democrat revisionist thinker at the turn of the century.

By the summer of 1942, Tony Crosland had volunteered for the Royal Welsh Parachute Regiment as part of the newly formed First Airborne Division, which was to be deployed as a front line unit to reinforce the British Eighth Army. John Keegan, the military historian, analysing parachute operations in the Second World War, concluded: 'parachuting to war is essentially a dicing with death, in which the odds are loaded against the soldier who entrusts his life to silk and static line'.[9] Because the casualty rate was known to be so high, soldiers had to volunteer. In a letter to Philip Williams in July 1942, he explained his decision: 'This time a year ago I should have regarded any such prospect with the utmost distaste and repugnance . . . But a second year of army life . . . has changed the ratio of my interests: politics have gone down to just that extent that military affairs have gone up . . . This combination of growing interest in, and self-identification with, the army was psychologically the determining factor, though mixed with many others – vanity, bravado, browned-off-ness with the infantry, a feeling of the utter absurdity of spending three years of one's life in khaki without getting an interesting psychological experience for one's pains . . .'[10] The unhappy rebel of 1940–41 had become the committed volunteer of 1942.

Roy Jenkins was called up by easy stages. After he left Oxford in the summer of 1941, the army authorities ordered him to stay on at the Oxford University Senior Training Corps (which they had already made him join in his third year at Oxford) to pass the undemanding Certificate B. Twice a week, he travelled down from London to Oxford to attend his Training Corps course and see friends at Balliol or the Oxford Union. To keep himself occupied, he got a job at the

American Embassy through his father, which involved analysing the impact of imperial preference (the British Empire's tariff system) on the US economy. It was not until February 1942 that he was summoned to an artillery Officer Cadet Training Unit (OCTU) at Alton Towers in North Staffordshire, a nineteenth-century Gothic extravaganza.

Jenkins found little difficulty in adapting to army life, to having to wear battle-dress at all times, eat from mess-tins, and sleep in stuffy Nissen huts. He described himself 'as an adequate but not distinguished cadet'.[11] After two months, his army duties were mitigated by weekend leaves, which enabled him to escape by the 1.02 p.m. Saturday train from Stafford in time to see Jennifer in Cambridge and get back to camp late on Sunday night. With characteristic precision, Jenkins noted the extraordinary wartime contrasts: 'Exactly an hour away from the bleak Alton parade ground one could be lunching with the pre-war napery and china of the London, Midland and Scottish Railway and watching the three spires of Lichfield Cathedral slip by.'[12]

After passing out at Alton Towers, he was commissioned, and, in the late summer of 1942, joined the 55th Field Regiment, Royal Artillery on the north edge of Salisbury Plain, where the regiment was under canvas and, in the run-up to the Dieppe raid, on full alert. Roy Jenkins later called this interlude, 'the peak of my strictly military career'. However, as so often in wartime, nothing happened, and, at the end of 1942, he was sent to a newly formed artillery regiment, in training at Clevedon near Bristol, where he spent the winter.

Jenkins spend most of 1943 on the South Coast. In the spring his unit was deployed on coastal defence in Sussex, though by this time an invasion was no longer seriously expected. He was transferred, at the beginning of the summer, to another artillery battery, which was formed from the Leicestershire Yeomanry and was on duty at Angmering-on-Sea, also in Sussex. The officers' mess, living up to its hunting background, maintained a grander style (even in wartime) than he had been used to in his previous postings; however, Roy got on reasonably well with his fellow officers, even though he had little in common with most of them. His relationship with his battery commander, who was seeking the Conservative nomination for Dover but was later killed in Italy, was based on wary mutual tolerance; his senior officer was prepared to turn a blind eye to Jenkins' refusal to subject himself to early morning PT, so long as Roy put on his PT kit to enter the bathroom which they shared.

Jenkins was thought well enough of as an officer to be sent as temporary ADC to the general commanding his division for six weeks in September and October. Returning to his battery at Angmering, he fell ill and, after going on leave to Pontypool, was diagnosed as having jaundice. When he came back on duty just before Christmas 1943, he was told that he was required for special intelligence work at the Code and Cipher School at Bletchley Park. He owed this posting to Sandy Lindsay, the Master of Balliol, who, despite Roy's poor marks in his final philosophy papers for which Lindsay had tutored him, correctly surmised, perhaps on the basis of his burst of hard work in getting his First, that he had the necessary powers of concentration to make a competent cryptographer. At the beginning of 1944, Jenkins, who had grown bored with training for something that never happened (though he also admitted that he did not have the urge 'to hurl himself against the enemy'), left Angmering with little regret, for a twelve-week course on codes and ciphers at Bedford as a preliminary to Bletchley Park.

For Healey and Crosland, the new direction in their army careers for which they had both volunteered led, in both cases, to active service in Italy. Denis Healey's training in Scotland as a Military Landing Officer responsible for getting troops, vehicles, guns and armour across beaches, was perfunctory. The only recent British experience of large-scale landings (at Dieppe) had been a disaster. So, in November 1942, Healey was sent to observe the Algerian landings of the British-American 'Operation Torch', following the entry of the US into the war after Pearl Harbor. Then, at last, on the evening of 13 April 1943, Healey's Beach Group embarked in Glasgow for North Africa, to prepare for an invasion of Sicily.

Crosland survived his paratroop training. He wrote to Philip Williams: 'The actual act of jumping is far worse than I expected, and not faintly comparable with anything I have experienced before. Sitting, tense and keyed up, waiting to drop through a hole in the fuselage into empty space, then the awful three seconds plunging helpless through the air before the chute opens – it has taught me at least the true content of phrases which before meant little to me, such as abject terror and cold sweat.'[13]

After initial training in the Derbyshire hills, Crosland spent the winter months of 1942–43 doing further parachute jumps, going for twenty-five-mile-long marches and generally undergoing a process of 'toughening up' on Salisbury Plain, supervised by a commanding officer who was both a fitness freak and a rigid disciplinarian. 'Even the most ferocious Jehovah in his most wrathful moods would have seemed a very ray of cheerful sunshine compared with our new CO,' was Crosland's comment.[14] His life was made more enjoyable by the occasional leave in Oxford where his mother was now living and by falling for an eighteen-year-old girl recently returned from Canada. Then, like Healey, Crosland went to North Africa with his regiment to prepare for the Sicily landings.

North Africa, where German and Italian troops finally surrendered on 13 May 1943, proved to be a frustrating period of waiting for Healey and Crosland. Crosland spent much of the time on exercises, including one designed to see how long troops could exist without water in desert conditions, an experiment hardly applicable to Italy. At the end of this exercise, he deliberately provoked the commanding officer by ordering his men to present arms instead of doing an 'Eyes Right'. As they were carrying anti-tank weapons, the result was a shambles.

Healey was first at divisional headquarters and then on the coast. He found time to paint and write up North African scenes in his diary: 'pink, saffron, black and scarlet flared in the stony fields below a pool of yellow flowers – it was a woman doubled under a load of hay'. Just before the invasion of Sicily, his division was addressed by General Montgomery, fresh from his triumph at El Alamein and the defeat of Axis troops in Tunisia: 'He did not impress us with his sharp, ferret-like face and pale-green eyes, wearing his vanity like a foulard,' wrote Healey critically.[15] For both Healey and Crosland, the waiting ended in something of an anti-climax. Healey landed in Sicily long after the initial successful assault, while Crosland's regiment was in full parachute gear waiting on the runway to take off when they were told that the drop ahead of them had been so successful that their operation was cancelled.

Though bitterly contested, the Italian campaign, with which

Crosland and Healey were to be involved for the next two years, was in reality a side show. By 1943, the main Allied priority was to prepare for an invasion of France, which, especially after the Normandy landings in June 1944, diverted men and resources away from Italy. Fighting in the Italian peninsula was, in any case, bound to be difficult; its length and its mountainous terrain make it ideal for defensive operations. One of the Second World War's most distinguished historians has written about the problems of the Italian campaign from the point of view of the Allies: 'The painters whose landscapes had delighted European collectors had left warnings to any general with a sharp eye of how difficult an advance across the topography they depicted must be to an army, particularly a modern army encumbered with artillery and wheeled and tracked vehicles.'[16] Captain Crosland understood the drawbacks only too well. 'This is a devil-begotten campaign,' he complained in his diary. 'There are innumerable rivers and steep gulleys running at right angles to our advance . . . So tanks are more or less ruled out. The result is the machine gun dominates the campaign and we are back to 1914 . . . What a far cry from the theory of Blitzkreig; and how disheartening it all is.'[17]

The Allies attempted to get round the natural advantages which the Appenines, Italy's central mountain range, gave to the defender, by exploiting their sea and air superiority to turn the enemy's flank. Following the fall of Sicily, the King of Italy had dismissed Mussolini and the new government under Marshal Badoglio opened negotiations with the Allies for an armistice, which was announced on 8 September. The Allies, who had already crossed the Straits of Messina and taken Reggio di Calabria on the toe of Italy, promptly landed at Salerno, just south of Naples. The Germans, who following the armistice had rushed extra divisions into Italy, put up a fierce resistance. Though Allied troops entered Naples on 1 October, the German commander managed to establish a defensive line for the winter across the peninsula.

On three occasions, Denis Healey was ordered to take part in the Salerno landing but each time the order was cancelled. The officer who took his place was killed within hours of reaching the beach at Salerno. Instead, Healey was appointed beachmaster for a subsidiary landing further south, designed to prevent retreating German forces from reinforcing their resistance at Salerno. Just before dawn on 8

September, Healey's landing craft beached at Porto di Santa Venere to find that the assaulting battalion had not yet arrived (it had, in fact, landed on the wrong beach, an hour and a half late) and that the Germans were raining down mortar fire, which continued all day and the next night.

Healey was also dive bombed: 'I felt myself lifted off the ground, there was a tinkling followed by thuds as debris hit the earth again . . . Then WHOOM, WHOOM, WHOOM, WHOOM, WHOOM. I counted the bursts, my muscles taut, found a helmet lying on the ground an inch or two in front and jammed it on my head. Stones and earth showered around and I felt a heavy blow on my right ankle. Then the drone faded. I got up and brushed off the dust. My ankle was numb and not very painful.'[18] Though there were many Allied casualties, Healey escaped serious injury, the minor beachhead was secured, and the Germans retreated. Healey was mentioned in dispatches.

As Healey was being dive bombed and shelled at Porto di Santa Venere, Crosland was landing safely at Taranto harbour on the Adriatic which had been delivered to the Allies by the Italians. However, the ship transporting other members of his regiment hit a floating mine in the harbour and many were drowned, including the commanding officer. Crosland was appointed adjutant and promoted to captain, as the previous adjutant had been injured in the disaster. He wrote in his diary: 'I shall not soon forget the sight and stench of those washed-up bodies, horribly and grotesquely swollen, limbs distorted, flesh decomposing: and the grim business of loading them on the lorries, travelling in the back of the lorry with that macabre load, and burying them in a huge communal pit, trying hard not to be sick.'[19]

In December 1943, Crosland's brigade was ordered up to the front line in the Abruzzi, north of the Sangro river on the eastern side of Italy. He wrote: 'I fear we shall be very cold and very uncomfortable: but I still have a certain exhilaration about a very novel experience.'[20] For the next few days, his regiment's exposed position in a salient was heavily shelled. Casualties included a truck driver, 'my old friend Johnson', who had his head blown 'right off'. Crosland noted in his diary: 'It's not a very pleasant experience, this first taste of shellfire. When I hear the warning whistle, I get a nasty feeling in the pit of my stomach . . . It's an inhuman impersonal sort of warfare, the menace of death that suddenly comes out of the blue and leaves you helpless to hit back.'[21] After watching the Germans repulse a New Zealand assault on their hill position he commented, 'The Germans certainly can fight back and they'll take a lot of beating on this and other fronts.'[22] On 11 December, the Royal Welsh Parachute Regiment was relieved and Tony noted, with guilty relief, the lightening of tension as his troops moved away from the front line.

The next day, Crosland, to his surprise and mortification, was removed by the acting commanding officer, Major Roderick, from his position as adjutant, which he much enjoyed, on the grounds he was insufficiently 'regimental', and made intelligence officer instead. Crosland appealed to the brigadier and asked for a transfer to another battalion. The brigadier, in a judgement of Solomon, persuaded him to wait until the commanding officer came back from leave and meanwhile guaranteed that he would not be demoted in rank. As Tony himself admitted in his diary, he did not bother to hide his disagreement with Roderick's decisions or his opinion of what he considered to be Roderick's excessive caution. In the circumstances, it was not surprising that Roderick wished to replace him.

A few days later, Crosland led his first patrol as intelligence officer, with the task of finding out whether the Germans had evacuated Guardiagrele, a nearby stronghold, south of Pescara. In order to answer the question set to him by the CO, Crosland soon realised that his patrol would have to pass through well-fortified enemy positions. Taking only the Italian-born interpreter with him, he crawled in the dark across deep gulleys and rivers. Dawn found them short of the German lines and near a shallow trench where they spent the day. 'It was not one of the pleasantest days I have spent. Bitterly cold – too cold to sleep. The trench so small that we suffered agonies from cramp. The continuous nervous tension of whether we had been spotted and whether a patrol would scotch us from behind.' When night fell, they climbed up to the road where they came under enemy fire.

Crosland rapidly and sensibly decided that he now had the answer to the question which he had been asked and, after a hazardous journey back, reported to the brigadier who was 'very pleased with our efforts, and very anxious about whether he would ever see us again'.[23] The brigadier took Crosland to see General Freyburg, Commander of the Second New Zealand Division, to tell him about the findings;

Crosland was impressed by Freyburg who asked penetrating questions about his patrol. It may have been Crosland's success on this occasion that led to a recommendation for a Military Cross which was, however, turned down by the War Office.

For the next two months, the Parachute Brigade continued to be used for patrols, establishing a reputation as a 'crack' unit. Crosland himself went on further dangerous patrols and also came under direct shell attack in the front line, sustaining a minor face wound. His understandable pride in his own and his unit's performance did not, however, colour his professional judgement on the failure of Allied troops to break through on the eastern front. 'I think this is going to become the forgotten front. Monty's much boosted Sangro offensive, that was to sweep on to Pescara, has now been completely stuck for a month . . . The right policy is clearly to move all possible troops from this front, which is stuck, to the Rome front, which is potentially mobile.'[24]

Meanwhile on the 'Rome front', Denis Healey, after a period on the staff at Bari and then at Naples, had been appointed Military Landing Officer to the British assault brigade for the Allied landing at Anzio, thirty miles south of Rome. The idea was to turn the Germans' western flank and open up the road to Rome and beyond. Healey was prominently involved in the planning which took place in the fine baroque palace at Caserta, north of Naples. A key issue discussed was how to avoid parachute troops being shot up by their own side, as happened during the Sicily landings. It was decided that the parachutists should be issued with the metal clickers then commonly found in Christmas crackers.

The Anzio landing was a great initial success, achieving complete surprise. On 22 January 1944, a large Allied force (including two American divisions and a big complement of British troops) got ashore safely, even capturing German officers in their pyjamas. Healey, though suffering from a broken tooth sustained in a lorry accident, played his full part. The American commander, General Lucas, however, failed to press home the opening advantage, and the Germans, hastily reinforced, managed to confine Allied forces to the beachhead. It was not until May that the main Allied army, having at last captured Monte Cassino, made contact with the Allied troops in the beachhead.

Healey's later conclusion was that a bolder commander might have entered Rome in the first few days, but he would have soon been repulsed by the Germans. The Allied forces, weakened by troops withdrawn for the Normandy landings, were never strong enough, according to Healey. However, he also pointed out that in order to provide reinforcements, the Germans had to weaken other more important sectors, including the Russian front: 'So Anzio on balance turned out to be a success.'[25]

Healey, with his job completed, left the beachhead after the first three days. His contribution as a key officer involved in both the planning and the execution of a logistically brilliantly successful landing was recognised when he was promoted from acting major to the substantive rank. He was once again mentioned in dispatches.

In August 1944, Tony Crosland took part as a paratrooper in a spectacular airborne landing in the South of France which preceded and was designed to link up with a French-American seaborne invasion between Cannes and Toulon. This was the so-called operation 'Anvil' which was advocated by the Americans as supporting action for the D-Day landings but which, in Churchill's opinion, had little strategic merit. Tony described his hazardous parachute jump in his diary for 30 August.

> The stillness was very eerie, made more so by the cloud which completely hid the coast below us. But I had no time to enjoy the stillness, as almost immediately I found myself oscillating violently towards another chute, and then found to my horror my legs colliding with his rigging lines and got momentarily caught up in them. I managed to kick myself free, but it gave me a moment of absolute panic, a fleeting nightmare of the two of us hurtling down together. A moment later the earth opened up into sight. Spasmodic firing from various directions, but this worried me much less than the terrific speed I was descending at.

Crosland landed badly, hitting his face on his helmet and straining a ligament in his left knee. But, after some more shots and a Tommy gun burst, he was directed by a Frenchman to a nearby village where he found his brigadier and most of brigade headquarters. The operation went almost without a hitch and, on schedule, the paratroopers linked up with Allied armoured cars which had been landed from the sea.

For Crosland, the high point of the campaign was the liberation of Cannes. Tony and a few others made their way in borrowed jeeps into Cannes, where they were met by wildly cheering crowds who thrust champagne into their hands. He commented, 'a night of pure pleasure at liberated Cannes: a fortnight which began as an operation and ended as a holiday on the Riveria'.[26] A fortnight after leaving Rome, he returned with most of his battalion and went on leave in the city.

A memorable feature of Crosland and Healey's Italian campaigns was the opportunity it gave them to visit the country's beautiful cities, taste its culture, and enjoy its landscape. It was a kind of wartime grand tour. Crosland loved Rome and Siena, was initially disappointed with and then captivated by Florence and enthralled by Neapolitan opera, a delight of which his Exclusive Brethren upbringing had previously deprived him. His diary contains lyrical descriptions of Italy – the charms of Ravello, the snow-clad peaks of the Abruzzi and the primroses and nightingales of springtime in the mountains.

Denis Healey also fell in love with opera to which he went with Jack Donaldson, his colonel in Naples and later a friend of Crosland's and Labour Arts Minister: 'For me the revelation was Puccini, whose music-dramas had a special resonance in wartime Italy. "Butterfly" was the story of so many Italian girls under the Allied occupation.'[27] Denis had a Neapolitan girlfriend who greatly improved his command of the language. The following year he was based with the Eighth Army in Siena, from where he explored the beauties of Tuscany, usually accompanied by a young upper-class captain in the First Aid Nursing Yeomanry (FANY), whose first name was Lavinia. On one expedition, they went to Montegufoni, the Italian home of the Sitwells. The best paintings from the Uffizi gallery in Florence had been stored there for the duration of the war and, as the caretaker let them into the drawing room, a shaft of sunlight illuminated Botticelli's *Primavera*. Healey described it as 'the most exciting moment of my life'.[28]

In Robert Harris's thriller *Enigma*, Kite, the Cambridge college porter, is highly censorious of the hero, Tom Jericho, one of the stars of

Bletchley Park, who has burnt himself out breaking German codes: 'It was disgusting, a young man of that age, not wearing uniform, hiding away in the middle of England.'[29] Roy Jenkins wore uniform but that did not protect him from criticism of his home posting. Writing to Philip Williams in February 1944, Tony Crosland, then on the Italian front, poked fun at Roy; hearing, probably from Arthur Jenkins, that Roy had been suffering from jaundice, he unkindly suggested that Roy thought that 'this should entitle him not only to a wound stripe, but also the 1939–44 star and I believe he is making representations to this effect in the highest quarter'.[30] In February, Jenkins had not yet gone to Bletchley as he was still on the preparatory course but neither then nor later would he have been able to explain to Crosland or to anybody else exactly what he was doing there. Bletchley Park was and remained top security; the first book on Ultra, the intelligence source at Bletchley derived from the interception and decryption of enemy machine ciphers (especially Enigma and Fish), was not published until the 1970s.

It is now, however, generally agreed that the British Government Code and Cipher School at Bletchley Park made a considerable contribution to the Allied war effort. Churchill attached the highest importance to Ultra. He always insisted on receiving the latest breakthrough as quickly as possible, asking imperiously 'Where are my eggs?'.[31]

Ultra played a critical role in turning the battle of the Atlantic in favour of the Allies in the spring and early summer of 1943; provided Montgomery with crucial intelligence about Rommel's intentions in North Africa; and helped Alexander in Italy, especially in revealing the German plan to counter-attack the Anzio beachhead. Arguably, Ultra's greatest contribution to the war in the West, however, came during the battle of Normandy, when Bletchley gave Montgomery regular information about the German strength and order of battle, crucially before the landings and then in August when the Germans counter-attacked at Mortain; the latter disclosure greatly assisted the destruction of the German armoured reserve and the encirclement in the Falaise gap of their army of the West by the American General Patton.[32]

Having got through the preparatory course at Bedford, Jenkins was sent to Bletchley Park, an undistinguished Victorian Tudor Gothic mansion in Buckinghamshire, just before the Normandy landings. By the time he arrived, the personnel there represented something like a cross-section of the British intelligensia. Churchill is supposed to have commented: 'I told you to leave no stone unturned in your recruiting. I did not expect you to take me so literally.'[33] There were brilliant Cambridge mathematicians like Alan Turing, Max Newman and Gordon Welchman; chess grandmasters like Harry Golembek, Hugh Alexander and Stuart Milner-Barry; historians like Asa Briggs (later Provost of Worcester and a peer, as well as an usher at Roy Jenkins's wedding) and J. H. Plumb (later Professor of Modern History at Cambridge); and literary figures such as the poet Herbert Read and the novelist Angus Wilson.

Roy Jenkins worked on the German military cipher known as Fish. Fish was different from Enigma in that it transmitted messages based not on Morse but on the impulses of the international five unit teleprinter code, and was thus even more difficult to break. It was also used only for communications between the Berlin High Command and the various commanders in the field, including Rundstedt, Kesselring, Manstein and Rommel, and was, therefore, of the greatest strategic importance to the Allies, especially just before and after the D-Day landings. Two sections were used to decode Fish. The first, Max Newman's section, consisted mainly of high powered mathematicians, assisted by Wrens and the vast machine, which was a forerunner to the modern computer, called Colossus; this section stripped the first layer of disguise from the intercepted messages by the techniques of probability mathematics. The second, Major Tester's section, to which Roy, who was a 'breaker', belonged, had the task of intepreting the still incomprehensible five rows of noughts and crosses into German.

It was exhausting three-shifts work; the night shift was the longest and the bleakest. Jenkins remembered 'quite a few absolutely blank nights, when nothing gave and I went to a dismal breakfast having played with a dozen or more messages and completely failed with all of them. It was the most frustrating mental experience I have ever had, particularly as the act of trying almost physically hurt one's brain, which became distinctly raw if it was not relieved by the catharsis of achievement'. On the other hand, he sometimes struck gold. There was one night in June 1944, at a critical period in the Normandy battle, when Roy made thirteen separate breaks. He thought that it was too good to be true, and grew superstitious towards morning, 'particularly when it became clear what the exact score was to be'. As he was taking the train from Bletchley to London as soon as he came off duty, he was afraid that he might be hit by a flying bomb, 'the unnatural success of the night might be a fine apotheosis before being caught by one'.[34]

In September, Roy, for no obvious reason except perhaps fatigue, went seriously off form and was relegated to the setting room where the code breakers' work was put into final shape. Paradoxically, this demotion coincided with his promotion to captain, which showed how little Bletchley was concerned with rank. However, to his relief, after a couple of months he was allowed back into the 'breakers' elite. Later Roy described what the Bletchley experience meant for him: 'We tried extremely hard, feeling that it was the least that we could do as we sat there in safety while the assault on the European mainland was launched and V-1s and V-2s descended on London. And trying hard meant straining to get the last ounce of convoluted ingenuity out of one's brain . . . It also meant doing everything as quickly as possible . . . a lot of information was of value only if it could be passed on within a day or so.'[35]

Over the winter of 1944–45, the Allied troops in Italy, weakened by the transfer of a quarter of their strength to France in the previous summer, were held up by determined German resistance on the so-called 'Gothic line' between Pisa and Rimini. Healey wrote that men, who had come through the desert and Monte Cassino without breaking, collapsed with the strain and bitter cold of fighting in the mountains. There was deep resentment when Lady Astor, Conservative MP for Plymouth, foolishly described them as 'D-Day Dodgers'. They replied with a song, whose last verse ran.

> If you look around the mountains, in the mud and rain
> You'll find the scattered crosses, some which bear no name.
> Heartbreak and toil and suffering gone,
> The lads beneath them slumber on,
> For they were the D-Day Dodgers – who'll stay in Italy.[36]

In November 1944, Healey was sent to Pesaro, south of Rimini, to plan a landing in northern Yugoslavia to cut off German troops escaping from Italy and also, Healey believed, to forestall the capture by Tito's partisans of Fiume. To his relief, the operation was cancelled, as it was opposed by the United States Chiefs of Staff. Denis spent the last months of the war on the staff of the Fifteenth Army Group in Florence. Tony Crosland was no longer in action either, as he had joined the Sixth Armoured Division at the end of 1944 as an intelligence officer specialising in aerial photographs. He had a week of leave in early March 1945 which he took in Florence. At dinner parties, he met members of the Florentine aristocracy whom he described, with characteristic brio, as 'genuinely cultured and completely bogus'.[37]

However, in April 1945, with Hitler facing catastrophic defeat in Europe on both the eastern and western fronts, the British Eighth Army finally broke through into the Po valley and succeeded in encircling most of the German forces left in northern Italy. The Sixth Armoured Division moved rapidly beyond the Po; Crosland, who was with them, commented in his diary entry of 1 May that it was the first real battle of movement in Italy since 1943. As the Germans surrendered and the war came to an end, Allied forces linked up with Tito's partisans at the Isonzo River and then pushed north into Austria. On 6 May, Denis Healey, in a bold piece of private tourism, took his jeep from the army high command in Florence northwards into Austria and Yugoslavia. Beyond Villach, he and his driver called in at divisional headquarters, where he found Tony Crosland 'slim and handsome in his parachutist's beret'.[38] He also saw hordes of refugees on all the roads, including individual German soldiers who had simply decided to walk home.

In the immediate aftermath of war, the manner in which these refugees, displaced persons, and defeated soldiers were treated was to haunt Tony Crosland for the rest of his life. Over the next four weeks, he witnessed at first hand the handover of literally hundreds of thousands of Croats, Slovenes and Chetniks to Tito and Cossacks, Ukrainians and White Russians to the Soviets.

At first, Eighth Army battalion commanders, without higher instructions, gave their protection to this extraordinary diverse horde, so anxious to surrender to the British. Tony Crosland described an army of Chetniks as 'a sight so medieval, so unusual, so Hollywood almost . . . of the men, many were giant bearded figures, others wore their hair long, so that it fell over their shoulders Elizabethan fashion . . . I had come to look on them as Fascists: whereas these people, or at least all the rank and file, were peasants and worker types, kindly and cheerful and anything but a collection of mercenary thugs.'[39]

Then orders came from the British High Command to give up the prisoners to Tito and the Russians. Crosland noted in his diary on 18 May:

> The problem of the anti-Tito Croats and Slovenes is almost causing a civil war within the British army . . . The armed lot south of the Drava were dealt with thus: our troops all withdrew North of the river, and behind them took out the centre section of the bridge . . . The unarmed lot were shepherded into trains and told they were going to Italy; they crowded on in the best of spirits and were driven off under a British guard to the entrance of a tunnel at the frontier; there the guard left them, and the train drove off into the tunnel.

He wrote to Philip Williams that it was: 'The most nauseating and cold-blooded act of war I have ever taken part in.'[40]

Crosland's diary entry for 29 May is equally shocking:

> I witness today the handing over to the Soviet Army of large numbers of Russian nationals who had been fighting in the ranks of the Wehrmacht . . . This was apparently agreed at Yalta . . . The scene of this particular handover was the bridge at Judenberg which is the frontier between our zone and the Russians. The road down to the bridge was lined for half a mile with armed British soldiers. Across the bridge was the Russian committee of welcome . . . One knew that these Cossacks had committed some of the worst atrocities of the war . . . one forgot all that, and felt nothing but pity . . . it all went off with only a single hitch – one man leapt out of his truck and hurled himself over the parapet . . . One by one the trucks crossed the bridge. The prisoners off-loaded and were marched off by the Russians. The bridge itself was like a paper-chase; when they knew beyond a doubt that it was true, they frantically tore up

and threw away all letters and photographs which might have incriminated fresh victims . . . I could hardly stand the whole scene, and nearly broke down.[41]

So Crosland and Healey's victorious two-year campaign, which had taken them the length of Italy, ended, at least in Crosland's eyes, in shame and dishonour.

The one on whom the war had an obvious, and, in many respects, beneficial impact was Denis Healey. Major Healey had clearly had a 'good war'. He adapted well to army life at all levels. He proved himself under fierce enemy fire at Porto di Santa Venere and as a vital part of a far smoother and more successful landing at Anzio. Army staff training taught him to analyse problems systematically. From combined operations, he learnt the importance of planning and how to improvise when, as so often, planning went awry. He had campaigned the length and breadth of Italy and found out how life was lived by all classes. He later called the army, 'a school in practical reality'.[42]

When Healey left Oxford, it was by no means certain that his future career would be political. He could well have become a university professor. It was the war which pushed Healey towards politics. The reason was partly personal: 'I had learned that I could think well only under stress.'[43] But he also wanted the opportunity to build a better world. And, as the pragmatic realist which he had become as a result of his wartime experience, that could only be through the Labour Party. Fortunately, despite becoming a Communist at Oxford, he also remained a member of the Labour Party which he had joined when he was in the sixth form at Bradford Grammar School.

So, when he was asked by Ivor Thomas, Labour MP for Keighley, to put his name on the candidates' list, he agreed. The Pudsey and Otley Labour Party invited him to their selection conference; he wrote movingly from Italy: 'If you could see the shattered misery that once was Italy, the bleeding countryside and the wrecked villages . . . you would realise more than ever that the defeat of Hitler and Mussolini is not enough by itself to justify destruction, not just of twenty years of fascism, but too often of twenty centuries of Europe. Only a more glorious future can make up for this annihilation of the past.'[44] On the basis of this eloquent letter, Denis was chosen as the Pudsey and Otley Labour candidate for the coming election.

Tony Crosland's wartime career was more mixed than Denis Healey's. Captain Crosland certainly proved himself a highly coura-geous and effective front-line officer in one of the army's 'crack' units, as well as a talented divisional intelligence specialist. But his ten-dency to question authority, so essential for intellectual inquiry, brought him into conflict with less able senior officers, notably with Major Roderick in the Abruzzi. More naturally reflective than Healey, Crosland's fascinating war diary reveals how much he was affected by the horrors of war. His lengthy correspondence with Philip Williams also shows that his wartime experience had consolidated a move away from Marxism, which had already begun at Oxford; many of the ideas which were to form the basis of *The Future of Socialism* appear in a pre-liminary form in their letters.

During the war, Tony Crosland, who at Oxford was already attracted to the idea of a political career, became firmly committed. He had much going for him. He was on the candidates' list, the party leader, Clement Attlee (whom he had met with Arthur Jenkins), had spoken well of him, and around a dozen constituency parties had invited him to selection conferences. However, three quarters of these invitations arrived in Italy only after the date set for selection (the let-ters had been sent by sea mail) and the remainder with only a day or two to go. Another problem was that he was not due any home leave. Roy Jenkins commiserated with him in a letter of 28 November 1944, describing his (Roy's) defeat by Major Woodrow Wyatt in the Aston selection conference: 'Wyatt won largely through being a major at twenty-six and having a better record than had I. God knows, though, it was modest enough compared with yours . . . I was also irritated (I do expect you will believe this) by the thought that you could have ful-filled all their demands about three times as well as Wyatt and would almost certainly have got the constituency had you been able to appear before the selection conference.'[45]

On the face of it, Roy Jenkins was least changed by the war. Unlike Denis and Tony, he had never come under enemy fire or been involved in an active service operation. His wartime experience prob-ably added little to his already strong ambition to get into the House of Commons, except to make him even more determined to get there as quickly as possible. After being beaten by Woodrow Wyatt at Aston, he failed by only one vote to win the Sparkbrook selection conference, and in April 1944 he beat Eddie Shackleton, later a Labour leader of the House of Lords, for the Solihull nomination.

However, even in Roy's case, the war left its mark. His gift for getting on with people of different views and backgrounds was fully utilised on regimental duties, while his ability to focus his powers of concentration on the task in front him, first demonstrated at Oxford, was further developed by his demanding work at Bletchley. Above all, like Healey and Crosland and many other young officers, he was determined to play his part in helping create out of the destruction of war a better Britain and a better world.

4

Into Parliament

In a parliamentary system, the first goal of a budding politician is to become a Member of Parliament. The Parliament of 1945–50, with its radical programme of legislation including the setting up of the National Health Service, the creation of the Welfare State, and the nationalisation of the major utilities, was an exceptionally exciting one of which to be a member, though only Jenkins of the three succeeded in being elected to it.

Both Roy Jenkins and Denis Healey fought the landslide election of 1945 as Labour candidates but, as they contested rock solid Conservative seats, they were defeated, in Healey's case quite narrowly. Later, Roy Jenkins won the Southwark by-election of April 1948 for Labour. Tony Crosland, who went back to Trinity, Oxford, after the war, first as a student and then as a don, was returned to Parliament as MP for South Gloucestershire at the General Election of 1950, which Labour just won. Denis Healey (who established a formidable reputation as International Secretary of the Labour Party) did not become an MP until after Labour had been turned out of office.

As the war came to an end, the coalition began to break up. Of the Labour big three – Attlee, Bevin and Morrison – Attlee, Deputy Prime Minister, and Ernest Bevin, Minister of Labour, would have preferred

Labour to remain in the coalition until victory had been achieved over Japan. However, Herbert Morrison, chairman of the Policy Committee of the NEC as well as Home Secretary, was closer to party opinion and spoke strongly and successfully for an immediate break at the crucial meeting of the NEC held during the Blackpool party conference of 18–20 May 1945.

Major Denis Healey and Captain Roy Jenkins were among a number of glamorous young men in uniform who attended that party conference as prospective candidates. Denis made a dramatic speech in which there was more than a trace of his Marxist past. He declared that 'the upper classes in every country are selfish, depraved, dissolute and decadent. The struggle for Socialism in Europe has been hard, cruel, merciless and bloody . . . Remember that one of the prices paid for our survival during the last five years has been the death by bombardment of countless thousands of innocent European men and women.' When he returned to his seat, his neighbour, George Thomas, later Speaker of the House of Commons, in a characteristically waspish aside, said to him, 'Denis, you have the most wonderful gift of vituperation.'[1] It was this conference speech which brought him to the attention of Hugh Dalton, Philip Noel-Baker and Harold Laski, three influential members of the NEC from different wings of the party, who all suggested that Healey apply for the job of International Secretary, confident that he would be defeated in the coming election.

Most of Labour's leaders, aware of Churchill's unique standing, doubted whether Labour could win the 1945 election. However, the deep unpopularity of the Tory Party, which was blamed for pre-war unemployment and poverty, as well as the newly acquired credibility of the Labour Party, which had played such a notable part, especially on the home front, in the wartime coalition, more than made up for Churchill. British voters, who wanted a better life than they had before the war, did not believe that the Tories would give it to them. The Gallup Poll, then little regarded, predicted a Labour landslide. In beautiful summer weather, Denis Healey and Roy Jenkins addressed well attended meetings of voters eager to hear what these young Labour officers had to say. Jenkins recalled 'two or three twilight open-air meetings outside pubs which had just closed, when great seas of faces looked up seeking a message appropriate to that time of relief, exhaustion and hope'.[2] The message of the two men was simple – the planning which had been necessary to win the war was also essential to solve the problems of peace.

Polling day was 5 July. The results were not, however, declared until 26 July, to allow time for separate polls for Lancashire towns affected by 'Wakes week', for public holidays in Scotland and, above all, for collecting the servicemen's vote which went overwhelmingly Labour's way. The Labour Party won a triumphant victory, winning 393 seats against 210 for the Conservatives. The floodtide, which swept Labour to victory in surburban and rural as well as city seats, nearly carried Denis Healey in at Pudsey, where he was defeated by only 1651 votes. At Solihull, Roy Jenkins, who had also begun to believe in the possibility of victory, was beaten more decisively, by 5000 votes. Tony Crosland wrote exultantly to his mother from Italy: 'What a day. Even I, in my wildest dreams, never expected a landslide like this.'

They quickly came down to earth, and indeed, in Roy Jenkins' case, suffered from what might be called post-electoral anti-climax. The feeling of disappointment was sharpened by the success of a number of their contemporaries or near-contemporaries who had also been in the armed forces, including Woodrow Wyatt at Aston, John Freeman at Watford, Christopher Mayhew at Norfolk South, Raymond Blackburn at King's Norton, Birmingham and Jim Callaghan at Cardiff South. It was a wonderful time to be a Labour MP, which made it all the more frustrating for those who had not been elected.

On 28 July, a meeting of the newly elected Parliamentary Labour Party at Beaver Hall triumphantly acclaimed Clement Attlee as Prime Minister and Leader of the Labour Party, thus dashing the hopes of Herbert Morrison who had ideas of supplanting Attlee. Two days later, Hugh Dalton, newly appointed Chancellor of the Exchequer and assiduous patron of young men, gave a dinner for twelve of the most promising new members, including Hugh Gaitskell, Harold Wilson, Dick Crossman, John Freeman, Evan Durbin, and Woodrow Wyatt. And on 16 August, John Freeman, moving the address in reply to the King's speech in his dark green Rifle Brigade uniform, proclaimed that 'today may rightly be regarded as D-Day in the battle for the New Britain'. His speech brought tears to Winston Churchill's eyes.

Meanwhile Healey, Crosland and Jenkins were still in the army,

Denis and Tony in Italy and Roy at Bletchley Park. After the dropping of the atomic bombs at Hiroshima and Nagasaki had led to the Japanese surrender, they had very little to do. Denis Healey tried to keep himself occupied at Allied Headquarters by reading, walking, going to the opera and talking to friends like Andrew Shonfield and Tony Crosland who were in a similar position. In a letter to Philip Williams, Crosland wrote: 'I have been seeing a certain amount of Denis Healey recently, and he has given me a lot of gossip about old Labour Club stalwarts. It appears he has swung away from the CP, and is very much in a state of flux. In fact one can hardly describe him at the moment as holding any coherent attitude.'[3]

At Bletchley Park, Jenkins, who now found himself quite unable to break the ciphers which the Russians, in their turn, were sending out to their generals on the captured Fish machines, settled down in a remote room to read the key 'tombstone' volumes, such as Morley's *Gladstone*, Garvin's *Joseph Chamberlain* and Lady Gwendoline Cecil's *Salisbury*, which then formed the core of English political biography. It was an immersion which was to prove of great value to him in the future. He summed up his five months of waiting to leave the army 'as a combination of public uselessness and private utility'.[4]

Of the three, Denis Healey had the most attractive immediate prospects of employment. The army wanted him to join a team writing up the official history of the Italian campaign. However, although he would have been promoted to lieutenant-colonel and have lived in an Austrian castle, he would also have been separated from Edna Edmunds to whom he had become engaged. He could also have gone back to Oxford to take up a senior scholarship at Merton College and to study the philosophy of art. But an academic life no longer appealed.

Instead, he decided to follow up the suggestion of prominent NEC members and apply for the job of International Secretary of the Labour Party. With support from the Chancellor of the Exchequer, Hugh Dalton, the Chairman of the Party, Harold Laski, and the Health Minister, Nye Bevan, he was appointed on 20 November 1945. This was a crucial decision for Healey. It would help make his personal reputation and shape his future direction. Accepting a job at Transport House as International Secretary meant that, he was, in effect, opting for a career in Labour politics.

Following the election, Tony Crosland was in a quandary as to what to do next. He wrote to Philip Williams in August: 'Failure to get back for the election has rather altered my plan for life. I have always rather assumed that I would go straight out of the army into active politics . . . I am therefore . . . tending to plan on the basis of not going into politics until early middle age.'[5] However, after the Japanese surrender, news came through that the government was considering allowing several thousand arts students serving in the army to resume their studies. Crosland commented that he had not previously thought of going back to Oxford but, as it meant exchanging 'one's last and probably barren year of army life for a slightly less barren year at Oxford', he was now prepared to return to Oxford, 'even with Trinity thrown in'.[6] After some uncertainty, by the end of 1945 he was back at Trinity as an undergraduate. It was as if the war years had never happened.

Roy Jenkins was fortunate to obtain early release from the army. Because of connections through his father with the Prime Minister, Clement Attlee, he was offered a job as an economist with the newly re-established Industrial and Commercial Finance Corporation (ICFC) by its Chairman, Lord Piercy, who had worked for Attlee when he was in the War Cabinet. As Roy now had nothing to do in the army except read political biographies and no immediate prospects in civilian life after Solihull had failed to return him to Parliament, he decided to accept the offer. It was not becoming an industrial banker which attracted him but the fact that it qualified as a 'Class B' early release and would therefore get him out of the army and enable him to live with Jennifer whom he had married in January 1945.

Their wedding, arranged by Jennifer's parents, had been a relatively grand occasion, especially for wartime. It took place in the Savoy Chapel and there was a reception afterwards at the Savoy Hotel, at which Attlee made a typically terse principal speech. Michael Ashcroft, who died young, was best man. Despite the festivities, the war still made its presence felt. While the register was being signed, a V-2 rocket exploded across the river and, later that evening, another rocket landed uncomfortably close to Markham Street, Chelsea, where Roy had gone to fetch some clothes from the house where Jennifer lived. On hearing of Roy's marriage, Tony Crosland, who was still in

Italy, commented patronisingly to Philip Williams, 'Roy, bless his sweet heart, is now safely married.'[7] At the beginning of 1946, Roy joined the ICFC and soon after the young Jenkins found a flat over a café in Marsham Street near Westminster.

Denis married Edna in the week before Christmas 1945. Both had had affairs during the war but, according to Denis, this strengthened rather than weakened their relationship. They spent their honeymoon at the Buck Inn in Upper Wharfedale. It was so crowded that the young couple had to sleep in the loft of the barn next door. Healey recalled in his memoirs that their style was somewhat cramped because Edna had to spend much of her honeymoon tending to a painful boil which he had developed at the base of his spine. They were back in London for the New Year and quickly found a bedsit off Manchester Square, from which Denis went to work at Transport House and Edna at Bromley Girls' High School. Edna was earning eleven pounds a week, Denis only seven, a disparity of which Denis was somewhat ashamed.

London in 1946 was shabby and still suffering from war damage. But, as the capital of the nation which had stood alone against Hitler and had emerged from the war as one of the major victor powers and with a new Labour government committed to social progress, it was, Denis Healey wrote, 'pullulating at that time with change and excitement'.[8] At Soho restaurants or at Bush House, an enthralled Healey met European intellectuals and politicians who had escaped the concentration camps and were still working in London, often as journalists and broadcasters. In the evenings, he and Edna went to the Old Vic, then at the peak of its reputation, to see great actors such as Lawrence Olivier, Alec Guinness and Ralph Richardson or entertained friends in their tiny attic. The Jenkins also went to the theatre but they preferred the cinema. They dined out in Soho and at restaurants near Westminster. Although neither the combined income of the Jenkins' nor of the Healeys was more than £1,000 a year, low inflation and restrictions on the cost of restaurants and food meant that their standard of living was relatively good. And, despite the limit on the amount of money to be taken abroad, both couples had holidays on the continent in 1946. Roy and Jennifer went to Ascona at the Swiss end of Lake Maggiore and Denis and Edna, after attending the Italian Socialist Party conference at Florence, had a more romantic second honeymoon, first at Sorrento and then on the island of Capri.

As International Secretary, Denis Healey rapidly became more influential than all but a handful of Labour backbench MPs. Healey's task at Transport House was to rebuild relationships between the Labour Party and sister socialist parties in Europe and to help in re-establishing the Socialist International. He also had the responsibility of providing the link on foreign policy, Commonwealth and colonial issues between the Labour government and the Labour Party outside Parliament. Healey derived his clout from his relationship with the Foreign Secretary, Ernest Bevin, second only to the Prime Minister and arguably his superior in terms of prestige. Denis admired him greatly.

Bevin, formerly General Secretary of the Transport and General Workers, had been brought into the War Cabinet by Churchill in 1940 as Minister of Labour. He built up his ministry into a great office of state which effectively mobilised national manpower and also raised the status of industrial workers. Bevin had expected to become Chancellor of the Exchequer in the Labour government but, at the last moment, Attlee switched him to the Foreign Office. Twenty-four hours later, Attlee and the new Foreign Secretary flew to Berlin for the Potsdam conference, convened by the Allies to decide the post-war settlement.

With the shoulders and hands of a manual labourer, Bevin had the mind and authority of an international statesman. George Brown, another of his admirers, wrote about him, 'He was a man with little or no taught advantages, who relied wholly upon his own brain, his own imagination and his capacity for envisaging things and people. He had a natural dignity that offset his endowment of determination and ruthlessness.'[9] But Bevin's formidable personality could not make up for the post-war decline in British power or, following the emergence of Russia as a superpower, ensure international security, especially in Europe. Bevin had few illusions about the Soviet Union.[10] However, it needed all his nerve and resolution to stand up for British and European interests in the face of the determined Russian effort to take over Eastern Europe.

Denis Healey was one of the few Labour Party members who saw at first hand what Communism in Eastern Europe was really like. In the freezing January of 1947, he went to Hungary where he met the Communist leader, Malyas Rakosi, who was busy undermining the other political parties by what he called 'salami tactics'; first dividing off the left from the other parties, then the hard left from the soft left (sending the latter into exile and jailing trade union leaders) and then forcing a fusion of the social democratic rump with the Communists. In November 1947, he attended the Brno Congress of the Czechoslovak Social Democrats which overwhelmingly rejected fusion with the Communists. But, a few months later in March 1948, the infamous Prague coup installed a Communist dictatorship in Czechoslovakia. At Wrocław in Poland, Healey watched the Polish Socialist party vote against fusion with the Communist party. But this was followed by show trials of leading Socialists as well as a purge of the nationalist-inclined Communist leader, Wladyslaw Gomułka. The Polish Socialists were duly forced to merge with the Communists who then took over the country.

Healey's role as International Secretary of the Labour Party, then unrivalled in prestige, gave him an influence disproportionate to his years with Western European socialist leaders. His most important task was to help the German Social Democrats (SPD) re-establish themselves. He persuaded Labour's National Executive to invite their fiery chairman, Kurt Schumacher, to London in November 1946 and helped organise support for the SPD's admission to the Socialist International in June 1947. He was less successful with the Italian Socialists who, despite his efforts, split, mainly on the issue of relations with the Communists, and, as a result, were severely weakened electorally.

In May 1947, the Labour Party published a pamphlet, *Cards on the Table*, written by Healey, which set out a vigorous defence of Bevin's foreign policy.[11] In part, Healey's pamphlet was a response to a left-wing attack on Bevin in another pamphlet, *Keep Left*, written by Richard Crossman, Michael Foot and Ian Mikardo, signed by another twelve MPs (including Woodrow Wyatt) and published by the *New Statesman*. *Keep Left* criticised Bevin for what the pamphleteers saw as a 'dangerous dependence' on the USA and called for the creation for a 'Third Force', based on an alliance between British and French Socialists which would be strong enough 'to hold the balance of world power, to halt the division into a Western and Eastern bloc and so to make the United Nations a reality'.[12]

In *Cards on the Table*, Denis Healey bluntly pointed out the facts of international life. Since the war there had been 'a sustained and violent offensive against Britain by her Russian ally'. Russia had launched a series of propaganda attacks against the United Kingdom at the UN, as well as opposing the UK in important strategic areas, such as Trieste, Northern Persia, the Dardanelles, Greece, Turkey and Eastern Europe. He also made it clear that co-operation with the United States was based not on ideology but on practical grounds. 'The aim of an Anglo-American understanding is to prevent war by proving to Russia that an aggressive anti-British policy is doomed to frustration. Our hope is that sooner or later the Russians will realise that the policy they have pursued since 1945 is both impractical and unnecessary.' Healey dismissed as unrealistic the idea that Britain could pursue an independent policy as leader of a European socialist bloc. Both Britain and Europe depended on the United States for reconstruction and recovery and 'while we shall do everything possible to restore Europe as a vital and independent factor in world politics, we cannot base our policy on the assumption that this aim is already achieved.'

Cards on the Table was an important milestone in Denis Healey's development. Greatly appreciated by Ernest Bevin and his two junior ministers, Hector McNeil and Christopher Mayhew (who were Healey's main line of communication with Bevin), it not only gave firm support to an embattled Foreign Secretary before his party conference speech but, more strategically, also helped set the scene for the revolution in foreign policy which culminated two years later in the setting up of the North Atlantic Treaty Organisation (NATO).

In June 1947 General George Marshall, the US Secretary of State, made his historic speech at Harvard, offering American assistance for European post-war reconstruction. Ernest Bevin, who first heard the report of Marshall's speech on his bedside radio and immediately realised its importance, led the prompt response to Marshall's offer. The Organisation of European Economic Cooperation (OEEC) and the successful implementation of the Marshall Plan which helped reconstruct Europe followed. Similarly Bevin, reacting swiftly to the Communist coup in Prague, was the main architect of the March 1948 Brussels Treaty which united the UK with France and the

Benelux countries in the Western European Union and committed British troops to German soil for fifty years. In April 1949 came the prize for which Bevin had been working so hard – the North Atlantic Treaty Organisation through which the United States became directly involved in the defence of Western Europe.

In his autobiography, Healey wrote, 'I was lucky, in Dean Acheson's words, to have been "present at the creation".'[13] As one of Bevin's trusted 'irregulars', he was given a free run of the Foreign Office where he met leading officials, such as Gladwyn Jebb and Evelyn Shuckburgh. He wrote the Labour Party's memorandum on the Marshall Plan and helped organise a meeting of key European Socialists at Seldon Park which issued a strongly worded declaration in support of the Plan, as well being sent by Bevin (in company with Morgan Phillips, General Secretary of the Labour Party) on a mission, just before the crucial 1948 Italian General Election, to put pressure on the Italian Socialists to disassociate themselves from the Communists who had attacked the Plan.[14]

Healey contributed to a number of leading European socialist newspapers and broadcast for the BBC in French and sometimes in German and Italian which added to his already considerable reputation on the continent and supplemented his meagre Labour Party income. It is, however, significant that Denis's closest friends during this period were Americans, especially Dave Linebaugh and Sam Berger, who were diplomats at the United States Embassy in London. By the late 1940s, the pre-war Oxford Communist and the semi-Marxist major of the 1945 Labour Party conference had been changed by his experience of Soviet tactics in Eastern Europe to an enthusiastic supporter of NATO and United States involvement.

While Healey was being fully stretched by his post at Transport House, Jenkins was feeling increasingly frustrated by his job in banking and busily planning to get into Parliament. Jenkins' task at the Industrial and Commercial Finance Corporation was to act as assistant to one of the four controllers who oversaw the application for finance from small and medium companies. After being transferred within a year from one to another controller, and then to a third (which Jenkins later wrote, 'was not a compliment to the success of my performance'), he established a 'modus vivendi' with the third, John Kinross.

However, Roy continued to be restive, applying unsuccessfully for two university posts, one as assistant lecturer in philosophy at Manchester and the other as lecturer in economics at Trinity College, Oxford (to fill a vacancy created when Tony Crosland was made a fellow of Trinity in 1947), as well as for a job as a BBC talks producer.

Attlee came to his rescue by launching him on a part-time writing career. As a preliminary to a biography, he asked Jenkins to edit a volume of his speeches made between May 1945 and November 1946. The fee was £50. After receiving the cheque from Attlee personally (which he was slow to acknowledge) he received the following typed letter from the Prime Minister: 'Dear Roy, I sent you a cheque for £50 a week ago. I have not had an acknowledgement. Yours ever, C. R. Attlee.' After a hasty letter of apology, Jenkins was able to proceed with the arrangement that he should write Attlee's biography; he was given the free run of the Prime Minister's private papers in his No 10 Downing Street study. The book was written between November 1946 and November 1947 in the evenings at the Jenkins' Marsham Street flat and at weekends either at Jennifer's parents' house in Hampstead Garden Surburb or at Roy's family home at Pontypool. It was published by Heinemann in April 1948.

As a biography, *Mr Attlee* suffered from two disadvantages. It was only an interim one, covering Attlee's career up to the time he became Prime Minister. And not only had the author's father been Attlee's PPS but the author himself hoped to become a Labour MP. However, Roy Jenkins avoided many of the pitfalls. His portrait of Attlee was sympathetic but not uncritical. The Labour leader came across as a conventional, middle-class Victorian without a trace of charisma in his make-up but who was, nevertheless, honest, disinterested and tough-minded enough to stand up to Churchill during the war and to face down and control his more gifted colleagues in the Labour Cabinet. *Mr Attlee* was well received, Richard Crossman in the *New Statesman* commenting favourably on Jenkins' judgement that 'Attlee was a Socialist because it was to him scandalous that all could not enjoy the spacious playing fields, the firm formative influence and good clothes and decent accommodation that had been his.'[15] Roy Jenkins' first book was a successful enterprise in that, without blighting his political prospects, he showed that he had the potential to become a serious writer, even if *Mr Attlee* was not a serious book.

A chance to land a safe Labour seat occured when his beloved father, who had been made a junior minister by Attlee, died suddenly from a neglected prostate in April 1946. Roy and his mother were shattered by Arthur Jenkins' death but were persuaded that Roy should go for the Pontypool nomination. After six weeks of intense campaigning during which he addressed at least twenty party meetings and miners' lodges and other trade union branches as well as calling on key individuals, Roy was eventually defeated at the final selection conference in June by 134 votes to 76. Afterwards Jenkins described his candidature as a 'mistake' because it divided the local party and his failure to win the nomination as a 'lucky miss' because he would have inevitably been compared with his father and found wanting.[16]

His Pontypool setback did not deter Jenkins from seeking a seat. For Roy, the chamber of the House of Commons, especially with the Labour Party under Attlee in power, was the centre of national life and he was determined to get there as quickly as possible. He was 'a young man in a hurry'.[17] In March 1948, he struck lucky. The MP for Central Southwark in London announced his immediate retirement through ill health. Although the seat was a safe one, it was due to disappear through redistribution at the next General Election; and, as the London Labour Party had decreed that the successful canditate had to undertake not to fight the newly created combined seat at the General Election, Jenkins, who was confident enough to risk all to get into the Commons even for less than two years, had a straight run against a local alderman and won the selection conference by 20 votes to 8. After a short ten-day campaign, he held the seat at the by-election comfortably on a low turnout. By early afternoon of Friday 30 April 1948, Roy Jenkins had become, at the age of twenty-seven, the youngest member of the House of Commons. On the following Tuesday afternoon, he was introduced by the London whip and by the Prime Minister himself, a tribute more to Roy's father than to Roy himself but, by any standards, an almost embarrassingly impressive entrance.

A month later, Jenkins made his maiden speech at the committee stage of the Finance Bill, then a big occasion taken entirely on the floor of the House. It was a brief but fluent contribution in support of the main item of Stafford Cripps' 1948 Budget, the so-called 'special contribution', a non-recurring capital tax on better-off individuals that Cripps was introducing partly as a sweetener to encourage trade union wage restraint. As is customary with maiden speeches, Roy referred to his constituency, linking his working-class constituents to his main theme by arguing that those with the broadest shoulders should bear the greatest burden of Crippsian austerity. He concluded with a flourish: 'I claim for this tax that it is a tax which inflicts real hardship on no person in this country . . . it is a useful tax, a tax which fits well and purposefully into the framework of a bold and challenging Budget.' In accordance with tradition, the MP for Oxford University, Sir Arthur Salter, who was called next to speak, congratulated the new member on his speech, and the fact that he had made it without notes. It was a self-confident, suitably loyalist and intelligently technical beginning. Roy Jenkins was clearly a young MP to watch.

Tony Crosland's decision in 1945 to go back to Trinity College, Oxford, however disappointing it might have seemed at the time, turned out to be a wise one. Oxford made Crosland's reputation as a political economist as well as an almost legendary don and led indirectly to his election to Parliament in 1950.

As a battle-hardened veteran sporting a red parachute beret, he must have seemed a 'star' figure to young undergraduates fresh from school. He quickly again became chairman of the Democratic Socialist Club and, succeeding where he had failed in 1940, President of the Union. The 8 May 1946 edition of *Isis*, the undergraduate magazine, featured an 'Idol' article about the new president (*Isis* idols were portraits of Oxford glitterati) who clearly impressed his interviewer. On being asked what he considered his greatest achievement during the war, Crosland flippantly replied 'the liberation of Cannes'. More seriously, he admitted that his favourable pre-war attitude towards the Communist Party had been changed by the war. The article was accompanied by a photograph of Crosland smoking a pipe.

Crucially for his future, Tony Crosland got a First in PPE in only one year and was invited to stay on at Trinity, to start with as a lecturer in economics and then in 1947, when his economics tutor, Robert Hall, left to become an economic adviser to the Labour government as Fellow in Economics. Tony quickly made his mark, working hard during the day and playing hard at night. This was Roy Jenkins' description of Crosland at Oxford after the war: 'As a young don, he with one or two contemporaries formed something of a cult group, of which the distinguishing characteristic was the unusual combination of hard intellectual endeavour and undisciplined, even rather riotous, relaxation.'[18]

As an economist, Crosland published two papers while he was a fellow at Trinity, one on 'Prices and Costs in Nationalised Industries' and the other on 'The Movement of Labour in 1948'. He also contributed less technical articles to left-wing journals, such as *Socialist Commentary*, calling for the nationalisation of over 50 per cent of industry; his revisionism did not yet involve the downgrading of public ownership. His close friend, Ian Little, who wrote the highly regarded *A Critique of Welfare Economics*, described Crosland as 'an orthodox Keynesian'.[19] John Vaisey, also a well-known economist, said that 'the economics . . . that Crosland learned was of a relatively simple kind: an elementary knowledge of market-theory; some modern welfare economics . . . from Ian Little; and a great deal about so-called Keynesian demand management from Hall and others . . . who were actually doing the job of managing the post-war economy. Strangely enough, Crosland's two political mentors, Hugh Dalton and Hugh Gaitskell, both knew far more economics than he did.'[20]

The point about Crosland was that, although he was a lecturer and fellow in economics, he was very much a political economist, interested more in the policy implications of economics than the theory. Michael Young, another close friend and head of Labour's research department from 1945 to 1951, introduced him to sociology at about this time. Crosland saw sociological analysis as the key to tackling inequality. His diaries show that he continued to think long and hard about the direction of Socialism. Having rejected Marx, he was also ambivalent about the Webbs. 'I like blue books and I like research – but it all becomes unattractive when it is *unrelieved* by any recreation or alternative interest . . . No, I shouldn't have liked the Webbs. I should have admired them, been fascinated by them, enjoyed talking shop with them . . . But with what a feeling of relief and release I should have walked out of their house.'[21]

Tony Benn, who was an undergraduate at New College, was tutored by Crosland. Like many other students, Benn was impressed by the handsome economics don whose way of winning people over was to insult them. Crosland insisted on calling Benn 'Jimmy': 'We can't have two Tonys here,' said Crosland.[22] Such was his tutor's charm that this made no difference to their relationship and they often used to go to films together.

For Crosland at Oxford, pleasure started at 7.30 p.m. on the dot. His regular companion in 'riotous' living, which included considerable amounts of alcohol, was Raymond Carr, then fellow of All Souls' and future author of the classic account of the Spanish Civil War. On Friday nights, they ran a poker school that met in Tony's rooms at Trinity to which undergraduates were invited. Susan Crosland, his second wife and biographer, commented, 'Others might think a young don should set an example. Tony felt passionately that you ought to be free to do things that affect only yourself – or to the extent that others don't mind if they have the same freedom.'[23]

Tony Crosland's idea of pleasure included having a succession of girlfriends. His method of approach was confrontational, inviting a response. If that was not forthcoming, he quickly dropped the girl. William Rodgers, who went as an undergraduate to Magdalen in January 1949, remembered how Crosland combined 'the attractions of a red beret denoting his war experience with a reputation for "girls who left his college rooms at dawn"'.[24]

However, friends also said that his earlier sexual ambivalence was still present, at least until he met his first wife, Hilary Sarson. It may have been partly this element in Tony's make-up that attracted Hugh Dalton, who was to prove such a reliable patron to him. Dalton, Chancellor of the Exchequer from 1945 to his resignation over a Budget leak in November 1947, was a larger-than-life personality, with piercing pale blue eyes and a booming voice, who had helped to guide the Labour Party to a sensible policy on rearmament in the 1930s and to prepare it for power in the 1940s. Son of a Canon of Windsor and educated at Eton and King's College, Cambridge, he was taught by Keynes, influenced politically by Keir Hardie and the Webbs and became an adoring friend of the poet Rupert Brooke, who died during the First World War. 'The radiance of his memory still lights my path,' wrote Dalton many years later.[25] Unhappily married, he took great pains to encourage younger male politicians, especially if they were clever and handsome. Dalton first met Crosland at the Oxford Union in the summer of 1946 when Tony was President. 'Make a note! Make a note! Name's Crosland. I want him here,' said the Chancellor excitedly to his private secretary and Crosland was invited to 11 Downing Street.[26]

Nicholas Davenport, the financial journalist, and his attractive actress wife, Olga, used to gather together left-wing politicians, economists, writers and film stars to their beautiful country house, Hinton Manor near Oxford. During the summer of 1947 they invited Dalton, exhausted by a sterling crisis, to spend his sixtieth birthday with them. Tony Crosland came over to dinner 'in his bright red sports car, wearing the red beret of the Parachute Regiment. We had an entertaining evening of drink and talk . . . As he drove away, I could see in Hugh's eyes the rekindling of his romantic love for gallant and handsome young men.' Davenport added: 'After another weekend occasion, when Tony had left abruptly to catch a train with a girl to London, leaving Hugh and me alone to dine, Hugh actually refused to eat or speak. He paced about the room as if he had been jilted as a lover.'[27]

Dalton and Crosland developed a complex relationship in which Hugh was the over-attentive father and Tony the wayward son. Roy Jenkins described it as a kind of sadomasochism: 'Tony was cruel to him, called him an old windbag to his face. Hugh would take it and come back for more.'[28]

After his enforced resignation in November 1947, Dalton had time to further the careers of his protégés, especially Crosland. In September 1948, he told Tony that he had hopes of 'fixing up you and others' for parliamentary seats.[29] On Crosland's behalf, he was helpful in making introductions in the South Gloucestershire constituency, which was likely to become a safer seat as a result of redistribution from Bristol's surburbs and where the sitting member was retiring on grounds of ill health. Dalton even warned off Roy Jenkins who, with his Southwark Central constituency disappearing, was himself anxiously looking for a new seat at the next election. In September 1949, Crosland comfortably won the South Gloucestershire nomination. He thanked Dalton profusely for his support; Dalton replied that 'favouritism is the secret of efficiency' and predicted a bright future for Tony in politics, 'if you have fair luck and don't drink too much'.[30]

Meanwhile Roy Jenkins had become somewhat desperate in his search for a seat, even suffering from psychosomatic pains, after having been turned down twice at selection conferences. In October 1949 he landed the newly created but safe Stetchford division of Birmingham, a success which understandably transformed his morale. Both Crosland and Jenkins comfortably won their seats at the February 1950 election at which the Labour government had its majority reduced from over 150 to just 6. Jenkins was already an experienced campaigner, having fought both the 1945 General Election and his 1948 by-election. Crosland quickly found his feet, developing a nice line in self-confident repartee at public meetings. He addressed a mixed crowd of gentry and farmworkers at Badminton, home of the Duke of Beaufort. 'Why is it, Mr Crosland, that when my daughter had her gas cooker repaired, it was necessary to send three fitters to do the job?' Tony was asked by one of the Duke's houseguests. 'I can only suggest, Madam, that if your daughter's beauty resembles yours in any way, two were gazing at her in admiration while the other was working,' replied the Labour candidate.[31] Crosland was returned as MP for South Gloucestershire with a majority of about 6000, while Jenkins held Stechford, a safer seat, even more easily by 12,400 votes.

The 1950–51 Parliament was a come down from that of 1945–50. The great Labour majority of 1945 had disappeared and the Attlee government, with its leaders plagued by ill health and visibly tiring, was continually harried and kept up late by a revived Tory Party. Appropriately, Crosland made his first speech during the 1950 Budget debate. Dalton advised him not to include too many figures and to mix appreciation of the government's policy with his own suggestions, in a tone combining 'determination and humility'.[32] Crosland's 'maiden', like that of Jenkins, was a success but there was not much humility about it. 'I believe it is a tradition of this House that maiden speeches should not be controversial. But . . . there is nothing . . . which should deter me from throwing a few pebbles at the Right Hon. and learned gentleman the Chancellor of the Exchequer,' said the new member and proceeded to criticise Cripps for too restrictive a Budget.[33]

At the beginning of their parliamentary careers, neither Jenkins nor Crosland could be typecast as typical right wingers. Roy, who, like Tony, wrote articles in favour of further nationalisation, was one of a number of MPs who gathered around Nye Bevan, the charismatic Health Minister, in the smoking room of the Commons between 5.30 p.m. and 7.30 p.m., while Tony, who was a contributor to both *Tribune* and the *New Statesman*, was also impressed by Nye. After hearing Bevan speaking at the Durham Miners' Gala, Crosland told Philip Williams that Bevan was 'a very great man. I could listen to him by the hour.'[34] They admired him not only as a brilliant speaker and creative minister but also a possible future leader of the Labour Party.

During the frequent late- and all-night sittings of the 1950–51 Parliament, Jenkins and Crosland joined an eclectic group of parliamentary canasta players (canasta was a then fashionable card game imported from the United States). The players included Woodrow Wyatt who, after being a signatory to *Keep Left*, was moving to the right, Tom Driberg, who was a High Anglican left-wing member of the National Executive Committee, and John Freeman, junior Minister of Supply and supporter of Bevan. In the summer of 1951, Driberg, despite being an active homosexual, got married with much fanfare at a London church. The members of the canasta group attended the wedding, Crosland, Jenkins and Wyatt acting as ushers, while John Freeman gave away the bride.

However, Bevan's resignation from the Cabinet on 22 April 1951, on the issue of charges for teeth and spectacles, split the canasta group politically. John Freeman left the government with Nye Bevan and Harold Wilson, while Tom Driberg was an enthusiastic Bevanite supporter. By contrast, Crosland, Jenkins and Wyatt were appalled by the irresponsibility of Bevan's decision. On the evening of 19 April, Jenkins and Wyatt walked out of New Palace Yard in a state of shock, having just heard the news of Bevan's impending resignation. Jenkins, Wyatt and Crosland agreed later that night that his departure would be a disaster for the Labour government. They believed that Bevan had acted less out of principle and more out of pique; when Cripps had resigned, Bevan had been passed over for the Chancellorship in favour of Hugh Gaitskell and, a few months later, following Bevin's illness, for the Foreign Secretaryship, to which Attlee had reluctantly and disastrously appointed Herbert Morrison.

Bevan's opposition to Gaitskell's 1951 rearmament Budget and the health charges that were introduced in his Budget was arguably more sensible than Jenkins and Crosland then allowed. Many commentators now think that the rearmament programme following the outbreak of the Korea conflict overstrained the British economy just when it was recovering from the war.[35] However, for Jenkins, Crosland and Wyatt, the priority in 1951 was the stormy international situation, with the Korean war at a critical stage and the Cold War in Europe still very intense after the Berlin blockade. Viewed in this context, Bevan appeared to be putting his personal ambition before the national interest. Bevan's resignation was the start of a decade of Labour infighting which effectively kept the party out of office for nearly fourteen years. It also determined the political direction not only of Jenkins and Crosland but of Healey as well, in the Labour civil war which followed.

In his autobiography, Denis Healey wrote that he hesitated a long time before deciding to run for Parliament.[36] He had been put off by the internecine battles of the National Executive Committee which he had witnessed as International Secretary and was little attracted by the frustrating life of the backbencher MP. He sought a job that would allow him something of the scope which the International Secretaryship had given him.

One example of Healey's influence was his authorship of *European Unity*, a famously controversial Labour Party statement published in June 1950, which uncompromisingly rejected European economic and political union and was ambivalent about the Schuman Plan that helped launch the European Community. The Schuman Plan, named after the French foreign minister who proposed it, was in fact the brainchild of Jean Monnet, who has been described as having 'done more to unite Europe on a permanent basis than all the Emperors, Kings, Generals and dictators since the fall of the Roman Empire'.[37] Monnet's idea was to pool French and German coal and steel resources under one supernational authority, thus guaranteeing peace between the two countries and providing 'the germ of European unity'.[38] He persuaded Robert Schuman to adopt the plan as his own, and, at a press conference in Paris on 9 May 1950, with the support of the French and West German cabinets, Schuman put forward proposals for an international authority to regulate the coal and steel production of the two countries and of any other country which might wish to participate.

The Schuman Plan presented the Labour government with a major dilemma. On the one hand, they did not wish to be seen to oppose such a constructive idea to end the old conflict between France and Germany, which was why Attlee gave the plan a guarded welcome in the Commons. On the other hand, there was a general consensus among ministers, such as Attlee, Bevin and Morrison, and leading officials, like Strang, Makins and Plowden, that the Schuman scheme would not only involve the United Kingdom in an unacceptable loss of sovereignty but lead inevitably to European political federation, anathema to the British ruling élite. The government, therefore, decided to seek negotiations, but without accepting the principle of a supranational authority.

On 1 June the British bluff was called. Schuman, with the support of the Benelux countries and Italy as well as Germany, presented the United Kingdom with a virtual ultimatum; either the British accepted the pooling of coal and steel production and the institution of a new supranational authority as their 'immediate objective' or they would be excluded from the negotiations. A hastily arranged cabinet meeting under Herbert Morrison's chairmanship (Attlee was on holiday and Bevin ill in hospital) rejected the French terms. As a result, the UK stood aloof from the first successful initiative to promote European integration. Dean Acheson, US Secretary of State at the time, called the British decision 'the greatest mistake of the post-war period'.[39]

It was into this political and diplomatic maelstrom that Healey's document *European Unity* was launched. Its publication caused a furore, especially on the continent. It was published just before a government White Paper setting out in emollient terms its position on the Schuman Plan. The tone of *European Unity* was, in contrast, not just anti-federalist but distinctly anti-European: 'In every respect except distance we in Britain are closer to our kinsmen in Australia and New Zealand on the far side of the world, than we are to Europe. We are closer in language and origins, in social habit and institutions, in political outlook and in economic interest. The economies of the Commonwealth countries are complementary to that of Britain to a degree which those of Western Europe could never equal.' It also stated: 'No Socialist party with the prospect of forming a government could accept a system by which important fields of national policy were surrendered to a supranational European representative authority, since such an authority would have a permanent anti-Socialist majority and would arouse the hostility of European workers.' This was taken by critics as implying that Britain's Labour government would co-operate only with European Socialists.

Healey pointed out in his memoirs that, at the instigation of Hugh Dalton, his draft was altered by the National Executive and that Dalton's press conference was 'even more aggressively sectarian'.[40] However, Healey undoubtedly shared many of the assumptions of Labour Ministers.[41] He had already written strongly against European federalism in his pamphlet *Feet on the Ground* in September 1948. He was less than impressed either by the political and economic perform-ance of France and Italy or by their Socialist parties. And he put far greater emphasis on the United Kingdom's relationship with the United States and the Commonwealth than with continental Europe. However, in the Commons debate on the Schuman Plan on 26 and 27 June 1950, while Edward Heath made his maiden speech in favour of British participation, both Roy Jenkins and Tony Crosland also sup-ported the government line of Britain keeping out.

Later that summer, Hugh Dalton, now Minister of Town and Country Planning, led the Labour delegation to the newly set up Council of Europe at Strasbourg. He brought with him as his deputy Jim Callaghan, a promising junior minister at the Admiralty, the recently elected Crosland as economic adviser, and Denis Healey as the party's foreign affairs expert. Interestingly, he did not take Roy Jenkins who, at that stage, was considered less promising than the other two. Following the British government's refusal to join the Schuman Plan and their opposition to European federalism, the Labour delegation was much criticised by continental delegates, so much so that Dalton reported back to Bevin on 'the strength of the anti-British Labour feeling' at Strasbourg.[42] To Attlee, he spoke warmly of the contribu-tions made by Callaghan, Crosland and Healey.

One August weekend, Dalton escaped from the humidity of Strasbourg and took Callaghan, Crosland and Healey on an expedi-tion to Le Donan in the Vosges. Dalton wrote: 'On arrival, we walked up a valley behind the hotel and, at the top, found Denis, seated like a sphinx, on top of a stone edifice called Le Musée. Then we turned and ran back down the valley, spurting in the last lap before reaching the hotel; we had had a lovely sweat, an ardent thirst, a magnificent view; and now we had a wonderful dinner, after which we sat up talk-ing till a late hour.' Accounts by Healey and Callaghan make it clear that a good deal was drunk and that Dalton revealed a great deal about himself. Healey's comment about Dalton was: 'sad man'.[43]

Later that summer, Dalton sent two pages of his diary to Tony Crosland in which he showed the intensity of his feelings:

Tonight Tony is dining in King's with Kaldor . . . Am thinking of Tony, with all his youth and beauty and gaiety and charm and energy and social success and good brains – and a better economist and a better Socialist than Kaldor, and with his feet on the road to political success now, if he survives to middle age – I weep. I am fond and more proud of that young man than I can put in words. I think of him – I've said this earlier – as something between a beloved only son and a gay and adorable younger brother.[44]

Crosland had gained much from his relationship with Dalton but this was going too far. At dinner in Strasbourg in November, Tony, who was a student of Freud, accused Dalton of sexual repression. In a letter to Crosland written after a wakeful night, Dalton apologised for 'fussing' him too much. Dalton sympathised with Crosland for finding life in the 1950–51 Commons 'disappointing, boring and narrowing' and tried to cheer Crosland up by assuring him that he would get office when Labour returned to power.[45]

Crosland's tendency to heavy drinking did not go unnoticed. A. J. P. Taylor, who had married Tony's sister, Eve, took upon himself to warn Crosland about his behaviour and claimed that Attlee had not appointed him to the government, 'because he has seen you drunk too often in the smoking room'.[46] Tony replied sharply that it was none of Taylor's business. He received a similar warning from a political opponent, Bob Boothby, who was also a delegate at Strasbourg; Boothby conceded that it might not be his concern but he wrote because of his regard for Crosland, his irritation at a waste of talent and his fear of 'you going the same way as too many others in the profession'.[47]

The Parliament of 1950–51 came to an end when Attlee, who felt that his government could not continue with such a small majority, called a General Election in October. Though Labour won more votes than the Tories, Churchill and the Conservatives got back to power with a majority of seventeen. Both Jenkins and Crosland were returned with slightly reduced majorities.

Healey, who remained at Transport House during the election, was

on a visit to Strasbourg in December when he received a telephone
call, asking if he would accept a nomination to be the Labour candidate
for a by-election in south-east Leeds. Despite his initial hesitation
about Parliament, he agreed. He had explored other alternatives, such
as Professor of International Relations at Aberystwyth and Foreign
Editor of the *Daily Herald*, and he no longer wanted to work at
Transport House now that Bevin was dead and Labour out of power.
After a deadlock when the favourite, a local councillor, failed to get an
overall majority, Healey won the adjourned selection conference comfortably
and went on to win the February 1952 by-election, with a
majority of 7000 on a low turnout. All three were now MPs, with good
prospects of office, if and when Labour returned to power.

5

Opposition and
The Future of Socialism

Opposition is usually a frustrating experience for clever, ambitious politicians, all the more so if the governing party is in power for a long time. After the narrow Tory election victory of 1951, Hugh Dalton predicted that the Labour Party would soon be back in office.[1] But the Conservative Party, accepting much of what Labour had done and more in tune with postwar affluence, won three successive elections: in 1951 under Winston Churchill, in 1955 under Anthony Eden, and in 1959 under Harold Macmillan. Denis Healey's comment about the period is apposite: 'We used to describe the period of Conservative government from 1951 to 1964 as "Thirteen Wasted Years". The first eleven of those years were wasted by the Labour Party.'[2] Following Nye Bevan's resignation, Labour spent too much of the 1950s in fratricidal conflict and too little on adapting itself to the changes which the Labour government of 1945–51 had in part helped bring about. Though it was, in many respects, to be a depressing decade for them, Crosland, Jenkins and Healey all became influential members of the revisionist wing of the Labour Party.

After the 1951 defeat, Labour MPs had to get used to opposition. Former ministers, accustomed to government cars and red dispatch boxes, and MPs, whose main task had been to support the government in the division lobbies, had to find themselves a new role. In the 1950s, the pressures of parliamentary and constituency life were much less than now. Although there was a shadow Cabinet or parliamentary committee, far fewer MPs had front-bench responsibilities. There were no departmental select committees. And constituency obligations were much less onerous than they are today.

Roy Jenkins wrote that, following the Tory victory in 1951, 'the shock of moving to the Opposition benches, which I had never previously experienced, was considerable'.[3] His immediate reaction was to accept an invitation to join Hugh Gaitskell's shadow front-bench finance team which included former ministers like Douglas Jay and other promising MPs, such as his friend Tony Crosland. Their main task was to oppose the first 1952 Budget of the Tory Chancellor of the Exchequer, R. A. Butler. Roy's effectiveness in moving amendments to the Finance Bill (the committee stage was then taken on the floor of the House) was such that it earned him the respect and friendship of Gaitskell, already emerging as a possible successor to Attlee.

Jenkins, who had come into Parliament as an Attlee loyalist and who, for a year or two, was part of Bevan's smoking room circle, had by 1953 become a fully fledged Gaitskellite. The tribal warfare, which dominated the first part of the 1950s, inevitably affected relations with the Bevanites. Although he remained on reasonable terms with Dick Crossman, Michael Foot and John Freeman, Roy recalled, with some regret, that Bevan and he 'hardly addressed a word to each other throughout the decade' and that Jennie Lee, Nye Bevan's wife, was 'even more resentfully sharp-clawed'.[4]

Gaitskell once described Bevanism as 'only a conspiracy to seize the leadership for Aneurin Bevan'.[5] Although Gaitskell was hardly objective about Bevan, there was some justice in what he said. The loose collection of semi-Marxists, left-wingers, pacifists, individualists and malcontents in the *Keep Left* group was transformed by Bevan's resignation into a more formidable group, capable, now they had Bevan at their head, of mounting a serious challenge for the leadership.

However, there were serious Bevanite policy issues, mostly concerned with foreign affairs and defence. In March 1952, fifty-seven Labour MPs defied the party whip and voted against the Conservative government's Defence White Paper. Two years later, German rearmament and the prospect of a South-East Asia anti-Communist alliance also provided flashpoints. The right-wing majority in the Parliamentary Labour Party bitterly resented the Bevanites but the rebels were far more popular in the constituency parties, which were wooed by a travelling circus of left-wing MPs organised by the *Tribune* weekly journal.

In 1954, opposition to German rearmament, which attracted party support beyond the Bevanites, caused Jenkins difficulties with his constituency party. Roy strongly supported the leadership position. He believed that the tense situation in Europe and the need for German rehabilitation made German rearmament essential. However, on 23 February 1954, a packed meeting of the Parliamentary Labour Party gave the leadership a majority of only two. The management committee of the Stechford party met that same day and unanimously carried a pro-Bevanite resolution. In the knowledge that Jenkins had voted for the leadership, a motion was then put down that a special meeting be called 'to discuss the relations of the member with the constituency'.

Rather than prevaricate, Jenkins boldly decided that matters should be brought to a head and went to Birmingham to defend himself at the next meeting of his management committee. Devoting his speech partly to the case for German rearmament and partly to his right as an MP to vote in the way he judged even if his constituency party did not agree with him, he swung the delegates his way and the motion calling for a special meeting was defeated by thirty votes to two. Thereafter, Roy had few problems with his Stechford party.

In his autobiography, Jenkins described himself as an old-style member. He normally visited his constituency about once a month and also for a week in September. Roy usually stayed with a local couple, the Hitchmans, in their semi-detached house in the heart of the Stechford constituency, which was mainly skilled working class. There had never been a question of him living there nor even of having a pied à terre. Although Jenkins hardly ever raised constituency issues on the floor of the House, he dealt efficiently with correspondence and held monthly surgeries. Though a relatively conscientious constituency member, Jenkins' priorities were always national rather than local.

During the 1951–55 Parliament Jenkins acquired a growing reputation as a writer. After the defeat of 1951, he produced a short (55,000 words) book on the achievements and prospects of the Labour Party called *Pursuit of Progress* which was published by Heinemann in

April 1953. Analysing Labour Party history, its main message was that, in any left-wing party, there was an inevitable tension between utopianism and reformism and that, though there was a necessary role for the utopians, practical advance was only achieved when the reformists were in control. He accepted that there would be periods of Tory government and that the advance of socialism would have to be carried out 'by a process of fits and starts'. The Jenkins of *Pursuit of Progress* was a politician on the move. He could see that the 1945–50 settlement was no guide to the future but he had not yet worked out a viable alternative. If this was not the comprehensive revisionist work for which younger Labour MPs and supporters were beginning to call, it was well reviewed and at least demonstrated that Jenkins was prepared to put his pen at the disposal of the Gaitskellite cause.

His next book, *Mr Balfour's Poodle*, which was published a year later in February 1954, was a more serious literary enterprise. It was a well-researched and lively narrative account of the constitutional and political struggle between the House of Lords and Asquith's Liberal government from 1909, when the Lords rejected Lloyd George's Budget, and 1911, when the Parliament Bill became law. Jenkins' work, whose title was derived from Lloyd George's aphorism, 'The House of Lords is not the watchdog of the constitution; it is Mr Balfour's poodle', was designed to appeal to the general reader, though its scholarship was of sufficient calibre for it to be recommended by modern history lecturers to their pupils and to be still in print nearly fifty years later. Roy had been attracted to the subject by the passing of the 1949 Parliament Act which had reduced to one year the delaying powers of the Lords and he had shrewdly noted the absence of a popular history of the 1911 crisis. He researched and wrote much of the book in the tranquillity of the House of Commons Library.

Much more than his earlier two books, *Mr Balfour's Poodle* can be said to mark the real beginning of Roy Jenkins' career as a professional writer. It was favourably reviewed by R. C. K. Ensor in the *Sunday Times*, by A. J. P. Taylor in the *Guardian*, by Leonard Woolf in *The Listener* and by Harold Nicolson in the *Observer*. It was, however, a private letter of fulsome praise from Harold Nicolson before publication which gave Jenkins the most pleasure, as Nicolson, himself a considerable literary figure, was then one of the top two or three broadsheet reviewers in the country.

Perhaps most important of all, the success of *Mr Balfour's Poodle* led to a suggestion by Mark Bonham Carter, the Liberal politician and publisher, that Roy's next book should be about Sir Charles Dilke, the radical Victorian politician whose career had been destroyed by a sensational divorce case, and that Collins, for whom Bonham Carter was a senior manager, would be interested in publishing it. After he had read *The Times'* reports of the case and the two-volume standard life published in 1917, Jenkins became fascinated by Dilke's downfall and agreed to write his biography. Roy's career as a political biographer was launched.

In addition to writing books, Roy turned to journalism, including a weekly London letter (for five pounds an article) for a Bombay journal edited by his cousin by marriage. In 1953 he also received an attractive offer from Spendon Lewis of the John Lewis Partnership, who had been impressed by his *Pursuit of Progress*, to join the firm either in an executive or advisory capacity. After initial hesitation, Jenkins agreed to work for one and a half days a week, giving economic and general advice for £1000 a year. In those days, it was unusual for Labour MPs to have paid employment outside politics. But, for only a relatively small expenditure of time, Jenkins had doubled his income.

By the middle fifties, the Jenkins family had taken settled shape. Charles, their eldest son, was born in 1949, Cynthia, their daughter, in 1951 and Edward, their youngest, in 1954. In December 1948, they had moved out of their small flat in Marsham Street to a much bigger apartment in a Victorian mansion in Cornwall Gardens, South Kensington. In 1954, after the death of Roy's mother and the sale of the family house in Pontypool, the Jenkins were able to buy a fine late Victorian six-bedroom house in Ladbroke Square, Notting Hill for £5250, where they were to live for the next twenty-three years.

As well as a splendid L-shaped first-floor study-cum-drawing room, the house had a large ground-floor dining room where Roy and Jennifer regularly entertained their friends, including the Gaitskells, the Beaumarchais from the French Embassy, J. K. Galbraith, the American economist, the Benns (who lived nearby), the Crossmans, Woodrow Wyatt (between wives) and the Healeys. In a sense, it was a re-creation, albeit on a grander scale, of Roy's parents' generous hospitality at Pontypool. There was a notable absentee. Although Jenkins and Crosland still saw a great deal of each other, the Jenkins had decided that it was better to see Crosland on his own: 'Famous for his flounces and his unconcealed disapproval of those he might be asked to meet, he was too hazardous a guest for dinner parties.'[6]

For a time after he had entered Parliament, Denis Healey continued to have doubts about the place. In the 1950s, the House of Commons was still run like a gentlemen's club, for the convenience of well-off Tory MPs who had outside jobs. There was no secretarial allowance and Denis did not even have a desk for his papers. Until he became a Cabinet minister in 1964, he wrote all his letters in longhand. He supplemented his meagre parliamentary salary by earnings from journalism, radio and television.

However, whatever the job's shortcomings, Denis brought considerable advantages to his new career. Unlike Roy and Tony who had experienced parliamentary life with Labour in government and had to get used to being in opposition, Denis went straight on to the opposition benches. And, with Britain still a world power, albeit a declining one, there was a premium on Labour MPs who were experts, like Healey, in foreign affairs. In his first years in Parliament, he spent much of his time in the chamber listening to and sometimes speaking in debates, especially on foreign affairs. In the 1950s, it was customary to have four or five major foreign affairs debates, often lasting two days, in which great speakers like Churchill and Bevan as well brilliant backbenchers like Bob Boothby and Dick Crossman argued with passion about the big international questions of the day such as the H-bomb, German rearmament, the Russian invasion of Hungary, or the Suez crisis.

Healey made his maiden speech on the contentious issue of Germany. He said that, in the long run, German rearmament was inevitable and that the dilemma for the West was to derive a framework within which it could safely take place. Denis showed his mettle by warning Anthony Eden, then at the height of his reputation as Conservative Foreign Secretary, against a European Defence Community (later, as Healey predicted in his speech, rejected by the French) as a means of harnessing the Germans. With prescience, Healey argued instead for German membership of NATO: 'I am one of those who believe that the even closer unity of the Atlantic peoples is one of the most fruitful developments of the postwar era. And I am convinced that it offers to us the one real chance of solving the perennial problem of Germany.' Denis was congratulated by the next speaker, the Conservative MP and writer, Fitzroy Maclean: 'Hon. members have often listened to his speeches before but hitherto they had been delivered by his Right Hon. friends on the front bench. Now . . . he has made good and emerged as an orator in his own right.'[7]

In truth, though Healey's contributions were always meticulously researched and read well in Hansard afterwards, in the chamber they too often tended to sound like lectures rather than parliamentary speeches. When Healey made his first speech from the Labour front bench, Anthony Eden, then still Foreign Secretary, said that, 'It was all the Foreign Office's best briefs rolled into one, and expressed much better than they are usually put before me.' All the same, Denis's outstanding ability and knowledge made him an obvious candidate for the front bench not only as a foreign affairs spokesman under Attlee but later as Gaitskell's shadow Colonial and Commonwealth spokesman and Wilson's shadow Defence Secretary. More than Roy or Tony, Denis rapidly became indispensable to the Labour leadership.

During the 1950s, Healey, adding to his contacts made as the Labour Party's International Secretary, developed a unique network abroad. Every year, he gave lectures in the United States. In Washington, he got to know the US foreign affairs establishment, Dean Acheson, Truman's Secretary of State, George Kennan, the State Department's expert on Russia and George Ball, Under Secretary of State to successive Democrat administrations. Denis also wrote a monthly column for the radical New York journal, the *New Leader*, which helped give him an entrée to the city's Jewish intellectual world. In these ways, he strengthened his links with the United States.

Denis Healey was a frequent attendee at the international conferences that sprang up during these years. At the NATO parliamentarians' conference, he met Stewart Udall, Democrat congressman and later Kennedy's Secretary of the Interior, and John Lindsay, the Liberal Republican who became Mayor of New York. Healey was a founder member of the Bilderberg conference, the brainchild of Juzek Retinger, Polish friend of Churchill and international fixer par excellence. The aim of these conferences, the first of which was held at Bilderberg in the Netherlands, was to bring the leaders of

Europe and North America closer together. Here, Healey mingled with European and American politicians, businessmen, bankers and trade unionists.

Denis also went to the British-German Königswinter conference, started by Frau Lilo Milchsack, wife of a German industrialist, to help improve relations between the two countries. The conference met annually at Königswinter, a riverside resort near Bonn, and Healey became friends with German politicians like Helmut Schmidt, journalists like Marion Dönhoff who wrote for *Die Zeit* and generals like von Seger und Etterlin who had commanded the German troops at Monte Cassino. Critics of Healey frequently commented on his tendency to 'name drop'. What they often overlooked was that, back in the 1950s or early 1960s, he had already become well acquainted with many of those whose names he was later accused of 'dropping', before either they or he had become famous.

Although Healey made his political reputation in foreign affairs, he played his part in the internal feuds which split the Labour Party following Bevan's resignation. In 1951, he was calling for a new direction for the party:

> The Labour Party may hope to carry the Welfare State and
> planning further than the Tories, but for a long time physical
> and psychological factors will fix rigid limits. Future
> nationalisation no longer attracts more than a tiny fringe of
> the Labour Party itself; it positively repels the electorate as a
> whole. Even among Labour economists there is a growing
> revolt against physical controls in favour of the price
> mechanism. A policy based on class cannot have a wide appeal
> when the difference between classes is so small as Labour has
> made it.[8]

This was a clear and early indication that Healey was firmly on the side of those who sought to revise Labour's ideology and policies in the light of changing circumstances.

Healey recognised Nye Bevan's great abilities but he saw Bevanism as a flight from reality and was highly critical of what he considered to be Bevan's 'irresponsibility about defence and deliberate exploitation of the anti-Americanism always latent in the Labour party'.[9] The two men had a fierce row one summer evening in 1952 which began at an American Embassy dinner party and ended after midnight on the terrace of the House of Commons. Nye called Denis 'a red-faced boy from Transport House', to which Denis responded in kind. In October, at the Morecambe party conference, which marked the high point of Bevanism, Healey, already showing a talent for invective, attacked Bevan publicly: Bevan's anti-Americanism, said Healey, was 'jingoism with an inferiority complex: I ask you to throw away the stale mythology of these political Peter Pans. We cannot solve the problems of foreign policy on a diet of rhetorical candyfloss.'[10]

Three years later, his hostile attitude to Bevan put his survival in Parliament at risk. Redistribution had eliminated one of the safe Labour seats in Leeds and the selection conference for the new constituency of Leeds East took place a few days after the Parliamentary Labour Party (PLP) had withdrawn the whip from Nye Bevan for abstaining, despite a specific decision by the PLP, in a debate on the H-bomb. Healey's constituency party was far to the left – its right wing was sympathetic to Bevan, while the left was Trotskyite. Healey's situation was complicated by the fact that one of his fellow Leeds MPs, with whom Denis worked closely, was Hugh Gaitskell, Bevan's chief critic and rival for the leadership. The first question put to Healey by a sullen selection conference was how he had voted in the PLP meeting. Denis took the challenge head on by telling them that, though they did not have the right to ask, he had, in fact, voted for the whip being withdrawn and that they would have done the same if any Labour councillor had behaved in Leeds as Bevan had done in Westminster. Healey was given a majority of two to one and was never in serious trouble with his local party again, though from time to time he quoted the message sent to Frederick the Great by one of his generals after being ordered to carry out a disastrous attack: 'Please tell His Majesty that after the battle my head is at his disposal, but during the battle I propose to use it in his service.'[11]

Though, like Jenkins and Crosland, Healey always saw himself as primarily a national politican, he enjoyed his duties in his mainly working-class Leeds constituency and considered that he derived strength and understanding from his local work. He once wrote: 'Every MP should act as a Miss Lonelyhearts. The busier a politican is with national or international affairs, the more important is his constituency case work.'[12] Most of the problems with which he had to deal in the 1950s were concerned with housing. Waiting lists for council houses were still outrageously long; later, defects in postwar housing and a huge backlog of repairs became predominant. In his relations with his constituents, Denis received considerable help from Edna. He later paid her a warm tribute: 'It took time for me to win the confidence of my party activists. Edna's warm outgoing personality made up for my own weaknesses. She worked hard in the constituency and spoke better than I at election meetings. At that time I could only make my audience think. She could make them laugh and cry.'[13]

Denis and Edna now had a growing family. Jenny was born in 1948, Tim in 1949 and Cressida in 1953. Once the children came, the Healeys moved from their attic in Bloomsbury to Highgate, first at 46 Langbourne Avenue, Holly Lodge Estate and then to 16 Holly Lodge Gardens. The house in Holly Lodge Gardens had an attractive garden with views over London; it also was next to Highgate cemetery where Karl Marx was buried.

Unlike the Jenkins, the Healeys did not do much entertaining, though there was a memorable Sunday lunch party at Holly Lodge Gardens with the Jenkins and the Benns after which Denis took their guests to see Karl Marx's grave. Healey was away so much, either in the constituency or abroad, that he tended to keep his spare weekends free for the family. It was in the middle 1950s that the Healeys, equipped with a new Hillman Husky estate (their first car) and a tent, started taking continental camping holidays. They would stay for a week by a lake in the Alps, usually near Annecy or Montreux, then have a week high up in the mountains, then finish with a week by the Mediterranean or by an Italian lake. With his camera, Denis recorded these happy occasions, Edna with the children at Grindelwald, Jenny and Tim drawing on a table at a farm near Klagenfurt, a full moon over the Gran Paradiso, Val d'Aosta.

In the 1951–55 Parliament, Tony Crosland did not trouble to conceal his boredom with the life of an opposition MP. In 1952, he had worked hard as a member of Gaitskell's shadow finance team. He also took trouble over his Budget debate speeches. The Tory minister, Edward Boyle, later praised his 1955 Budget contribution as one of the best debating speeches he had ever heard in the House.[14] Crosland ferociously attacked the Chancellor, R. A. Butler for his irresponsibility in buying votes by reducing taxation in April, after having previously tightened monetary policy in February.

But Tony was a poor attendee at the Commons. He was contemptuous of the low level of parliamentary debate and depressed by the internal Labour Party warfare. Susan Crosland described his attitude to Parliament in the 1950s: 'With his flat only fifteen minutes' drive from the House, he could stroll into the chamber long enough to listen to the few speeches that interested him, occasionally deliver an incisive speech of his own, stroll out again and go home . . . When he came back for evening divisions he would sometimes be accompanied by one or other young woman who was clearly not interested in politics.'[15] When Dick Crossman criticised him for coming drunk into the House in the evening, Tony replied, 'How else is one to endure being here?'

This was a time when Crosland was unhappy in his private life. In the autumn of 1952, he married Hilary Sarson, with whom he had had an intermittent affair for several years. Although there was a strong physical attraction between them, Hilary did not share Tony's political and intellectual interests and Tony had had deep misgivings about getting married to her. The marriage got off to a disastrous start. At the wedding lunch at the *Gay Hussar* restaurant, the well-known left-wing haunt in Soho, Hilary was made miserable by Hugh Dalton's booming remarks about Tony's previous girlfriends,[16] while the honeymoon consisted mainly of a motor tour of southern Spain with the economist Nicky Kaldor and his wife Clarisse, during which Kaldor continually put Hilary down. Bill Rodgers recalled a 1953 New Year's party, with Tony 'morose and steadily getting drunk in the company of his new and first wife, Hilary, to whom he rarely spoke'.[17] Hilary had hoped that buying the top-floor flat of 19 The Boltons, South Kensington would convert Tony into a monogamist but he was soon discreetly seeing other women and, after about a year, Hilary moved out.

Tony now resumed his womanising ways openly, whether with daughters of the aristocracy or the film starlets whom he met at cocktail parties. In his memoirs, Woodrow Wyatt, then a friend, remarked, 'Tony's girls were a wonderment to me: nearly always very pretty and frequently fair and blue-eyed, occasionally with brains as well: he hardly ever loved the numerous girls he went to bed with.'[18] Fellow Labour MPs may have been envious of Tony's sexual conquests but they were also critical of Tony's failure to pull his weight in the Commons.

However, if some wrote Tony off as an arrogant intellectual, there were others in the Labour Party who admired him for his intelligence and style. Apart from Hugh Dalton, the most important of these was the shadow Chancellor, Hugh Gaitskell, who quickly recognised Crosland's potential both as an economist and as a thinker and was amused and attracted by his hedonistic private life. It would certainly be wrong to write off this first period of opposition as wasted for him. It was during this time that Tony Crosland wrote his most original political work and began to emerge as Labour's leading revisionist thinker.

In May 1952, a few months after Labour's election defeat, *New Fabian Essays* came out. These essays, modelled on the original 1889 *Fabian Essays in Socialism*, had been planned and written while Labour was still in power and they were a conscious, if somewhat uneven, attempt by a number of younger Fabians, including Crosland, Jenkins and Healey, to set out the way ahead. Dick Crossman edited the book and wrote a typically provocative introductory essay: 'The Labour Party has lost its way not only because it lacks a map of the new country it is crossing, but because it thinks maps unnecessary for experienced travellers.'[19] In his contribution on *Equality*, Roy Jenkins argued in revisionist fashion that socialism should be defined in terms of greater equality rather than nationalisation. Jenkins' essay was also anti-Marxist-Leninist in that it stressed how the Soviet Union had less equality than any of the Western welfare states. The main message of Denis Healey's *Power Politics and the Labour Party* was that socialists needed to understand the realities of power politics in international relations and how, with the recovery of Germany and Japan and the rise of China, the position of the United Kingdom was bound to weaken in the postwar world.

Crosland's essay, *The Transition from Capitalism*, was, however, the most authoritative and original of the collection. In it, he put forward themes which he was to develop more fully in *The Future of Socialism*. First, capitalism, so far from collapsing as predicted by Marxist analysis, had continued to expand. Second, since 1945, capitalism had itself been transformed by a number of forces (including the extension of the power of the state, the coming of full employment, the expansion of social services, the growth of managerialism, the rise of the technical and professional middle class and the role of the unions) into a new form, which Crosland, somewhat inelegantly, called 'statism'. Britain was, however, still a class-ridden society and more equality was required, 'not simply equality of opportunity on the American model, but equality of status in the widest sense – subjective as well as objective . . . The purpose of socialism is quite simply to eradicate this sense of class, and to create in its place a sense of common interest and equal status.'[20]

Crosland concluded by outlining new areas for socialist concern – the maldistribution of property (as opposed to income), poor industrial relations, and, above all, reform of the education system. 'Nothing more amazes visitors from genuinely equalitarian countries (such as Sweden or New Zealand) than the existence in Britain of a social hierarchy of schools,' pointed out the future Secretary of State for Education. Although *New Fabian Essays* was well reviewed, its impact was blunted by the Bevanite row: by May 1952 commentators were more interested by Labour's fratricidal war than in its possible future direction. However, Tony Crosland's essay was recognised as the most interesting contribution of the collection by the *Manchester Guardian*, *The Times* and the *Evening Standard*.

In 1953, Crosland published a 200-page study, *Britain's Economic Problem*. In it, he argued that the deterioration in the foreign exchange position had deep-seated causes, including a shortage of goods and raw materials, a shift in demand for manufactured goods, and the predominent position of the United States in the postwar world. What was required was long-term investment to strengthen the UK's industrial base. Dalton wrote in his diary, with some justice, that no other MP could have written so well on the subject, while a former Labour Treasury minister, Douglas Jay, called it 'the best book since the war on the British struggle for solvency'.[21] If his Fabian essay had revealed his promise as a theoretican, *Britain's Economic Problem* was a well-timed reminder that Crosland was one of Labour's few trained economists. As such, he was likely to be a strong candidate for an economic job in another Labour government, stronger indeed than Roy Jenkins, who, with his sharp political antennae, was quick to recognise

Crosland's superior claim, at least in Hugh Dalton's and Hugh Gaitskell's eyes.[22]

The problem for Crosland was that, following redistribution, he was uncertain of being in the next Parliament. Like Roy and Denis, Tony was, in the style of the 1950s, a reasonably assiduous local constituency member who dealt conscientiously with the suburban and rural problems of south Gloucestershire. When visiting his constituency in his sports car, he stayed with the Donaldsons. Jack had been Denis Healey's colonel in Naples but was now a local farmer, while his wife Frankie was a writer on farming matters who later became a well-known biographer. Twenty-five years later in his memorial address on Crosland, Jack Donaldson described Crosland's visits: 'He was never an easy guest. He was always determined to put off meals until he felt sufficiently relaxed to enjoy them, and he used to deploy his considerable armoury in delaying tactics until sometimes we had lunch an hour or more late. He closed all conversations which did not interest him, and he never refrained from complaining of any lapse in the standards of comfort of the house.'[23] Yet the Donaldsons and their teenage children were captivated by Tony and looked forward immensely to his next visit.

When, at the beginning of 1955, the Boundary Commission allocated some of his safest south Gloucestershire wards to Bristol in exchange for Conservative wards from Stroud, Crosland estimated that redistribution would create a seat with a Tory majority of between two and three thousand. After his hopes were dashed that a neighbouring Labour MP in a more promising seat would retire, Crosland decided to desert south Gloucestershire in favour of Southampton, Test, which had also been adversely affected by redistribution. This was a bad misjudgement because, at the May 1955 election, the Tory majority in his new seat was some four thousand greater than in his old seat, though, even if he had stayed on, it is doubtful if he could have held south Gloucestershire.

In one way, Crosland's defeat at the 1955 election was a blessing in disguise. It enabled him to finish the big book about contemporary socialism on which he had been working for the last two years. Tony's method of writing was highly disciplined. 'He could concentrate intellectually for fourteen, fifteen hours a day, pacing himself with breaks to make a pot of tea, walking to some café for a meal.'[24] The flat at 19

The Boltons was organised around his work. He wrote in longhand in one of two comfortable but battered armchairs. Manuscripts were arranged systemically in piles on the seat of a deep sofa, on its arms and on the ground in front of it; if one of Crosland's riotous parties was planned, a considerable operation was required to remove the papers, while still maintaining them in their proper order.

In the autumn of 1954, Crosland had abandoned the Westminster parliamentary session to take two months' 'sabbatical' in the United States. Both Healey and Jenkins had also gone on long trips to the new superpower, Denis in September 1949 and Roy from August to October 1953; but Healey was not then an MP, while Jenkins' visit was in the parliamentary recess. All three were immensely impressed by the experience. Healey later wrote: 'That first visit to the United States gave me a love for the country and its people which has survived many political disappointments.'[25] Jenkins believed that his first trip to the States was 'a major formative influence in my life; it could be regarded as a fairly sound investment of not much more than $3000 by the US Government.'[26] Crosland looked at American society with a sociologist's eye. He was greatly attracted by the social mobility, educational opportunity and classlessness of the United States compared to the United Kingdom of 1954. 'The facts about America are hardly in dispute. Objectively, class differences in accent, dress, manners, and general style of life are very much smaller. Subjectively, social relations are more natural and egalitarian and less masked by deference, submissiveness, or snobbery.'[27] It was the creation of a more egalitarian, classless Britain that was to be the main subject of *The Future of Socialism*.

Crosland's book was highly ambitious. Ever since his wartime correspondence with Philip Williams, he had wanted to write the definitive work for his generation on revisionist socialism. Consciously following the example of Edmund Bernstein, the revisionist German Social Democrat whose *Evolutionary Socialism*, published in 1899, had decisively refuted the Marxist theory that capitalism was about to collapse, *The Future of Socialism* was long (over 500 pages) and comprehensive. Drawing not only on economics but also political theory, history, sociology and industrial psychology, his book also covered the policy areas of education, the social services, industrial relations, as well as of economic and fiscal policy. He saw sociology as especially important. 'I am convinced that this is the field, rather than the traditional fields of politics and economics, in which the significant issues for socialism and welfare will increasingly be found to lie.'[28]

The underlying thesis of the first part of the book was that the harsh world of the 1930s had been transformed by the war and the postwar Labour government. Expanding on his Fabian essay, he showed how the Marxist theory of capitalist collapse, so firmly believed by socialist intellectuals before the war, had been clearly disproved. On the contrary, output and living standards were rising steadily. At the same time, the commanding position of the business class had been reduced by the increased powers of government and the improved bargaining strength of labour. Managers not owners now ran industry. The combination of rising living standards, redistributive taxation and welfare benefits and services had substantially reduced primary poverty. Crosland argued that, in the 1950s, ownership of the means of production was largely irrelevant. 'I conclude,' he wrote authoritatively, 'that the definition of capitalism in terms of ownership has wholly lost its significance and interest now that ownership is no longer the clue to the total picture of social relationships: and that it would be more significant to define societies in terms of equality or class relationships, or their political systems.'[29]

One of the key points about *The Future of Socialism* was the clear distinction it drew between ends and means.[30] 'Ends' were defined as the basic values or aspirations and 'means' as describing the institutional or policy methods required to promote these values in practice. It was incorrect to try and define socialism in terms of a policy like nationalisation which, Crosland pointed out, had been introduced for very different purposes both in Nazi Germany and the Soviet Union. The revisionist task was to subject the means to searching criticism and scrutiny in the light of changing conditions. Uncomfortable as it might be to acknowledge, the means most suitable in one generation could be wholly irrelevant in the next.

Modern socialism, Crosland concluded, was about improving welfare and promoting social equality: 'The socialist seeks a distribution of rewards, status, and privileges egalitarian enough to minimise social resentment, to secure justice between individuals and to equalise opportunities; and he seeks to weaken the existing deep-seated class stratification with its consistent feelings of envy and inferiority, and its barriers to uninhibited mingling between the classes.'[31] Significantly, he gave first priority to educational reform, including introducing comprehensive secondary education and opening up entry to private schools. 'If socialism is taken to mean a "classless society", this is the front on which the main attack should now be mounted.'[32]

In his conclusion, he called for cultural changes to make Britain a more cultured and civilised country and for a greater emphasis on private life and leisure. In a celebrated passage on the Webbs, which was as revealing about him as it was critical of the two Fabians, he wrote 'Total abstinence and a good filing system are not now the right signposts to the socialist utopia: or at least, if they are, some of us will fall by the wayside.'[33]

Forty-five years later, it is easy with the benefit of hindsight to criticise *The Future of Socialism*. Crosland was too optimistic about economic growth. 'I no longer regard questions of growth and efficiency as being, on a long view, of primary importance to socialism,'[34] he confidently proclaimed. His definition of equality has been criticised as being too doctriniare and rigid, though Crosland, in his book, sought not an unrealistic equality of outcome but to remove unfair and unnecessary barriers. He also ignored racial and sexual equality. He appeared sometimes to be an uncritical supporter of public expenditure (though he later made significant qualifications). He was too complacent about Conservative opposition to socialist ideas and policies, ruling out 'a wholesale counter-revolution'.[35] Above all, he had nothing to say about the international context in which Labour governments had to operate. Croslandism was 'revisionism in one country'. Yet accepting that it was a tract for its times, its authority, lucidity and sheer style have ensured that *The Future of Socialism* is still read today.

Published to coincide with the October 1956 party conference, *The Future of Socialism* was an immediate success not just with moderate socialists but across a wide swathe of liberal opinion. The *Financial Times* said that Crosland had left his critics in the Labour Party flailing in his wake. In the *Spectator*, Graham Hutton wrote that the book showed what Labour might become. On the BBC's European service, the academic William Pickles said it was the most important book on its subject since Bernstein.[36] Even Dick Crossman, a Bevanite fellow traveller and rival Labour Party theoretician, admitted to Crosland that his ideas were 'diabolically and cunningly left-wing and Nye should have been clever enough to think them up'.[37]

In an assessment thirty-two years later, Roy Jenkins was right to say that *The Future of Socialism* influenced a whole political generation:[38] its combination of hope with realism, ideals with practical policies, gave it a wide and enduring appeal. However, in the context of the 1950s, it had a more immediate purpose – to provide the intellectual basis for Hugh Gaitskell's attempt to modernise the Labour Party.

6

Hugh Gaitskell's Supporters

Crosland, Jenkins and Healey were all committed supporters of Gaitskell, Labour's leader from December 1955 to his early death in January 1963. Crosland and Jenkins were intimate personal friends, members of what came to be known as the 'Hampstead' or 'Frognal set'. Healey was not quite so close but more important politically than either Crosland or Jenkins. A fellow Leeds MP, he was a trusted foreign policy and defence expert to whom Gaitskell turned for advice and support. All three agreed with Gaitskell that the Labour Party's ideology and policies urgently needed bringing up to date and they tried to help him do it.

Gaitskell was a strong leader who aroused both great enthusiasm and great controversy within the party.[1] For Crosland and Jenkins especially, he was the lost leader, the political hero who bravely tried to modernise the Labour Party. His qualities of high intelligence, rationality and integrity combined with courage and passion, made him an inspiring man for revisionists to follow. They believed that, if he had lived, he would have won the 1964 election and gone on to make an outstanding Prime Minister. Philip Williams, whose biography of Gaitskell was published in 1979, ended it with the words, 'Gaitskell might have been the great peacetime leader that twentieth-century Britain has badly needed, and sadly failed to find.'[2] Yet to the Bevanite left, he was public school, right wing, a machine politician who stole the leadership from Nye Bevan, lost the 1959 election partly by his own mistakes and inadequacies and then wilfully tried to turn the party into a British version of the American Democrats and deservedly failed. According to Bevan's biographer, Michael Foot, Gaitskell and Gaitskellism offended against everything that Bevan stood for.[3]

Hugh Gaitskell's rise to the leadership of the Labour Party was even more meteoric than Tony Blair's. Elected to Parliament in 1945, he became Chancellor of the Exchequer in October 1950 and leader five years later. Gaitskell gave his own explanation: 'The leadership came my way so early because Bevan threw it at me by his behaviour.'[4] There was much in this judgement. Attlee had wanted Bevan to succeed him but Bevan's erratic judgement and conduct ruled it out. There were, however, other factors. Herbert Morrison was expected by some to succeed Attlee but Attlee's strong opposition and Morrison's own weaknesses undermined his chances. More crucially, following the 1952 party conference at Morecambe, at which the Bevanites won six out of the seven constituency places on the National Executive, Gaitskell made a controversial speech at Stalybridge, in which he warned against Communist infiltration and made a fierce attack on the Bevanites. This speech made him leader of the moderate faction inside the parliamentary party and the favourite of the big unions, who, in 1954, voted him into the party treasurership and increasingly saw him as their candidate for the succession.

After the May 1955 election defeat (in which Crosland had lost his seat), both Crosland and Jenkins became convinced that it was essential that Gaitskell should succeed Attlee, who was now in his seventies, as soon as possible. Gaitskell initially believed that Morrison, with whom he had worked in alliance since Labour lost power in 1951, should have the first turn; but Crosland and Jenkins believed that a Morrison leadership would not only be a disaster for the party but would also leave the way open for Bevan. On 7 June, the Gaitskells dined alone with the Jenkins at Ladbroke Square and Roy tried his hardest to get Gaitskell to change his mind and stand in the leadership ballot of Labour MPs (at that time the method of choosing the leader) when Attlee announced his resignation.

As the year went on, Morrison's position deteriorated and Gaitskell's support among MPs increased. In October, Gaitskell spoke eloquently at the Margate party conference, explaining, in revisionist fashion and to Bevan's chagrin, that he had become a socialist not so much because of nationalisation but because of his belief in social justice and dislike of the class system. Later that month, he made a devastating attack in Parliament on the Tory Chancellor, R. A. Butler, for his irresponsible and opportunistic management of the economy: 'he began in folly, he continued in deceit, and he has ended in reaction'.[5] The pressure on Gaitskell from Labour MPs, including the ex-Bevanite Harold Wilson, to put his hat in the ring became intense. By early November Gaitskell had been persuaded and he took Morrison out to lunch to tell him that he had decided to stand. Morrison, totally misreading the situation, told him to go ahead, though warning him, 'you'll be out on the first ballot'.[6]

When Attlee finally resigned on 7 December, Morrison made a last-minute attempt to get Gaitskell to stand aside. Bevan was also prepared to step down if Gaitskell did. This self-interested manoeuvre was rejected by Gaitskell, who won the ballot of Labour MPs easily, winning 157 votes to Bevan's seventy and Morrison's forty. It was an emphatic win for a man of the new generation (Gaitskell was forty-nine) whom most Labour MPs thought the best bet to lead the party to victory at the next election.

Gaitskell began his leadership in a conciliatory manner by holding out an olive branch to the Bevanites. He appointed Harold Wilson as shadow Chancellor and persuaded Nye Bevan to become shadow spokesman for the Colonies. Dick Crossman and Kenneth Younger, a former Minister at the Foreign Office, became part of Alf Robens' informal shadow foreign affairs team, working with Denis Healey, whom Gaitskell relied on for foreign affairs and defence advice. Other younger supporters of Gaitskell did less well. Crosland and Wyatt were out of Parliament, but Jenkins was not given a front-bench post until after the 1959 election.

Yet Jenkins, Crosland and Wyatt had a closer personal relationship with Gaitskell than did most members of the shadow Cabinet. Crosland and Jenkins, in particular, had instant access to the leader's office, lunched or dined with Gaitskell at least twice a month, and were invited to Sunday evening parties at Hugh and Dora Gaitskell's home in Frognal Gardens in Hampstead. Some Labour MPs, including Harold Wilson, became jealous of the so-called 'Hampstead set' and exaggerated its influence. The reality was that, while Gaitskell shared a revisionist vision with the bright younger MPs with whom he liked to associate, his decisions were his own and not those of Jenkins and Crosland or anybody else. Indeed Roy and Tony were critical of Gaitskell's support for withdrawing the whip from Bevan in 1955, were doubtful about his tactics over Clause IV of the party constitution in 1959–60, and thought he was wrong about Europe in 1961–62. For the new Labour leader, Jenkins and Crosland, together with Woodrow Wyatt, Christopher Mayhew, Douglas Jay and Patrick Gordon Walker, were like-minded but candid friends with whom he enjoyed discussing a variety of topics, including politics but also ranging much wider over literature, painting and music. Despite being leader, Hugh Gaitskell insisted on retaining his friendships: 'Kings who had favourites were never popular,' he admitted in 1960, listing among his faults, 'kicking against the pricks of loneliness – in other words wanting to continue to have friends – real ones. I put that as something I want especially to try and keep.'[7]

Roy Jenkins was devoted to Gaitskell. Nearly forty years after his death, Gaitskell's photograph still stood on the mantelpiece of Roy's dining room at East Hendred. In his autobiography he said: 'I admired and indeed loved him more than anyone else with whom I have ever worked in politics.'[8] Ten years after Gaitskell's death, Jenkins wrote a biographical essay on Gaitskell for *The Times* in which he assessed his qualities. 'He had purpose and direction, courage and humanity. He was a man for raising the sights of politics. He could raise a banner which men were proud to follow, but he never perverted his leadership ability. He was that very rare phenomenon, a great politician who was also an unusually agreeable man.'[9] As Gaitskell was fourteen years older than Jenkins, there was no question of rivalry. On the other hand, the age gap was narrow enough for there to be shared interests. For Gaitskell, Jenkins' main attraction as a friend was his connections outside politics, something which Gaitskell felt had been lacking in his own life. 'As a result, he was enthusiastic about my non-political success, half respected my political advice, but did not feel any great need to promote my conventional political career.'[10]

Roy's view, one shared by others, was that Tony Crosland, as with Hugh Dalton, was Hugh Gaitskell's favourite. Woodrow Wyatt wrote: 'There was a scintilla of platonic homosexuality in his affection for

Tony, which Socrates would have understood. Hugh not only loved his mind but also his looks and the eternal undergraduate youthfulness of his raffish parties at the Boltons.'[11] Crosland, as befitted the author of *The Future of Socialism*, was both Gaitskell's main intellectual guru and also his boon younger companion, 'Mr Gaitskell's Ganymede' as the *New Statesman* called him, to Crosland's annoyance.[12] For his part, Crosland greatly respected Gaitskell for his leadership qualities. On the night of his death, Tony said in a television interview: 'You had complete confidence in him. You trusted him. You knew absolutely where you were with him and of how many other politicians in Britain at the moment could you say the same?'[13] Crosland, however, sometimes criticised Gaitskell for alleged lack of intellectual rigour and frivolity. And he often queried whether he was radical enough to lead the Labour Party. Susan Crosland summed up her husband's relationship with Gaitskell. 'The two men admired, loved, maddened one another. They shared what might be called an egalitarian attitude to people, their manner unaffected by someone's position – though Tony carried to extremes his treatment of others with concentrated attention or unconcealed dismissiveness according to mood or his assessment of their personalities. Both men threw themselves into their work. Both had a large capacity for enjoyment. The main contention between them was Tony's concern that Hugh was insufficiently radical for a left-wing leader.'[14]

Denis Healey's relationship with Hugh Gaitskell was more formal and businesslike. He was not a member of the 'Hampstead set', though he was invited to Frognal parties. But as a fellow Leeds MP (Alice Bacon, chairman of the party's organisational sub-committee, and Charlie Pannell, an Amalgamated Engineering Union MP, were the others), Healey had local interests in common with the leader. On constituency visits, Healey and Gaitskell both stayed with the Gillinsons, enthusiastic promoters of the visual arts in Leeds, so Healey got to know Gaitskell well. Denis loyally backed Gaitskell in the big disputes of his leadership, especially over unilateral disarmament, but he had his doubts about his long-term suitability as leader of the Labour Party. 'I was worried by a streak of intolerance in Gaitskell's nature; he tended to believe that no one could disagree with him unless they were either knaves or fools. I have always doubted whether the fierce puritanism of his intellectual convictions would have enabled him to run a Labour government for long, without imposing intolerable strains on so anarchic a Labour movement.'[15]

Gaitskell took Healey more seriously than either Crosland or Jenkins as a politician. Healey wrote, with characteristic self-confidence, that he helped form Gaitskell's position on a number of crucial international issues, such as Suez, the Common Market, Russia and the H-bomb.[16] In time, he might well, as he claimed, have become Gaitskell's Foreign Minister. Whereas Gaitskell sometimes had doubts about the commitment to politics of both Crosland and Jenkins, he saw Healey as a possible future leader of the Labour Party.[17]

Gaitskell's diaries show that, early in his leadership, he already had a high opinion of Healey. On 14 February 1956, he agreed with Alf Robens, the new shadow Foreign Secretary, that Denis Healey was by far and away the best of the informal team: 'Very sound indeed, very clever, and very firm.' On 28 February, in an unusual display of confidence, Gaitskell took Denis out to lunch to discuss how to prevent Alf Robens repeating the disastrous speech he had made the previous afternoon in a foreign affairs debate. He asked Healey to organise the team by producing a monthly review of the foreign affairs situation, ensuring regular meetings, and acting as Robens' 'permanent secretary', 'advising him all the time'.[18]

The first big test of Gaitskell's leadership was over the Suez Crisis, which divided British politics more deeply than any foreign policy issue since Munich. Healey's verdict on Suez was that it was in conception, 'a demonstration of moral and intellectual bankruptcy' and in execution, 'a political, diplomatic and operational disgrace'.[19] Denis played a crucial role in helping define Gaitskell's opposition to the Eden government over the Crisis, as well as himself making a number of key speeches and interventions. On 1 August 1956, following the takeover by the Egyptian leader Gamal Abdel Nasser of the Suez Canal on 26 July, Gaitskell had a long talk with Healey. Gaitskell reported in his diary:

> To begin with I thought there was a bit of difference between
> us, and perhaps there still is in emphasis. He was inclined to be
> anti-government and also less inclined to be worried about
> Nasser; more pacifist, more neutralist, shall I say, than

expected. However, after a talk it soon transpired that there was no great difference between us. He readily admitted the great dangers if we did nothing to resist Nasser; he fully agreed that the prestige factor was very important and that the effect in the Middle East would be very serious (but) . . . he took the view that if we were to use force in an unjustifiable way, we would have the whole of the Middle East against us, and much of the rest of the world also.[20]

After the conversation with Healey, Gaitskell's speech in the first Commons debate on 2 August was finely balanced. He strongly condemned Nasser's actions in seizing the Canal and, for fear of being thought unpatriotic, did not attack the government directly. However, though he agreed that military precautions were justified, he said, echoing Healey's advice, that it was British policy not to use force in breach of international law or contrary to world public opinion. 'While force cannot be excluded we must be sure that the circumstances justify it and that it is, if used, consistent with our belief in, and our pledges to, the charter of the United Nations and not in conflict with them.' Healey's speech was more openly critical of the confusion in government policy towards Nasser. 'I believe Colonel Nasser and, indeed, the Arab world as a whole, have some justification for being totally perplexed about what the real attitude of this country is . . . because our policy has somersaulted at least twice a year and in the last year four times.' He also explicitly warned the Conservative Party 'against unilateral military action by Britain, to try to bring back the nineteenth century'.[21]

Significantly on 7 August, following briefings to the press that the government were going to use force against Nasser, Denis Healey and Douglas Jay wrote a strong letter to *The Times*, questioning the extent of the government's military preparations and condemning the use of force, unless supported by the UN. *The Times* letter was Jay's idea but bringing in Healey was at Gaitskell's suggestion, though Healey was not aware of this at the time. Denis had agreed to join Douglas Jay in writing the letter partly because he wanted to stiffen Gaitskell who was away on holiday, though by this time Gaitskell hardly needed stiffening. He himself wrote a firm letter to Eden on 10 August, letting him know that the Healey/Jay letter represented his views. 'Lest there should still be doubt in your mind about my personal attitude, let me say that I could not regard an armed attack on Egypt by ourselves and the French as justified by anything which Nasser has done so far or as consistent with the Charter of the United Nations'.[22]

As the Suez drama unfolded over the next weeks, with Eden and the majority of the Cabinet determined to use force to topple Nasser and desperately seeking a plausible pretext to do so, Gaitskell, advised by Healey, shifted from his initial cautious posture of 2 August to demanding, in his Commons speech of 12 September, an outright pledge from the government not to use force contrary to the Charter. 'Is he (Eden) prepared to say on behalf of HMG that they will not try to shoot their way through the Canal?' asked Gaitskell, winding up for the Opposition.[23]

Despite Gaitskell's warnings, backed up strongly by Healey, and the public opposition of the United States, Eden was determined to bring matters to a head. On 29 October, following secret collusion between the United Kingdom, France and Israel, Israeli tanks, supported by French planes, invaded Sinai; on 30 October, an Anglo-French ultimatum, ostensibly issued to separate the participants but in fact a ploy to justify seizing the Canal, was rejected by Nasser and British planes bombed Egyptian airfields; on 31 October, the British and French vetoed an American resolution in the Security Council calling for a ceasefire; and at dawn on 5 November, British and French paratroopers landed in Port Said. However, on midnight on 6 November, the British were forced by American economic pressure to agree to a ceasefire, still seventy-five miles from Suez. Eden's Suez adventure had ended in what the then Tory Chief Whip Edward Heath, called 'a humiliating failure'.[24] On 9 January 1957, the Prime Minister resigned on grounds of ill health.

Gaitskell was outraged by the government's behaviour and, in a series of passionate parliamentary speeches as well as in a powerful reply for the Opposition on 4 November to a ministerial television broadcast by Eden, he denounced the Conservative administration's 'criminal folly' in breaching the UN Charter, dividing the Commonwealth, undermining Anglo-American relations, encouraging by example the Russian invasion of Hungary and greatly damaging the reputation of the United Kingdom. For many, Gaitskell's powerful and principled oratory helped restore a sense of national honour and pride which had been so shaken by the Eden government's duplicity.[25] Michael Foot, never Gaitskell's greatest admirer, praised him for his 'relentless, passionate marshalling of the whole legal and moral case against the government's expedition to Suez',[26] while Asquith's daughter, Lady Violet Bonham Carter, thanked him in a letter 'for your magnificent speeches. It was not only for your party you were speaking – you "spoke for England" – for England's real and best self.'[27]

During the Suez Crisis, Healey not only acted as one of Gaitskell's main advisers but also as one of the party's most authoritative parliamentary spokesmen on the issue. On 30 October, the day of the Anglo-French ultimatum, in the first overtly hostile intervention from the Labour benches, he told the Prime Minister that 'it would be a crime and a tragedy if at the moment when freedom is being suppressed by Russian tanks in Hungary, this government did anything without international support which led to a similar impression being given to world opinion.'[28] On 1 November, he asked the Speaker if he could please tell him what was the parliamentary expression which came closest to expressing the meaning of the word 'liar' after the government had denied his charge that they had failed to consult the Americans. When Port Said fell to British and French troops the same day as the Russians captured Budapest, he asked Eden if he had exchanged congratulations with Bulganin, the Soviet leader.

Denis also spoke outside the Commons, including at big meetings at York and Oxford on behalf of the Labour leadership. Healey kept in touch with Conservative backbenchers who opposed Suez, such as Nigel Nicolson and Edward Boyle, as well as the rebels of the right wing Suez group like Julian Amery and Hugh Fraser, who thought Eden was not tough enough. Denis Healey wrote that 'in the whole of my political life I have never been so angry for so long as I was during the Suez affair'.[29] A young Tory politician, Reggie Maudling, claimed that steam actually came out of Healey's ears. When driving to the Suez protest meeting at York, he heard on the car radio the last appeal for help from Hungary. Denis wrote that he had to pull over to the side of the road until he had stopped weeping. All this emotion at least had the effect of improving the quality of Healey's speeches – the strength of his feelings led to him speaking more like a passionate human being and less like an academic lecturer. Suez raised Healey's profile and standing both in the Labour Party and Parliament, and, above all, with Gaitskell.

When Gaitskell delivered his Godkin lectures at Harvard in January 1957, his closest advisor was Denis Healey. Their most original idea was for the demilitarisation of Central Europe, including Poland, Hungary, Czechoslovakia and East and West Germany. This was a considered and imaginative response to the Hungarian uprising, an initiative which Healey developed further in a Fabian pamphlet *A Neutral Belt in Europe* and which others, including the American foreign affairs expert, George Kennan, and the Polish Foreign Minister, Adam Rapacki, also took up. However, neither the Americans nor the Russians were prepared to take the risks involved and the initiative ran into the sands. Healey also went with Gaitskell on some of his visits abroad, most notably to Russia with Nye Bevan in 1959, the trip during which Macmillan announced a General Election. The press wanted a statement from Gaitskell who, uncharacteristically, was suffering from drinking too many vodkas at a collective farm outside Moscow. Healey and Bevan tried but failed to wake him, so Bevan had to stall the press for three hours until Gaitskell came down to issue a short prepared statement. In his autobiography, Denis commented on Gaitskell's passion for dancing on these foreign visits, including a late-night visit to a dingy nightclub in Ljubljana in 1960, where Gaitskell whirled Edna Healey remorselessly round the floor.

While Denis Healey's parliamentary reputation rose, Roy Jenkins, despite his close friendship with Gaitskell, became what he later called 'semi-detached' from Parliament. Part of the reason was that Gaitskell had appointed Harold Wilson as shadow Chancellor and Jenkins no longer felt inclined, as he had under Gaitskell, to devote himself to the detail of Finance Bills. Despite his strong feelings about the Suez Crisis, Jenkins did not get involved in any of the numerous statements and debates on the issue. His biggest parliamentary interest between 1957 and 1959 was trying to get a reform of the law of censorship on to the statute book. It was (and is) very unusual for a backbencher's initiative on a controversial subject to get through Parliament. But Roy's ability to assemble a formidable and committed cross-party coalition, combined with his skill at negotiating with ministers, especially the Home Secretary, R. A. Butler, as well as several large slices of luck, led to the Bill receiving royal assent on 29 July 1959. This was an impressive parliamentary achievement, which was a forerunner of the liberal reforms introduced when Jenkins was Home Secretary in the 1960s. In his autobiography, Healey paid tribute to his skill and courage as a backbencher in piloting his Bill through Parliament, though noting Roy's lack of interest at that time in 'the cut and thrust of politics'.[30]

If Jenkins became somewhat detached from the Commons during the Gaitskell period, there was an important development, arising from his parliamentary duties, which was to have a big influence on his future. In the summer of 1955, he was chosen by his party to be a delegate to the Council of Europe at Strasbourg. Between his appointment and the spring of 1957, he spent a total of about seven weeks either at Strasbourg or at committee sessions held in European cities as far apart as Berlin and Palermo. This was the crucial period leading up to the Treaty of Rome which established the European Common Market, and Jenkins learnt a great deal from his ringside seat. His speech to the full Assembly in October 1956 took the then orthodox British line that the United Kingdom, because of its Commonwealth ties, would have to remain aloof from the new European project but at least, unlike the Tory government, he warmly welcomed the process which had been started at the Messina Conference in June 1955. However, his Strasbourg experience clearly had an effect on his thinking, for, when Macmillan set up the European Free Trade Association (EFTA) in 1958, Jenkins opposed the initiative as inadequate, and by the time his book, *The Case for Labour*, came out he had become a committed supporter of British membership of the Common Market, unlike his party which backed the government's position.

It was during those years that Roy Jenkins became increasingly well-known as an author, as well as a freelance journalist, becoming a regular contributor to the *Spectator*, then in a liberal phase. He was in demand as a performer on radio and on the new medium of television. During 1955 and 1956 he did the background research (mostly at the British Museum) for the Dilke biography which he had been commissioned to write by Mark Bonham Carter for Collins. He wrote the book, the first of Jenkins' series of political biographies, in the following eighteen months and it was published in October 1958. *Dilke* got good reviews and, with its unusual mix of politics and sexual scandal, sold well in both Britain and America.

He also wrote *The Labour Case*, one of three Penguin party political specials published for the 1959 election. With considerable skill, Jenkins' short book (50,000 words) deployed the Gaitskellite argument for increased economic growth as a way of improving economic performance, raising living standards and supporting extra expenditure on education, health and reducing poverty, including increasing pensions. It also included two chapters on post-Suez foreign policy which were read before publication by Denis Healey. Altogether this was a far more convincing work than his book of similar scope and length, *The Pursuit of Progress*, published six years before. It was better written and more coherent. It was clearly revisionist, in that the only nationalisation measure mentioned was the renationalisation of steel. Perhaps most significant of all, the authentic Jenkins voice began to emerge for the first time. In the preface, he described himself as holding 'rather moderate views'. The case for a return of a Labour government was argued without the usual party political polemics. And, for the first time in print, he put forward some of the key elements of his political credo.

In the opening chapter, in words that are still relevant today, he urged the British not to waste their substance in chasing old glories such as Suez. 'The chief danger for a country placed as we are is that of living rather sullenly in the past, of believing that the world has a duty to keep us in the station to which we are accustomed, and showing bitter resentment if it does not do so . . . The best prophylatic against this dangerous national nostalgia is a firm faith in the future, a sense of living in a buoyant and expanding economy, and joining with other similar placed countries to promote a more sensible, co-operative and prosperous world.' Hence the argument for involving the United Kingdom with the movement for European integration. In the closing chapter, entitled 'Is Britain Civilised?', Jenkins set out with conviction and passion the agenda that was to form much of his programme as Home Secretary a few years later, including the abolition of the death penalty, reform of homosexuality legislation, divorce law reform, and changes in laws relating to theatre censorship and abortion. Jenkins concluded in a ringing declaration of his liberal faith; 'Let us be on the side of those who want people to be free to live their own lives, to make their own mistakes, and to decide, in an adult way and provided they do not infringe the rights of others, the code by which they wish to live.'[31]

The period between 1955 and the 1959 General Election was much more frustrating for Crosland who was out of Parliament. *The Future of Socialism* was extremely well received, quickly giving him star status among Labour's intelligentsia. On the Fabian lecture and weekend schools circuit, Crosland was in great demand. Bill Rodgers, then General Secretary of the Fabian Society, wrote later that it was Crosland who made the most charismatic impact on his generation. 'His capacity to reject with contempt a flawed argument presented with bogus authority, or to strip away the sentiment from a conventional political assumption was greatly admired. So, too – although with awe rather than approval – was his ability to be stunningly rude to women when he was simply bored by them.'[32]

Even though he was out of Parliament, his close friendship with Hugh Gaitskell gave Crosland the ear and support of the party leader. Gaitskell asked him to help draft parts of *Industry and Society*, the key party document on public ownership which was endorsed at the 1957 party conference. The purpose of the document was to get away from the Morrisonian 'shopping list' approach to public ownership and produce a formula on which the party could unite. Crosland clearly inserted the idea of the state gradually building up shareholding in major public companies as an alternative to specific nationalisation commitments. For Gaitskell, Crosland had provided 'a politically effective fudge' on public ownership which could bring the party together without providing the Conservatives with too much electoral ammunition.[33]

Gaitskell also appointed Crosland to be Secretary of an Independent Commission, set up by the Co-operative Movement at its annual congress in 1955, to investigate ways of modernising itself.[34] Crosland, who saw the Commission, which Gaitskell chaired, as a practical exercise in revisionism, threw himself with vigour into his new appointment, visiting twenty-five local Societies to see for himself the extent to which the Co-ops were failing to keep pace with private retailing. When the Commission completed its work in the spring of 1955, it paid tribute to 'the great energy, exceptional ability and complete intellectual integrity of its Secretary'. The report, which was praised by the *Economist* as 'an impressive document', recommended the adoption of modern management structures and techniques, a reduction in the number of local societies and the establishment of a retail development society to provide central direction.

However, his work for the Independent Commission ended in disappointment. The forces of conservatism within the Co-op management saw the report as an attack on their position, shortsightedly condemning it as an attempt to make the Co-op 'a glorified capitalist concern'. By the autumn of 1958, Crosland was forced to admit that the decision of the central executive to set up further studies into the report's key recommendations amounted to its virtual rejection. His role as Gaitskell's backroom guru also had its disadvantages. When Labour was doing well, Crosland could at least derive satisfaction from knowing that Gaitskell was taking the party in a revisionist direction. But when, under the leadership of Macmillan and with the help of a pre-election boom, the Conservatives began to recover, critics, such as Harold Wilson, blamed Gaitskell's advisers, especially Crosland.[35]

Crosland's private life continued to be colourful, including bohemian parties at The Boltons with writers, economists, painters, film stars and actresses. Gaitskell, who was entranced by the company, was often the only politician invited. Gaitskell also sometimes used Crosland's flat for his affair with Ann Fleming, the society hostess who lionised him. She joked that when she went to bed with Gaitskell she liked to imagine that she was with the more glamorous Crosland. Tony Benn, a friend of Crosland since his Oxford days and now a young MP, wrote in his diary on 25 May 1957 after attending one of Crosland's parties:

> Tony is, of course, a very unhappy person. His years in the war gave him the excuse for thinking that his youth had gone and he has been trying to catch up since 1945. At thirty-nine it is rather silly. He is unusually gifted as an economist and has a very clear mind with a very great faith in his power of reason. But the proof of his unhappiness is his curious death wish, which he showed when in the Commons, and which now takes the form of affecting to be bored with current politics. If he

gets back into Parliament he will get high office. If he does not, then his life could be a very tragic one.[36]

In fact, Tony Crosland's luck was about to change.[37] In the late 1950s, he got to know Susan Catling, an attractive American married to an Irish journalist working in London. And the prospect of a seat in Parliament suddenly came up. When Kenneth Younger, the MP for Grimsby, went to tell Hugh Gaitskell that he wished to leave Parliament in order to become Director of the Royal Institute of International Affairs, Gaitskell immediately asked the size of Younger's majority and, on being told that it was above three thousand, he commented, without discussing Younger's plans, that it was a good prospect for Crosland. Although Crosland had had doubts after the success of *The Future of Socialism* about returning to Parliament, he was persuaded by Gaitskell that he could make a bigger contribution as an MP and possible future minister than by returning to being an academic.[38] With the leader's support, Crosland won the Grimsby nomination with a clear majority over four other rivals, including Bill Rodgers, General Secretary of the Fabian Society, who was runner-up.

With the possible exception of 1992, 1959 was Labour's most traumatic defeat since 1931. The party had gone into the election with such high hopes. Since Bevan's appointment as shadow Foreign Secretary in November 1956, it had appeared united behind Gaitskell. It ran an energetic campaign, with both Gaitskell and Dick Crossman, who was campaign co-ordinator, making outstanding contributions. Yet, instead of a Labour victory, the Conservatives won for the third successive time and with an increased majority of 100. Although Gaitskell was blamed for making a pledge during the campaign not to increase income tax (a pledge that was supported by Harold Wilson, the shadow Chancellor), even the left accepted that the real reason was affluence. When Macmillan said, 'most of our people have never had it so good', it struck a chord with the voters; for the prosperous majority, 'Don't let Labour ruin it' was a potent slogan.

Before the election, Gaitskell had told Tony Benn who was in charge of media publicity, to build up Crosland, Jenkins and Healey – 'the up and coming generation'.[39] Both Healey and Jenkins won their seats comfortably, though with reduced majorities. Crosland, however, only just hung on at Grimsby, winning by a mere 101 votes after a recount with an above average swing against him. Jenkins went to Grimsby to help the new candidate. There is a photograph from that visit of Roy and Tony chatting with Grimsby housewives on their doorsteps. Roy is smiling engagingly at the women, while Tony is standing with his hands on his hips, looking down almost bashfully at his feet. At the count, Crosland's complexion changed colour; according to one of his helpers, 'I watched that lad change from red to white to green to grey.'[40] However, Crosland's survival in a bad political year was to ensure him a relatively safe seat for the rest of his life.

Gaitskell, whose dignified acceptance of defeat initially enhanced his reputation, badly mishandled the aftermath of the 1959 election. Given the scale of that defeat, there was certainly a strong case for the Labour Party doing what the German Social Democrats did in 1959 (after their own defeat in 1957) and sending a signal to the voters that it had come to terms with changing social and economic conditions. But instead of planning a long-term campaign around a carefully thought-out strategy, Gaitskell, perhaps because of his post-electoral exhaustion, allowed his friends to sound off in public with their own views which his enemies then misrepresented as the leader's, thus helping build up opposition to reform.

An initial 'post-mortem' meeting of Gaitskell's friends was held at Frognal Gardens on the Sunday morning after the election, at which Tony Crosland and Roy and Jennifer Jenkins were present. At some stage, the participants, who also included Douglas Jay, Patrick Gordon Walker, Hugh Dalton, and the chief whip, Herbert Bowden, sat in a circle and gave their views on the defeat. The discussion, in Jenkins' judgement, 'was conducted much more casually than conspiratorially'.[41] Reasons given for Labour's defeat included the unpopularity of nationalisation, the unpopularity of the unions, the unpopularity of local councils and more generally of the party's 'cloth cap' image. Jay advocated dropping further nationalisation, loosening the link with the unions and changing the party's name. Somebody, probably Dalton, suggested that a new formula should replace the existing Clause IV, part 4, of the Labour Party constitution which called for the common ownership of the means of production, distribution and exchange. By all accounts, Gaitskell said very little.

However, news of the meeting quickly got out and to the left it provided clear evidence of a right-wing 'plot' to change the nature of the Labour Party. Their suspicions were strengthened the following Monday by a *Panorama* interview with Jenkins who opposed further nationalisation and suggested loosening the link with the unions and by an article by Douglas Jay in *Forward* which proposed dropping steel nationalisation and adding 'Reform' or 'Radical' to the name of the party. In fact, Gaitskell did not agree with either of Jenkins' or Jay's specific proposals. Instead, he favoured the idea of a revision of Clause IV, part 4. Jenkins and Crosland, both of whom subsequently loyally backed up their leader, thought that changing the party objectives in this way might be more trouble than it was worth. 'Why draw everyone's attention to this shibboleth?'[42] Crosland asked Gaitskell. Healey, who was consulted as well, was also against changing Clause IV. Later, he called the proposal Gaitskell's 'ghastliest mistake'.[43]

When Gaitskell spoke to the November party conference at Blackpool, the dice were already heavily loaded against him. The leader spoke only for himself, as there was no platform position. The left was uniformly hostile; while in the centre, Crossman was ambivalent, Wilson, who was worried about rumours of losing his shadow Chancellorship (the *Sunday Times* had even suggested that he would be replaced by Roy Jenkins), suspicious, and Nye Bevan, already ill, above the battle. Crucially, the unions, on whom Gaitskell had so often relied for support in the past, were strongly resistant to constitutional change. His criticism of Clause IV as it stood was unanswerable – 'it implies that we propose to nationalise everything but we do not' – and his formulation of a new Clause IV was not much different from that which Tony Blair successfully carried through conference in 1995. But it was clear that there was not then enough support, even after such a disastrous defeat as 1959, for revising the clause.

The debate that followed was marked by bitterness, a warning of battles to come. One of the best and bravest speeches from the floor was made by Denis Healey, not so much in support of changing Clause IV, but, as he would so often attempt to do in the future, trying to bring delegates back to the real world.

There are too many people who have spoken from this rostrum in these last two days who seem to think it is all right to do without votes. If they want to luxuriate complacently in moral righteousness in opposition they can do it – but who is going to pay the price for their complacency? In Britain it is the unemployed and the old age pensioners. You will have your TV set, your motor car and your summer holidays on the continent – and still keep your socialist soul intact. The people who pay the price for your sense of moral satisfaction are the Africans, being slowly forced into racial slavery, the Indians and the Indonesians dying of starvation. We are not just a socialist Sunday School. We are a great movement that wants to help real people living on this earth at the present time.

Jenkins, who also spoke, said: 'We exist to change society. We are not likely to be very sucessful if we are horrified at any suggestion of changing ourselves.'[44]

In the end, Gaitskell was forced by the weakness of his position, a weakness that was accentuated by the growing and divisive debate on unilateralism, into an unsatisfactory compromise. Clause IV, part 4, was retained but was supplemented by a new statement of aims. Was Gaitskell wrong, as Crosland, Jenkins and Healey all believed, to have tried to change Clause IV? It may be that, given the strength of conservatism inside the Labour Party at that time, such a change was never practical politics. There is an alternative view that it was not so much the objective that was unrealistic but the manner in which Gaitskell set about it. If there was ever to be a real chance of changing the clause, then the leader had to have both the big unions and potentially hostile rivals like Bevan and Wilson on his side, as well as rallying moderate opinion inside the party. Relying on his Frognal Gardens Praetorian Guard to turn opinion was never going to be enough.

A crisis over nuclear defence, which almost overwhelmed Gaitskell's leadership, came quite suddenly around Easter 1960. At the end of April, the Tory government, which three years before had abolished conscription and adopted a defence policy that overwhelmingly relied on the nuclear deterrent, abandoned Blue Streak, the fixed land-based rocket. This amounted to the virtual end of an independent British delivery system and therefore also of a wholly independent British nuclear deterrent and gave a big boost to the unilateralists. The Campaign for Nuclear Disarmament (CND) held a highly successful third Aldermaston march that Easter which helped highlight the issue of unilateral disarmament and had a major impact on the Labour movement. Easter was also the start of the union conference season. The shopworkers and the electricians' union, influenced by the Communists, both went unilateralist, as did the engineering union a few weeks later. The biggest union of all, the Transport and General Workers' Union, was now led by a committed unilaterist, Frank Cousins, so it looked increasingly likely that Gaitskell would be defeated at conference, at which the unions then had the overall majority of the vote.

In fighting off the unilateralists, Gaitskell no longer had the active support of his deputy, Nye Bevan, who had been so effective in opposing them at the 1957 conference but was suffering from the cancer from which he died in July. To make matters worse for the Labour leader, he was in Israel when the Commons debated the abandonment of Blue Streak at the end of April, even though Roy Jenkins had tried to persuade him to stay and modify policy during the debate.[45] In his absence, George Brown, the defence spokesman, and Harold Wilson, winding up for the Opposition, both made it clear that the argument for an independent British nuclear deterrent had received a devastating blow. Criticism of Gaitskell's leadership, no longer confined to the left, mounted.

It was about this time that Crosland, with the leadership in some disarray, appointed himself as a kind of unofficial chief-of-staff to Gaitskell, sending him a stream of often critical memoranda over the next few months. In May Crosland wrote:

Recent events demonstrate that your leadership still lacks a proper system of intelligence and forward planning . . . In the seven months since the election, we have suffered a major defeat over Clause IV; we are now fighting an unplanned defensive battle over the H-bomb; we have achieved not one single one of the positive reforms which the moderates wanted (a change in the composition of the NEC and/or an explicit change in the balance of power between the NEC and Parliamentary Party, a new set-up at Transport House, a systematic study of survey material, etc etc); your own position is weaker, and you yourself more criticised, than at any time since you assumed the leadership; and the morale of the right-wing of the party is appallingly low.[46]

On 12 May after the House had risen, Gaitskell, with Crosland and Gordon Walker, went to a gloomy meeting at Roy Jenkins' home at Ladbroke Square. According to Gordon Walker's diary, a depressed Gaitskell told the others that he was concerned lest George Brown, in his efforts to win over conference, compromised too much on policy. Crosland replied that 'it was essential to keep in step with Brown and Robens – otherwise we would be a powerless rump'. Following the Ladbroke Square conversation, Gordon Walker commented in his diary: 'I began to fear that (Gaitskell) has the seeds of self-destruction in him . . . a death wish.'[47]

His friends, however, were not prepared to let Gaitskell destroy himself. Crosland, in particular, worked tirelessly to prop up his leadership. Apart from writing a major article, *The Future of the Left*, in the March issue of *Encounter* and a Fabian pamphlet, *Can Labour Win?*, in May, in both of which he urged the party to come to terms with social change, he helped set up the Campaign for Democratic Socialism (the CDS) to support Gaitskell and his policies.

At Easter he met Bill Rodgers, then in his last week at the Fabian Society, at the Two Chairmen pub near the Society's office in Dartmouth Street, and they agreed to try and organise moderate opinion in the party. In the next few weeks, they put together an informal organising board, composed of Roy Jenkins, Patrick Gordon Walker and Douglas Jay; friends of Bill Rodgers including Dick Taverne (future Labour MP and Minister) and Michael Shanks, Industrial Editor of the *Financial Times*; and four others from an Oxford group, including Brian Walden, later MP and broadcaster, and Tony Crosland's Trinity friend, Philip Williams. At Roy Jenkins' request, Denis Howell, who had lost his seat at the 1959 election, was also invited to join the organising board; the board agreed to draft a manifesto around which supporters could rally. In Bill Rodgers' view, 'Tony's role was critical. He gave the intellectual lead reflected in the text of the manifesto and, together with Philip Williams, was mostly responsible for its drafting. He also showed a discipline and single mindedness of which most of us had been previously unaware.'[48] CDS was launched at the end of October, soon after the Scarborough conference where Gaitskell was defeated on defence.

However, despite his defeat, Gaitskell's impressive and passionate speech at Scarborough helped prepare the ground for his success the subsequent year. He began by accepting that the cancellation of Blue Streak undermined the case for an independent British deterrent. He argued that the key issue was neutralism. 'If you are a unilateralist in principle, you are driven to becoming a neutralist . . . either they (the unilateralists) mean that they will follow the cowardly hypocritical course of saying, "We do not want nuclear bombs, but for God's sake, Americans, protect us," or they are saying that we should get out of NATO.' Turning to the leadership question, he asked, 'Supposing all of us, like well-behaved sheep, were to follow the policies of unilateralism and neutralism, what kind of impression would that make upon the British people . . . There are some of us, Mr Chairman, who will fight and fight and fight again to save the party we love.'[49] Such was the persuasive impact of his oratory that he won over many constituency delegates during his speech, thus minimising the scale of his defeat. The *Daily Herald*, a pro-leadership paper, called it 'Gaitskell's finest hour. He turned what looked like an exultant triumph for his enemies into the hollowest of paper victories.'[50]

When the Labour MPs returned to Westminster, Wilson, despite being opposed to unilateralism, challenged Gaitskell for the leadership of the party as a 'unity' candidate opposed to Gaitskell's confrontational leadership. Crosland wrote to Gaitskell: 'In the next ten days, we have one single overriding object, to make sure that his vote is as low as possible and yours as high as possible. Our possibilities over the next twelve months will depend entirely on this; and to achieve this we must resort to any degree of chicanery, lying etc etc.'[51] In fact Gaitskell's speech at Scarborough had given his supporters new heart and Gaitskell won decisively by 166 to 81 for Wilson. Gaitskell's fightback was gathering momentum.

Healey may have had his misgivings about Gaitskell's style of leadership.[52] Even so he played an important part in Gaitskell's recovery. Healey had been elected to the shadow Cabinet in 1959 and, following Bevan's death, had been appointed, at his own request, shadow

Commonwealth and Colonial Secretary. However, he was acknowledged to be the party's leading defence expert, who had worked with other defence 'intellectuals' in Britain and the United States on issues of nuclear balance and arms control throughout the 1950s. He had helped set up the Institute of Strategic Studies in London in 1958 and, in 1961, he wrote a Fabian Pamphlet, *The Race Against the H-Bomb*, in which he argued that neither of the superpowers could achieve security in a nuclear arms race. At the Scarborough conference, he gave Gaitskell practical support by making a powerful speech against neutralism and in favour of the leadership's position.

Following Scarborough, Healey played a key role as one of Gaitskell's nominees as a shadow Cabinet member on a drafting committee (which was composed of four each from the shadow Cabinet, the NEC and the General Council of the TUC). It was Healey who drafted the majority, Gaitskellite document, 'Policy for Peace', which was presented to the 1961 Blackpool conference. It accepted that Britain should no longer attempt to remain an independent nuclear power since this neither strengthened the alliance, nor was a sensible use of limited resources, but it stressed both the need for British membership of NATO and for NATO to continue to have nuclear weapons, unless or until the Soviet Union also gave up its own nuclear weapons. Healey not only wrote the leadership defence document but spoke up powerfully both in the PLP and outside Parliament for it.

Meanwhile, assisted by the efforts of trade union moderates and by the organisational work of the Campaign for Democratic Socialism both at union conferences and in the constituencies, the tide turned decisively in Gaitskell's favour. At Labour's 1961 Blackpool conference, the official defence policy was carried by nearly 3–1. It was a triumph for Gaitskell, which restored his authority as leader and, for the first time, helped impress his personality on the country. All three protagonists, especially Crosland and Healey, had played a significant part in Gaitskell's famous victory.

The last great drama of Gaitskell's leadership, which was over the Common Market, divided his three supporters. Jenkins and Crosland were for British entry, while Healey was against. On 22 July 1961, the Conservative Cabinet belatedly decided to apply for entry. Although Macmillan emphasised that he was entering into negotiations in order to see if the UK's terms could be met and safeguards secured, especially for the Commonwealth and British agriculture, it was from the start his intention to take the United Kingdom in if he possibly could. After the débâcle and failure of the European Free Trade Association, Macmillan now believed that Britain's future lay in the European Economic Community.

Gaitskell was much more ambivalent. Intellectually, he could see a case for British entry, above all on political grounds, but he was at heart a Commonwealth man who was deeply influenced by the Commonwealth governments' hostile reaction to the course of the negotiations. He never felt himself primarily a European ('I probably feel that I have more in common with North Americans than with the Europeans,' he once said) and, although he saw the advantages of a Franco-German understanding, he often regretted the creation of the European Community, telling some CDS supporters who were also European enthusiasts that the subject was a 'bore and nuisance and it has always been so'.[53] He was also determined that, after the Clause IV and unilateralist rows, he would try to keep the Labour Party as united on the subject as he possibly could and he was aware that, though there was a determined group of his closest supporters in favour, the majority was probably against British entry. This was one reason for his insistence on tough terms.

In contrast, Roy Jenkins enthusiastically supported the UK joining the European Community, both on economic and political grounds, and emerged during this period as Labour's leading pro-European. In July 1960, he had resigned from a minor front-bench Treasury spokesmanship in order to be able to speak in a European debate. At the beginning of 1961, six months before the Macmillan application, Jenkins helped set up the all-party Common Market campaign, with Lord Gladwyn, former ambassador in Paris, as chairman and himself as deputy chairman. Roy also became chairman of the Labour Committee for Europe. In these two capacities, he took a leading role in the growing Common Market debate, making speeches up and down the country as well as in the Commons and appearing on television. He also wrote on the issue for newspapers and magazines, including a magisterial refutation of the 'anti' case in *Encounter*.

Jenkins' relationship with Hugh Gaitskell was inevitably affected by their differences over the EEC. In April 1962, Jenkins tried to move

Gaitskell on the issue by arranging for Jean Monnet, the French architect of the European Coal and Steel Community, to address the XYZ
dining club of economists, politicians and Labour City sympathisers.
Gaitskell, who was a prominent member of XYZ, attended the dinner.
The evening was a total disaster. Monnet wanted to explain the philosophy behind the European Community, while Gaitskell insisted
on asking detailed questions about issues such as the EEC's impact on
undeveloped countries. Thinking that Gaitskell's questions did not
address the basic issue, Monnet said, 'You must have faith.' Gaitskell
replied, 'I don't believe in faith. I believe in reason and you have not
shown me any.'[54] Gaitskell went away unimpressed and Jenkins drove
Monnet back to the Hyde Park Hotel in deep depression.

Then in September, Gaitskell, following meetings with
Commonwealth leaders, toughened his stance further. His two
acolytes, Jenkins and Crosland, were both concerned by his increasingly 'anti' position. In his *The Conservative Enemy*, a collection of
essays published that year, Crosland, calling himself an instinctive
European, made clear his pro-European stance in words which still
find their echo today: 'We cling to every outmoded scrap of national
sovereignty, play the obsolete role of an imperial power, and fail to
adjust to the new, dynamic Europe . . . The cause is partly our oppres-
sive, traditional pattern of class relations, partly the psychological
difficulty of adapting from great power to second-rate international
status, partly the complacent ignorance bred by an insular tradition.'[55]
In September, Crosland wrote to Gaitskell spelling out his view that,
though membership of the EEC might improve growth prospects, the
case for British entry was mainly political: Britain needed above all to
find a new role. Trying to pull the leader back to a more neutral position, Jenkins had an unsuccessful lunch (also in September) with
Gaitskell at the Garrick Club. It went on until four o'clock but the
more they talked, the wider the gap became. 'We parted friendlily,'
wrote Roy Jenkins, 'but a temporary separation, personal as well as
political, began that day.'[56]

Jenkins and Crosland as well as other pro-Europeans were deeply
upset by Hugh Gaitskell's speech on the Common Market at the 1962
Brighton conference, in which he opposed entry on the terms negotiated by the Conservative government. On the surface, it was an
analysis of the pros and cons of entry. But in strongly emotive passages

that helped give the speech its dramatic force, he looked back to the contribution which the Dominions had made in the First World War: 'We at least do not intend to forget Vimy Ridge and Gallipoli.' He accused the government of selling 'the Commonwealth down the river'. And, in passionate though inaccurate rhetoric, he said that joining the European Community could mean, 'the end of Britain as an independent European state . . . the end of a thousand years of history'.[57] When Gaitskell sat down, he received a lengthy standing ovation. However, as Dora Gaitskell said to Gaitskell's Leeds colleague Charlie Pannell, 'All the wrong people are cheering.'[58] Roy Jenkins stood but did not applaud, while Bill Rodgers, the organiser of CDS, sat firmly in his seat. In the debate that followed, Jenkins made a courageous and passionate speech on behalf of the pro-European minority, reminding delegates that every socialist party in the six was in favour of the European Community and that five out of the six member states wanted the UK in.

Although he did not share Gaitskell's romantic chauvinism, Denis Healey supported his conclusion, in part because he still believed that the Commonwealth, under British leadership, could play an important role in world affairs. He argued that the Europeanism of the Tories was 'imperialism with an inferiority complex'. Above all, he saw the issue as a distraction because he was certain (and had advised Gaitskell accordingly) that de Gaulle would veto British entry. When, a few days before Gaitskell's death, de Gaulle rejected the British application, Healey wrote: 'The nation can no longer delude itself into thinking that the painful changes in both domestic and external policy required to invigorate its flagging economy will automatically be imposed by entry into the EEC.'[59] But if Britain could modernise its economy, then Healey foresaw there would be another attempt to join the Common Market after de Gaulle had left the scene.

After Brighton, Gaitskell had the world at his feet. His party was united behind him. The left was enthused by his anti-Common Market stance, while the pro-marketeers, like Jenkins and Crosland, were still bound to him by personal and political loyalties. Both Gaitskell and the Labour Party were riding high in the polls and it seemed that he had a good chance of becoming the next Prime Minister. Tragically, he was struck down by a rare immunological disease, *lupus erythematosus*, and died, after a short illness, on 18 January 1963.

Roy Jenkins, who was in the United States, was phoned by the *Daily Express* with the news and asked for a comment. Jenkins, who was devastated, declined. The insensitive reporter was surprised and said, 'Harold Wilson, who was in New York, was able to give us a very moving one without difficulty.' Roy, remembering all too clearly that Wilson had challenged Gaitskell for the leadership, replied bitterly, 'But you have to remember that he was very fond of Gaitskell.'[60] After the memorial service at Westminster Abbey, Crosland was seen, 'long, dark coat flying behind, striding off alone and in deep distress along Victoria Street'.[61] As Attlee and Healey walked together across from the Commons to Westminster Abbey, Attlee sadly told Denis that he had expected Gaitskell to go to his memorial service, not the other way round.

During the Gaitskell period, Healey had risen furthest. At forty-five the youngest member of the shadow Cabinet, his grasp of foreign policy and defence issues already made him indispensable to any Labour leader. At the same time, he had shown considerable courage both at the 1959 and 1960 party conferences in putting forward, in trenchant style, his views about the future of the party and about neutralism. He had emerged both as a moderniser who grasped the changes in society and a pragmatic realist who understood the workings of power both at home and abroad. If Gaitskell had become Prime Minister, he might well have become Foreign Minister in time. Under any other Labour Prime Minister, he was certain to be a senior Cabinet minister.

Crosland had become Labour's leading revisionist intellectual, who had not only written *The Future of Socialism* but also acted as a one-man think-tank to Gaitskell. And, as his leadership of the Campaign for Democratic Socialism demonstrated, he could show considerable discipline, drive and organisational power if he believed in the cause. As he later said about Roy Hattersley, there was 'very big political potential there'.[62] With his new commitment to a parliamentary career and his private life becoming more stable, there was a greater chance of that potential being realised. Certainly, he would have been an economic minister in a Gaitskell government, possibly, after a year or two, Chancellor of the Exchequer.

Despite his close relationship with Gaitskell, Jenkins' political fortunes had prospered the least of the three revisionists. As he said himself, he had become semi-detached from politics. However, on the Common Market and on liberal issues, he had staked out positions of his own which were to be vital both to his own future and to British politics. The death of Gaitskell was a great personal blow to Jenkins, as it was to Crosland. Yet, paradoxically, under Gaitskell's successor as leader of the Labour Party, his career was to flourish in a way which would have astonished Roy, and Tony and Denis as well, in the cheerless days after Gaitskell's death.

7

Harold Wilson's Ministers

When some of the leading Gaitskellites met at Tony Crosland's flat at 19 The Boltons a few days after Hugh Gaitskell's death, they were deeply divided over the choice of his successor. The obvious candidate of the right was George Brown, the deputy leader of the party. Brown was an exceptionally able and eloquent trade-union MP. He was also a bully, who was liable to fly off the handle, and often drank too much. John Harris, Gaitskell's former press aide, reported to the meeting that Gaitskell had found Brown a difficult deputy.[1] Roy Jenkins, who was still in the United States, was represented by Jennifer Jenkins: Roy's position was that he was 'unenthusiastically but firmly for Brown'.[2]

Crosland was appalled by the prospect of the volatile Brown as leader and argued for James Callaghan, the shadow Chancellor, whom he had got to know well when they were both delegates at the Council of Europe in the early 1950s. Tony admired Callaghan for possessing the political skills which he himself lacked. Crosland went to see Brown in his room in the House to explain why he was doubtful about supporting him. Typically, Brown exploded. Next day he wrote a letter of apology. 'I do hope I wasn't too vehement.'[3] Callaghan was a more emollient politician but, although he might have been better placed to beat Wilson than Brown because of his support in the centre, he did not yet have the standing in the party to poll more than Brown on the first ballot.

One thing on which all the Gaitskellites could agree was that they did not want Harold Wilson. He was very much the Gaitskellites' bête noire. They considered him an opportunist without firm political beliefs and had not forgiven him for having challenged Gaitskell for the leadership in 1960. Crosland complained that the choice was between a crook and a drunk.[4] For the less committed, Wilson had excellent qualifications for leading the Labour Party. A Cabinet minister at thirty-one, a former Chairman of the Public Accounts Committee, and both a shadow Chancellor and shadow Foreign Secretary, he had a thorough grasp of the issues. For many in the centre and the moderate left, Wilson's coolness and pragmatism were a refreshing contrast to the passion and idealism of Gaitskell. And, given the balance of forces within the Labour Party, it was probably easier to unite the party from slightly left of centre than from Gaitskell's revisionist position on the right of the party.

Once Callaghan had divided the centre-right by his decision to stand, Wilson became the hot favourite for the leadership. On the first ballot, Wilson led with 115 votes followed by Brown with 88 and Callaghan with 41. Wilson's vote was only eight short of a majority. On the second ballot Wilson won decisively with 144 to Brown's 103. Jenkins supported Brown on both ballots. Wilson's biographer, Ben Pimlott, wrote that Crosland voted for Wilson on the second ballot.[5] However, according to Susan Crosland's account, Crosland, despite his doubts, backed Brown in the second ballot: 'It was emotionally impossible for him to vote for Harold Wilson.'[6] Healey shared Crosland's concerns about Brown: 'Like the immortal Jemima, when he was good he was very very good, but when he was bad he was horrid.'[7] Healey therefore voted for Callaghan on the first ballot, but, in contrast to Crosland, backed Wilson on the second ballot, though without much enthusiasm.[8] Whatever his reservations, Denis thought that Wilson was far more likely to unite the party and win the General Election than the erratic Brown.

Healey was right. Wilson proved to be an outstanding leader of the Opposition. He brilliantly exploited the growing weakness of the Conservative administration. Harold Macmillan's government was undermined by a faltering economy, by the failure of his attempt to join the Common Market, and by the scandal that arose when the Minister of War, John Profumo, was forced to resign after he admitted lying to the Commons about his affair with a call-girl. When Macmillan had to stand down because of ill health, his successor, Sir Alec Douglas-Home, who had renounced his earldom to become Prime Minister, appeared bumbling and amateur, a figure from another age.

By contrast, Wilson seemed the personification of the dynamic, meritocratic Britain for which writers like Michael Shanks in *The Stagnant Society*, Brian Chapman in *British Government Observed*, and Tony Crosland himself in *The Conservative Enemy* had so persuasively argued. The new Labour leader was assured in the House, fluent on television (arguably Wilson was the first top-flight politician in Britain who was good on television), always well briefed, a professional to his finger tips. At the time, many of the younger generation saw him, wrongly as it turned out, as a kind of Yorkshire version of the charismatic US President, John F. Kennedy. Following his election to the leadership, Wilson's ratings soared and Labour established a commanding lead in the polls.

Under Wilson, Healey's political career continued to prosper. At the time of Gaitskell's death, he was already one of the top half dozen members of Labour's shadow Cabinet. When Gaitskellite MPs met to decide on their candidate to oppose Wilson, two of their wives had expressed their regrets that Healey was not senior enough to be a candidate himself.[9] On becoming leader, Wilson gave the shadow Foreign Secretaryship, which George Brown coveted, to Patrick Gordon Walker, a leading Gaitskellite. When Brown upbraided Gordon Walker, Gordon Walker replied that if he had not accepted, Wilson would have given the job not to Brown but to Healey.[10] In any event, Denis landed the shadow Defence Secretaryship, the post for which, apart from shadow Foreign Secretary, he was best qualified. Healey's political future seemed assured. Provided Labour won the next election, he was bound to become a senior Cabinet minister.

If it made good sense for Wilson to offer positions to the senior Gaitskellites, like Healey and Gordon Walker, it was not obvious that he needed to look after Gaitskell's closest companions, especially Jenkins and Crosland. Still grieving for Hugh Gaitskell, Roy Jenkins had become almost totally detached from politics. He got on with writing his next book, a biography of Asquith, doing a number of long, ground-breaking articles for the *Observer* (his account of the 1962 takeover battle between ICI and Courtaulds won a Granada Award of the Year), and pursuing what he called his 'over-active social life'.[11] In July 1963, he was offered the editorship of the *Economist*. A flattered Jenkins told the chairman, Geoffrey Crowther, that he would think it over during the summer recess which he was spending in France writing *Asquith*. Stopping off in Paris on his way back to London, he met a close friend, Marie-Alice de Beaumarchais, wife of the French diplomat, who told him to go and see Wilson. 'He will want you for your own sake but in any case why on earth don't you go and ask him instead of deciding in the dark?'[12]

This was good advice. On 12 September, in a crucial meeting for Jenkins' future, Roy saw the new leader of the Opposition in his room in the Commons. Wilson handled Jenkins brilliantly. Flatteringly, he appeared to be genuinely impressed by the *Economist* offer but told Roy that he was looking forward to forming a broad-based government in which he hoped Jenkins would be a prominent member. Roy, of course, could not hope to be in the Cabinet at first, but the road to promotion would be wide open. Wilson would understand if he accepted the *Economist* offer, though he very much hoped that he would not. Impressed by Wilson almost despite himself, Jenkins decided to remain in politics.

Crosland found it even more difficult than Jenkins to come to terms with Wilson. As one of Gaitskell's campaign managers when Harold Wilson had contested the leadership in 1960, he had not troubled to hide his disdain for the challenger. His moving television tribute to Gaitskell on the night of Hugh's death contained an implied criticism of Wilson: 'Most of the others are dwarfs and pigmies beside him.' His remark about the 1962 leadership election being a contest between a crook and a drunk not only accurately reflected Crosland's assessment at that time of the two men but almost certainly got back to Wilson.

The victory of the 'crook' was a devastating political blow to Crosland. From being a close confidant of Gaitskell, he was completely excluded from the leader's magic circle which now, under Wilson, consisted of former Bevanites and centrists like Dick Crossman, Barbara Castle, Peter Shore, Tony Benn, and, Roy Jenkins' former tutor, Thomas Balogh. Philip Williams wrote to Tony soon after Wilson's election, urging him, if he decided to stay in politics, to open communications with the new Labour leader, but Crosland politely but firmly rejected the advice. He was not yet ready to parley with Wilson. However, in May, Tony Benn reported a revealing conversation with Crosland. 'I had a long talk to Tony about his attitude to Wilson, who he thinks has done very well and would like to help in any way he could. I must try to pass this on to Harold since Tony is too good to waste. But the simple fact is that with Hugh's death his old courtiers feel in the cold – exactly as I felt with Hugh.'[13]

There is no evidence that Crosland had or even sought a direct meeting with Wilson, similar to the one that Jenkins had had. But, as the chances of Labour winning the next election grew, Tony found other ways of working with the new regime. Both Callaghan, the shadow Chancellor, and Brown, who was to lead the Department of Economic Affairs, a new ministry devised by Wilson as a counterbalance to the Treasury, sought help from Crosland.

In 1962, Tony had asked his close friend, the welfare economist Ian Little, then Fellow of Nuffield College, to arrange a series of special economic seminars at Nuffield for Jim Callaghan, who knew little about economics. In addition, leading economists such as Nicky Kaldor from Cambridge, Robert Neild, director of the National Institute of Economic and Social Research, and Donald Macdougall, economic director of the newly set up National Economic Development Council, met Crosland to discuss current economic issues, especially devaluation. Separately they each put the case for devaluation to Callaghan. They all believed that, if Labour's plans for growth were not to be derailed, then a decision to devalue should be taken as soon as Labour came to office. The shadow Chancellor listened but remained non-committal.

Like Jenkins, Crosland stood for the shadow Cabinet for the first time in the autumn 1963 elections. He was surprised and hurt to be approached by Bill Rodgers, his old ally from CDS days, now Labour MP for Stockton and organiser of the parliamentary right, who advised him not to stand in case it hurt the chances of Roy Jenkins.[14] Tony ignored Rodgers' advice and polled 72 votes to Roy's 64, not enough to get either into the shadow Cabinet. This was the first overt sign of the intense personal rivalry which, in the post-Gaitskell world, was to undermine the friendship of Crosland and Jenkins.

In February 1964, Tony Crosland married Susan Catling. According to the journalist Anthony Howard, Wilson had let it be known that he preferred Tony to regularise his domestic situation.[15] It is unlikely that this was a factor in their decision, as Tony and Susan had been contemplating marriage for several years. The big question, which preoccupied both of them, was whether, once married, Crosland, who was accustomed to single life, would feel 'fenced in'. Overcoming their mutual hesitation, they got married at Chelsea Register Office, with the widows of Crosland's two former patrons, Dora Gaitskell and Ruth Dalton, as witnesses.

It had been assumed by both Tony and Susan that Tony would benefit from an occasional 'adventure' and 19 The Boltons was kept on when Tony moved into Susan's house in Holbury Street, Chelsea. They were both surprised when Tony's flat was not used. The first time Tony went to The Boltons proved to be the last. The flat was freezing cold and there was nothing to eat and drink. 'No one looking at you would guess how cunning you are,' Susan reported Tony as saying on his return to Holbury Street. 'In principle you accede to poor old Toto retaining a fragment of his freedom. Then you make absolutely certain that his life will be so disagreeable when he returns to his bachelor flat that he never wants to go there again.' By the end of 1964, they had moved into a larger, Victorian house in Lansdowne Road, Notting Hill, which provided a study for Tony and rooms for Susan's two daughters from her first marriage, Sheila and Ellen-Craig. The marriage was a huge success, giving Crosland the stability and direction which he had hitherto lacked. Crosland became more a serious politician and less the theoretician and enfant terrible that he had been until then.

The 1964 election was a cliffhanger. In a series of speeches, beginning with his conference address at Scarborough in 1963, Wilson, like Blair in 1997, had promoted Labour as the party of modernisation and opportunity, intent on breaking down the barriers of class and privilege. But, as the spring of 1964 turned to summer, Labour's lead in the polls began to slip. When NOP put the Tories fractionally ahead at the end of August, it seemed that the Conservative government's tactic of postponing the election until the last possible moment was paying off. Labour's advantage was that Wilson was a much better campaigner than Douglas-Home. There was also a feeling on the doorstep that it was time for change. On the other hand, Labour had been out of office for so long that for many voters actually making the change seemed a big gamble.

As a senior member of the shadow Cabinet, Healey played a prominent role in the campaign. He was filmed answering questioning at a coffee-morning party in North London for one of Labour's party political broadcasts and, with Patrick Gordon Walker, discussed foreign affairs and defence issues on a radio programme. However, Conservative Central Office refused to allow the Defence Secretary, Peter Thorneycroft, to debate the deterrent with him on ITV's *This Week*, which suggests that, on this issue at least, the Conservatives feared him. Healey was in demand as a speaker in a number of constituencies, where his robust campaigning style made him a favourite with party members.[16]

Denis was immensely relieved on election night when early results showed a swing to Labour, though, when he was interviewed for BBC television from his count at Leeds Town Hall, Robin Day seemed more interested in Krushchev's fall from power, which had been announced a few hours earlier. Denis went to bed at three in the morning with the pundits predicting a Labour majority of up to twenty. But, as he and Edna drove down to London later that Friday morning, Labour failed to win several close-run rural seats and the lead melted away. By the time they arrived at the Healeys' Highgate house, the overall majority was only four. Healey had scarcely time to unpack before he was called to No 10 Downing Street to be offered the Ministry of Defence by the man who, at forty-eight years of age, had just become the then youngest Prime Minister of the century.

In contrast to Douglas-Home's administration, the Wilson Cabinet seemed to be a ministry 'of all the talents'. George Brown became First Secretary of the newly established Department of Economic Affairs. His appointment was balanced by James Callaghan, the apparently unflappable and sensible Chancellor of the Exchequer. From the left, there was Richard Crossman, intellectually gifted if often unpredictable, and Barbara Castle, who had genuine 'star' quality. Wilson also appointed a solid bloc of former Gaitskellites and Morrisonian right wingers. 'He gave no preference to his old Bevanite chums,' commented Denis Healey. 'If anything, he did the reverse.'[17]

Healey, whose appointment was on the list of the first six Cabinet ministers announced on Friday evening, was, at the age of forty-seven, the youngest member of Wilson's Cabinet. After the long years of apprenticeship, first at Transport House and then in opposition in Parliament, Denis had at last arrived in power. 'I felt like a man who, after driving his Jaguar for hours behind a tractor on narrow country lanes, finally reaches the motorway,' wrote Healey.[18]

Denis's first weekend was hectic. He was sworn in as a Privy Councillor. He was then briefed by the Permanent Secretary, Sir Henry Hardman, and by the Ministry's Chief Scientific Adviser, Solly Zuckerman. On Sunday evening, he dined at Zuckerman's flat in Chelsea to meet the Chief of Defence Staff, Lord Mountbatten. The evening was interrupted by calls from the Prime Minister trying to persuade Zuckerman to become Minister of Disarmament. The conversation ranged over the whole field of defence policy. This was the first substantial meeting which Denis had had with the glamorous Mountbatten, the Royal who had been the last Viceroy of India and was now the senior serving officer at the Ministry of Defence. Even the self-confident Denis Healey found him, 'a formidable personality to have as my senior service advisor'.[19] On Monday morning, he went to the Ministry and took possession of his office on the sixth floor, overlooking the Thames.

Crosland and Jenkins had to wait to find out whether they would get a place in Wilson's government. Neither had played a significant role in the election campaign. Tony had concentrated on holding his highly marginal seat at Grimsby and succeeded in increasing his majority from 101 to 4098, while Roy spoke for a few pro-European Labour candidates outside Birmingham. On the Friday night after the election, Jenkins took part in a television programme which was interrupted, somewhat to his discomfiture, by an announcement of the first six Cabinet appointments, including Denis Healey. But there was no news about Roy. At noon on Saturday, he went for a drink with Crosland at Susan's house in Chelsea. To Roy's relief, Tony had not heard anything either, though Jenkins admitted to being jumpy about the telephone calls that Crosland received while he was there. In the afternoon, the Jenkins took a drive around Richmond Park to calm their nerves. On their return, Roy was told by his younger son, Edward, that there had been a message to ring No 10 Downing Street

just after they had left for their drive. 'I expect it's too late now,' added
Edward cheerfully. Roy immediately phoned Downing Street and was
summoned for 10.30 a.m. on Sunday.

Meanwhile Tony Crosland was also waiting for the call. He had
thought that he might be made number two to Jim Callaghan at the
Treasury or go to the Department of Economic Affairs under George
Brown. But, like Jenkins, he could not be certain of office under
Wilson. In the event, it was Susan Crosland who answered the crucial
phone call. A plummy voice said, 'It's the Pope. May I speak with your
husband?' It was George Brown telling Crosland that he was to be
made Minister of State at the Department of Economic Affairs (DEA)
and summoning the Croslands to George Brown's Marble Arch flat at
10.30 that evening.[20] The logic behind Tony's appointment was that
neither Wilson nor Brown wanted Callaghan to be reinforced by
Crosland, while Brown in his new department needed all the help he
could muster. As compensation, Callaghan got the economist, Robert
Neild, as a temporary civil servant.

Meanwhile, Brown had also phoned Jenkins, not only to invite the
Jenkins to his flat as well but to tell him that he was to be offered the
Ministry of Aviation the next morning. Roy was delighted by this
news. He had written two big feature articles for the *Observer* on the
British Overseas Airways Corporation and the crisis caused by buying
the British VC10 aircraft, which Wilson had read. And running a
department of his own was preferable to being like Tony Crosland, a
mere number two. Indeed when Crosland heard about Jenkins'
appointment later that evening, he was considerably put out. Bill
Rodgers, who had landed the job of parliamentary secretary at the
DEA and was also present at the Saturday night meeting, reported that
Crosland was furiously jealous. He wanted his old friend to be in the
government but not in a superior position to him.

The Saturday night meeting at Marble Arch was explosive. George
Brown, in a wine-red velvet smoking jacket, was furious when Tony, in
his customary carpet slippers, began by telling George that he had
already discussed his own appointment and the broad division of func-
tions between the two economic departments with Jim Callaghan.
'Treason,' roared George. A more substantial argument arose over the
issue of devaluation. Wilson, Brown and Callaghan had met without
officials at No 10 on Saturday morning and had taken the fateful

decision against devaluation, despite a predicted balance of payments deficit of £800 million. Wilson was determined not to devalue and his two most senior ministers went along with the far more experienced Prime Minister. Their informal decision was confirmed later that morning when the three met again, this time with their permanent secretaries. Crosland, unaware of these meetings, raised the devaluation issue with Brown, arguing strongly that it was economically essential and, if the decision was taken straightaway, it could be blamed on the Tories. Jenkins supported Crosland but as he admitted later, 'not as strongly as I should have done because I had temporarily succumbed to the infantile disease of departmentalism and had my mind too much on aircraft'.[21] Brown refused to discuss the matter, saying that the decision had already been taken and the subject was never to be raised again. Tony was horrified by this news and, by the time he had returned to Susan's house in Chelsea, was in two minds about accepting the job as Brown's number two.

On Sunday morning, Roy Jenkins went to 10 Downing Street for his meeting with Harold Wilson. Wilson began with an apology for not putting Jenkins in the Cabinet, virtually promising that he would promote him in the next reshuffle. Wilson was so circumlocutory that he did not get round to making the Ministry of Aviation offer for nearly ten minutes. Jenkins recorded that, if he had not already been forewarned by Brown, he might have wondered whether he was to be given a job at all. Wilson said that he wanted Jenkins to clean up the mess in military and civil aircraft procurement that the Conservative government had left behind. Jenkins straightaway accepted, provided that he was also put in charge of civil aviation generally. Wilson immediately agreed.

Why was Wilson prepared to treat Jenkins so generously? Obviously, it made good political sense to bring the Gaitskellites into his administration. But that does not explain why he gave Jenkins his own department and not Crosland. One reason was that Jenkins had demonstrated considerable knowledge of the aircraft industry. Wilson also found Roy more congenial and easier to handle than Tony. Harold was uncomfortable with Crosland's intellectualism, while he was able to gossip with Jenkins about recondite political facts and the minutiae of the Victorian railway system. Certainly, when Crosland went on the Monday to No 10 to be appointed as Brown's second-in-command, the

Prime Minister did not make the same promise of early promotion to the Cabinet that he had given on the previous day to Roy. Crosland followed up the meeting at No 10 with a memorandum to Wilson setting out the case for devaluation. Tommy Balogh, who was working for Wilson as an economic adviser, later commented, 'It was a very courageous thing to do. People don't argue with Prime Ministers.'[22]

After meeting his permanent secretary on the Sunday, Roy made a relaxed start the following morning at his new ministry, which was housed in the Ministry of Defence building. The Department of Economic Affairs existed in name only. 'Who are you?' asked George Brown's private secretary to a tall figure in the doorway. 'My name is Crosland,' was the reply. The new offices at Storey's Gate had no chairs, no writing paper and only one typewriter. George Brown erupted at regular intervals. But Labour was now in power and the ministerial careers of Healey, Jenkins and Crosland had at last begun. Denis, a member of the Cabinet, was the obvious front-runner but Roy and Tony at least had their feet on the ladder.

Labour's small majority meant that Harold Wilson had to devote the first months to demonstrating that Labour could provide an effective government and, therefore, deserved to be re-elected with a decent majority. Denis Healey, who was usually critical of Wilson, especially in the period between July 1966 and 1970, said of his first two years as Prime Minister, 'he was at his best'.[23] Wilson appeared to be in almost total command – of his Cabinet, of his party, of Parliament, and of the national political scene. In Kennedy mode, he promised 'a hundred days of dynamic action' and was able to please the December party conference by telling delegates that the government had already carried out some of its pledges, including increasing old age pensions and social benefits. He was brilliant in debate in the Commons, roused his party by his conference speeches and dominated the media headlines. He made good use of television. In his first eighteen months, he gave five interviews on *Panorama* and made six ministerial broadcasts. The ninety-seven seat majority, which Labour won in 1966, was an impressive endorsement not only of the party but, above all, of the new Prime Minister.

Healey, Jenkins and Crosland quickly made their mark as ministers. Denis Healey who was to be Defence Secretary for six years, said he 'loved every minute of it'.[24] In 1964 he brought to his new job the knowledge and contacts on both sides of the Atlantic that he had built up since the early 1950s. His 'good' war also helped him in his relationships with his senior serving officers.

Healey's first departmental decision was whether to renew Mountbatten's appointment as Chief of Defence Staff. After asking the views of his senior officials, he found that only one of them favoured Mountbatten's re-appointment. Denis also disagreed with Mountbatten's determination to get rid of the separate service Chiefs of Staff and establish a single central organisation to carry out the administration of the three services. Healey suspected that Mountbatten's motive was to build up himself as the supremo of defence policy rather than the Secretary of State. When Denis told Mountbatten that he had decided not to reappoint him, 'he clapped his thigh and roared with delight; but his eyes told a different story'.[25] Despite Solly Zuckerman's brilliance, Denis found him unpredictable and disloyal. Healey managed to persuade Wilson to move Zuckerman from Defence to No 10. Denis had left no doubt who was in charge of his vast and unwieldy department, which in 1964 was responsible for 458,000 servicemen and women, and 406,000 civil servants.

In his first week in office, Healey had a top secret briefing on the Polaris missile. Labour had a manifesto pledge to renegotiate the 1962 Nassau agreement, concluded between Macmillan and Kennedy, to give the UK Polaris. In the run-up to the election, Wilson had denounced Polaris as neither independent nor British and inadequate as a deterrent. However, as Opposition defence spokesman, Healey had told Parliament in February 1964 that a Labour government would not necessarily cancel Polaris, and there is also reason to believe from conversations on Privy Councillor terms between Healey and Thorneycroft, the Conservative Defence Secretary, that Wilson had always intended to keep Polaris, under the cover of pooling it with the Americans inside a NATO force.[26]

On 11 November, a three-man Cabinet Committee on nuclear policy, composed of Wilson, Healey and the Foreign Secretary, Gordon Walker, met and decided to proceed with the construction of at least three Polaris submarines. Healey believed that, in the uncertain post-Krushchev era, a few Polaris submarines would increase

London's clout in Washington and 'tend to reinforce the credibility of the American deterrent'.[27] Wilson had never been a unilateralist, despite running for the leadership against Gaitskell in 1960, and strongly agreed. The Prime Minister took the issue to Cabinet on 26 November and received majority backing for a Polaris force. On 29 January 1965, the Defence and Overseas Committee accepted Healey's recommendation for four Polaris submarines. Thus was the great issue of nuclear weapons, which had so convulsed the Labour Party, summarily dealt with. Healey, alongside Wilson, played the leading role.

In 1964, the United Kingdom still had extensive political and military obligations outside Europe, with more British troops east of Suez than in Germany. At that time, Healey favoured this disposition of forces. When Harold Wilson said in his November Mansion House speech, 'We are a world power, and a world influence or we are nothing,' his Defence Secretary may not have approved of his vainglorious tone but he shared the Prime Minister's basic assumptions. As he wrote later, 'I myself believed that our contribution to stability in the Middle and Far East was more useful to world peace than our contribution to NATO in Europe.'[28] The threat to Malaysia from Indonesian infiltration was an especially important factor to Healey. Yet the 21 to 23 November defence conference at Chequers revealed that worldwide commitments – in Malaysia, Hong Kong, the Caribbean, the South Atlantic, Cyprus, Aden, and the Gulf as well as obligations to NATO – were straining UK defence resources almost to breaking point.

The economic weakness that the incoming Labour government had inherited meant that, from its first economic statement, there was intense pressure on defence spending. Healey was almost immediately instructed by the Cabinet to cut the expenditure planned by the Conservatives by sixteen per cent over the next five years. There were further cuts to come, so much so that, when Labour left office in 1970, the United Kingdom, for the first time in its history, was spending more on education than on defence and, in 1972, defence spending would be running a third below the level envisaged by Peter Thorneycroft. Obvious targets for savings were the prestige military aircraft projects initiated by the Conservatives – the TSR-2 strike and reconnaissance plane, the HS681 short take-off transport, and the P1154 vertical take-off aircraft. On this issue, Denis Healey and the new Aviation Minister, Roy Jenkins, worked closely together.

Roy Jenkins was assisted in making his mark by the fact that decisions on the aircraft projects that the incoming Labour government had inherited from the Conservatives were near the top of their agenda. The first and biggest decision was whether to proceed with the super-sonic Anglo-French airliner, the Concorde. Brown and Callaghan wanted to cancel it immediately. Roy recognised the escalating costs and the likely lack of demand for the aircraft but thought that it was wrong to present the French with a unilateral decision to cancel, without any consultation or proper review. He tried to persuade the Cabinet not to make an immediate decision to question the future of the aircraft but he failed.

On 29 October he was sent to Paris to explain the government's position to the French administration. At Heathrow, he was handed a Foreign Office telegram that contained the sentence: 'The Minister of Aviation should be prepared for the atmosphere of cold enmity with which he will be met in Paris.'[29] In fact, French ministers received Jenkins with courtesy, though making it clear that they had no inten-tion of either agreeing to cancel the project or even to review it. The French had a trump card up their sleeve. As the previous Conservative government had agreed that the Concorde arrangement should not be a commercial agreement but the subject of an international treaty, it was open to the French government to sue the UK government for substantial damages at the Hague Court of International Justice.

It was against this unpromising background that Roy made the first of a series of House of Commons speeches that quickly established his reputation as an outstanding parliamentary performer and greatly helped further his rise. The Conservative opposition had decided to exploit the situation by concentrating on Concorde during the debate on the Queen's Speech. When Jenkins rose to reply at 9.30 p.m., the House was packed. Despite the uncomfortable position in which he found himself, Roy was able to put the Tories on the defensive, and inspire his own side. Though he had little time to prepare, he made the case for a review with considerable authority. He was assisted by the pompous and overfrequent interventions of Julian Amery, the former and unsuccessful Minister of Aviation, to which Jenkins had a devastating response: 'The Right Hon. Member for Preston North must recognise that people are entitled to take a different view from him on this and other projects. His administration at the Ministry of

Aviation was not such that all his opinions are sacrosanct.'[30] The retort silenced the opposition, enthused Labour MPs, and marked the beginning of Roy's mastery of the House of Commons.

In January 1965, a Cabinet Committee, finally convinced by the firm public stand of the French, decided to reprieve Concorde, thus letting Roy off that hook. However, on 1 February the government announced that it was replacing two of the three British projects, the HS681 and the P1154, with their cheaper American counterparts (the TSR-2's cancellation was delayed until the April Budget). In the debate that followed, Jenkins led for the government and Healey wound up. Once again, Roy crushed the Opposition with a well-prepared and well-argued speech. He pointed out that the problems of the aviation industry were there before the election and were only hidden by 'the carelessness about public money' of the former Minister of Aviation and 'the breezy salesmanship' of the former Minister of Defence. According to Jenkins, they operated rather like a pair of motor dealers – 'One in the back of the shop over-trading with other people's money, and the other in the front of the shop trying to explain away the mileage readings on the speedometer.' He concluded: 'We must make our defence decisions in what appears to us to be the best interests of the nation as a whole, and stick to them.' Healey's winding-up speech was a characteristic mix of factual information and invective, but his delivery was less effective than Jenkins', so much so that he was criticised by Conservative members for reading his brief.[31]

On 13 April, Jenkins once again gave a masterly performance in winding up for the government in an opposition censure motion on the cancellation of the TSR-2. He described the TSR-2 as a good plane that had to die because it cost too much – it was not 'a prize project, but a prize albatross'. The decision to cancel was the right one which, 'if the previous government had faced up to their responsibilities, ought to have been taken long ago'. The Times called Jenkins' speech 'a thunderous tub-thumping display, which set the Commons alight'.[32]

Tony Crosland was also catching the eye in his number two job at the DEA under George Brown. According to Dick Crossman's diary entry for 13 December 1964, Crosland, like Jenkins, Brown and Wilson, was 'thriving on the responsibilities of office'. Within his department, he learnt to deal with the mercurial George Brown. 'The great role that Tony played in the early days,' said Brown's Principal Private Secretary, 'was to establish some order in which advice could at least be presented to George so that he would know the facts when taking a policy decision.'[33] He got discussion going on issues such as the import surcharge, the autumn Budget and even the great unmentionable, devaluation. Brown commented later, 'You couldn't have found two people more different in manner than Tony and me. He could irritate every part of me – drape his hand on the mantelpiece, look at me in that patronising way – but he couldn't make me dislike him. You knew where you were with Tony. He was the one bloke who would fight me to my face – in the Department, in private.'[34] Outside his department, he was also playing an active role. Wilson sent him by plane to Strasbourg to win the Council of Europe's support for the new government's import surcharge. He returned in time to wind up the debate on the subject in the Commons.

On 22 January 1965, the Labour government suffered a serious setback. The Foreign Secretary, Patrick Gordon Walker, who was looking for a way back to the Commons, having lost his Smethwick seat in the October General Election, was narrowly and unexpectedly defeated at the Leyton by-election.

Jenkins' first reaction to the Leyton result was one of sympathy for an old friend. However, at breakfast the next morning, the thought occurred to him that Healey could well be made Foreign Secretary and the ensuing vacancy at Defence might then involve him. A little later that morning, he had a call at his Ministry from Emanuel Shinwell, the Labour veteran who was then chairman of the Parliamentary Labour Party, saying that he had advised Wilson to make Jenkins Foreign Secretary. When, soon after, Roy received a summons to No 10, he began to take Shinwell's message seriously. But, as he waited in the little hall outside the Cabinet Room, Callaghan, who always enjoyed being in the know, walked by and told him that Michael Stewart, then Secretary of State for Education, was to become the Foreign Secretary and Jenkins was to be offered Education.

This news, which Wilson confirmed, presented Jenkins with a dilemma. He was not attracted by the Education job, especially as his children were at private schools. On the other hand, if he rejected the post, he would be turning down a seat in the Cabinet. After discussing

Wilson's offer over a sandwich lunch with Jennifer, he decided to turn it down, and Wilson assured him that his decision would not preclude a further opportunity to enter the Cabinet, possibly in a senior position. Wilson wrote later: 'By far the outstanding success among ministers outside the Cabinet was Roy Jenkins. I decided he must be invited, though I knew that his inclinations were far more in the direction of the Home Office than Education.' Wilson added that Jenkins wanted to wait until the Home Office became available: 'A brave decision; few politicians would refuse their first chance to join the Cabinet.'[35]

When that evening Jenkins heard that it was his friend and rival, Tony Crosland, who had been appointed Secretary of State for Education and had thus entered the Cabinet ahead of him, he suffered from much the same pangs of jealousy that Crosland had experienced in October when Jenkins had been given his own department at Aviation, perhaps made more acute by the knowledge that Crosland's elevation had been directly caused by his own refusal. Though Healey was enjoying his job at Defence, he would have been more justified in feeling disappointed in being passed over for the Foreign Secretaryship. Apparently Crossman suggested Healey to the Prime Minister but Wilson's response was, 'I wouldn't trust Healey in the Foreign Office with all those professionals. And anyway we can't let him run away from the Defence job.'[36] Clearly Wilson wanted to be his own Foreign Secretary and understood very well that Denis would be his own man.

Even if Crosland was only Wilson's second choice as Education Secretary, it was an inspired one. Wilson commented, 'He's got a good brain, he's written well about education and he will be a positive addition to the Cabinet.'[37] Crosland had certainly thought long and hard about education. In *The Future of Socialism*, he had written that creating a fairer education system was the key to promoting a more equal society. In *The Conservative Enemy*, he had argued that the Labour Party should make educational spending the overriding domestic issue of the 1960s and called for a policy of integrating the public schools into the state system. Now, as Secretary of State for Education, he had been given the chance to put his ideas into practice.

In an interview later about his start at the Education Department, Crosland said, 'What is important is that at an early stage officials should see that you are not willing to accept submissions automatically and without questions, but that you propose to criticise, to reject when you think necessary and to take initiatives of your own. In other words, they must see that you have a mind of your own and are determined to take the final decision yourself.'[38] Tony never enjoyed the initial weeks in any job. Early in 1965, Susan remembered him commenting as he came up the stairs of their Lansdowne Road house carrying three red boxes, 'If I had more ministers and more time it might be fun.'[39] To help him shape his views, he invited educational experts, economists and sociologists to Lansdowne Road. These gatherings 'acted often as pre-meetings to a crucial one in the ministry the following week . . . only when some sort of line emerged would the whisky come out and the conversation be allowed to become general and edge towards political gossip'.[40]

Crosland liked to read himself into a subject, consult experts and civil servants, and then take an informed view. This impressively rational process of decision-making inevitably took time – and time is not always available in government. The education portfolio, however, suited his method of working. Most of the big educational decisions facing him were long-term, and he was able to concentrate on a few key objectives.

The most important immediate decision facing him was secondary school reorganisation. Labour had fought the 1964 election on the policy of abolishing the eleven-plus examination and reorganising secondary education on comprehensive lines.[41] As the middle class expanded, educational aspirations had grown. But the eleven-plus exam had the effect of dividing children into either the successful twenty-five per cent minority who went to the grammar schools or the rejected seventy-five per cent majority (including many middle-class children) who had to go to the usually inadequate secondary modern schools. Not surprisingly, the exam had become increasingly unpopular. Moreover, research had shown that the secondary school system was unjust, inefficient, wasteful and divisive.[42] And, in addition, a number of local educational authorities had introduced comprehensive secondary education in their own areas; by 1965, twelve per cent of children were already in comprehensives.

When Crosland arrived at Curzon Street his predecessor, Michael Stewart, had decided to prepare a circular for local authorities.

According to Crosland's Parliamentary Private Secretary, Christopher Price, Michael Stewart had been considering the statutory imposition of comprehensive education and even laying down a single institutional model, the eleven to eighteen, 'all-in' secondary school.[43] Crosland's circular, the famous DES 10/65, which went through a number of redrafts, substituted a more flexible policy, which allowed local authorities a number of options.

Crosland not only rejected legislation but also the advice of his Minister of State, Reg Prentice, that the Department should 'require' local authorities to prepare plans to go comprehensive. Instead, he decided on the word 'request', relying on the momentum behind the policy. By the summer of 1966, Crosland's voluntary approach had proved successful. The majority of local educational authorities came forward with comprehensive schemes, while less than twenty had refused to do so. 'The great push had taken place,'[44] commented Wilma Harte, the civil servant with responsibility for reorganisation, so much so that even Mrs Thatcher, the Conservative Secretary of State in the 1970s, was unable to reverse the tide.

Crosland has been fiercely attacked for his comprehensive policy, especially in conservative circles.[45] Later his critics made much of his unfortunate throwaway remark to his wife that he was 'going to destroy every fucking grammar school in England' (revealed by Susan Crosland in her book about her husband)[46] and accused him of undermining educational standards for the sake of social engineering. In practice, as we have seen, his approach was not only gradualist and flexible but was the first serious attempt to provide good secondary education for the seventy-five per cent of children who failed the eleven-plus exam. Exam results in the 1970s and 1980s disappointed the hopes of the reformers (though they were much better in the 1990s), but this was not because of Crosland's structural changes; rather it was because they were not accompanied by reforms to the secondary school curriculum or by sufficient improvements in teaching standards and methods. In Crosland's day, the curriculum was still a ministerial 'no-go' area. And the big issue, as far as teachers were concerned, was to provide enough of them to cope with the postwar 'baby boom'.

He failed to produce a solution to the intractable problem of the 'public schools' about which he had written so passionately in *The*

Conservative Enemy. He had already rejected abolition as being anti-libertarian. Late in 1965 he set up a Public School Commission under the chairmanship of Sir John Newsom to advise on the best way of integrating the public schools with the state system. After Crosland left the DES, the Newsom Commission came forward with proposals for limited assimilation that were shelved by the government as being too costly. Crosland later said to a journalist, 'Once the state system is strong enough to compete, if parents want to send their children to some inferior fee-paying school for purely snobbish reasons, that's their affair.'[47]

Apart from secondary reorganisation, the other key decision taken by Crosland was in higher education. The Robbins Report of 1963 had proposed a major expansion of the universities. In his April 1965 speech at the Woolwich Polytechnic, Crosland came out instead for a pluralist model of expanding universities and a growing public sector of polytechnics, technical colleges and colleges of further education. This so-called 'binary' system was criticised not only by university vice-chancellors for being 'anti-university' (Crosland had said that Britain needed to get away from 'its snobbish caste-ridden hierarchical obsession with university status') but also by left-wing critics who argued that all he was doing was creating a new divide at eighteen. Crosland's response was that 'both the demand and the need is for a pluralist, not a unitary, system of higher education, and for alternative institutions which offer something totally different from the traditional universities'.[48] In 1966, Crosland announced the creation of thirty polytechnics, which were to be different from but not inferior to the universities, particularly in their response to vocational and industrial needs.

Whatever the verdict of history, either on the binary system or on comprehensive reorganisation, there is no question that, in his two-and-a-half years at Education, Crosland made a real impact. Toby Weaver, Deputy Under Secretary for Higher Education, said that Crosland had 'a rare combination of qualities: brains, courage, perspective and compassion'.[49] There was a general consensus within the government and the Labour Party that Tony Crosland had been a successful 'modernising' Secretary of State for Education, who had done more than any of his predecessors, with the possible exception of R. A. Butler, to open up educational opportunity for the majority.

*

Following his interview in the House of Commons with Wilson when he was offered Education, nearly a year went by before Roy Jenkins achieved his ambition of becoming Home Secretary. According to Jenkins, he saw Wilson in late September 1965 to ask him about the future of the Ministry of Aviation.[50] Jenkins had virtually completed his mission; decisions had been taken about prestige aircraft projects, Concorde had been reprieved and a high-powered independent inquiry on the aircraft industry under Edwin Plowden, set up by Jenkins, was due to report very soon. The Prime Minister told Roy that he would soon enter the Cabinet, as Sir Frank Soskice had said he would soon resign as Home Secretary. 'You surely wouldn't like to be Home Secretary?' asked Wilson, either teasing Jenkins or forgetting their earlier conversation in January. Jenkins replied that, on the contrary, he would like very much to be Home Secretary and explained some of the reformist ideas which were contained in the chapter 'Is Britain Civilised?' in *The Labour Case* which he had written for the 1959 election. Wilson appeared enthusiastic.

Roy Jenkins was appointed Home Secretary on 22 December 1965. It proved a brilliant choice. Roy was in buoyant mood over Christmas. At forty-five, he was the youngest Home Secretary since Churchill, as well as succeeding Tony Crosland as the youngest member of the Cabinet. He had a very clear idea of what of what he wanted to do with the job. His first priority was to sort out the Home Office, which had been a graveyard of the careers of his immediate predecessors, Sir Henry Brooke and Sir Frank Soskice. 'Poor old Home Office,' Soskice had minuted on one file, 'we are not always wrong, but we always get the blame.'

Jenkins knew that he had to improve both the decision-making process of the department and its public image. He needed a new principal private secretary (he brought in David Dowler from the Ministry of Aviation), a new head of press and publicity, and a special advisor with responsibility primarily for public relations. John Harris, a former Transport House official who had worked for both Gaitskell and Gordon Walker, now became Roy Jenkins' 'spin doctor'. Above all, Roy had to change the permanent secretary, Sir Charles Cunningham, who ruled the Home Office with a rod of iron. Under Cunningham, advice to the Home Secretary came on one or two sheets of blue paper, signed by the permanent secretary. There were no discussion of alternative options, no background documents and no indication whether there had been dissenting opinions. When Roy confronted Sir Charles, there was a monumental row, with the civil servant weeping tears of rage. But Jenkins got his way and, though he wanted to stay on a year after his sixtieth birthday, the permanent secretary was retired in May 1966.

In a television interview with Robin Day, Jenkins defined the central purpose of the Home Office 'as being that of striking a very difficult balance between the need to preserve the Queen's peace and the need to preserve the liberty of the individual'.[51] He made it clear from the first that being a libertarian did not mean that he did not also have a big responsibility as Home Secretary to try and protect society against crime. In May 1966, he announced a major police reorganisation, reducing the number of police forces from 117 to 49. In November, he published a Criminal Justice Bill which, for the first time, brought in majority jury verdicts, as well as streamlining court procedure and introducing tighter control over the use of shotguns. In August, he responded swiftly to the murder of three policemen at Shepherd's Bush in London. But in a speech at Hounslow in September, he made it clear that he was not going to be panicked by press campaigns. It was important, he said, to stick to the facts – there was no 'murder wave'. He concluded that: 'A highly equipped, well-organised police force is the best protection of themselves and the public, and our best hope of turning back the crime wave; and this must be supplemented by a system of justice which will protect the innocent, without making it easy for the guilty to escape or involving an unnecessary waste of the time and trouble of police and public.'[52]

It is, however, for his liberal reforms that Roy Jenkins' stewardship at the Home Office in the 1960s is remembered. The death penalty had been abolished in 1965 but while he was Home Secretary the Sexual Offences Act got rid of existing criminal penalties for homosexual acts between consenting adults in public; abortion was made legal; and bills giving teeth to the newly set-up Race Relations Board and abolishing theatre censorship by the Lord Chamberlain were prepared. These subsequently became law. As many such issues were traditionally reserved for private members' legislation, with the government remaining neutral, Roy Jenkins' strategy was to help backbenchers get their bills drafted, to give his personal support to these bills, and, crucially, to ensure that they received sufficient parliamentary time to become law.

In the 1980s, there was much Conservative criticism of the so-called 'permissive society' for which the Jenkins reforms were blamed. But this line of argument ignores just how repressive and out of line both with contemporary attitudes and with continental practice UK legislation in this area had become. As Wilson's biographer, Ben Pimlott, puts it, the effect of this exceptional period of reform 'was to end a variety of judicial persecutions of private behaviour, quietly to consolidate a mood change in British society; and to provide a legal framework for civilised social values'.[53] Jenkins rightly got the main credit.

Jenkins once contrasted the variable climate of the Home Office – sudden violent storms out of a clear sky – with the predictable long dark Arctic winter of the Treasury. His ability to cope with these crises – the *Torrey Canyon* wreck (the giant oil tanker that ran aground off the Scillies, threatening the beaches of southern England); the murder of the three policemen at Shepherd's Bush; and the escape of the spy, George Blake, from Wormwood Scrubs prison – and to defend himself and the government in Parliament in difficult situations greatly increased his stature with his party and the media.

In his scathing Commons reply to an Opposition censure motion on the Blake escape, he routed the Conservatives. Wilson remarked that 'the Opposition leaders could not have been more devastatingly castigated if he had produced irrefutable evidence that they had, severally and collectively, been responsible for springing Blake'.[54] Jenkins demolished the suggestion that his Tory predecessor had put special curbs on Blake which Labour had relaxed. Lord Butler had said that Blake should never have been put in Wormwood Scrubs; Jenkins pointed out that Butler had sent him there. He had been asked by the Opposition to include the Blake escape in the terms of reference of the Mountbatten inquiry; and he had agreed to it. His concluding attack on the leader of the Opposition, Edward Heath, who had instigated the debate, was so wounding that his old Balliol friend did not speak to him for a year. 'I believe that this problem will be met by the constructive measures we are taking, and taking quickly; but it will not be by that combination of procedural incompetence and petty partisanship which is the constant characteristic of Edward Heath's parliamentary style.'[55] By mid-1966, Jenkins was recognised as Labour's coming man.

While Jenkins and Crosland were enhancing their reputations as modernising Cabinet ministers, Healey was wrapped up in his work as Defence Secretary. 'Before long,' he wrote later, 'I was being described as essentially a technocrat rather than a politician. This did not worry me; technocratic seemed simply a pejorative word for competent, an adjective which not all my fellow ministers invited.'[56] Healey's task at Defence was to get on top of the department and to try and make its workings more rational; to maintain the United Kingdom's security obligations, including fighting an undeclared jungle war in Borneo; to scrap ineffective and wasteful projects; to cut back defence spending in line with Cabinet decisions; and, when the economic situation deteriorated during 1967 and the strain on military manpower became too severe, to withdraw from British commitments east of Suez in an orderly fashion and without losing the support of the services.

In the Labour Party of that time Defence Secretary was not a glamorous job, but Denis Healey was by far the best equipped for it. Indeed he was arguably the best Defence Secretary since the war. Neil Cameron, an RAF officer who was a member of Healey's Programme Evaluation Group (PEG) and later became Chief of Defence Staff, wrote that Denis brought to his post 'a very clear mind, a lot of charm, and an unwillingness to take no for an answer'.[57] Professor Michael Howard, a leading military historian, describing Healey's method of working, commented: 'He is impatient of formalities; if he wants a decision, he assembles the men concerned and gets it; and his choice of men concerned is not always what protocol would suggest. He will not wait for information to come up through the usual channels, but dives down into the machine himself. Policy is therefore not made by regular meetings of any formal body, but by ad hoc groups.' Roy Hattersley, one of Healey's junior ministers, said: 'Denis was a brilliant minister. He had huge grasp of the issues, was good at making up his mind and was a wonderful delegator. He might blame you in private but would always support you in public.'[58]

Healey continued the reforms, begun under his Conservative predecessor Peter Thorneycroft and Mountbatten, of breaking down the rivalries between the three services and trying to strengthen the centre. The ministers in charge of each of the services were downgraded to Parliamentary Under Secretaries, while Healey created two more senior Ministers of State, one responsible for equipment and administration, the other across the board. The powers of the permanent under secretary vis à vis the service departments were considerably increased. Healey also set up a Programme Evaluation Group, consisting of officers from each of the three services, as well as a scientist, a civil servant and an economist, to enhance the policy-making capacity of the Defence Secretary.

Healey dominated the service chiefs by the force of his intellect and personality. However, expenditure cuts inevitably led to clashes. The 1966 Defence Review cancelled the CVA-01, the strike carrier planned by the navy for the 1970s. The Navy Board were very bitter about Healey's decision and the Chief of Naval Staff, Sir David Luce, resigned, as did the Navy Minister, Christopher Mayhew, who had known Denis at Oxford. In his resignation statement, Mayhew broadened his attack on Healey to include the failure of the government to cut its commitments east of Suez. In August, however, there was better news for the Defence Secretary. The undeclared frontier war with Indonesia in Borneo came to an end, thus allowing the withdrawal of a substantial number of British troops and giving Healey the opportunity to reconsider the future of United Kingdom obligations east of Suez.

Between 1964 and 1966, the Labour Cabinet was dominated by the Prime Minister, and, to a lesser extent, by George Brown and James Callaghan. Given the inexperience of most of his ministers, Wilson saw himself as the centre-forward, who had to try and score all the goals himself.[59] In Cabinet, however, he let his colleagues talk (except on the big issues, like devaluation, which he did not allow to be discussed at all). Although Healey, of course, spoke on defence and foreign affairs, he wrote later that for the first year, 'he played little part in Cabinet discussions about . . . domestic issues'.[60] As to his style, he admitted himself that on his own subjects he was said to dominate his colleagues rather than persuade. Susan Crosland, presumably reporting her husband's views, said that Denis, when in the ascendant, 'could not resist one-upmanship'.[61]

When Crosland first entered the Cabinet early in 1965, he was more circumspect. 'I cannot offer comment because I haven't given the matter serious thought' was a typical Crosland remark. Callaghan told him he was too modest; on many issues, he was better informed than his colleagues. Tony took the hint. By April 1965 Crossman noted in his diary that Crosland was emerging in Cabinet 'as a man with something important to say on the economic side'.[62] Barbara Castle was delighted that he spoke out for higher public spending when the government put forward a package of public expenditure cuts in July 1965,[63] while Crossman wrote that, in the Cabinet discussion of George Brown's National Plan, much trumpeted as the centrepiece of the government's economic policy, it was Crosland who pointed out the impact that the government's cuts could have on the National Plan: 'Crosland is the only member of the Cabinet who comes right out with these honest-to-God economic judgements.'[64]

Writing in his diary in April 1965 when Roy Jenkins was not yet in the Cabinet, Crossman noted that as Minister of Aviation, he had steadily raised his status.[65] In the Cabinet as Home Secretary, he rapidly became a powerful figure, making clear his views on issues such as Common Market entry, which was back on the agenda following the 1966 election. However, it was the crisis of July 1966 that brought him to prominence on economic issues.

The July 1966 crisis, even more than the devaluation crisis of November 1967, was a defining moment for the Wilson government. A run on the pound led to the government introducing an austerity package, including cuts in public spending and a wages freeze, decisions that meant the virtual abandonment of the National Plan, a fatal loss of direction for the Labour government, and a devastating blow to the reputation of the Prime Minister.

Wilson remained determined not to devalue. However, George Brown now believed devaluation was essential for economic growth, while a rattled Callaghan, though still against devaluation, believed it might become inevitable. Crosland and Jenkins were strong devaluationists, as were Crossman, Castle and Benn (newly promoted to the Cabinet as Minister for Technology). Brown, not for the first time, was threatening to resign. By 14 July, Wilson, who was on a trip to Moscow, was facing a political as well as economic crisis.

Robert Neild, Callaghan's economic advisor at the Treasury, commented: 'At moments of crisis, people are caught in characteristic poses. Roy is at a grand country house, Nicky (Kaldor) is rushing back and forth between Cambridge and London. Tony is at home with his wife and family.'[66] Jenkins indeed spent the weekend at Sevenhampton near Swindon with Mrs Ann Fleming, Gaitskell's former girlfriend, but his fellow guests were not politicians or press magnates but John Sparrow, the warden of All Souls', Stuart Hampshire, the distinguished philosopher, and his close friends, Mark and Leslie Bonham Carter. Roy spoke by telephone to both George Brown and Jim Callaghan. George was threatening resignation and wanted Roy to resign as well, while Jim preferred deflation rather than devaluation.

On Saturday afternoon, Roy saw Robert Neild, who tried unsuccessfully to sell him the case for a postponement of devaluation. On Sunday afternoon Crosland and Jenkins met at Tony's home in Lansdowne Road and found that they were both in favour of immediate devaluation. On Monday evening Tony and Roy both had conversations with Dick Crossman at the House of Commons. Crossman asked Jenkins whether, as Wilson alleged, he and Crosland supported devaluation merely in order to get into Europe. Roy replied, 'A floating pound gives a certain freedom of action, either to enter Europe or to do anything else, and what we are trying to regain this week is freedom of action.'[67]

At Tuesday afternoon's Cabinet meeting, which met for four-and-a-half hours, devaluation was fully discussed for the first time. According to the accounts of Crossman, Callaghan and Jenkins, only six ministers were in favour of either immediate devaluation or floating; these were Brown, Crossman, Crosland, Jenkins, Castle and Benn. Wilson, however, got the erroneous impression that Jenkins was advocating devaluation later.[68] Jenkins noted that Healey appeared to have an open mind.[69]

Defeat for the devaluationists was also a defeat for the Labour government. The decision not to devalue in July 1966 meant that the government was forced to squeeze the economy and sacrifice growth, Labour's raison d'être, in order to maintain the value of sterling, a parity which in the end proved unsustainable. Politically, the events of July 1966 were also a major defeat for Wilson. Even if both the Labour Party and the Prime Minister were to stage something of a recovery before the 1970 election, Wilson, apparently in charge of events before the July crisis, now almost always appeared on the defensive.

Although Callaghan had declared in his April 1967 budget that the ship was back 'on course', events such as the June Six Day War in the Middle East, a European Commission report on Britain's application for Common Market membership implying the need to devalue, and a deteriorating balance of payments forced the government's hand. On 16 November, the Cabinet agreed to devalue by fourteen per cent to a new parity of $2.40 to the pound. As a matter of honour, Jim Callaghan, who had resisted devaluation for so long, was determined to resign as Chancellor. The question was who was to succeed him.

In his book on the Chancellors, Edmund Dell, then a junior minister, wrote that, in 1967, there were three possible candidates – Healey, Crosland and Jenkins.[70] Healey was the least obvious choice. He was clearly doing a good job at Defence, had no economic qualification and had not yet achieved mastery of the House or built up a following in the Parliamentary Labour Party. However, it is clear from Susan Crosland's account that Denis Healey thought he had a chance. During the crisis, Edna Healey told Susan that she felt so worried about Healey's prospects that she had to go to bed for a day.[71]

In many eyes, Crosland was the front-runner. He was clearly the best economist of the three men. Three months earlier, he had been promoted to President of the Board of Trade and, unlike Jenkins, made a member of Wilson's Steering Committee on economic policy, appointed after the July 1966 crisis. He had the support of the outgoing Chancellor. He had been called upon to open the debate on devaluation on 21 November and had made a brilliant speech in which he said that devaluation offered a new strategy based on expansion and export-led growth. Tony reported to Susan on the evening of 19 November: 'Jim talked in front of the others about my being Chancellor in a week or so. He says that he and Harold have agreed that the odds on this are 95 to 5.'[72]

But, to Crosland's great disappointment, Wilson appointed Jenkins instead. One reason was that it enabled Wilson to make Callaghan Home Secretary in straight swap. Another was that Wilson found Roy easier to get on with than Crosland: Jenkins was Wilson's Gaitskellite.[73] However, perhaps the most important reason of all was that Jenkins was the most effective in the House and was the darling of the liberal press, and he was therefore considered by Wilson as more likely than Crosland to impose his authority on the Chancellorship, at a critical time for the government.

Jenkins' promotion to the second most important job in the government was a crucial moment in the see-sawing balance between the three men. At Oxford, Healey and Crosland had both been senior and more prominent than Jenkins. During the time of Gaitskell, Roy, though personally close to the Labour leader, was still very much an also-ran. Under Wilson, he had proved himself a highly successful Home Secretary, but Healey and Crosland were also recognised as competent Cabinet ministers. Now, suddenly, thanks to Wilson's support, Roy, the youngest of the three, had pulled decisively ahead.

How did the promotion of Jenkins affect his relationships with Crosland and Healey? The friendship between Jenkins and Crosland never fully recovered from Jenkins' appointment over the head of Crosland to the one job that Crosland coveted most in politics. In a conversation with Dick Crossman earlier in June, Tony had complained that he and Roy 'have ceased to know each other at all intimately and I think he is behaving in a very funny and remote and ambitious way'.[74] Now the younger man, who had for so long been the junior partner in their relationship, had leapfrogged over the elder. To add salt to Crosland's wounds, only a few hours after hearing the news, he had to fly to Paris to deputise for the Chancellor at an OECD meeting.

When the two finally met a few days later, Crosland was bitter. Had he known that Jenkins was to be Chancellor, he told Jenkins, he would never have agreed to move from Education to the Board of Trade. Now, any economic achievement would be attributed to Jenkins and perhaps to Wilson, but certainly not to Crosland. Jenkins later commented that 'it would be idle to pretend that these events of November 1967 did not leave a scar on Crosland which had the effect of crucially damaging the cohesion of the Labour right over the next eight or nine years. Had he and I been able to work together as smoothly as did Gaitskell and Jay or Gaitskell and Gordon Walker a decade before, it might have made a decisive difference to the balance of power within the Labour Party and to the politics of the early 1980s.'[75]

Jenkins and Healey had never been as close as Jenkins and Crosland, so there was not the feeling of personal betrayal in Healey's reaction, as there was in Crosland's. Healey's diary for 21 November merely noted tersely: 'Roy and Jim swop jobs – some relief'. All the same, he later admitted that he had a pang of regret when the Treasury job went to his younger Balliol contemporary.[76] Where necessary, Healey was prepared to work with Jenkins as Chancellor, but that did not mean that he accepted Roy as leader of the centre-right, modernising faction of the party. As always, Denis continued to have a strong belief in his own abilities and, in any case, was a loner who did not join groups or cabals or even bother to set up his own.

Wilson had taken a big political risk in promoting his most dangerous potential rival, Roy Jenkins, to the Chancellorship but, in preferring Jenkins to Crosland and Healey, he also succeeded in dividing the three leading Gaitskellites from each other, to the long-term detriment of the revisionist cause in the Labour Party.

Chapter 8

The Ascendancy of Jenkins

From 29 November 1967, when Roy Jenkins was appointed Chancellor of the Exchequer, until Labour's defeat at the General Election of 18 June 1970, Jenkins was the dominant figure in the Wilson administration. Two examples from the heavyweight press illustrate Jenkins' ascendancy. The *Sunday Times* leader for the November weekend in which Roy became Chancellor went so far as to suggest not only the future of the British economy and of the Labour Party, but even that parliamentary democracy itself depended upon his success at the Treasury. The *Economist* cover for 13 June 1970, published a few days before the election, carried the headline 'In Harold Wilson's Britain'. However, the message of the cover photograph, which pictured a relaxed Wilson and a sleek and confident Jenkins walking briskly together in front of St Margaret's, Westminster, was that the two men were clearly equals. The implication was that if, as everyone then expected, Labour won the election, it would be as much because of Jenkins' achievements as Chancellor as because of the popularity of Wilson, and that, in due course, Jenkins was likely to succeed Wilson as Prime Minister.

It would be hard to overstate the sense of crisis that the 1967 devaluation brought with it. Even if the policies needed to strengthen the weak balance of payments were obvious enough, requiring a combination of deflation to dampen domestic demand and release capacity for exports and incomes control to ensure that the competitiveness acquired by devaluation was not squandered, Jenkins had only a narrow margin for error.[1] The Bretton Woods fixed-exchange-rate system allowed only a two per cent band below the central rate of the pound. The Bank of England reserves available to defend the new parity were small. And there were only three years at the most before the election to turn the economy around. Jenkins' assessment of the situation facing him was therefore apposite: 'We were always near to the edge of the cliff, with any gust of wind, or sudden stone in the path, or inattention to the steering, liable to send us over.'[2]

What added to the government's difficulties was Wilson's dramatic loss of credibility following devaluation. It was not only that devaluation was a major personal disaster for the Prime Minister. He compounded the defeat by refusing to admit it. In a television broadcast immediately after devaluation, Wilson's tone was 'too complacent by half'.[3] It was during this broadcast that he said, 'It does not mean that the pound in the pocket is worth fourteen per cent less to us now than it was' – a sentence, which, even if correct in purely domestic terms, was used against him to great effect for the rest of his career. After devaluation, Wilson's political weakness led to dissension in the Cabinet, unrest in the parliamentary party, persistent attacks in the media, and disastrous results in the public opinion polls and in by- and local elections.

Roy Jenkins was forty-seven when he became Chancellor in circumstances which, provided he was successful in his new job, potentially opened up the road to the leadership of the party and the premiership. Jenkins brought to the Chancellorship high intelligence, historical perspective, steely ambition and the ability to make and stick to decisions. Above all, he was authoritative in Cabinet and commanding in the Commons.

When, after the SDP breakaway, Harold Wilson came to speak for Roy Jenkins' Labour opponent in the 1981 Warrington by-election, he was asked whether or not Roy had been a good Chancellor. Wilson's reply was, 'yes, up to 7 p.m.' Both Crossman and Castle in their diaries also implied that Jenkins did not work long hours.[4] However, in his autobiography, Roy wrote that he worked harder as Chancellor than ever before or since. He was at his desk at the Treasury from 10.00 a.m. to 8.00 p.m., and worked on his boxes both late at night, in the morning and for five or six hours a day on Saturdays and Sundays. Jenkins had learnt from his last year at Oxford cramming for his First and from his Bletchley experience the secret of intense concentration under pressure. He also knew how to get the best out of himself. Though usually a decisive decision-maker, Roy preferred to think through problems. He also liked to recharge his batteries by going out to lunch or dinner during the week and by going down to his and Jennifer's Oxfordshire home at East Hendred for the weekend.

Roy Jenkins' political reputation was based at least in part on his ability to make impressive and stylish House of Commons speeches. His preparation was almost always meticulous. When he knew he had to make a big speech, he went into a two-day virtual purdah when nothing mattered except its preparation. He once told Tony Crosland that before a major speech he worked on the twenty-to-one principle: 'Allow twenty times as long for the preparation of the speech as the speech itself will be.' Immediately before a speech he would wring his hands together in an attack of acute nerves but from the moment he began to speak it was a different matter. 'I try to feel the House, to play the House, like a matador playing a bull, for if you slip, it's very difficult to get up again.' He was not only a fine phrase-maker but was also ruthless in debate, more often than not routing the Tory opposition. His dominance over his Conservative opposite number, Iain Macleod, himself a formidable debater, was such that one Conservative newspaper likened their clashes to that of the mongoose, Riki Tiki Tavi, and the cobra in Kipling's famous story.[5]

But even if he was now a committed and highly ambitious minister, Roy still retained a 'hinterland'. He no longer had time for writing, though his *Asquith*, written before the summer of 1961 and January 1964, was published to acclaim after he became a minister, and a collection of his speeches and essays, edited by Anthony Lester, came out in 1967. His social life, however, remained extremely important to him. Questioned about his taste for 'sophisticated and elegant living' by Robin Day in a television interview following his appointment as Home Secretary, Jenkins replied: 'If by elegant one means does one like things to be attractive rather than unattractive, yes I do. If by sophisticated one means does one like to know a wide range of people, inside and outside politics, then yes I do.'[6] Jenkins liked socialising with his friends, many of whom he had known since Oxford and who had now become part of the liberal establishment – dons, lawyers, diplomats, civil servants, authors and leading journalists from the *Guardian*, *The Times* (then of a more liberal disposition) and the *Observer*. Unlike most politicians of his generation, he genuinely enjoyed the company of women, much preferring mixed to all-male dinners. Roy had especially close relationships with Leslie Bonham Carter, wife of his Oxford friend and Liberal politician Mark Bonham Carter, and Lady Caroline Gilmour, daughter of the eighth Duke of Buccleuch and wife of the left-wing Conservative MP and later Cabinet minister Ian Gilmour.

His home at East Hendred was a vital base, acting as a weekend retreat for thinking and relaxing and, as his parents' house at Pontypool had been, as a place to invite his friends for tennis, croquet, and talk. Jennifer Jenkins had bought the house, an old vicarage, in an auction in September 1966. The purchase had been partly financed by the sales of *Asquith*. In a diary entry for April 1968, Crossman records a visit to East Hendred:

> We drew up ten minutes early in the back courtyard of a rather ramshackle old vicarage with a croquet lawn. Inside we found a very family party; Jennifer's father and her mother; then a tall willowy young man at New College, who is the eldest son, Charles, with his girlfriend; next Cynthia, who is at St Paul's; and finally young Edward, who is at the City of London School . . . I hadn't at all expected this family atmosphere . . . So Roy has a real family to cope with at home . . . Roy gave us some excellent claret . . . and in the noise of the family talk he told me about his conversation with the Prime Minister.[7]

When Jenkins reviewed the second volume of Crossman's diaries in 1976, he pointed out that their vicarage was not 'ramshackle'; it was, in fact, a neat, whitewashed rambling house with room for a tennis court and croquet lawn. Roy, who used to play fiercely competitive tennis with Tony Crosland on the Ladbroke Square court, was now able to improve his unorthodox left-hand tennis serve and become increasingly expert at the tactics of croquet.

According to Edmund Dell, in the few months after devaluation, 'the government drifted'.[8] Roy Jenkins admitted later that he ought to have acted immediately to cut consumption, in order to release resources for exports as quickly as possible.[9] The Treasury had presented his predecessor, Jim Callaghan, with an urgent package of measures to accompany devaluation but Callaghan had refused on the grounds that he lacked the credibility to implement such a package. Jenkins' advisors failed to re-present the new Chancellor with the package, perhaps because of demoralisation or exhaustion or both, but the permanent secretary, Sir William Armstrong, and the Governor of the Bank, Sir Leslie O'Brien, later suggested the tightening of hire purchase or the use of the regulator (by which all indirect taxes could be increased or lowered by ten per cent by an Order in Council) before the April Budget.

In an emergency debate on 5 December 1967, Jenkins had told Michael Foot, then a left-wing rebel, that, though further room had to be made in the economy for exports: 'We did not want to dig a hole and have it empty. We want it to be there only when the export demand is ready to fill it, and we think that the Budget is likely to be about the right time for this further excavation.'[10] As Jenkins accepted in his autobiography, this apparent precision about timing was economic nonsense: 'So far from waiting with this lofty assurance I ought to have been shovelling earth out like mad from the moment of my appointment.'[11] He was probably influenced in his reply to Foot by the Prime Minister's own preference for delaying taking deflationary measures until the Budget.[12]

Whatever the reason, Roy Jenkins' failure to squeeze consumption immediately was a major error. He wrote in his autobiography: 'It encouraged a spending spree of anticipatory buying. It also missed the best moment for the bracing imposition of the burdens of austerity in a mood of national sacrifice. It probably delayed the improvement in the balance of payments by no more than two or three months, but as we were very close to the rocks of another devaluation when the ship eventually turned this could have been decisive.'[13] In the first two weeks of January, all Jenkins' energy was taken up by a marathon series of Cabinet meetings, at which his package of public spending cuts worth £800 million was discussed. Public expenditure had increased by one-sixth in real terms between 1963–64 and 1966–67 and needed to be brought back under control if devaluation was to work. The cuts involved a number of harsh decisions, including a restoration of prescription charges, postponement until 1973 of the raising of the school-leaving age to sixteen, restrictions on both housing expenditure and roads, and, most difficult of all, withdrawal from east of Suez and the cancellation of the order for fifty American F-111 strike aircraft. There was little dissent over the principle of such a package. The difficulty, as always, was getting agreement for the specific measures.

Jenkins had the consistent backing only of the Prime Minister, who, however, left almost all the advocacy to the Chancellor, and of Dick Crossman, who, as Lord President and Leader of the House, was not a spending minister and gave enthusiastic and vocal support to Jenkins throughout. Callaghan, who might have been expected to line up behind his predecessor, opposed Jenkins on three out of the four main issues.

Tony Crosland's attitude was, however, the more depressing for Roy. Here was his oldest friend in politics and, as President of the Board of Trade, the second most important economic minister in the government, challenging the Chancellor at a moment of crisis. Crosland demanded and got a general discussion of the economic background to the cuts. But at the Cabinet meeting of 12 January he went further and argued for only half the cuts for which Jenkins was asking. Crossman noted: 'Roy's reply was fairly devastating. Even with £800 million cuts, he said, he would have to impose more than half the necessary cut in demand by increasing taxation in the coming Budget. And it was at this point that he revealed that the trade deficits in the last three months of 1967 had come to over £300 million, the same as in the autumn of 1964 when Maudling was having his election spending spree . . . Cabinet just had to accept the size of his public sector cuts.'[14]

As former Education Secretary, Crosland was also one of the leaders of the revolt in the Cabinet against delaying the raising of the school-leaving age (RSLA). Crosland was supported by Michael Stewart, another former Education Secretary, and by two ministers, George Brown and Ray Gunter who had not been to university. When Crossman, who was backing the Chancellor, asked Crosland who would be affected by postponement, Tony replied: 'Only 400,000 children. But they're not our children. It's always other people's children. None of us in this room would dream of letting our children leave school at fifteen.'[15] Jenkins pointed out that no one had suggested any other way of extracting £40 million out of the education budget and that there were a number of teachers and parents of children at comprehensive schools who would welcome what was after all only a short-term postponement. At a further Cabinet meeting, it was the vote of the current Education Secretary, Patrick Gordon Walker, which decided the issue in favour of the Chancellor.

Crosland then attempted to blackmail Jenkins by threatening to withdraw his support for cancelling the F-111, unless the Chancellor gave way on the postponement of RSLA. Tony said to his wife Susan, 'I shall tell him that I'm only willing to risk selling a certain number of beliefs down the river to save the present economy. I suppose it is blackmail really.' Although Jenkins himself felt uneasy about postponing raising the school-leaving age, he immediately rejected Crosland's ploy.[16] 'I could not understand the logic of this proposition and rejected it on the spot . . . believing that if I started to make deals of this sort I would quickly be cut up like a salami sausage.'[17] Subsequently only the Leader of the House of Lords, Lord Longford, resigned over the issue.

This was hardly Crosland's finest hour. Of course, he had a case on postponement but he knew very well that, following devaluation, tough action had to be taken swiftly. He had earlier advised Callaghan accordingly.[18] Yet he opposed both the size and the content of the Jenkins spending package which was very similar to the one that the Treasury had prepared for Callaghan. Even sympathetic Cabinet colleagues like Tony Benn thought that Crosland's behaviour was 'niggling'.[19] It is difficult not to conclude that Tony Crosland was still smarting from being passed over for the Chancellorship and was taking it out on Roy Jenkins, whom he took to calling 'the Iron Chancellor'.

Denis Healey's reaction to Jenkins' promotion and to his spending package was more straightforward. As Roy told Dick Crossman, defence was a prime target for Treasury spending cuts and it was Denis's duty as Secretary of State to fight as robustly as he could for his department. But he was prepared to accept his responsibility as a senior minister to help get the spending cuts package through Cabinet. Jenkins, who was aware that Denis had coveted the Chancellorship (though he would have preferred the Foreign Office),[20] shrewdly invited Healey to a 'softening up' lunch in a private room at Brown's Hotel on 14 December. Roy disclosed the broad outlines of his strategy, including withdrawal from east of Suez.[21] According to Denis Healey, Jenkins also told him that, following the row over supplying arms to South Africa, Healey was now the Prime Minister's 'Public Enemy Number One'. Jenkins and Healey agreed to stand together, presumably against any threat from Wilson to Healey's position,[22] an indication that, at least in the 1960s, the two men were able to work together.

Jenkins' approach to Healey was a mark of the growing importance of Denis's role in the government. Healey dominated his department. He also had a big influence on the direction of foreign affairs. It was a Foreign Office joke that the FO was divided into two groups – those who thought that Healey should be Foreign Secretary and those who thought he already was. Denis was also increasingly intervening in Cabinet economic discussions, in part because of their impact on defence spending. After the July 1966 crisis, Wilson had appointed him to the newly formed Cabinet Economic Committee. Healey had gradually come round to the inevitability of devaluation and was one of a group of ministers set up to implement the decision once it was taken in principle, including a package of spending cuts. Horrified by the implications for defence, Healey attacked Callaghan savagely in Cabinet Committee 'for his misdirection of the economy over three years, and how did we know that what was proposed would do any better'.[23]

If Healey was critical of Callaghan, his opinion of Harold Wilson had reached rock-bottom, especially after the row over the sale of arms to South Africa in December 1967. Healey believed, with justification, that Wilson had deliberately stirred up the parliamentary party in order to strengthen his own weak position. In effect Wilson had turned Labour MPs against Brown and Healey over a decision, taken in principle by the Cabinet Defence and Overseas Policy Committee and endorsed by Wilson, to sell naval weapons to South Africa. After two stormy Cabinet meetings in which Wilson was bitterly criticised, especially by Brown and Healey, the decision was reversed. Although Healey later conceded he was wrong to have supported the sale of arms to South Africa, he stuck to his view that the

December Cabinet crisis was as much about Wilson's style of government as about arms.

At weekends, Healey was glad to escape from the frustrations of political life and from Admiralty House, where the Healeys had a flat during the week, to the small gatehouse of an Edwardian mansion near Withyham, on the border between Kent and Sussex. Here Denis walked in Ashdown Forest and talked with his children, especially Cressida who had hated leaving their home and friends in Highgate. The Healeys' rural oasis may have preserved Denis's sanity but all the same it was a sceptical and sometimes belligerent Healey with whom his Oxford contemporary and new Chancellor had to work.

Despite having been a strong supporter of the east-of-Suez strategy, Healey now broadly accepted the case for withdrawal, though he bargained fiercely over the timing. The critical issue for him was the cancellation of the F-111 order. The problem this raised for Healey was that he had promised the F-111 to the Royal Air Force as compensation for the earlier cancellation of the TSR-2 and he feared that Sam Elworthy, the RAF chief who had become the Chief of Defence Staff, would resign. The first Cabinet vote produced a majority of only one in favour of cancellation. Healey asked for and was given a pause for reflection.

However, the second vote increased the majority to three. Although in the meantime Healey had swung the vote of Lord Longford, Jenkins had persuaded Gordon Walker to reverse his vote and the Prime Minister had nobbled Cledwyn Hughes. During the discussion Healey had threatened resignation but after the decision he did not carry out his threat, partly because he feared that his successor might be Dick Crossman, an old sparring partner of his. Resignation would, in any case, have been difficult to justify, especially as withdrawal from east of Suez removed the operational requirement for the F-111. When, after the decisive Cabinet meeting, Jenkins took Healey back to the downstairs study of 11 Downing Street for a drink, he found that Denis drew a sharp distinction between the threat of resignation in argument and what happened once the decision was made. 'Of this I was glad,' wrote Jenkins, 'for I would have regarded his loss as a major weakening of the government and the forces of sense within it.'[24] On this occasion, at least, Roy was prepared to take the trouble to hold out the hand of friendship to Denis.

Though it was Wilson and not Jenkins who announced the public spending cuts to the House on 16 January 1968, it was due to Roy's skill and determination that the package of about £800 million in cuts over two years had survived a bruising series of Cabinet meetings virtually intact. However, the Budget statement on taxation decisions did not come for another two months and so markets were left in ignorance of the government's overall post-devaluation strategy for a full four months after devaluation. Not surprisingly, sterling remained under threat as Roy worked on his first Budget. Significantly, he consulted only Wilson, Crosland and Healey. Bringing Crosland and Healey into his confidence, he had three conversations with Tony and discussed the shape of his Budget with Denis at East Hendred over the weekend of 10–11 February. Jenkins commented that the Healey stay was 'an indication of the importance I attached to his position in the government, for, despite . . . over fifty years of close acquaintanceship this was, and remains, a unique occasion'.[25]

As Roy decided on his Budget dispositions, a sterling/dollar crisis suddenly blew up which led to a farcical but damaging political problem for the Wilson government. Partly as a result of the deficit financing of the Vietnam War, the dollar came under sustained pressure in late February and early March as holders of dollars moved into gold. Inevitably, the weakness of the dollar affected the pound. Another devaluation looked inevitable. Late on Thursday 14 March, President Lyndon Johnson requested that the world's main gold market in London should be closed the following day. Jenkins decided to exploit the opportunity afforded by Johnson's request to close the foreign exchange market as well. Arrangements were made for a post-midnight Privy Council at Buckingham Palace to make the necessary Order in Council proclaiming a Bank Holiday. Wilson tried (how hard is clouded in mystery) to find George Brown, the Foreign Secretary, to associate him with the decision. Brown could not be located and Peter Shore, Secretary of State for Economic Affairs, and a protégé of Wilson's, went with Jenkins and Wilson to the Palace.

After midnight, Brown was at last found in the Commons. He flew into one of his rages when he heard what had happened and, gathering together a group of Cabinet ministers including both Crossman and Crosland, attempted to summon Wilson to explain himself. After some hesitation, Wilson refused to come and instead invited the ministers over to No 10 Downing Street. About ten minutes later they arrived, with Brown almost incoherent and Crosland looking glowering. Jenkins quietly and calmly set out what had happened and why, quickly satisfying most of the ministers present, though Crosland and Stewart complained about the lack of consultation. Brown, however, continued shouting, protesting bitterly about Wilson's style of government. Eventually he said to the Prime Minister, 'You know you've done wrong,' and left the Cabinet room, slamming the door behind him. Although a number of his colleagues tried to prevent him, Brown, not for the first time, handed in his resignation and Wilson, for the first time, accepted it.

The Prime Minister promptly offered the Foreign Secretaryship to Michael Stewart. During an evening telephone conversation, Jenkins suggested to him that Healey would make a much better choice but Wilson had already made up his mind, as Jenkins found out when he turned on the television fifteen minutes later. On Sunday evening, Healey saw Wilson at No 10 and asked him whether Stewart's appointment was permanent. When the Prime Minister replied that it was, Healey said, 'Michael is only there temporarily, and you will be having me in the Foreign Office next autumn and I want you to make George Thomson Minister of Defence in my place.'[26]

Tony Benn commented in his diary on Jenkins' performance during the crisis: 'Roy's behaviour was very detached and rather impressive. He's got his eye on the main chance and thinks Harold will destroy himself and that he, Roy, will then take over.' After the Brown drama, Benn gave Crosland a lift home and recorded: 'He hotly denied there was any alliance to replace Harold. He and Roy were at daggers drawn and there were great disagreements. But I'm sure Tony, in his heart, thinks Harold will go.'[27]

As Wilson's reputation fell, Jenkins' continued to climb. After a magisterial performance at 3.00 a.m. on the night of the Brown affair which helped quieten the Commons, Jenkins' Budget speech on 19 March was a tour de force. The Budget raised taxation by about £923 million, mainly by increasing indirect taxes, though there was a one-off levy on investment income. Despite this being the then biggest hike in taxation ever imposed in a single Budget, it was received with rapture by Labour backbenchers. As Edmund Dell put it, 'Never has pain been inflicted with greater elegance.'[28] The key to Jenkins' enthusiastic reception was that his speech set out with clarity and panache a credible post-devaluation economic strategy. At last the Labour government and Labour MPs were being given a sense of direction. After listening to Roy's Budget speech and watching his television performance Crossman commented: 'I felt that it's possible that we've now scraped the bottom and are at last moving upward.'[29]

But, contrary to Crossman's prediction the summer of 1968, the year of student revolts across Europe, also proved to be a time of acute political discontent in the UK. The economic background was one of bad trade figures and of continuing pressure on the pound. The political fall-out was considerable. In February 1968, Gallup put the Tories twenty-two per cent ahead. In May, after Brown had gone, their lead rose to twenty-eight per cent.[30] By-election results were appalling and the May local elections disastrous. Many Labour backbenchers began to believe that, with Wilson as leader, Labour faced catastrophe at the next election and their seats were threatened. Then on 10 May, the day after the local elections, Cecil King, chairman of the Mirror Group, signed a front-page denunciation in the *Daily Mirror* demanding Wilson's resignation. Although King himself was forced to resign by his own board a few weeks later, the pressure on the Prime Minister continued and his position looked shaky.

In the hothouse atmosphere of Westminster, summer is the classic time for plots. Wilson was paranoid about plotting, often imagining conspiracies where there were none. This time he was correct. Many of the younger Labour MPs, especially those from the 1964 and 1966 intakes, believed that Roy Jenkins was now the obvious alternative to Wilson, whom they thought had become an electoral liability. Discussion about the leadership was widespread in the smoking and tea rooms, in the bars and on the terrace of the House of Commons.

The emergence of Jenkins as the favourite candidate of younger members of the centre-right of the Labour party was not inevitable. MPs like Bill Rodgers, Dick Taverne and David Marquand had admired Crosland for *The Future of Socialism*, for his uncompromisingly intellectual approach to politics, and his irreverent glamour. They also much respected his achievements as Education Secretary. But they began to feel disappointed with Tony: 'When you spoke to him, he no longer seemed as interested in you as before,' said Dick

Taverne.[31] Bill Rodgers wrote that 'he seemed to have lost some of the fearless, visionary independence of his earlier years. He was more calculating in his political judgements, often making the opinions supposedly held by his working class constituents in Grimsby the touchstone of his own.'[32] Even before Jenkins became Chancellor, Tony Crosland was aware that Roy was forging ahead of him and resented it.

At meetings of the 1963 Club, an informal dining group formed to preserve Gaitskell's legacy and which both Jenkins and Crosland usually attended, David Owen, a young member of the 1966 intake, noted the strong personal rivalry between the two, 'delphically conducted but ever present within a friendly gathering'.[33] Tony became increasingly unhappy that the club was being used as a springboard for Roy's ambitions. At one point during the 'silly season' of August 1967 when there was much press speculation about leadership contenders, especially Jenkins, Crosland turned somewhat petulantly on his PPS, Christopher Price and asked: 'Why the fuck don't I ever read about Crosland for PM; what the hell are you doing about it?'[34]

Centre-right Labour MPs were also impressed by Healey. His grasp of defence issues and his decisiveness as a minister were well recognised (Hattersley, Owen and Taverne who all served under Denis spoke highly of him) and many of them thought he ought to be Foreign Secretary. They were also aware of the strength of his personality and were amused by his earthy humour, especially if it was directed against others. But, even more than Tony, Denis was a loner who displayed little interest in building up the network of relationships that might have helped him shore up his support base. This was a severe handicap for a potential leader of the Labour Party.

In 1968, Jenkins had decisive advantages as a leadership contender. He was a commanding figure in Cabinet; he was a far better parliamentary performer than either Crosland or Healey; and, above all, as the new Chancellor, he was untainted with the failures that had led up to the devaluation and had set out in his Budget a clear strategy which could, given time, lead to Labour's recovery. Also, unlike Healey or Crosland, he was prepared to put himself out for those who he considered as allies or protégés. Although Roy Hattersley regarded Crosland as his friend, it was Jenkins rather than Crosland who spoke to Wilson in favour of Hattersley's promotion to the government.[35] As

Bill Rodgers put it, 'Roy was loyal to his friends and attentive to their interests.'[36] Increasingly, the younger revisionist intellectuals as well as older members of the centre-right impressed by his competence, looked to Jenkins as their leader, rather than Crosland or Healey.

In May, the Jenkinsites (as they increasingly came to be called) went into full plotting mode. Jenkins wrote that: 'There was a dedicated group of commandos, waiting as it were with their faces blackened for the opportunity to launch a Dieppe raid against the forces of opportunism (i.e. against Harold Wilson).'[37] Their numbers included Patrick Gordon Walker, sacked by Wilson in the spring reshuffle, Christopher Mayhew, who had resigned as Navy Minister over defence cuts in 1966, Austen Albu, an ex-minister, a number of current junior ministers such as Bill Rodgers, Dick Taverne and Roy Hattersley, and younger backbenchers like David Owen, David Marquand and John Mackintosh, described by Dick Crossman as 'three of our ablest right wingers'.[38] They set up an inner core of ten, which was supposed to spawn further sub-groups. By the middle of June, they believed that they had a list of over a hundred MPs who wanted to get rid of Wilson.

But the rules of the Labour Party contained no mechanism for getting rid of a Prime Minister. For a coup to be successful, it had to have overwhelming support not only from the backbenchers but from the Cabinet as well. Roy Jenkins described the summer mood in the Cabinet as 'one of fretful discontent with Wilson, reluctant respect for me as Chancellor, but without any approach to a settled desire to make me Prime Minister'.[39] The problem for Jenkins was his relative youth. Backing Roy would put paid to the pretensions of other possible contenders, not only of Callaghan, who in 1968 was still smarting from the devaluation debacle, but also of Crosland and of Healey.

Bill Rodgers commented on the Jenkins–Crosland–Healey triangular relationship: 'Many of the younger Gaitskellites wished that Roy Jenkins, Tony Crosland and Denis Healey could sink their differences, sideline their ambitions and learn to work together. Here were three men of similar age and outstanding talent who could save the nation. There was no great ideological gulf between them and, if it came to the point, they ought to be able to agree who should replace Wilson.'[40] The trouble was that all three wanted to be Prime Minister. To topple Wilson, Tony Crosland and Denis Healey would have had to yield the palm to Roy Jenkins, who had been their junior at Oxford and had only recently been promoted over their heads. So, despite Wilson's shortcomings (of which Crosland and Healey were well aware) and the dismal electoral outlook for the Labour Party, Tony and Denis preferred the uneasy status quo to serving under Roy. In June 1968, the behaviour of these three revisionists established a recurring theme in their relationship. When personal ambitions collided, mutual co-operation was precluded.

Roy himself was sceptical about the prospects of a coup succeeding in 1968. Although he did not want to lose the support of the plotters, he knew that, without Crosland's and Healey's support, he did not have enough senior backers in the Cabinet and that, equally important, Wilson was unlikely to go quietly. The political and economic situation was so fragile that a botched coup could have led to the end of the Labour government. Jenkins saw Patrick Gordon Walker twice during this period, once on 27 May and the second time on 4 July. On the first occasion, he listened with obvious interest to Gordon Walker's news about the plotters and let Gordon Walker know about Cabinet opinion. On the second, he advised the plotters against action. Gordon Walker noted in his diary, 'he did not want to say, at any time, that we should move. He wanted to be consulted and might advise against action – but, otherwise, would leave it to us. He clearly did not want to be implicated in actually launching an action.' The commandos were stood down. It was probably about this time that Jenkins told Healey: 'I will never be caught with a dagger in my hand unless it is already smoking with my enemy's blood.'[41]

The question, raised by Jenkins himself in his autobiography, remains whether if, like Thatcher, Macmillan and Lloyd George, he had been more ruthless, Roy could have successfully engineered a coup d'état that summer. Despite his considerable support in the PLP (which did not, however, extend to the left), it remains doubtful if such a coup could have come off without more Cabinet backing, especially the support of Crosland and Healey.

There was one moment when the cautious Jenkins might have been provoked into an open breach with the Prime Minister. Wilson had become paranoid about leaks, though it was Tony Crosland who pointed out that most of them came from No 10. On 15 June Jenkins delivered a speech about the House of Lords (whose future was being

discussed by an all-party group under the chairmanship of Dick
Crossman). The speech received favourable publicity in the Sunday
newspapers and Wilson was jealous. He told the Chancellor at a private meeting that he intended to introduce legislation to curb the
powers of the Lords. Wilson's intention was promptly leaked to the
media. At Cabinet the next Tuesday, Wilson deplored the leak in
terms which showed how vulnerable he felt: 'I know where a great part
of the leaking and backbiting comes from. It arises from the ambitions
of one member of this Cabinet to sit in my place. But I can tell him
this: if he ever does sit in my place he will find that the difficulties
which have been created by the present atmosphere in the Cabinet are
such that life will be as intolerable for him as it is for me.'[42] Wilson's
suspicion of Jenkins and his resentment of the success of John Harris,
Roy's press officer, in getting favourable stories about Jenkins into the
newspapers had overcome his better judgement.

Jenkins did not rise to the bait in Cabinet but stayed behind after
the meeting when he told Wilson that what he had said was insuffer-
able. He added that he deplored the Prime Minister's way of
conducting business, which made personal relations intolerable. As it
happened, Roy said, he was not responsible for the leak but he knew
who was. He demanded that the Prime Minister retract his charge in
a statement, which they would discuss beforehand, to Thursday's
Cabinet. Otherwise it would be a resignation matter for Jenkins.

By Wednesday evening when the two men met again, Wilson had
backed down completely, having found out that the leak had come
from the Conservative leader of the House of Lords, Peter Carrington,
who had been informed by Dick Crossman. In conciliatory mood,
Wilson said that, for the sake of the government, it was important that
their relations, which had been appalling the previous month, were
improved. Harold then said that he did not intend to remain Prime
Minister for too long and that he expected Roy to succeed him: 'We
cemented the better atmosphere with about twenty minutes conversation on nineteenth century railways,' Jenkins noted.[43] The following
morning, Wilson made an apologetic statement to Cabinet.

It was fortunate for Wilson that his reconciliation with the
Chancellor came when it did. For three days later, Ray Gunter, a
Cabinet minister who had been extremely upset by his removal to the
Ministry of Power from the Department of Labour in the spring

reshuffle, resigned, protesting about Wilson's style of government. If Jenkins' quarrel with the Prime Minister had been still unresolved, it would have been likely to have come out into the open, probably leading to a leadership battle and even the collapse of the Labour government.

In the autumn of 1968, the government faced an economic crisis which threatened a disastrous second devaluation. Jenkins anxiously watched every month's trade figures (June was good, July bad, August and September good) but he became concerned by mid-October that the consumption trend was too high, so he decided to tighten hire purchase controls. As it was nominally a Board of Trade matter, the decision went to the small Cabinet economic strategy committee, Misc. 205. Here Jenkins and Crosland clashed again. 'His view,' noted Jenkins, 'was that we ought to do something different from the proposition under discussion, maybe more drastic, maybe less, but certainly much later.'[44] As a consequence, action came ten days after it should have done and Crosland, who announced the changes in the Commons, got the blame. At about this time, Barbara Castle, who had been impressed by Crosland when he was at the DES, called him a 'curious bird', some-one who said a lot of the right things but never fought, while the Prime Minister, hardly an unbiased observer, told Crossman in September that he regarded Crosland as a disappointment, often contributing an idea in Cabinet but not a policy or a decision.[45]

Bad October trade figures left the UK exposed when a new inter-national currency crisis erupted. The problem this time was that the deutschmark, the symbol of the rising postwar Germany economy, was undervalued not only against the franc but also against the pound. To avoid a humiliating second devaluation, the ideal solution for the British was a German revaluation. The German government called a conference of finance ministers in Bonn but announced beforehand that they were not prepared to revalue. Overreacting, Wilson and Jenkins summoned the German ambassador late at night to give him a dressing-down. Wilson told Herr Blankenhorn that the German decision was 'irresponsible' and 'intolerable', while Jenkins said, 'If your refusal to revalue forces us to let the pound float down, as it may well do, we could not in those circumstances afford anything like the present level of military expenditure in Germany.'[46]

The Bonn conference proved to be a failure and, on 22 November, Jenkins flew back to announce to the Commons a new £250 million package, including using the regulator to increase indirect taxes by ten per cent, a lower ceiling on bank lending, and a deposit scheme on a third of imports. For a short time, markets steadied but on 5 December when Jenkins was on a weekend trip to the north-east of England, the City was convulsed with rumours that either Wilson or Jenkins had resigned and pressure started to build up again against sterling. By Tuesday, reserves were almost exhausted. However, at lunchtime, the rate steadied and, in mid afternoon, after a bravura performance by the Prime Minister at Question Time, the market turned decisively up.

By 4.30 p.m. when Jenkins, showing that his old friendship was still alive, went to see Crosland in Westminster Hospital (Tony had slipped on ice outside his home in Lansdowne Road and broken his elbow), the Chancellor, previously apprehensive about the outcome of the crisis, was in ebullient mood. On Thursday, excellent trade figures calmed market nerves and staved off a second devaluation. According to Healey, Roy Jenkins had been so depressed at the end of November that he had told Denis that if the pound collapsed again Britain's only hope would be a coalition led by Healey and Reggie Maudling, the Conservative shadow Home Secretary.[47]

1969 was the year in which the UK balance of payments at last came good. January's trade figures were satisfactory but the February and March ones were bad, so on 15 April in his second Budget, which was much less well received than his first, Jenkins tightened the screws once again, taking a further £340 million out of the economy, mainly by increasing indirect taxes. Following these measures, the balance of payments surplus for 1969 was £400 million and public finance went into substantial surplus for the first time since the war. Even after the Budget, the turn-round in the balance of payments was, however, slow in coming and in May there was again pressure against sterling. Roy, so resilient throughout 1968, found this new crisis hard to bear, especially as he had to negotiate a further stand-by credit from the IMF.

On the evening of Friday 16 May, on a train returning from Birmingham, where he had been doing his monthly 'surgery', he decided that, unless the May and June trade figures showed a decisive improvement, the strategy which he had pursued since he had been appointed would have failed. More drastic policies involving a real cut in living standards rather than just a standstill would be required and a new Chancellor would be needed to implement them. He doubted whether even a reconstituted Labour government would have the moral authority to impose these new measures. 'I then had no desire to participate in a coalition, which many people were advocating. It was merely that I could begin to see, as an added complication in a web of gloom, the emergence of a case for it.'[48] It was the nadir of Roy's Chancellorship.

Fortunately, the turn around in the balance of payments came in time to save the Chancellor and the government. Both the May and June figures were good, while the Board of Trade statisticians also reported a significant underestimate of exports going back several years. On 18 July, Roy Jenkins was able to announce that, as a consequence of the improvement, foreign exchange reserves had grown by a net £1 billion. There was another flurry of excitement centred on the fate of the deutschmark in August and September. But two further good months of balance of payment figures, with August's especially so, as well as the decision of the Bundesbank to let the deutschmark float until there was a new German government, enabled the Treasury to weather the storm without great difficulty. After flying back from the annual IMF meeting in Washington, Roy Jenkins, though not a natural party conference speaker, was able to present a favourable account of his stewardship to the party conference at Brighton which was very well received by delegates. 'By 12.50 p.m., or 7.50 a.m. Washington time, it was over and I was in the bar of the Grand Hotel, Brighton savouring a well deserved dry martini and one of the best moments of my chancellorship.'[49] Jenkins' persistence and courage had not only brought about a transformation in the balance of payments but had also given the Labour government a much-needed shot in the arm. For many in the party, both inside and outside Parliament, Jenkins' performance as Chancellor was the shining light in an otherwise dark landscape.

1969 was also the year of Barbara Castle's ill-fated industrial relations proposals, which infuriated the trade unions, divided the parliamentary party and the Cabinet and nearly toppled Harold Wilson. It also divided Jenkins and Crosland, though Healey was on Jenkins' side of the argument. In addition, it laid bare a structural fault in the Labour

Party which, over the next two decades, was to call into question its credibility as a governing party. The question which was increasingly asked was how could the Labour Party, so closely tied to the unions, also claim to represent the national interest.

The background was as follows: reform of industrial relations was clearly a relevant issue for a modernising Labour Party and, in response to public and media concern about the number of unofficial strikes, Wilson had set up a Royal Commission on Trade Union and Employers' Associations under Lord Donovan. In 1968, the Donovan Commission reported that the major problem of British industrial relations was its failure to come to terms with the growth in shop floor power.[50] It proposed that companies should be obliged to register collective agreements and that a Commission on Industrial Relations should be set up to examine and give advice on problems arising out of registration of agreements, trade union recognition, deficiencies in factory procedures and industrial relations generally. The Donovan report, firmly rooted in the voluntary tradition, came out firmly against legal intervention.

For Barbara Castle, appointed by Wilson in his 1968 spring reshuffle as First Secretary for Employment and Productivity, the issue was whether the Donovan approach was adequate, given the growing number of unofficial strikes in key export industries, such as shipping, the docks and motor manufacturing, and also the inflationary pressures in the economy. The new First Secretary, an interventionist by temperament, decided that something more was needed. At the end of 1968, she published a draft White Paper, called *In Place of Strife*, which, as well as most of the Donovan ideas, also included proposals for pre-strike ballots, for a twenty-eight day 'conciliation pause' in unofficial strikes, for powers to impose a settlement where unofficial action resulted from inter-union disputes and an Industrial Board to impose financial penalties if the new rules were breached.

The Prime Minister, aware of the approach of a General Election and anxious if possible to outflank the Tories on this issue, gave Barbara Castle enthusiastic support. She noted that 'when Harold read it, he was delighted. He thought it out-manoeuvred the Tories – he thought of it first and foremost as a very skilful weapon for defeating Heath.'[51] Compared with the much tougher industrial relations legislation introduced by Conservative governments in the 1970s and

1980s, the Castle proposals seem relatively mild. However, it quickly became clear that they would be vehemently opposed by the trade unions. The question was whether the government had the strength and cohesion to drive the legislation through against trade union opposition.

The position of the Home Secretary, Jim Callaghan, who was a former trade union official, was crucial. He was instinctively opposed to legal intervention. His post of treasurer of the party also brought him into close contact with trade union leaders. In political eclipse since the devaluation, he soon emerged as a formidable opponent of the In Place of Strife proposals. Callaghan argued in Cabinet that legal sanctions would not stop unofficial strikes; that they would not pass through Parliament; and that they would create tension between government and unions at a time when morale was low.[52]

On 26 March 1969, he publicly cast his vote at the National Executive Committee of the Labour Party against Cabinet policy, an unprecedented move for a Cabinet minister. His action helped carry a motion against the In Place of Strife proposals. Wilson briefed the press that he had slapped Callaghan down. He also dropped him from the inner Cabinet. In reality, Callaghan was in too strong a position to be sacked. He had the support of the TUC and the NEC, while opposition was growing inside the PLP. Jenkins remembered Callaghan being televised walking through the crowds at Victoria Station to his Sussex train, 'with a defiant dignity which made me realise how formidable a politician, freed of the incubus of the Exchequer, he had become'.[53]

From the outset, Jenkins had given the Castle proposals strong support, partly because of his Cabinet alliance with Barbara Castle and partly because he saw the need for action on industrial relations. However, Roy considered that the leisurely timetable of consultation followed by legislation in the following session proposed by Wilson and Castle was a serious mistake. If the issue was so vital, then there should be no delay. His view was that trade union reform was so sensitive for a Labour government that 'it could be carried through only on the run'.[54] He persuaded Wilson and Castle that he should announce in his Budget statement that a short bill should be rushed through the Commons without delay, even though such a bill would inevitably emphasise the penal aspects of the package. As a sop to the unions, he would also say that the statutory powers taken over incomes in the 1968 Act should be abandoned when they expired at the end of 1969.

Crosland's attitude to *In Place of Strife* was sceptical. He was well aware of the need to modernise the unions but thought it extremely unwise to legislate on the issue so late in the Parliament. He voiced his doubts in Cabinet on 3 January, arguing that the economist Andrew Shonfield's minority recommendation to the Donovan report that the Commission on Industrial Relations should be given powers in relation to unofficial strikes be considered, and, as the pace quickened, he lined up with Callaghan, though he was critical of the Home Secretary's open defiance of Wilson and his public glad-handing of trade union leaders. 'Jim is behaving like a caricature of an old wheeler-dealer. Sometimes it's difficult to stomach,' Tony told Susan.[55]

However, according to Dick Crossman, Crosland worked closely with Callaghan: 'Tony and Jim do see a lot of each other and I know it because my room in the House is on the same landing as theirs. They are in cahoots with Douglas Houghton, the chairman of the party, and it has been their triangle which has really endangered Harold in this crisis.' Crossman speculated on Crosland's motives: 'Tony, who has never forgiven Harold for making Roy Chancellor, has never lost hope that if Roy goes he will be Chancellor in his place. His best chance would be the breaking up of this government and Callaghan taking over.'[56] Allowing for Crossman's hyperbole, those comments have the ring of truth.

Throughout 1968 and the early part of 1969, Healey was heavily involved in the implementation of the east of Suez withdrawal. In his July 1968 White Paper, he had announced plans for the withdrawal of forces from Singapore and Malaysia and in January 1969 he announced the end of commitments in the Gulf and set December 1971 as the date for the final withdrawal from Singapore. However, despite his preoccupation, Healey gave broad support to the *In Place of Strife* proposals. Wilson had told Denis, whom he had considered for the Ministry of Labour job before offering it to Barbara Castle, that he had decided on union reform because he had given up hope of making incomes policy work. Healey, in a letter to Wilson on 14 January, argued that it would be better to try and get at least some of the industrial relations legislation on the statute book in 1969 rather than waiting until the following year.[57] However, as trade union and party opposition grew, Denis became more cautious. In meetings of the inner Cabinet, he was recorded as stressing the need for discussions with the TUC and, at one point, he remarked that 'if he had realised the impact the proposed Bill would have on party morale he would not on balance have supported it in the first place'.[58]

The growing party hostility to In Place of Strife also worried Roy Jenkins. For Roy, the issue was complicated by the almost total collapse in the Prime Minister's authority both within the PLP and the Cabinet. The plotting of 1968 inside the PLP now resumed again, with the difference that this time there were two alternative crown princes – Jenkins and Callaghan. Some of Jenkins' supporters, including Tom Bradley, Jenkins' PPS, and Roy Hattersley, were urging him, for the sake of his leadership chances, to abandon the Bill.

Jenkins wrote later: 'Nevertheless I was not tempted to renege on the Bill in order to replace Wilson. Apart from anything else, this would be fatal for the future. The real count against Wilsonism was that it was opportunistic and provided leadership by manoeuvre and not by direction. To replace him by outdoing his own deficiencies would make a discreditable nonsense of the whole enterprise.'[59] There was a further more mundane point. Clearly, if Jenkins and Callaghan could combine together, they could bring Wilson down. But if Harold was toppled, no one could be certain whether Roy or Jim would succeed him. On 9 May, Jenkins told Bill Rodgers that he was not prepared to serve under Callaghan.[60] The day before John Harris, Jenkins' press aide, had told the Jenkinsite conspirators that Roy did not want them to move. So, despite his weakness, Wilson was saved by rivalry between the two obvious crown princes.

Even if Jenkins was not prepared to act against Wilson, the prospects for the In Place of Strife proposals were becoming desperate. On 5 June, Roy told a dinner party hosted by the Christopher Mayhews and attended by the Gordon Walkers and the Marquands that the battle could not be won. At an all-day crisis Cabinet on 17 June, the Chancellor remained silent during the morning session. At 4 p.m., he met Barbara Castle to tell her of his defection; in view of their close working relationship, he felt he owed her that. According to Jenkins, she did not recriminate but 'accepted the news like St Sebastian receiving another arrow'. At the afternoon session, Wilson behaved 'with a touch of King Lear-like nobility'. In the end, the Prime Minister and Barbara Castle were forced into a humiliating climbdown, which involved having implausibly to accept the TUC's so-called 'solemn and binding' undertaking to limit unofficial strikes as a victory. Jenkins concluded later: 'It was a sad story from which he (Wilson) and Barbara Castle emerged with more credit than the rest of us.'[61]

It was indeed a sad story. Callaghan's purely voluntarist position may have been popular with the unions but was hardly a viable long-term response to the UK's industrial relations problem. Crosland's argument about the detail and timing of In Place of Strife was more tenable, while Jenkins can be criticised for not holding out to the last, though at least he was the last rat to leave an already sinking ship. What is indisputable is that the failure of Labour's industrial relations proposals in 1969 did the party lasting damage, because it established in the voters' minds that the party was incapable of carrying through measures which the trade unions opposed, even if these were thought to be in the national interest.

After Wilson's humiliation over In Place of Strife, he was determined to get his own back on those ministers who had opposed him. On 2 July, Crossman reported that the Prime Minister had talked as though he was determined to remove Callaghan, Marsh (the Minister of Transport) and Crosland from the Cabinet: 'He is infuriated by Crosland and I must say that Tony's behaviour at the Board of Trade has been more than usually irritating. He has been inefficient but nonchalant and cavalier, just not seeming to mind. He seems thoroughly browned-off, sick at not being Chancellor, sickened by the Chancellor's policy, and having failed to become Chancellor, he now seems to have got into that peevish frame of mind which I believe is one of the bases of the leaks.'[62]

In September, Crosland had a silly row with Jenkins, over publication of the trade figures.[63] The Chancellor complained that Crosland had announced the trade figures in the House without proper consultation with the Treasury. Jenkins wrote sharply to Crosland that his behaviour was 'almost unbelievable' and he added that 'you can hardly expect good relations between the Board of Trade and other departments'. Crosland replied that he was astonished and saddened to receive 'so hectoring and pompous a communication from an old friend and Cabinet colleague', adding that 'as everyone in the Treasury knows perfectly well you are very lucky to have had me at the Board of Trade; and the degree of constructive tension between our two departments is just about right'. It was indeed sad that Jenkins considered it necessary to write such a formal letter to Crosland rather than simply picking up a telephone. On the other hand, given the extreme precariousness of the government, Crosland should, as a matter of courtesy and common sense, have consulted Jenkins over the presentation of the trade figures.

Relations between Crosland and Jenkins had become so bad that Roy feared that he would be blamed if Wilson decided to sack Tony, a move that the Chancellor, in reality, strongly opposed. However, Crosland did not think that Jenkins was trying to get rid of him. He told his wife: 'despite our mutual malice on some things, there is a limit to Roy's self-centredness. He might hope I would be demoted within the government, but he always said at the end of the day, "I think you're mad if you drop Tony". Roy would actually say, "it would be *wrong* as well as foolish".' In fact, instead of sacking Crosland in his October reshuffle, Wilson gave him overlordship of a new super ministry, taking in housing, transport, local government and regional planning. A few days later, he was invited to join the inner Cabinet. Wilson's fury over his *In Place of Strife* humiliation had subsided. His relations with Callaghan had improved, following the Home Secretary's impressive handling of riots in Northern Ireland and, though he was pleased to have removed Tony from an economic department, the Prime Minister was not in a strong enough position to sack the Cabinet minister who was Callaghan's closest ally.

In 1969 Denis Healey, whom Wilson had regarded as 'Public Enemy Number One' in 1968, began to be courted by No 10. This was a recognition both of his importance in the government and of his use to Wilson as a counter-weight to Jenkins and Callaghan. In April, Denis was asked to become Party Chairman without portfolio, a poisoned chalice which he understandably refused. The Defence Secretary also found himself invited to No 10 for several of Harold's discursive chats.[64] Then in the autumn, Wilson appointed Healey to the Campaign Committee, composed of ministers and members of the NEC, to consider strategy and organisation for the coming election.

Despite these overtures from Wilson, relations between Jenkins and Healey remained cordial, with Jenkins even suggesting that, if he went to the Foreign Office, Healey should replace him as Chancellor. However this plan, and the prospect of Jenkins succeeding Wilson as Prime Minister, depended on a Labour victory.

With the balance of payments now in surplus, Labour gradually recovered in the polls. The Conservative lead which had averaged over nineteen per cent in July 1969 was down to twelve and a half per cent by September, with NOP, Gallup and ORC showing Tory leads of eleven per cent or less.[65] After a successful Labour Party conference, the Tory advantage narrowed to four per cent in an ORC poll. Although this proved to be a flash in the pan (as the higher swing to the Tories in the by-elections held at the end of October showed) Wilson's personal ratings improved and, with the rise of his popularity, the threat to his political position inside the parliamentary party was removed. The Prime Minister, recovering some of his old bounce and verve, began to plan for a 1970 General Election.

The Budget was obviously crucial to Labour's electoral strategy. The problem for the Chancellor was one of expectations. Now that the balance of payments had come right after 'two years' hard slog' there was inevitably a feeling, not confined to anxious Labour MPs, that there ought to be a Budget bonanza. Yet, Jenkins saw little room for an extra fiscal stimulus. Wage rises were already averaging twelve per cent, partly as a result of over-generous settlements in the public services. And the Chancellor did not want to put at risk his achievement in turning round the balance of payments by a give-away Budget which he regarded 'as a vulgar piece of economic management below the level of political sophistication of the British electorate'.[66]

On 8 March, Budget prospects were discussed at the inner Cabinet meeting at Chequers. According to Crossman's diary, a group, including Crossman, Crosland, Castle and Shore, argued for a more generous Budget, which would enthuse working-class supporters. Crossman commented:

> Roy was exactly as I expected, conventional, rigid, narrow,
> low-risk, balance-of-payments conscious, not, I believe,
> expecting to win in this way but saying there is no other way

that leaves intact all that economic policy has gained. It was
quite clear he had swung Harold to his side and that Callaghan
and Healey were also with him. Healey was extremely assertive
throughout, in a sense intellectually vulgar, tough, hearty and
reactionary . . . I suppose Tony Crosland and I were the two
who put our philosophy perfectly clearly, in a way too clearly,
because it was disliked and repudiated not only by Roy, Denis
and Harold but also by the working-class people, Fred Peart
(who had succeeded Crossman as Leader of the House) in
particular.[67]

Perhaps because of Crosland's opposition, Jenkins gave Tony a lift
back from Chequers and explained to him the outlines of his Budget.
Apart from the Prime Minister, he also consulted Denis Healey once
again and Barbara Castle, as well as Willie Ross, the Secretary of State
for Scotland, and Tony Benn, who had become overlord of a beefed-
up Ministry of Technology and was now counted as an economic
minister.

Roy's Budget speech on 14 April was well received by his own side,
though Labour MPs preferred the first part in which the Chancellor
described the economic improvements of the last year to the second
part in which he set out his specific proposals. Jenkins was able to present an impressive record. Borrowing of about £2 billion in 1967–68
had been transferred into a surplus on the public sector accounts of
nearly £600 million. Though the final figures were not yet available,
the balance of payments surplus for 1969–70 was at least £500 million,
while the economy had grown steadily by an average of three per cent
over the last two years. Personal consumption, which had grown by
only four per cent, had been held back to make room for exports,
which had grown by twenty-four per cent over the period. The
Chancellor warned the House about inflationary prospects. However,
he felt able to give away £200 million in a full year, mainly through
increases in personal tax allowances. As the Chancellor sat with his
aides in his room enjoying a post-Budget whisky, his PPS, Tom
Bradley, reported that the feeling in the tea room was one of disappointment. When, later that week, Roy remarked to John Harris that
there did not seem to be much force in the Tory attack, the
Chancellor's press advisor replied, 'No, there does not need to be

because they are not frightened of the Budget.'[68] But, contrary to Tory hopes, the Budget proved popular with the voters. The post-Budget Harris poll put Labour ahead for the first time for three years; according to Gallup, sixty per cent believed that the Budget was fair.

The pressure for an early General Election grew. When the inner Cabinet had met at Chequers on 8 March, they had discussed possible election dates. Healey declared for the autumn, unless a window of opportunity opened up at the end of June. Jenkins said that there ought to be organisational planing for June and policy planning for October. Crosland and Crossman argued for waiting until October. Wilson, who enjoyed tactical discussions of this kind, was concerned about the football World Cup in June, but said that there would be the risk of rising prices in October. He added, 'In June the evenings are light right up to the close of the polls.' Crossman noted: 'Harold is anxious for an early election and he intends to have one.'[69]

On 4 May, Jenkins advised the inner Cabinet that the economic factors were neutral as between June and October and that they should await the results of the 7 May local elections. A day before those elections, however, the Prime Minister made it clear to the Chancellor that he had made up his mind in favour of June. 'He was firmly down the runway towards an early election and it would have required some dreadful news to get him to reverse engines.'[70] The borough elections, in which Labour made a net gain of 443 seats, were good enough to have the Prime Minister 'purring like a Persian cat'.[71] On 14 May, with five polls giving Labour an average of three per cent lead, Wilson informed the inner Cabinet that he had decided on 18 June as the date for the election. There was no dissent. John Harris, Jenkins' press aide, had tried to persuade the Prime Minister to choose 11 June on the grounds that the government might be damaged by anti-apartheid rioting at the Lord's Test Match against the South Africans. He was also presciently concerned that the May trade figures, due to be published on 15 June, might be bad. Unwisely both Wilson and Jenkins brushed these worries aside.

On almost every day of the 1970 election campaign the sun shone on Labour Party workers who, after a depressing three years, were now in an optimistic mood. Harold Wilson, who concentrated on walkabouts, campaigned in a relaxed, folksy almost non-political manner: 'His style was not so much "presidential" as that of a stage personality who could share old jokes with his fans.'[72] Roy Jenkins, who was being promoted by Wilson as the Chancellor who had put the British economy back on the right track, addressed meetings in many of the main cities. His television broadcast on 9 June was highly rated in the Conservative private polls: 'Mr Jenkins epitomised the cautious, responsible, successful image at which the Labour campaign seemed to be aimed.'[73] Denis Healey also played a prominent part in the campaign, flanking the Prime Minister at most of Labour's morning press conferences and travelling all over the country for the rest of the day. As a Cabinet minister, Tony Crosland also had a programme of national engagements, though according to figures supplied by agents after the elections, attendances at his meetings were less than for either Jenkins or Healey.[74]

Labour continued to believe in victory right up to election day itself and the polls gave them every encouragement. There was, however, one piece of news, announced in the last week of the campaign, that, with hindsight, should have made them extremely anxious. On the final Monday, the May trade figures were released, showing a deficit of £31 million. Although £18 million of this figure was accounted for by the exceptional purchase of two American jets, the deficit gave some substance to Edward Heath's dire warnings about the state of the British economy.

That evening Heath made an excellent, final TV broadcast, much superior to Wilson's complacent and vacuous effort the following evening. On the morning of 16 June, Conservative private polls found not only that the Tory leader's broadcast had been well received but that more people now believed that a Conservative government would be better placed to handle a new economic crisis than would a Labour one.[75] When Jenkins had been told at the beginning of the campaign that the trade figures were bad, he considered treating the jumbo jets in a special way, possibly spreading the impact over the period of payment rather than on the date of delivery. But the head of the government statistical service was opposed, so both Jenkins and Wilson decided, probably wrongly, not to take this course of action.[76]

As Labour's leaders attended their constituency counts on election night, the first few results showed a strong swing to the Tories. Jennifer Jenkins, who had been watching television, said to Roy, 'We've lost, you know.'[77] Tony Benn, who was at his Bristol count, noted in his diary, 'In a fraction of a second one went from a pretty confident belief in victory to absolute certainty of defeat. It was quite a remarkable experience.'[78] At Grimsby, Tony Crosland, after being mesmerised by a succession of Labour defeats on television, snatched a few hours' sleep in his hotel bedroom. When the alarm clock went off, he was 'dead asleep . . . face down, one arm flung out'.[79] Roy Jenkins dozing on his bed, decided he was 'surprised but in no way incredulous about the result'.[80] The next morning, back in Downing Street, he went through from No 11 to No 10 where he found Wilson 'calm and unrecriminating'. At 4 p.m., there was a desultory and depressed meeting of the inner Cabinet at No 10. When Tony Benn asked if he could take a picture of Wilson in the Prime Minister's chair, Jenkins and Healey quickly left for a farewell drink in No 11. As Denis arrived for the meeting, he had characteristically responded to the boos of the crowd outside No 10 by giving the V sign: 'This gesture had an unexpected effect. He got a tremendous cheer for it.'[81]

Why did Labour lose? Crossman's immediate reaction was that 'Harold's comfy, complacent, good-humoured mixing with the crowds hadn't been able to sustain itself for more than a fortnight and by the end of the second week the voice of doom, the endless repetitive reminders of rising prices, broken promises, unfavourable trade figures, all took their toll.'[82] Writing twenty years later, Healey's judgement was much the same: 'Bad trade figures in the last week may have given credibility to Heath's final attack on Labour's handling of the economy.'[83] However, as the standard work on the 1970 election pointed out, if one month's trade figures could create a scare enough to frighten a million voters away from Labour, the electorate must have been already in a fickle and sceptical mood. The underlying problem for Labour in 1970 was that after a prolonged period of unpopularity its recovery in the polls was only very recent and shallowly based, so it did not take all that much to undermine it.

Healey was right when he concluded that the election was lost by the government rather than won by the Opposition. The Wilson administration was certainly intellectually highly talented. Eight of the Cabinet had First Class degrees from Oxford, including Crosland, Healey and Jenkins, as well as the Prime Minister. In retrospect, its record looked better than it did at the time. There was a substantial increase in social spending; education, health and social security benefits all increased their share of the national product, with education expenditure for the first time going ahead of defence spending. Mainly as a result of Crosland's period as Education Secretary, educational opportunity was increased significantly. Because of increases in cash benefits, pensioners, larger families and the unemployed gained more in terms of real disposable income than the rest of the population.

There were significant reforms in the area of personal liberty, mostly associated with Jenkins's tenure at the Home Office. The Labour government helped open up society: 'Wilson did not create a classless society, but he helped to give birth to a more open one. Both by his personal style, and by the actions of his government, he dented old-fashioned class prejudice, and reduced the restrictive practices and social deference that had continued to blight British professional and public life in the early 1960s.'[84] In external affairs, the government's achievements were more patchy. However it was under the Wilson government that Britain gave up its role east of Suez (a change implemented by Healey, even if he had not originally desired it) and began to come to terms with its status as a medium-sized European power.

However, despite its undoubted social and educational achievements and its eventual success (after its failure to devalue and the waste of its first three years) in combining a respectable degree of growth with a healthy balance of payments, its campaign failed to convince a significant number of its working-class supporters to come out and vote, as I discovered when 'knocking up' for the Labour candidate in a marginal seat. In part, Labour paid the price for the squeeze on consumption needed to turn around the balance of payments. In part, it was the lack of a strategy for the next term. Potential Labour voters did not find the slogan 'Now Britain's strong let's make it great to live in' convincing, especially after nearly six years of Labour government.

After the election, Roy Jenkins was accused by left-wing activists of losing Labour the election by failing to produce an electioneering Budget. His colleague, Edmund Dell, who argued that his 1970 Budget should have been more restrictive rather than more generous, took a different view: 'Any justification in the accusation that Jenkins lost Labour the 1970 General Election lies not in the relative austerity of his pre-election Budget but in his delays in taking action after devaluation, and in his defection over *In Place of Strife*, so that Labour faced

Denis Healey, aged five.
(*Denis Healey Collection*)

Tony Crosland at about the same age.
(*Tony Crosland Collection*)

Roy Jenkins, aged six, on the day his father (standing on the right, above his mother) was released from Cardiff gaol. Roy did not find out about his father's imprisonment until some years later. (*Roy Jenkins Collection*)

The undergraduate Healey with friends in the Lake District. Denis is on the extreme left, his brother Terry is on the extreme right next to his Californian friend from Balliol, Gordon Griffiths, and Gordon's sister Mary is next to Denis. (*Denis Healey Collection*)

The Czechoslovakian statesman, Eduard Benes, addresses the Oxford Union in March 1940. Roy Jenkins is seated at the secretary's table, while Tony Crosland is behind him on the right. (© *Madron Seligman*)

Tony Crosland wearing his paratroopers'
beret, on leave in Rome in 1944.
(*Tony Crosland Collection*)

Major Denis Healey and Captain Roy
Jenkins at the 1945 Labour Party
conference. (*Hulton Getty*)

Denis Healey addresses the 1945
Labour Party conference. His fiery
speech helped get him the job of the
party's international secretary.
(*Hulton Getty*)

Roy marries Jennifer at the Savoy Chapel, January 1945. Hattie Jenkins is next to Jennifer, with Sir Parker Morris, Jennifer's father, at her side. (*Roy Jenkins Collection*)

Denis marries Edna at Marylebone Parish Church, December 1945. (*Denis Healey Collection*)

Tony marries Susan (Crosland's second marriage) at Chelsea Register Office, February 1964. The widows of his two patrons, Ruth Dalton (on Tony's right) and Dora Gaitskell (on Susan's left), are also present. (*Tony Crosland Collection*)

An elegant Roy Jenkins addresses dockers at the central Southwark by-election, which he won in April 1948. (*Roy Jenkins Collection*)

Denis Healey campaigns, wearing a hat, at his Leeds by-election in February 1952. (*Denis Healey Collection*)

Tony Crosland with Roy Jenkins in Grimsby at the 1959 General Election. Crosland had lost his seat in 1955, giving him the time to finish *The Future of Socialism* before returning to Parliament in 1959. (*Tony Crosland Collection*)

Gaitskell makes his 'fight and fight again' speech at the 1960 Labour Party conference: Crosland and Jenkins were committed acolytes of the Labour leader, while Healey was his close ally. (*Popperfoto*)

A cheerful Denis Healey leaves No 10 after being appointed Defence Secretary and Labour's youngest Cabinet minister by Prime Minister Harold Wilson. He was to remain in the same post until Labour's defeat in 1970. (*Hulton Getty*)

Tony Crosland is made Economic Secretary at the Department of Economic Affairs, under George Brown. In January 1965 he entered the Cabinet as Secretary of State for Education after Jenkins had turned down the job. (*Hulton Getty*)

Aviation Minister Roy Jenkins smiles as he leaves for New York in April 1965. He became Home Secretary in December 1965. (*Topham/Associated Press*)

Chancellor Jenkins leaves No 11 Downing Street to deliver his first Budget in March 1968. Jennifer is in front and his parliamentary private secretary, Tom Bradley, behind. (*Hulton Getty*)

Tony Crosland, seen here campaigning in Grimsby with Susan, at the 1966 election. In 1967 he had expected to become Chancellor instead of Jim Callaghan. His relationship with Roy never fully recovered when Wilson made Jenkins Chancellor instead. (*Hulton Getty*)

The *Economist* cover for 13 June 1970. Though it is entitled 'In Harold Wilson's Britain' it is clear that, in the magazine's opinion, Jenkins was also entitled to the credit for the expected Labour victory. In fact, it was the Tories who won. (*The Economist*)

Back in Opposition in July 1970 the two crown princes, Jenkins, Deputy Leader, and Healey, shadow Foreign Secretary, flank a tired-looking Wilson. (*Hulton Getty*)

The split on Europe looms: German Chancellor Willy Brandt comes to London in May 1971 to try to persuade Wilson, Jenkins and Healey to back British entry into the Common Market. Wilson remains non-committal, but Jenkins and, at this stage, Healey are in favour. (*Popperfoto*)

Jenkins alone in his railway compartment after voting for British entry into the Common Market, together with sixty-eight other Labour MPs, despite a Labour three-line whip against the motion. Crosland abstained, while Healey voted with the party line. In April 1972 Jenkins resigned as Deputy Leader. (*Popperfoto*)

Crosland, now Secretary of State for the Environment, looks bored but formidable at a Labour Party press conference in the October 1974 election, which Labour narrowly won. (*Hulton Getty*)

At the same election the Chancellor, Denis Healey, sticks to his unwise claim that inflation had dropped to 8.4 per cent. Wilson looks on wryly. (*Popperfoto*)

A few days after the election Home Secretary Jenkins, accompanied by his wife, visits the shambles of the wrecked Guildford pub where an IRA bomb had killed five and injured sixty-five. (*Hulton Getty*)

Denis Healey, seen here in the rain with Edna, stood in the 1976 leadership election which was won by Jim Callaghan. Denis got 30 votes in the first ballot and 38 in the second, before being eliminated. (*Popperfoto*)

Tony Crosland, posing with Susan, also stood. He got 17 votes. (*Hulton Getty*)

Roy, here concentrating on tennis at East Hendred, was the front-runner only a few years before, but in 1976 he finished well behind Callaghan, with 56 votes to Jim's 84. (*Hulton Getty*)

Roy Jenkins makes a point at a 'Britain in Europe' press conference during the 1975 referendum campaign. In 1977 Roy left British politics to become President of the European Commission. (*Popperfoto*)

The President of the Commission with the German Federal Chancellor in 1978: Jenkins helped persuade Schmidt to launch the Exchange Rate Mechanism (ERM). (*Roy Jenkins Collection*)

Chancellor Denis Healey appears breezy and confident on 29 September 1976: in fact, he had just been forced into a humiliating application for $3.9 billion of standby credits from the IMF. (*Popperfoto*)

Callaghan's new Foreign Secretary, Tony Crosland, enters No 10 Downing Street for a meeting: Crosland led the opposition to the IMF conditions but was out-argued by Healey. (*Popperfoto*)

This Garland cartoon illustrates Healey's increase in authority following the recovery of the British economy after the IMF settlement. (*Nicholas Garland*)

Prime Minister Callaghan, Home Secretary Jenkins, and Foreign Secretary Crosland await the arrival at Victoria Station of the French President, Valéry Giscard d'Estaing, in June 1976; unlike Callaghan, Roy seems amused by Tony's refusal to wear morning dress. (*Daily Mail*)

A solitary Crosland briefs himself before a NATO Foreign Ministers' meeting in September 1976. (*Popperfoto*)

Susan Crosland with her two daughters at the memorial service in Westminster Abbey for her husband in March 1977. (*Popperfoto*)

Healey and Foot together a few days before the November 1980 Labour leadership ballot. Healey's defeat by Foot triggered the Social Democratic Party breakaway and led to the electoral catastrophe of 1983. (*Topham/Press Association*)

A dishevelled Healey acknowledges the cheers of his supporters in September 1981, after beating Benn for the deputy leadership by an eyebrow. (*Popperfoto*)

After 1983, Healey served the new leader Neil Kinnock as Foreign Affairs spokesman. Here, an uneasy Kinnock looks on as Ronald Reagan mistakes Denis for the British ambassador in Washington. (*The White House*)

The 'Gang of Four' – William Rodgers, Shirley Williams, Roy Jenkins and David Owen (left to right) pose for the camera in Limehouse in January 1981, as they prepare to leave the Labour Party and set up the SDP. (*Topham/Press Association*)

A triumphant Roy Jenkins, who proved a courageous campaigner, thanks his Glasgow Hillhead constituents after winning the March 1982 by-election for the SDP/Liberal alliance. (*Topham/Press Association*)

An optimistic Jenkins is applauded by David Owen at the SDP's first conference. Two years later Owen forced Jenkins to resign the leadership and by the end of the 1980s the SDP had disintegrated amid bitter recrimination. (*Hulton Getty*)

Jenkins in his pomp as Chancellor of Oxford, June 1987. (*Roy Jenkins Collection*)

Healey hams it up with Barry Humphries and Roger Moore for LWT's *The Dame Edna Christmas Experience*, December 1987. (*Topham/Press Association*)

the election at a time of rapidly rising prices when even the widely acclaimed balance of payments surplus had only recently been acquired and still appeared precarious.'[85] Jenkins accepted his share of responsibility, recognising that it 'was broadly my policies on which Wilson had chosen to fight and on which he had lost'.[86] However, Wilson's fateful decision, contrary to the advice of Crosland and Jenkins, not to devalue either in October 1964 or, at the latest, in July 1966 was arguably the crucial factor in Labour's defeat. If the government had devalued earlier, there would have been the opportunity of nearly four years of export-led growth (instead of two) and Labour would probably have won the election.

The party's defeat in 1970 was both a tragedy and a crucial turning point for Labour revisionism. If it had won, it would have proved that the modernising, social democratic project, backed by Jenkins, Healey and Crosland, was a success. Labour really could have become the natural governing party, which Wilson claimed it already was. With Jenkins at the Foreign Office, Healey at the Treasury and George Thomson in charge of the Common Market negotiations (as Wilson planned after the election), Labour would almost certainly have taken Britain into the Common Market in the early 1970s, thus avoiding the damaging internal splits which followed in opposition. Crosland, who would probably have been Secretary of State for the Environment, might have had the impact in this area which he had had at Education. And, as the main architect of the victory, Jenkins would have been in pole position to succeed Wilson who had told Roy before the election that he intended to retire during the next Parliament and that he hoped Jenkins would succeed him. As it was, the defeat of 1970 ended Roy's ascendancy and removed his best chance of succeeding Wilson as Labour Party leader and Prime Minister. Opposition, which was to be haunted by the shadow of Europe, was to lead to new tensions and rivalries between Jenkins, Crosland and Healey which fatally undermined their relationship.

9

The Spectre of Europe

The crisis over Europe, which was to engulf the Labour Party in 1971–72 and fatally divide the three men, came to a head slowly. The party, especially former ministers, had been certain of victory in the 1970 election and had to get used to being in opposition. Defeat was an especially traumatic experience for Wilson and, according to one of his aides, 'he took a long time to come to terms with it'.[1] Roy Jenkins, who still believed that he might become leader, was more disorientated than dismayed: 'I had some sense of what it must be like to emerge from a long prison sentence . . . free but feeling it was a strange world which had moved on since I had last experienced it, and that the freedom was balanced by a lack of familiar props of support.'[2] Denis Healey spoke of the 'bewildering shock' of going from six years of absorbing work to 'the limbo of opposition'.[3] According to his wife, Susan, Tony Crosland felt 'stricken for a couple of months', though Susan herself had a guilty feeling of liberation: 'My high heels clattered gaily as I tripped down Lansdowne Road. "I'm free, I'm free."' Tony himself said the defeat was a 'great humiliation'.[4] Suddenly there was no office to go to and no work to do.

Financially, former Labour Cabinet ministers, deprived of their ministerial salaries, and, unlike some of their Tory counterparts, without the support of private incomes or lucrative City or industrial jobs, suddenly felt hard up – the more so as they needed to reconstruct at least a shadow of the system of the supporting staff to which they had become accustomed as ministers and which they would require if they were to become effective Opposition leaders and spokesmen. With commendable industry, Wilson wrote a 500,000-word account of his term of office as Prime Minister for which he received over £200,000; this money, which was a very substantial sum in the early 1970s, helped finance his private office.

With his literary reputation, Jenkins quickly managed to put together a £20,000 package of commissions (chiefly from his publisher and from *The Times*) which helped pay for a second secretary and for John Harris's services part-time. Healey agreed to write ten articles a year for the *Sunday Times* and to produce a book on defence (which he never finished, partly because a third of it was stolen with his suitcase at Heathrow). Crosland considered looking for a part-time job in industry or the academic world to compensate for the two-thirds cuts in his salary but nothing suitable came up so, like Healey, he turned to occasional journalism and TV interviews.[5] Tony was fortunate that Susan's *Sunday Times* profiles were well paid.

An immediate issue facing the Parliamentary Labour Party in opposition was the election for the deputy leadership, whose previous incumbent, George Brown, had been defeated at the General Election. The track-record of deputy leaders in succeeding to the leadership was not a good one but Jenkins was advised by his friend and lieutenant, Bill Rodgers, to stand, on the grounds that the deputy leadership would give Roy an increased status, including a seat on the National Executive Committee, as well as the inside track in the succession to Wilson. Jenkins, whose relationship with Crosland had improved in the heat of the election campaign, asked his old friend for his support. Tony told Roy that he would have to deliberate long and hard whether to give his vote to Callaghan or Jenkins, leaving Jenkins with the thought that, by the rules of canvassing, Crosland would have been marked down as 'against'. Callaghan, however, decided not to contest the deputy leadership but 'lurked like a big pike in the shadows, powerful, perhaps menacing but restrained'.[6] Callaghan may have been influenced in his decision not to run by Wilson's support for Jenkins. In the event, Roy won easily on first ballot with 133 votes to 67 for Michael Foot and 48 for Fred Peart, which meant that he could go off on his Tuscan holiday with the feeling of Mr Toad peep-peeping away in his motor.

In the elections for the shadow Cabinet, Denis Healey was runner up and was made shadow Foreign Secretary by Wilson, the position which he coveted and for which he was the best qualified person in the party. In September, he went to South Africa as a guest of the National Union of South African Students. His visit was partly to make up for what in opposition he now saw as an error – advocating selling naval weapons to South Africa. On his trip, he met Nelson Mandela in his Robben Island prison, Steve Biko (who was later murdered), and Chief Buthelezi. He found Mandela well informed and in good spirits: Denis noted that 'his moral authority, even over his warders, was immense'.[7] At Labour's Blackpool conference, Healey strengthened his position by being elected to the NEC as a constituency representative, a surprising success for a politician who was regarded by activists as a 'right winger'. He was clearly now one of the top three or four in the Labour hierarchy, and, with Jenkins and Callaghan, was being talked about as a possible successor to Wilson.

Opposition gives the opportunity for new faces and ideas to emerge. At an impromptu party at Lansdowne Road on the weekend after the election defeat, Tony and Caroline Benn told the Croslands, 'We've never been happier.' When Susan asked Tony what on earth they meant, her husband replied, 'He is happier in opposition. There's no other time he can make his move.'[8] Though Crosland was far more at ease in office than Benn, after the initial shock he, too, began to see that opposition could give him the chance to raise his profile. He resolved to become, even out of office, a full-time politician. He had come third in the shadow Cabinet elections and, like Healey, stood for the NEC in the constituency section, narrowly failing to be elected. In January 1971, his Fabian pamphlet 'A Social-Democratic Britain', based on a lecture given in November 1970, was published. This represented an attempt to stake out a middle ground in the Labour Party between what he saw as Jenkinsite economic orthodoxy and the so-called 'new politics' of Benn, who was beginning his move to the left.

'A Social-Democratic Britain' was primarily a restatement of Croslandism.[9] 'What we need,' he wrote, 'is not some great shift of direction but a clear affirmation of those agreed ideals.' As before, these included an exceptionally high priority for the relief of poverty, a wider ideal of social equality and strict social control over the environment. Crosland admitted that he had been too complacent in *The*

Future of Socialism about growth, which was 'an essential condition of any significant re-allocation of resources'. While accepting his share of responsibility, he attacked the Labour government's record on growth as 'wretched' and argued that in future growth should be given priority. The key, if squeeze and deflation were to be avoided, was a prices and incomes policy agreed between party and unions.

Writing as shadow Environment Minister, Crosland rejected the fashionable anti-growth nostrums of the environmentalists, arguing that the extra resources to tackle pollution and dereliction could come only from growth. In a side-swipe at Benn, he also played down the 'new agenda' issues, such as participation, student revolt and womens' lib, as not being central to Labour's objectives. His Fabian pamphlet raised a furore amongst environmentalists, whom he had accused of being mainly from affluent backgrounds and indifferent to the needs of the majority. The pamphlet was however, well received, the *Observer* praising it as a constructive contribution to the debate about Labour's future.[10] All the same, critics detected a certain conservatism creeping into Crosland's thinking. Arguably, the times now called for a further instalment of revisionism but the Crosland of the 1970s was now too much of a mainstream Labour politician to make the attempt.[11]

Apart from his thoughts on political strategy, Crosland was also taking his shadow Environment role extremely seriously. He told Wilson that he would devote much of his time to housing. A bevy of housing experts started to come to meetings at Lansdowne Road and, soon after, he embarked on a stream of articles and pamphlets on different aspects of housing policy. Towards the end of the first year of opposition, Tony was unexpectedly discovered to have high blood pressure. When the specialist explained that this was not surprising, given the lifestyle of a top-level politician, Tony replied only half-jokingly, 'Nothing to do with the nation's affairs. If anything is responsible for altering my blood pressure, it's my wife's children and their friends, most of whom, as far as one can make out, are deranged or delinquent – often both.'[12] In fact, Tony was proving himself an understanding step-father to Susan's two daughters, who were going through the usual traumas of adolescence at Holland Park comprehensive.

Then, in the early summer of 1971, the Common Market issue erupted and life for the three revisionists was never the same again. The

attitude of the Labour Party in opposition was in part shaped by the
determination of the new Conservative Prime Minister, Edward
Heath, to take the United Kingdom into the European Community.
Heath was a long-standing 'European'. He had made his maiden
speech on the need for European unity and on the desirability of
British participation in the Schuman Plan and he had been
Macmillan's chief negotiator in his abortive attempt to join in
1962–63.

Although the Tory manifesto at the 1970 election had merely
promised a negotiation – 'no more, no less' – Heath almost immediately opened negotiations with the original six members, with the
objective of gaining entry as quickly as possible and sorting any difficulties later. The key moment was the Paris summit on 20–21 May
with de Gaulle's successor as French President, Georges Pompidou.
Heath convinced Pompidou that the UK was serious about being a
constructive member of the European Community. Although detailed
negotiations continued, Heath's attention now turned to getting
British entry through Parliament. As the Conservative majority was
only thirty and there were likely to be forty Tory dissidents, he would
need Labour votes as well.

Pro-Europeans in the Labour Party, above all Jenkins, argued that
Heath's successful application had been foreshadowed and substantially assisted by the preparation for entry which had already taken
place under the previous Labour government.[13] After all, Wilson had
applied for entry in April 1967 (only for the application to be vetoed
by de Gaulle a few months later) and, after de Gaulle's resignation in
April 1969, he had geared up Whitehall for another attempt. A White
Paper on the cost of entering the Common Market was published in
February 1970, negotiating briefs were ready and a draft speech of
application had already been prepared for the newly elected Labour
Foreign Secretary (who was likely to be Roy Jenkins) to deliver in
Luxembourg on 30 June. In 1971, George Thomson, former Minister
for Europe who would have been the government's chief negotiator if
Labour had won, publicly stated that the terms negotiated by Heath
would have been acccpted by a Labour government if they had been
offered.

But the anti-European forces, which had been quiescent while
Labour was in government, grew in strength, especially among the

unions, whose most powerful general secretaries, Jack Jones of the Transport Workers and Hugh Scanlon of the Engineers, were both against entry. In autumn 1970, the party conference rejected only narrowly an anti-entry resolution. In late February 1971, Jenkins, who had become increasingly concerned about the gathering party storm over Europe, had a meeting with Wilson. Jenkins said, 'I am sure you understand that I am fully committed to going into Europe and will, if the terms are anything like reasonable, be determined to support them. I think you will find that the party in opposition is not prepared to go along with this. I therefore believe that the only way out will be a free vote without recrimination.' Wilson replied, 'I am more optimistic than that. I hope that we may be able to get the party officially to vote in favour, but at the worst, the very worst, we can fall back on a free vote.'[14]

Jenkins and Wilson, however, came at the European issue from very different perspectives. Roy believed it would be morally wrong for Labour to take one view in government and then adopt a different position in opposition. For him, membership of the European Community was absolutely crucial, both economically and for Britain's role in the world. It was not only a vital element in the policies of a modernising, revisionist Labour Party; it had also become one of those great issues which transcend party. If it came to a clash between his party's short-term interests and Britain's European future, Jenkins would choose Europe. In 1962, Wilson had been against Harold Macmillan's original application but in government he had changed to being broadly in favour of entry, a position which, according to his press aide, he continued to maintain in private.[15] But in opposition, his priority, given his style of leadership, was always likely to be to keep the party together and to maintain his leadership. As the hostility to the Common Market grew, Wilson gradually began to shift his position once again.

The crucial figure in Wilson's calculations was Jim Callaghan, who, though an Atlanticist, had supported the Labour government's applications for entry. 'Jim was the real villain of the piece on Europe, not Harold,' said David Marquand, a pro-market Labour MP.[16] On 25 May, Callaghan, always a shrewd judge of party opinion as his behaviour over *In Place of Strife* had already showed, made a fiercely anti-European speech at Southampton, in which he set out his opposition

to British membership in sweeping terms. Joining the Common
Market would mean 'a complete rupture of our identity' and a threat
to 'the language of Chaucer, Shakespeare and Milton'. He concluded:
'If we are to prove our Europeanism by accepting that French is the
dominant language in the Community, then the answer is quite clear
and I will say it in French to prevent any misunderstanding, 'Non,
merci beaucoup.' Callaghan's biographer comments, 'It was not his
finest hour, and his memoirs do not mention it.'[17] All the same,
Callaghan's move had a significant impact not just on Wilson but on
Healey and Crosland as well.

Until the end of the 1960s, Denis Healey had always taken a somewhat sceptical line on British participation in the European
Community. He had been against joining the Schuman Plan and he
opposed both the 1962 and 1967 applications, partly on the pragmatic grounds that they would be vetoed by de Gaulle. However, after
de Gaulle's resignation in 1969 and Healey's appointment a year later
as shadow Foreign Secretary, Denis began to take a more positive
approach. In February 1971, he went to Bonn with Roy Jenkins to
attend a meeting of Jean Monnet's Action Committee for a United
States of Europe and, afterwards, they met Willy Brandt, who had
become German Chancellor and whom Healey greatly admired, to
discuss British entry.

On 11 May, with about a hundred other Labour MPs, he signed a
pro-European letter in the *Guardian* and, on 26 May, he wrote an article in the *Daily Mirror* in which he explained why he had changed his
mind on the Common Market: 'I know it's unfashionable. Some of my
friends say it is politically inconvenient. But the world has changed a
lot in the last five years, and so has the Common Market.' A key
factor for Denis was the arrival in power of Willy Brandt as Federal
Chancellor: 'Britain's influence could be decisive if we are working
with people like Willy Brandt inside the Common Market.' Expressing
his hope that the British application would be successful, Healey concluded: 'Joining the Common Market won't solve any of our problems.
But if the terms are right it will give us a better chance of solving
them.'[18] However, by July, Healey had swung against entry at least on
the Heath terms, and announced that he would vote with the anti-
marketeers when the crucial decision came in the autumn. In his
autobiography, Denis wrote that his attempts 'to direct attention to

the real issues were regarded by the zealots on both sides as opportunism'.[19] But, given what he had written in his *Daily Mirror* article in May, it is difficult not to conclude that his July position was as much dictated by the swing of party opinion as by an analytic consideration of the terms.

In contrast to Healey, Crosland had long been an advocate of British membership of the European Community, mainly on political grounds. In *The Conservative Enemy*, he had called himself 'an instinctive European' and argued that we should 'link our destinies with a dynamic and resurgent Europe'.[20] With Jenkins, he had argued strongly against Gaitskell's stance in 1962 and also supported the Labour government's application for entry in 1967. Like Healey, he had signed the May *Guardian* letter and, like Healey, he had spoken up for entry at the joint meeting between the shadow Cabinet and the National Executive Committee at the Great Western Hotel, Paddington on 16 May. Jenkins described Crosland's speech, which opened the debate, as being 'cool but firm and effective'.[21]

However, when they drove home together, it became clear to Roy that Tony was less firm than he had appeared at the meeting. He began to develop the line that, while he was in favour of entry, the European issue was a relatively minor one which should not divert attention from the major issues of domestic policies which concerned his Grimsby constituents. Above all, the Common Market should not be allowed to endanger the unity of the Labour Party nor keep a Tory government in power. At about this time, Crosland wrote himself a note: he wanted the Tories to secure British entry but feared that Labour's pro-Europeans would be greatly damaged if they were seen to be defying mainstream party opinion, especially if they were accused of keeping the Tories in office.[22] Like many Labour MPs, Crosland was facing a tough choice. Should he line up with Jenkins who regarded British entry as a matter of high principle or should he back the majority who argued that opposing Heath came first?

On 9 June, Jenkins had an hour-long meeting with Wilson to discuss the European issue. The deputy leader appealed directly to the leader of the Labour Party to stick to the pro-European position that they had taken in government. Roy spoke frankly: 'What is most damaging to your reputation and position in the country is that you are believed, perhaps wrongly, to be devious, tricky, opportunistic. If on a major issue of this sort you take the hard, difficult, consistent, unpopular line, it will do your long-term reputation an immense amount of good.'[23] Jenkins then committed the pro-Europeans to backing a pro-European Wilson. Harold Wilson, who had begun their conversation by saying that he was in fact in a more difficult position than Roy because he, unlike Roy, had a choice, apparently took this unusually frank advice in good part. Jenkins came away believing that, though he might have failed to persuade Wilson to support the Heath terms, he had at least secured 'a licence, almost a blessing, for the course I intended to pursue'.[24] But their tacit agreement did not last through the summer.

Despite the opposition of both Wilson and Jenkins, the National Executive Committee agreed to hold a special conference on the Common Market on 17 July. In the run-up to the conference, both the pro and anti camps began to take up positions. Crosland's caution was resented by Jenkins, who wanted him to stand up and be counted. It was no good supporting something unless you supported it with enthusiasm, Roy said to him. Tony replied, 'I have always supported something with enthusiasm if I felt enthusiastic. I do not support things with enthusiasm if I do not feel enthusiastic. You may like this or not. That's the way I am.'[25] Crosland drafted a speech explaining that, while he was still pro-European, he would not vote to keep Mr Heath in power. He added that if he listed all the things for which he had fought for more than twenty years – greater equality, the relief of poverty, more public spending, educational reform, housing policy, the improvement of the environment – he did not find that 'any of these will be decisively affected one way or another by the Common Market'.[26] Urged by pro-market friends, such as Roy Hattersley, David Owen and his PPS, Dick Leonard, not to deliver such a lukewarm speech publicly, Crosland instead used it at a private meeting of his General Management Committee.

However, on 11 July, the *Sunday Times* carried a damaging story with the headline 'Crosland, Healey, No to Market'. James Margach, the paper's political correspondent, correctly reported the Healey announcement that he had once again switched sides and would be voting with the antis in October. The *Sunday Times* said that Crosland would also vote with the anti-marketeers, though Tony had, in fact, not yet made up his mind between voting against or abstention. The report, accurately reflecting Crosland's views, also made a reference to his warning that an 'élitist' faction of right-wing intellectuals was in danger of separating itself off from the Labour movement.

Tony's use of the word 'élitist' was particularly resented by the Jenkinsites, many of whom were already under mounting pressure in their constituencies. According to Susan Crosland's account, the pro-Europeans did not mind so much about Denis Healey who openly boasted of being an opportunist. It was Tony Crosland's 'apostasy' which rankled: 'Tony was known as a honest intellectual; when he qualified their case, he became the threat.'[27] A meeting of the 1963 Club on 20 July turned nasty: Crosland was accused of being driven by jealousy of Jenkins and of having become a careerist devoted to personal advancement.[28] When Tony and Susan attended a dinner of the informal XYZ Club of Labour MPs and outsiders interested in economics, they were cut dead by the Rodgers and the Tavernes. Susan commented, 'There was something comic about the little phalanx of backs.'[29]

The summer of 1971 was a crucial moment. If Crosland, Jenkins and Healey had managed to agree on a modus vivendi over Europe, the history of the Labour Party in the 1970s and the 1980s might have been different. An agreement would probably have involved Jenkins taking a less extreme position and Crosland and Healey adopting a more consistent pro-European stance. But if the three men had stood together, the divisions in the party over Europe could well have been accommodated without isolating the Jenkinsites and without undermining the cohesion of the centre-right in the Labour Party. Their failure to work together fatally weakened the forces of revisionism and opened the door to the left.

The July special conference on the Common Market revealed the sharp split in the party over the issue. Michael Foot and Peter Shore spoke eloquently for the antis, but some of the best oratory came from the pro-marketeers. There was a brilliant speech by John Mackintosh, MP for East Lothian and constitutional expert, who confidently asserted that British membership would bring economic growth with it and poured scorn on the sovereignty argument as being anachronistic. Given his views, the deputy leader, Roy Jenkins, was not allowed to speak on behalf of the NEC. However, Harold Wilson, for the first time, came out against entry on Heath's terms: 'I reject the assertion that the terms this Conservative government have obtained are the terms the Labour government asked for, would have asked for, would have been bound to accept.'[30] His biographer commented: 'Nobody believed him. Everybody knew he was speaking not from the heart, but under extreme pressure.' Jenkins later wrote: 'It was like watching someone being sold down the river into slavery, drifting away, depressed but unprotesting.'[31] For pro-Europeans inside the Labour Party, this was Wilson at his most unappealing. Healey, who had more sympathy for the leader of the Labour Party's situation, said that, at one shadow Cabinet meeting during that year, Wilson told his colleagues, 'I've been wading in shit for three months to allow others to indulge their conscience.'[32]

The effect of Jenkins' enforced silence and of Wilson's speech at the conference was to galvanise Roy into passionate oratory. At 6.30 p.m. on Monday 19 July, he and Barbara Castle were to address the Parliamentary Labour Party (PLP) on the Common Market; this was one of two concluding debates to wind up a series of PLP meetings on Europe. Roy spent most of the Sunday carefully preparing a twenty-minute speech which, following an over-lengthy and somewhat rambling contribution by Barbara, he then delivered without using notes. One young pro-European MP said that Barbara Castle was totally demolished by Jenkins. Another spoke of 'Roy's Nuremberg rally speech'.[33] Jenkins later called it 'an uncompromising, even an inflammatory speech making no attempt to paper over the cracks'.[34]

In obvious contradiction of Wilson, Roy said a Labour Cabinet would have accepted the terms offered to Heath and warned: 'You cannot turn down entry now and pick it up again, whether under a different government or not, in two or three years' time. The opportunity if we lose it now will be gone for at least a decade and possibly a lifetime.' He then turned the fire witheringly on Callaghan who had put forward economic growth as an alternative to EC entry: 'Jim Callaghan offered running the economy flat-out for five years. That is not a policy: it is an aspiration.' Finally, he dealt with the left: 'At (Saturday's) conference the only alternative we heard was socialism in one country . . . That's not a policy either; it's just a slogan, and it is one which becomes not merely unconvincing but hypocritical as well when it is dressed up as our best contribution to international socialism.' Even Benn called the speech a powerful one and said it was a 'direct attack on Harold Wilson and also on Healey and Crosland, who had climbed off the fence against the Market'.[35] Its impact on the pro-Europeans (over a hundred) in a packed meeting of about two hundred and fifty was electric. Roy's speech was interrupted every two or three sentences by spontaneous applause and its conclusion was marked by an astonishing eruption of emotion and banging on desks.

Roy Jenkins was so committed to the European cause and so frustrated by the movement of party opinion away from the pro-Europeans and Wilson's failure to oppose it that he had made a more impassioned speech than even his close friends thought him capable of. But the left and the anti-marketeers found it deeply offensive. When, later that evening, Roy passed the table at which Barbara Castle was dining in the Commons with Dick Crossman, she said, 'Roy, I used to respect you a great deal, but I will never do so again.'[36] There was even talk on the left of organising the constituencies and conference against the Jenkinsites. Benn commented, 'It took you right back to 1951 or 1961 – the party at its worst.'[37]

Wilson was badly shaken not only by Roy's speech but by the demonstration of support for Jenkins by a large section of the PLP which he mistakenly regarded as a deliberate and organised challenge to his authority. At Tuesday's final PLP Common Market debate, at which Willie Ross, the Scottish spokesman, and George Thomson were speaking, Wilson opened by making a bitter and undignified attack on the pro-Europeans. He demanded the right to require 'comradeship, mutual respect and the avoidance of personalities – public or behind cupped hands' and 'even after last night' (a clear reference to Jenkins's speech) called for unity in the party.[38]

Later that evening, Crossman, who, though he was still in Parliament, had become editor of the New Statesman, came round to see Jenkins at Ladbroke Square. He described Wilson as a 'broken' man. Speaking for himself, Dick advised Roy to resign as deputy leader because he would find it easier. He added, 'Of course, you think you are a Gaitskell and you are nothing of the sort. You are much more a Bevan than you are a Gaitskell. You have all the Welsh capacity for wrecking. But maddeningly for the rest of us you are a Bevan with the big difference that you have the press and the establishment on your side.'[39] As editor of the New Statesman, and anti-marketeer, Crossman had his own agenda. But his remarks highlighted Jenkins' dilemma. The more he upped the stakes on Europe, the more he endangered his own position and that of the pro-European minority within the party.

As Parliament broke for the summer recess, the pro-Europeans braced themselves for the party conference at Brighton at the beginning of October, the meeting of the Parliamentary Labour Party in the middle of the month and, above all, for the crucial Commons vote on entry on 28 October. The pro-Europeans did not want to set themselves up, like nineteenth-century Peelites or the Liberal Unionists, as a separate party in Parliament. As soon as Europe was out of the way, they intended to join their fellow Labour MPs in helping to defeat the Tories. But they saw entry to the European Community as overriding their normal party loyalty and were not prepared to attempt to bring the Heath government down on the issue. In that sense, they were becoming, as Wilson charged, a faction within the party. The stand of the pro-Europeans was generally unpopular with party activists, especially after the party conference had decided against entry, and a number of MPs, including Dick Taverne, George Thomson, Dick Leonard (Tony Crosland's PPS) and Jim Tinn, Bill Rodgers' neighbour on Teesside, were in trouble with their constituency parties.

Bill Rodgers, Roy's faithful lieutenant, put his considerable ability into the task of keeping the band of pro-European MPs together. On 9 June, *The Times*, briefed by Rodgers, reported that thirty Labour MPs were rock-solid for Europe and the day after Rodgers called a meeting attended by nineteen backbench Labour members. By the end of the session, Rodgers had begun collecting names for a letter to the chief whip, with a view to persuading him to allow a 'free vote'. Earlier, the chief whip, Bob Mellish, had told Dick Taverne and Bill Rodgers that a 'three-line' whip would be imposed only over 'his dead body' but, with the prospect of conference voting overwhelmingly against entry on the Conservative terms, he changed his position. As expected, the Brighton conference voted by five to one against entry.

Although the pro-European rebels, much to Wilson's fury, were favourably written up by the press as politicians who were prepared to put principle before party, the conference vote inevitably had the effect of increasing the pressure on them. Even so, by 12 October, Rodgers was able to show Bob Mellish a letter supporting entry on current terms with fifty-seven Labour signatures on it; he also told the chief whip that he should expect between sixty-five and seventy MPs to vote for entry. On 18 October, Edward Heath, with whom Rodgers had been in private communication, announced a free vote for Conservative MPs, calculating that this would encourage the Labour dissidents to go into the lobbies with the Tory government. However, both the shadow Cabinet and the PLP voted, in both cases narrowly, to impose a three-line whip. The question was how many Labour MPs would defy it.

Some Labour MPs argued that, instead of voting against a three-line whip, the pro-Europeans should abstain, which would allow the motion in favour of entry to pass but by a much smaller majority. Abstention, unlike voting against a three-line whip, was sanctioned in the party's standing orders. Both Fred Mulley, a committed European, and George Thomas, who was not, saw Roy Jenkins in the days before the crucial vote to urge this course of action. Jim Wellbeloved, a mainstream MP who shared an office with Bill Rodgers, tried to persuade him that a mass abstention would be more impressive than a smaller number voting for entry. David Owen put much the same case to the Jenkinsites. Tony Crosland said to Jenkins, 'It's irresponsible of you not to allow abstention to be seriously discussed by the group. You could make your European stand without voting for Heath.' He added, 'You might reflect that in the long run you are damaging yourself as well as the Labour Party.'[40] But Jenkins, who was convinced that 28 October was one of the decisive votes of the century, said that he had no intention of spending the rest of his life answering the question of what he did in the Great Division by saying, 'I abstained.'[41]

Roy Jenkins later wrote that the six-day Common Market debate, as opposed to the vote itself, seemed to him to be an anticlimax. That was partly because he was not allowed to speak from the front bench, now the Labour Party position had been decided against him. This also applied to other front-benchers such as George Thomson, Shirley Williams and Harold Lever. However, Bill Rodgers, who spoke on the first day, said that, unlike many well-trailed debates that failed to fulfil their promise, 'there was a great sense of occasion'.[42]

Reading the debate thirty years later, one is struck by the impressive performance of Labour's pro-marketeers. They were bitterly attacked by anti-marketeers in their own party, who kept intervening in their speeches. Yet the pro-Europeans put their case with considerable force and authority. Notable contributions were made by two former Foreign Secretaries, Michael Stewart, who said that a Labour Cabinet would have accepted the Heath terms, and Patrick Gordon Walker. But perhaps the bravest and most eloquent speeches were made by the younger pro-market MPs whose careers were at risk, like John Mackintosh, David Marquand, Roy Hattersley, David Owen, Phillip Whitehead and Michael Barnes. Owen said that the major argument for entry was political, while Marquand emphasised how membership could lead to further growth. Mackintosh dealt head-on with the sovereignty issue which, contrary to the impression given later by Euro-sceptics, was a major feature of the debate: 'The real point is that no nation has untrammelled sovereignty . . . What matters to the public is not the legal power to act but whether the consequences may mean anything.' He concluded that his vote in favour of entry would be a small act in 'a small and insignificant public career; yet my affirmative vote will be one of the things which will give me the greatest pleasure in my life'.

On the final day of the debate, Jenkins characteristically relaxed from the tension by eating with his friends. He lunched with John Harris and Roy Hattersley at his club, Brooks, in St James Street. Hattersley was worried about the prospect of strong-arm tactics by the more aggressive members of the left and was proposing a bodyguard to whisk Jenkins away into a departing car. Later Roy and Jennifer had dinner with the Thomsons at Lockett's, a convenient restaurant near the House of Commons. They were joined by Dick Taverne, who had come from his Lincoln constituency party meeting where he had been threatened with deselection if he voted for entry. Jenkins then went to listen to the wind-up speeches, with Callaghan for the Opposition and Heath for the government, and sat next to Wilson. Earlier in the day, Crosland had also sat near Wilson during the Leader of the Opposition's speech, so that, as he told his wife, 'everybody knows I was there and am not sick'. Crosland had, in the end, decided to abstain. When he told Jim Callaghan of his decision, Jim said it was 'a terrible mistake; however mixed my feelings about Europe, I should establish myself in people's minds as a party man forever distinct from the Jenkinsite right'.[43] Crosland thought so long and hard about complex issues that he was often in danger of falling between stools. Having performed his double somersault, Healey voted with the Labour Opposition.

When the division was called at 10.00 p.m., Roy Jenkins walked into the government lobby with the chairman of the Parliamentary Labour Party, Douglas Houghton, also a committed European. A group of angry Labour members gathered to watch Jenkins as he came out of the division lobby, but there was no violence (though after the vote Roy was called a 'rat' by Reg Freeson, who was later to be deselected by the hard left). The result of the division was that the government had an impressive majority of 112. Out of 356 'ayes', 69 were Labour. In addition, 20 Labour MPs abstained. The Labour 'Europeans', led by Roy Jenkins, had written themselves indelibly into history.

The 28 October vote had a damaging impact on the relationship between Jenkins and Crosland. Many of the pro-Europeans were very angry with Tony for abstaining. Bill Rodgers, at his most heavy-handed, said to Dick Leonard, Crosland's PPS, 'He's behaved like a shit and we must punish him.' Punishment included voting Crosland off the shadow Cabinet. When Leonard pointed out that the only result would be replace him with someone whom the Jenkinsites disagreed with a great deal more, Rodgers repeated, 'He's got to be taught a lesson.'[44] Jenkins took a cooler, more measured approach.

In November Roy and Tony had dinner together. Fearful of the consequences of a permanent split on the right, Roy offered an olive branch: 'I'm much better at tactics, you're much better at policy,' said Jenkins. If Tony would join the Jenkinsites, it would be possible to attract wider support, building up to a majority in the PLP. With Crosland on board, the pro-European Jenkinsite faction would be capable of defeating both Jim Callaghan and Michael Foot in a future leadership election. For Tony, the implication of Roy's approach was that he could become number two to Roy if he could 'only be decisive enough' to join the Jenkinsite faction. Crosland declined, partly, as he admitted to his wife, Susan, out of pride and vanity.[45] Certainly, the idea of being second fiddle to his friend who, for so many years, had been his younger acolyte rankled. But, according to Crosland, the main reason was that 'their idea of a Labour party is not mine. Roy has actually come to dislike socialism . . . It is Roy's misfortune that because of his father, he's in the wrong party. As a Liberal or

Conservative he might make a very good leader.' Anyway, the Jenkinsites would not – and should not – win over the party: 'The most that could happen is that the party would be split for a generation.' The Jenkinsites, who could have voted Crosland off the committee, wisely held their hand over the shadow Cabinet elections, though Tony slipped from third to eighth. It was clear, however, from their unsuccessful meeting that any idea of an alliance between Crosland and Jenkins had gone for good, thus opening up the prospect of a damaging division on the right of the Labour Party.

Significantly, Jenkins did not think it was worth approaching Healey. Although they had worked well together in government and Jenkins had backed Healey to succeed him as Chancellor if Labour had won the 1970 election, Jenkins had never been as close to Healey as he had to Crosland. In Roy's view, Denis's behaviour over the Common Market had been blatantly opportunistic. The convert to a pro-market position in the *Mirror* article of 26 May had become a strident opponent two months later. Tony Benn, himself emerging as an anti-marketeer, called Healey's 26 July speech in the pre-recess debate, 'most awful'.[46] Two months after he had argued that he was in favour of entry, he was now saying that the costs of entry were prohibitive. Denis's contribution to the historic October debate was little more convincing.

Healey later admitted, 'I would regard the episode as probably the most damaging to me of my entire career.'[47] In the shadow Cabinet elections, he fell from being runner-up the year before to bottom of those elected, which was an indication of what pro-Europeans, who would normally have voted for him, thought about his behaviour. All the same, Denis was a rival to Roy for the leadership in a way that Tony was not. Despite his somersault over Europe and though, unlike Jenkins, he was a loner without the support of a faction, his sheer ability, energy and staying power were bound to make him a serious contender. And, in any case, Healey did not believe that Jenkins was cut out to be Labour leader, being 'ill-suited to the politics of class and ideology which played so large a role in the Labour Party'. However, with hindsight, Healey regretted that mutual jealousy prevented him and Jenkins from co-operating more effectively.[48] It was certainly to have harmful consequences for the Labour Party.

A case can be made for the Healey–Callaghan–Wilson position

over Europe. There is no doubt that if Wilson had backed the Heath terms, as Jenkins had urged him to do, party conference and well over a third of the PLP would have fiercely resisted. In those circumstances it is open to doubt whether the leader could have forced it through his party. A more ambiguous position, involving a free vote, would have been more in character for Wilson, and would have made things easier for the Jenkinsites, at least in the short term. The position, which the leadership adopted, of opposing entry on terms negotiated by Heath on a three-line whip, may have been implausible but at least had the merit of keeping open the principle of entry, albeit in an extremely roundabout and inglorious way. At the same time, the party could be kept relatively intact: as Healey put it, 'in opposition the overriding duty of the leader is to keep the party together'.[49] However, as Healey himself admitted, his own political reputation, as well as that of Wilson and Callaghan, suffered as a consequence, while uncommitted voters were justified in asking whether a party that did one thing in government and another in opposition was to be trusted with power again.

After the 28 October vote for the principle of entry, even the boldest of Labour pro-Europeans were reluctant to support the legislation implementing the decision. Jenkins accepted that their position was at once illogical and comprehensible. Most of the pro-Europeans were party loyalists, unaccustomed to voting against a three-line whip, and they wanted to get back to familiar territory: 'We judged we could make a dash for Europe without endangering our long-term relations with the Labour Party.'[50] In the spirit of that strategy, Jenkins stood again for the deputy leadership instead of resigning (and standing against Wilson for the leadership, as one colleague urged him to do). Jenkins failed by only two votes to get an overall majority on the first ballot. However, on the second ballot, his lead over the runner-up, Michael Foot, was relatively narrow. It was thought that some MPs (probably including Callaghan and his close allies) subsequently abstained so as to prevent Roy achieving too great a triumph.

However, Jenkins' success in getting re-elected as deputy leader, despite having voted against a three line whip, was no more than the lull before the storm. On 17 February 1972, the European Communities Bill, which put into legislative form the decision to enter taken the previous October, had its second reading. In contrast to the massive majority of 112 in favour of the principle, the government's majority fell to only eight. Although there were a few Labour abstentions, most Labour pro-Europeans voted against the implementing legislation. Roy Jenkins remembered it 'as a day of misery'.[51] Bill Rodgers was in tears when he went into the division lobby against the second reading of the Bill, and Harold Lever was physically sick. As the Bill went through its remaining stages with numerous divisions, the pressure on the pro-Europeans was bound to increase, especially as they were relying on the courage of a few older Labour abstentionists, such as George Strauss, Austen Albu, Carl Johnson, Freda Corbet and Christopher Mayhew, to ensure that the legislation enabling the United Kingdom to enter the Community got through unamended.

Understandably, Roy Jenkins considered whether he should resign and, by so doing, release himself from the obligation to vote with his party on the European Communities Bill. During the October debate, there had been agonised discussions about whether Roy and other shadow Cabinet ministers ought to resign before the big vote. However, on that occasion Jenkins had apparently been persuaded not to resign by a pledge of support from Ted Short, Education Secretary in the Labour government and now a shadow Cabinet member, who told him: 'We hardly know each other and didn't get on in government, but I have the highest regard for your stand and will do all that I can to help.'[52] Now, following the second reading of the European Communities Bill, Roy 'was in a state of mounting discontent, both with myself and with the Labour Party'.[53] His unease about his position was made worse by the fact that, at a PLP meeting before the deputy leadership election, he had committed himself to voting with the party in subsequent divisions, provided he was not called upon to undo his vote of 28 October. He told the PLP that if unexpectedly he found it necessary not to vote with the party he would step down from the front bench. However uneasy he felt, Jenkins assumed, as the Easter holidays approached, that he would get through the passage of the Bill without having to resign.

It was the referendum issue that pushed Jenkins to resignation. The referendum was the brainchild of Tony Benn, the born-again left winger. In the Wilson governments of the 1960s, Benn had been the arch technocrat, serving first as Postmaster-General and then as

Minister of Technology. Although anti-market in the early 1960s, he swung round to a pro-European position by the mid 60s, strongly supporting Labour's application for entry. He said then that the UK had to cut Queen Victoria's umbilical cord and appealed for technological co-operation in Europe. In opposition, as part of his move to the left, he swung back again. Speaking in the October 1971 House of Commons debate, he said, 'I make no apology, in the course of having thought about this issue, for having changed the emphasis of my view at different stages.'

A new element in Benn's strategy was the referendum, which he began to espouse with great fervour, both on constitutional grounds and as a means of 'uniting the Labour Party'. In April 1971 he was unable to get a seconder when he put his proposal for a referendum to the NEC. However, as the row inside the Labour Party over the Common Market grew in intensity, support for the idea increased. When it first came before the shadow Cabinet in November 1970, Jim Callaghan, the former naval officer, had presciently remarked, 'Tony may be launching a little rubber life-raft which we will all be glad of in a year's time.'[54]

On 15 March 1972, the shadow Cabinet rejected by eight votes to four a Benn proposal that the Labour Party should support an amendment to the European Communities Bill, requiring a referendum before the UK entered the Community. Benn swallowed his disappointment and, on 22 March, exploiting the news that there would be a referendum in France over enlargement, he used his position as chairman of the party to persuade the NEC by thirteen votes to eleven (with Wilson, Jenkins, Healey and Callaghan absent) to pass a resolution inviting the PLP to consider supporting amendments to the Bill in favour of a referendum.

In view of the NEC resolution, the shadow Cabinet reconsidered its position on 29 March and proceeded to reverse its previous decision of a fortnight before by eight votes to six.[55] The defeated minority was made up of five hard-core pro-Europeans (Roy Jenkins, George Thomson, Harold Lever, Shirley Williams and Douglas Houghton) plus Tony Crosland, who said he was against a decision in favour of a referendum now, because it would involve another somersault. Denis Healey, who had voted against a fortnight before, was absent and Willie Ross, who was strongly against a referendum, had been persuaded by Harold Wilson to stay away from the meeting. Ted Short, who had abstained at the earlier meeting, came late to the meeting and voted for a referendum. According to Jenkins, Jim Callaghan reserved his position on the referendum but said he was in favour of voting for an amendment to beat the Conservatives and was influenced by Harold Wilson's wishes. The key swing vote was that of Harold Wilson, who spoke early in the discussion; he argued that the situation had been changed by the NEC decision and now strongly advocated voting for the Tory backbench amendment for a referendum which was due to come before the House after Easter.

What led to Wilson's change of line on the referendum? When he first heard about Benn's proposal in November 1970, he said, 'I understand you are suggesting a plebiscite on the Common Market. You can't do that.'[56] Like the other party leaders, he had spoken strongly against a referendum during the 1970 General Election. His shift of position may partly have been motivated by the prospect of embarrassing the Conservative government. He may also have been looking ahead to the election and the need to provide a mechanism that might get a divided party off the hook on which it had impaled itself and at the same time keep Britain in the Community. His press aide, Joe Haines said, 'Right from the start he believed that he could win a referendum on the Market, for staying in.'[57] Roy Jenkins' view, which seems plausible, was that Wilson, increasingly anxious about Roy mounting a challenge to him, was also using the issue as a means of provoking his resignation.

On 11 March, Jenkins had made a speech at Worsley in the constituency of a prominent Jenkinsite, John Roper. It was the first of a series of seven speeches, which was designed to act as a rallying call and was later turned into the book *What Matters Now*.[58] One of the speech's concluding sentences was: 'In place of the politics of envy, we must put the politics of compassion; in place of the politics of cupidity, the politics of justice; in place of the politics of opportunism, the politics of principle.' Despite Jenkins' public denial, both the press and Wilson took the reference to 'opportunism' to be a direct attack on the Labour leader. Wilson, who was always obsessed by possible threats to his leadership, may have decided to launch a pre-emptive strike. If so, it succeeded in its intention.

After ten days of brooding at East Hendred over the Easter recess,

Jenkins resigned, complaining about a constant shifting of ground by the NEC and the shadow Cabinet, above all on the referendum. George Thomson and Harold Lever resigned with him from the shadow Cabinet, as did David Owen, Dickson Mabon and Dick Taverne from the Labour front bench. Bill Rodgers had already been sacked by Wilson for his pro-European 'whipping' activities four months earlier. Neither Shirley Williams nor Roy Hattersley resigned. Shirley was promoted to shadow Home Secretary instead of Jenkins and Roy Hattersley to shadow Defence Secretary in Thomson's place.

Jenkins' motives in deciding to resign were mixed. In his autobiography he put forward three arguments for his opposition at that time to a referendum. First, it could put the whole issue of entry in doubt, thus undermining the vote of 28 October. Second, he was resistant on principle 'to the importation of the novel device of the referendum into our constitutional arrangements'.[59] Third, he feared a referendum would accentuate the divide in the Labour Party, even driving the pro-Europeans out of the party. However, according to Tony Benn's diaries, Roy did not speak out strongly at the crucial shadow Cabinet meeting on 29 March, confining himself to saying that he did not rule out a referendum in the event of an election manifesto requiring one, but he did not want one now.[60] Benn's reaction to Roy's resignation was that he had resigned not so much because of the referendum issue but because he realised that he could not continue as deputy leader of a party when he disagreed with a central part of its policy.[61]

Although Tony Benn had, of course, his own agenda (including his ambition to succeed Wilson himself), there is an element of truth in his judgement. In 1972, Roy Jenkins was almost certainly more strongly against referenda than Benn thought. But all the same the issue itself was more the breaking point than the main cause. As Benn rightly surmised, it was the difficulty of his underlying position which led to his resignation: 'I was convinced that Foot, Shore and Benn in particular were resolved to go on and on raising any issue they could think of which would embarrass the Labour Europeans. And with Wilson having apparently committed himself to go along with them, their majority was not in doubt.' Jenkins concluded, 'The prospect for me for the summer was that of being made to jump through a series of humiliating hoops, with the inevitable erosion of any position I had in the country, and a consequent increasing difficulty of ever again being able to find any firm ground on which to stand.'[62] An additional factor was that Roy Jenkins had been under great emotional strain, especially after having to vote against the second reading of the European Communities Bill.[63] Resignation at least had the merit of relieving him of that pressure.

Jenkins' closest associates had conflicting views about his resignation. George Thomson (who had already accepted an offer from Heath to become one of the first two British European Commissioners) and Harold Lever were strongly in favour, as were Dick Taverne and Bill Rodgers (who was, however, careful not to try and influence Roy's decision towards resignation). Shirley Williams and David Owen, who both saw the case for a referendum, and Roy Hattersley, who was concerned about the impact Jenkins' resignation would have on the party, were opposed to it.

The resignation of Jenkins was indeed a turning point. For Jenkins personally, it was a major and, as it turned out, fatal setback to his chances of succeeding Wilson. As an effective Chancellor and deputy leader, Roy had been the front-runner in the succession stakes. Now, he slipped back behind Jim Callaghan and probably Denis Healey as well. A number of MPs from the centre of the party, who had previously respected Jenkins for his parliamentary and ministerial skills, thought that Roy and his friends had been 'self-indulgent'. Echoing Crosland's complaint, there was talk in the Commons tea room and bars of middle-class élitism and 'being out of touch' with grassroots opinion. As Wilson's biographer acutely put it, 'Jenkins was signalling by his self-removal, that he was no longer a party man.'[64] It looked as though Jenkins' only hope of the leadership was now by a direct challenge to Wilson either before the election or after a Labour defeat at the next election. Yet, in his resignation interview with Wilson, Roy specifically ruled out standing against the Labour leader in the autumn of 1972, a clear indication that, as he had already demonstrated in July 1968, Jenkins lacked the single-minded ruthlessness for a coup d'état. Indeed, his resignation itself showed that he had lost the will to fight his corner.

The major beneficiaries of Roy's departure were Wilson, who had rid himself of an increasingly troublesome deputy, and Callaghan, who had seen his main rival for the succession commit what he considered to be virtual political suicide. Denis Healey also benefited from

Jenkins' demise, as Wilson appointed him shadow Chancellor in Roy's place. Tony Crosland who, though voting against the referendum amendment at the shadow Cabinet, had immediately made it clear that he had no intention of resigning over the issue, was in Japan for an environmental conference when Jenkins resigned. He had also wanted the shadow Chancellorship and rang up Harold Wilson from Tokyo to say so. As Tony explained to his wife, 'Harold was at his worst, evasive, rattled, all over the shop, saying, "You understand there are many permutations, and I have to fit three people into two jobs, etc".' Susan Crosland commented, 'That Harold had been evasive was not surprising: Denis Healey had already asked for the shadow Chancellorship and got it. Jim Callaghan, the third person in the permutations, had already asked for the job being vacated by Denis – shadow Foreign Secretary – and got it.'[65]

For the second time, Crosland had been passed over for the job that he coveted, though this time it was the shadow post. Wilson's appointment of Healey who, in contrast to Crosland knew little about economics, reflected not only his own predeliction (he got on better with Healey than Crosland) but also the power realities. In party terms (a more important factor than expertise when Labour was in opposition) Healey was simply a more prominent political personality than Crosland.

It is significant that Healey was eager to exchange a position, shadow Foreign Secretary, for which he was supremely well qualified, for another, for which, as he admitted, he was no more qualified than 'the average newspaper reader'.[66] It is true that if Labour had won the General Election of 1970 it is likely that Wilson would have appointed Healey as Chancellor instead of Jenkins, and probably Jenkins would have gone to the Foreign Office. But it is one thing to become Chancellor, with all the backing and advice of Treasury officials; quite another to do the shadow job with little full-time support, except from his two able front-bench colleagues, Joel Barnett and Robert Sheldon.

However, the shadow Chancellorship (and, hopefully, the Chancellorship if the next election was won) was such a key role that Healey had to stake his claim to it. If Wilson went after the election, then Healey, as Chancellor, would be in a good position to succeed him. But if somebody else (perhaps Crosland, or even Shore) took the post, there would be yet another crown prince. Healey, always confident in his own abilities, was in no doubt that he could pick up enough about economics to make a good fist of the Chancellorship. In opposition, he hoped to get away with attacking the weaknesses and contradictions in the policies of Anthony Barber, the Tory Chancellor.[67]

Jenkins' resignation also opened up a second position, that of the deputy leadership. On his return from Japan, Crosland put his hat in the ring. The Jenkinsites, however, decided to stop him. David Owen was in a minority of one in urging that they ought to vote for Tony, on the grounds that he was the best man. Instead, the group agreed to support Ted Short, because he had behaved better than Crosland over the Common Market issue (though Short, in contrast to Crosland, had voted for a referendum) and, very much to the point, Short would be more of a stop-gap figure than Crosland.

Jenkins felt particularly strongly about Crosland's behaviour because when Roy had tried to enlist his support over Easter Crosland had shrugged his shoulders and said he was off to Japan to study urban planning. Roy commented sharply, 'If Short had been a little uncomprehending, Crosland had been the pharisee.'[68] Jenkins, like nearly fifty other pro-Europeans, did not see why Tony should benefit from his exit. Tony issued a defiant statement: 'I am not running in order to keep someone else out. I am running to win – on a non-sectarian ticket.'[69] However, on the first ballot Ted Short came top with 111 votes, Michael Foot got 110 and Crosland was bottom with 61 votes and was, therefore, eliminated. The Jenkinsites had blocked Tony.

Some years later, Roy explained to Dick Leonard, Tony Crosland's PPS, that though he had kept Crosland from becoming deputy leader, he did not see himself or the Jenkinsites as playing the spoiling role. If Tony had been willing to help Roy, then Roy could have become leader. He didn't blame Tony for feeling as he did: at Oxford, Tony was the more prominent figure. But, in Jenkins' view, it was Tony, by refusing to back Roy, who had spoiled things for him.[70] But that was not quite the whole story. In his autobiography, Roy admitted to being uneasy about his treatment of Crosland.[71] In a world of pragmatic *real politik*, there was certainly a case for not voting for Tony Crosland. But if the issue was solely one of merit, then there was no question that Tony should have had the Jenkinsite vote. For, judged both in terms of ability and of modernising, revisionist credentials, Crosland was a potential leader of the Labour Party and Short was not.

What happened at the vote of 28 October 1971 and then over Roy's resignation in April 1972 and the subsequent deputy leadership election highlighted the split on the centre-right of the Labour Party between those who gave priority to Europe and those who were either anti-European or at least prepared to put their party loyalties and personal ambitions before their European beliefs. The fracture of the old Gaitskellite coalition on the European issue (already foreshadowed at Labour's 1962 party conference) was to have momentous consequences, leading to a dramatic increase in the influence of the left in the 1970s and early 80s and, arguably, in 1981 to the SDP breakaway.

Jenkins, Crosland and Healey each made their contribution to this disastrous split. Jenkins, by his principled and determined (his opponents would say obstinate and self-indulgent) stand on 28 October 1971 in defying a three-line whip and then by his resignation as deputy leader over the referendum in April 1972, helped accentuate the divisions over Europe. Crosland, by his cautious, non-committal approach, washed his hands of responsibility, refusing to take seriously the possible consequences of Jenkins' resignation, apart from the possibilities it opened up for his own advancement. Healey's behaviour was opportunistic, involving two switches of approach in as many months. He was also a direct beneficiary of Roy's resignation. Even if there was an argument for the Wilson–Callaghan–Healey position, none of the three, with the possible exception of Wilson and certainly not Callaghan nor Healey, made any attempt to accommodate the pro-Europeans in the party, an omission that was to have highly damaging consequences for the future. After the 28 October vote and Roy's resignation, relations between Jenkins, Crosland and Healey, which, despite Crosland's jealousy over Roy's promotion to the Chancellorship in 1967, had been mostly relatively good during the 1960s Labour government, were never the same again. Conflicting ambitions, personal pique and vanity, as well as differing approaches to the European question, kept them apart.

10

Return to Office and the 1976 Leadership Election

The period after Roy Jenkins' resignation in April 1972 was a dispiriting one for revisionist social democrats as the left grew in strength and influence and Jenkins became more alienated both from his two Oxford contemporaries and from the party. After Labour's unexpected victory in February 1974, Crosland, Jenkins and Healey became senior ministers. However, the Labour leadership election of 1976 in which all three stood and which Callaghan won, highlighted their continuing failure to combine together.

The key figure in the resurgence of the left was the energetic and persuasive Tony Benn who used both his chairmanship of the Labour Party (1971–72) and his post as shadow Secretary of State for Industry to put forward plans for extensive nationalisation and large-scale industrial intervention. The most far-reaching proposal, the brain-child of a left-wing economist, Stuart Holland, was for a massive interventionist National Enterprise Board (NEB), which, by taking a public stake in all kinds of businesses, would, it was argued, transform the economy, increasing growth, sustaining investment and technology and helping the regions and employment. As well as setting up an across-the-board system of compulsory planning agreements with private industry, the National Executive also came forward with a scheme for the NEB to take a controlling interest in twenty leading companies.

Crosland and Healey strongly opposed Benn's ideas. At a joint meeting of the shadow Cabinet and the NEC in May 1973, Crosland derided the proposal to nationalise these top companies as 'half-baked' and asked sarcastically, 'why don't we nationalise Marks & Spencer (which then had a high reputation) to make it as efficient as the Co-op?'[1] The author of *The Future of Socialism* also pointed out that there was no link between public ownership and greater equality. Maybe the public would accept nationalisation in individual cases, but not in general. When the NEC met later that month, the new shadow Chancellor Denis Healey recommended that the reference to nationalising the top twenty companies be dropped. However, his amendment was defeated by seven votes to six. Tony Benn wrote in his diary: 'The party is now firmly launched on a left-wing policy,'[2] though, on the following day, Wilson issued a press statement that said that it was inconceivable that the party would go into a General Election supporting Benn's proposal.[3]

As well as moving to the left, Labour in opposition became far more dependent on the unions. It was perhaps inevitable that Labour would be committed to repealing the Conservative Industrial Relations Act, even though the Tory legislation based many of its clauses on Labour's *In Place of Strife*. But Labour's rapprochement went well beyond the industrial relations field. In February 1973, the party and the unions published a joint declaration of aims, including a wide-ranging system of price controls, big increases in public spending on pensions, health, housing and transport and substantial extensions of public ownership. Harold Wilson, who said that the declaration provided the basis for a 'great compact' between a future Labour government and the unions, was eager to show that, unlike the Conservative Prime Minister, Edward Heath, he could still work with the unions. But it was a deal on the union's terms. Labour was promising to deliver on a whole range of costly items; the unions merely agreed to take these commitments into account when bargaining for their members.

The new importance of the unions in the party's strategy worried Crosland, who said at one shadow Cabinet meeting that it was not Marxism that was the problem, because nobody really believed in Marx, but whether the Labour Party ought to be so tightly linked to the unions. Benn commented, 'He [Crosland] wants a consumer-orientated

Swedish type of socialism, and yet it is this link with the workers, in my judgement, which offers the only serious chance of major social, political and industrial change.' Crosland's comment on his former pupil was, 'Nothing the matter with him except he's a bit cracked.'[4]

Denis Healey shared some of Tony Crosland's misgivings about the power of the unions. In his assessment in his autobiography, he wrote: 'The trade unions were now emerging as an obstacle both to the election of a Labour government and to its success once it was in power.'[5] But, in his role as shadow Chancellor, he saw it as one of his main responsibilities to be on good terms with the most powerful trade union leaders, especially Jack Jones of the Transport Workers and Hugh Scanlon of the Engineers. In June 1973, Tony Benn, who was entertaining Jack Jones and Geoffrey Goodman of the *Daily Mail* to dinner, was surprised to learn of Jack Jones's high regard for Healey. Jones, adopting what Benn described as the Healey position, criticised Benn for his support for more nationalisation: 'Why don't you make a speech on pensions instead of all this airy-fairy stuff?' asked the Transport Workers' leader.[6] As well as getting on with union leaders, Healey hoped that he would be able to enlist their support for an incomes policy on the lines of the Swedish and Austrian models, in which strong trade unions co-operated with Social Democratic governments over a range of policies, including pay.

Denis was feeling his way as shadow Chancellor. He warned the 1972 party conference to be cautious about making election promises and made it clear that Labour would need a policy for prices and incomes. In 1973, he told conference there were going to be 'howls of anguish from the eighty thousand who are rich enough to pay over seventy-five per cent on the last slice of their income', though he did not say (as he was accused of saying) that his main aim was to make the rich howl with anguish or that he would squeeze the rich until the pips squeaked. In Parliament he spent most of his time attacking the Tory Chancellor, Tony Barber, a task that became easier after the oil price hike of autumn 1973. However, when Barber was forced to introduce a crisis spending-cuts package in December 1973, Healey's response was inadequate both in terms of rhetoric and content. As he later admitted, 'Many of my colleagues wondered whether I was up to the job.'[7] Certainly, Labour's most knowledgeable foreign affairs expert did not sound as if he had yet mastered economic policy.

In contrast, Tony Crosland was very much on top of his brief as shadow Environment Secretary. He produced a series of policy statements on housing. He led the committee stage attack on the Tory government's Housing Finance Bill, winning concessions from the government. Dennis Skinner, then a fierce young left-wing Derbyshire miners' MP known by the press as 'the Beast of Bolsover', paid Crosland a rare compliment: 'To people on the outside, he looked as if he was coasting along; they took him at face value. When you worked with him, you realised he was pulling more than his share.'[8] Even if Tony was not yet in a top shadow position, he was one of only a handful of opposition spokesmen who could speak with genuine authority in the House, as when he destroyed intellectually the government's plans for an air and seaport at Maplin on the south-east coast.

Relations between Crosland and Jenkins remained tense.[9] Foolishly, Tony Crosland was not initially invited to speak at a January 1973 dinner commemorating Hugh Gaitskell at which Roy Jenkins was to be the main speaker. After protests, including one from Hugh Gaitskell's widow, Dora, the omission was rectified. According to Susan Crosland, Roy was not on his usual oratorical form at the dinner and Tony, whose speech was short and crisp, was much the more effective. Tony said waspishly to Susan, 'Roy set it up. He chose the venue, then the weapons. Then he was routed. It's a nice little cameo.'

A few weeks later, following a *Sunday Express* article that said the two men were not speaking, Roy rang up Tony and suggested a pre-dinner drink at Lansdowne Road. After the usual preliminaries, the two old friends and their wives got down to 'serious conversation'. Jenkins made a somewhat lame apology for the Gaitskell dinner episode that Susan shot down by asking, 'Can you imagine any circumstances, Roy, in which Tony would have arranged such a dinner for Hugh without mentioning it to you?' Then Crosland complained about a recent speech by Jenkins berating Labour's collective leadership for giving way to the left. This was resented, said Tony, by those who attended party committee meetings each week (in Tony's case nine) to prevent the left getting their way, while Roy remained in the sidelines and wrote elegant and well-paid biographical pieces for *The Times*. Roy then attacked Crosland over his resignation: 'You could have stopped me.' When the two men next met, this time in a House of Commons lift, Tony said, 'We must have another of those conversations soon. Very enjoyable.' Roy replied, 'I suppose that any bridge building must be preceded by major excavation.'

Following his resignation, Jenkins now found himself in the difficult position, later occupied by Michael Heseltine after he had walked out of Mrs Thatcher's Cabinet in the 1980s, of being a 'loyal' rebel. Harold Wilson told the Speaker, Selwyn Lloyd, that Roy would retire to East Hendred and write books. Jenkins proved him wrong. He remained active in the House and spoke at by-elections up and down the country, only refusing to speak against his old ally, Dick Taverne, when he resigned to fight a by-election at Lincoln as an independent democratic Labour candidate. He did, however, campaign for me, the Labour candidate at Chester-le-Street, where there was a by-election taking place on the same day (1 March 1973) as at Lincoln.[10] Jenkins' canvassing style was idiosyncratic but surprisingly effective. Roy would knock at a door which would be opened by a housewife. He would then quickly put her at ease – talking not about politics but about the splendour of her carpets. Crosland and Healey went to speak for the official Lincoln Labour candidate, who was comfortably beaten by Taverne. Crosland's old Oxford and CDS friend, Philip Williams, wrote to Tony to say how disappointed he was to see Crosland bringing respectability to Labour's campaign at Lincoln, where the issue was one of bullying activists trying to take away control from the PLP.[11]

But if, unlike Crosland, Jenkins avoided going to the Lincoln by-election, Roy's underlying problem was that he did not have his heart in the cause for which he was campaigning. As he wrote later: 'Every bad by-election strengthened my position, every good one weakened it.'[12] Not wanting Labour to win became part of Jenkins' mindset. For the first time, his loyal lieutenant Bill Rodgers became aware of a difference of emphasis with Roy. Although Rodgers was deeply disapproving of Labour's behaviour over Europe and of the potential inflationary agreement with the unions, he still did not want Labour to lose. Rodgers was influenced by an additional factor: 'There was also more than a vague irritation tucked away inside me that Roy and his generation – meaning mainly Crosland and Healey – had somehow failed us and that Shirley and I and our contemporaries should not be deprived of having our chance in cabinet.'[13] Action was required from Jenkins.

If Roy was to remain a major politician, he had to make a positive move – either to stand against Wilson in 1973, or at least stand for re-election to the shadow Cabinet. But by that autumn, it became clear that, with a General Election in the offing, ranks were closing behind Wilson's leadership. By failing to mount a challenge in 1972, Jenkins had missed his opportunity. The only alternative was to try and return to the shadow Cabinet, a course of action that was urged on him by his most important allies in the PLP; by the band of moderate trade union leaders whom Jenkins met on a regular basis; and by Willy Brandt when Roy saw him in Bonn in October. After all, the issue on which he had resigned had been for the moment resolved in his favour and a prominent seat in the shadow Cabinet would at least restore him to Labour's inner leadership group in time for the election.

Jenkins agreed to stand and was elected fifth with 143 votes, only seven votes from the top which, in the circumstances, was a satisfactory result, though Callaghan and Crosland finished ahead of him. The question for Wilson was which office to ask Jenkins to shadow. The Labour leader did not want to move either Callaghan or Healey which left only the shadow Home Secretaryship. Though Jenkins was loath to replace the incumbent, his close ally Shirley Williams, in the end it seemed the logical choice. The difficulty for Roy was that the subject no longer excited him nor gave him a strong enough platform from which to win a leadership election.

One possibility, much discussed by the leading Jenkinsites, was that if Labour won the election Roy should become Chancellor again, especially as Denis Healey seemed to be struggling in the role of shadow Chancellor. In the same December 1973 economic debate in which Healey fluffed his opening speech on the second day, Jenkins wound up for the Opposition with magisterial authority, not only virtually destroying the Tory Chancellor single-handedly by the force of his oratory, but also raising the question of whether the right man was shadow Chancellor. Afterwards, excited Labour members were heard to say that it was one of the most devastating attacks made in the Commons since the war, while, during Jenkins' speech, Tories remained silent, always a good indication of a really powerful Labour contribution.[14] Yet, despite his Commons success, Roy was chary about pressing his claims as Chancellor. This was not out of any concern for Healey's position. It was more that he knew how difficult the job of Chancellor was likely to prove in the economic conditions of the 1970s and he doubted whether he would be able to carry a Labour Cabinet without the support of Wilson and other senior colleagues. Perhaps the most important factor of all was that Jenkins did not believe that Labour, with its policies on nationalisation and inflation, deserved to win a General Election. In David Owen's view, this was 'an untenable position', which prevented Jenkins acting with full effectiveness in the tricky circumstances of 1973–74.[15]

Labour did not win the February 1974 election. The Conservatives lost it. The Heath government's economic strategy had already been gravely weakened by the inflationary consequences of Barber's 1972–73 'dash for growth' and by rapidly rising world commodity prices when it was hit by OPEC's quadrupling of oil prices. The miners, well aware of the improvement in their bargaining position that followed the oil hike, backed up a claim for a thirty-five per cent wage increase (well above stage three of the government's incomes policy) with an over-time ban and threat of an all-out strike. Heath, who had been defeated by the miners in 1972, was determined not to give away again. On 1 January 1974, he put the country on a three-day week and on 9 January he rejected an offer from the TUC not to use a settlement with the miners as a basis for other trade union claims. Despite, or perhaps because of his obstinancy, the country appeared to be behind Heath.

The question was whether he should cash in on this support by call-ing a snap election, as the hawks in his Cabinet wanted, or soldier on to the autumn. It is possible that, if he had called an election for 7 February, he would have won. Instead he delayed three weeks, waiting until the miners had decided on a pithead ballot for a strike, before finally deciding on a 'Who runs the country?' election on 28 February. In a Commons speech in January, Denis Healey vividly explained his old Balliol colleague's psychology: 'There is an element of strong rigid-ity in his make-up which tends to petrify his whole personality in a crisis. He should never have allowed himself to be manipulated into this dead end by an oddly assorted quartet of his colleagues, who are now trundling him like a great marble statue towards the precipice.'[16]

It may seem curious for a government to ask the voters, 'Who gov-erns Britain?' but most of Labour's leaders, especially Jenkins, were pessimistic about the result, and certainly so when on 10 January an

NOP poll put the Tories four points ahead of Labour. Harold Wilson, expecting to lose, fought a low-key campaign, encouraging his three crown princes – Callaghan, Healey and Jenkins – to play a full part at the morning press conferences. Jenkins, who spoke at meetings up and down the country, was pleasantly surprised to be given the whole of one of the five party political television broadcasts. Roy's last encounter with Wilson before polling day was on the final Sunday when they spoke at a big Birmingham town hall meeting. Jenkins noted that he 'seemed tired, depressed and expecting defeat, keeping going with some difficulty and gallantry until by the Thursday night he would have completed his final throw in politics'.[17]

But, though Labour polled fewer votes than the Conservatives, and its share of the popular vote was lower than at any election since 1931, it won five more seats than the Tories. Even so, Labour was still thirty-four seats short of an absolute majority. The minority parties, with thirty-seven seats, now held the balance in a hung Parliament. However, though the voters' answer to Heath's question had been inconclusive, it left more cards in Harold Wilson's hands than in Edward Heath's. After the Tory Prime Minister had tried and failed over the weekend to stitch together a coalition with the Liberals, who, in terms of votes if not of seats, had made the most significant advance of any party, on the Monday evening the Queen sent for the Labour leader who proceeded to form a minority government.

One of Wilson's key decisions was who to make Chancellor of the Exchequer. According to Jenkins, strong hints emerged from the Wilson entourage over the weekend that, given the very difficult economic inheritance, Harold Wilson was inclined to offer the Treasury to Roy, who, in contrast to Healey, would have the big advantage of having been a successful Chancellor in a Labour government.[18] Roy, whose political strategy had assumed a Labour defeat, was 'dismayed rather than excited at the prospect of going back into office'. He was still doubtful about the Chancellorship (if he was given a choice, he would have preferred the Foreign Office) but, if Wilson was actually prepared to offer him the job, it was his duty to accept it, especially as his supporters were urging him to demand it. On Sunday at East Hendred, Jenkins worked himself up to draft an economic policy memorandum, which he discussed with some enthusiasm with David Owen on a walk after lunch at the Owens' house at Buttermere.

However, by Monday it became clear that Wilson had decided to stick to the existing shadow Cabinet dispositions and to give the Chancellorship to Healey and the Foreign Office to Callaghan, with the Home Secretaryship left open for Jenkins. Wilson explained to Jenkins that he had hoped to persuade Callaghan to take charge of industrial relations and switch Healey from the Treasury to the Foreign Office but Callaghan had insisted on being Foreign Secretary. Wilson offered to sweeten the pill by reuniting the Home Secretaryship with the Northern Ireland Office but Roy, perhaps wisely, turned down that idea out of hand, though he indicated that he would probably accept the Home Office. Wilson concluded by saying that if Jenkins wanted to be a semi-detatched member of the government, the Home Office would be a suitable department from which to play such a stand-off role.

When the Jenkinsites met that evening, they greeted the news that Roy was likely to become Home Secretary with dismay. Bill Rodgers said it was a massive defeat for Jenkins, adding cruelly, 'How many votes are there in prison reform?' He also asked Roy bluntly, 'Did you make clear you wanted the Treasury?'[19] The truth was that Jenkins had not put up much of a fight either for himself or for his supporters, though he spoke up for Shirley Williams. As he admitted later, he ought at least to have made it clear that his acceptance of the Home Office depended on all his colleagues who had resigned with him also being given positions. As it was, he spent much of the rest of the week trying to negotiate for his colleagues from a much weaker position. It was a far cry from the self-confident Jenkins of the 1960s who had spoken up so boldly for his allies.

It is unclear whether Jenkins could have won the Chancellorship if he had fought for it. Given Callaghan's longstanding wish to become Foreign Secretary, Wilson's idea of making room for Roy at the Treasury by moving Denis to the Foreign Office was a non-starter. In his autobiography, Jim Callaghan said, 'As we had previously arranged, the Prime Minister asked me to go to the Foreign and Commonwealth Office',[20] without mentioning any attempt by Wilson to put him in charge of industrial relations. It may be that Wilson never in fact put the proposition to him. Callaghan, who had made himself indispensable to Wilson, was certainly in an extremely strong political position to get what he demanded. However, Jenkins was also vital to Wilson, especially at the moment of his formation of his minority govern-ment. Roy could have tried to insist on a straight swap with Denis Healey, with Healey going to the Home Office instead of Jenkins, if his heart had really been set on the Treasury. As it was, by accepting the Home Secretaryship for the second time, Roy fatally weakened his chances of succeeding Wilson.

The new Wilson government was highly experienced; no fewer than fourteen ministers were Cabinet veterans. The centre-right trio of Callaghan, Healey and Jenkins in the top jobs were balanced by three middle-ranking, left-wing Secretaries of State – Michael Foot at Employment, Tony Benn at Industry, and Barbara Castle at Social Services. Tony Crosland was appointed Secretary of State for Environment, becoming responsible in the government for the subject which he had shadowed in opposition. But, if the personalities in Wilson's Cabinet were impressive, the government was singularly ill-prepared for power.

The Labour Party had not expected to win the election, which it had fought on a manifesto that was not much more than a collection of slogans. The so-called 'Social Contract' with the unions committed the government to a number of expensive measures without an equiv-alent commitment in restraint of wages by the unions. Joel Barnett, Chief Secretary to the Treasury, said that 'the only give and take in the contract was that the government gave and the unions took'.[21] It was hardly the right way to deal with a national crisis, with the miners out on strike, the balance of payments in substantial deficit, and the public finances in a mess.

The classically educated Chancellor, Denis Healey, commented, 'It was like the Augean Stables.'[22] Inflation was high and rising. The impact of the oil shock and the commodity boom presented a severe enough problem. But these difficulties were compounded by the so-called threshold agreements contained in stage three of the Heath government's incomes policy. The purpose of these had been to guar-antee that, beyond a seven per cent threshold, price increases would be automatically compensated for by wage increases. In a low-inflation economy, these agreements might have made sense but in the post-oil shock world they were bound to escalate prices still further. By October 1974, retail prices were as high as eighteen per cent higher than a year before and this triggered off more threshold agreements. The Labour government added another inflationary impulse of its own. It settled the miners' dispute on the miners' terms, which had a 'ripple' effect on other wage settlements. By mid-1975, the year-on-year inflation rate had reached a catastrophic twenty-eight per cent, a much higher level than that of other Western governments.

Healey was to serve as Chancellor, the most demanding job in the Cabinet, throughout the entire period of the Wilson and Callaghan governments of the 1970s. Edmund Dell, then Paymaster General and a great admirer, wrote that there were three Healeys.[23] First, there was the 'political' Chancellor of the first year in office; then the 'heroic' Chancellor who dominated the struggle for an incomes policy in 1975 and for an acceptable agreement with the IMF; then there was the third Healey, who had come through the fire and was resurrected as a political Chancellor, with his eye on another victory and on the succession to No 10.

During his first period as Chancellor, from February 1974 to the spring of 1975, Denis admitted that he was learning on the job. He certainly made big mistakes. Partly because of forecasting errors made by the Treasury, his first Budget was mildly inflationary. It increased rather than reduced the balance of payments deficit, added to the public sector deficit, and put additional pressure on inflation. Healey made much of the advice from the IMF and the OECD that industrial countries should not add to the deflationary impact of the increase in oil prices by trying to eliminate the deficit on their balance of payments too quickly, though it is doubtful whether it was really applicable to the United Kingdom with its limited financial reserves, a vast balance of payments deficit and with inflation rising to hyperinflationary levels. Politically, Healey's reflationary Budget, including the increases in pensions, the introduction of food subsidies and extra money for housing as well as more public spending increases in July, set the scene for the October 1974 election, which Labour narrowly won. However, economically, Healey's decision not to deflate in 1974 helped set off the process which led inexorably to the autumn crisis of 1976 that almost ruined him.[24]

While Healey was learning to be Chancellor, Crosland was very much on top of things in his vast Department of Environment, having worked so seriously at the shadow portfolio. One civil servant reported that, 'He was in complete charge, he knew what he wanted done, and what he wanted from his officials was the administrative drive and ingenuity to get them done.'[25] Within a week, his officials were implementing Crosland's request to freeze rents and by the second week a programme to increase council-house building was underway. Next, he cancelled Maplin. Writing himself a note at Easter, he reflected on a surprisingly satisfactory return to government. Wilson was 'much improved', the Cabinet was one of 'exceptional quality', and he himself was more relaxed this time, 'knowing a lot' and having a broad idea of what needed to be done, unlike his time at the Board of Trade, when he was overwhelmed 'by ignorance'. The return of an official car improved his efficiency and it was 'nice not worrying about money'.[26]

By the summer recess, Crosland was less satisfied with his progress but pleased that he had at least presided effectively over his unwieldy department without major 'cock-ups'. The Tory Housing Finance Act had been repealed and he had produced a White Paper on the public ownership of development land. But he admitted that nothing had been done on transport and the shift in the distribution of the Rate Support Grant in favour of the metropolitan areas was, he concluded, 'morally and socially absolutely right, but politically definitely wrong'.[27] According to some of his colleagues, he was now playing a major role in the Cabinet. At the July Public Expenditure Cabinet, Joel Barnett, Chief Secretary to the Treasury, reported that 'much the more effective contribution to the discussion came from Tony Crosland' and, at the August Cabinet meeting to discuss the Industry White Paper, Tony Benn complained, 'Clever Tony Crosland knows it all, very much disliking the policy, of course.'[28]

Soon after Tony became a Cabinet minister again, his last book, *Socialism Now*, was launched in a blaze of publicity. As Dick Leonard pointed out, *Socialism Now* was very different from *The Conservative Enemy*, his book of essays published in 1962. *The Conservative Enemy* was the work primarily of a man of ideas – the revisionist intellectual who had written *The Future of Socialism*. *Socialism Now* was written by a top-flight politician, over half the book was devoted to his speeches on departmental subjects – housing, the environment, and education and industrial policies.

Most people, however, read *Socialism Now* for its opening 12,000-word title essay. Basically its purpose was defensive, to protect the revisionist castle against onslaughts from both right and left, especially from the left. The Crosland of *Socialism Now* had little doubt that his earlier definition of socialism was right. After examing in turn the relationship of ownership to power, equality, economic performance and social behaviour, he saw 'no reason to abandon the revisionist analysis of socialism in favour of a refurbished Marxism. Developments in Britain during the last decade have been acutely disappointing to a democratic socialist, but the explanation does not appear to lie primarily in the British pattern of ownership.'[29] His view was that British society had proved difficult to change and that the Labour government had not shown a strong enough 'will to change'. Crosland concluded that 'a move to the left' was needed, not in the traditional sense of old-fashioned Clause IV Marxism but 'in the sense of a sharper delineation of fundamental objectives, a greater clarity about egalitarian priorities and a stronger determination to achieve them'.[30] In a side-swipe at Tony Benn, he said that greater equality and 'not spawning new pieces of state bureaucracy' should divide Labour from the Tories.

On the whole, *Socialism Now* was well received. The *Sunday Times* carried extensive extracts from the book that Tony Benn claimed to be a major attack on Labour Party policy. Benn bitterly noted, 'This is clearly the way Fleet Street is going to build up its campaign: Crosland is the hero, I am the villain.'[31] Tony King, Professor of Government at Essex University, described Crosland as 'probably the most important socialist writer Britain has produced'.[32] However, there were others, including some who were sympathetic to Crosland and the revisionist position, who felt his analysis was much more effective than his prescriptions, especially on how to achieve faster growth. In my review for *Socialist Commentary*, I asked whether the better-off majority really wanted more equality for the deprived minority and whether it was possible to increase public spending significantly or put up taxes without provoking an inflationary spiral. I concluded that there was a strong case for a *Future of Socialism* Mark II but, 'as he admits himself, Mr Crosland has not written it. But that does not mean that it does not need to be done.'[33] Crosland's reply was, 'Keynes didn't write another general theory.'

It was a disconsolate Roy Jenkins who became the first recidivist Home Secretary since Sir John Simon in the late 1930s. After his defeat over his appointment to the government, he also found that his sure touch on Home Office issues had temporarily deserted him. Unwisely, he decided to delay a decision on the right of women settled here, whether of British birth or recent immigration, to bring in their husbands, even though men retained the right. He also announced an amnesty for illegal immigrants on a Maundy Thursday when few members were in the House, which incensed the Conservative Opposition. According to Jenkins, he performed 'like some allegedly considerable tennis player putting ball after ball straight back into the net'.[34] He went away for Easter with low morale and for a month or so was in such a state that he was unwilling to take any decisions at all.

He was rescued from this depressed mood by two things. First was the appointment of Anthony Lester as his political advisor. Lester was a lively and self-confident thirty-seven-year-old Fabian barrister who has since become the most prominent human rights lawyer of his generation. The second was a sudden Home Office crisis, which brought out the best in Jenkins. The two Price sisters, who had been convicted of causing two major bombing explosions, decided to starve themselves to death in Brixton prison unless they were sent back to complete their sentence in Northern Ireland. Although Roy was in favour of their being transferred, he did not wish to be seen to be yielding to IRA pressure. Following Anthony Lester's advice, he issued a statement saying that he was not prepared to act under threat and that if the sisters were determined to kill themselves the Home Office would allow events to take their course. Jenkins' firm stand paid off. The Price sisters started eating again; they were transferred to the women's wing at Durham within a few weeks; and then, without publicity, they were allowed to go to Northern Ireland in March 1975.

Apart from advising the Home Secretary about the Price sisters issue, Anthony Lester helped give direction to Roy's human rights commitment. By the end of the summer, the Home Office produced a landmark Sex Discrimination White Paper proposing the outlawing of sex discrimination in employment and education and setting up the Equal Opportunities Commission; it became law the following year. Jenkins also published the first ever scheme for the independent review of complaints against the police and, in his last parliamentary session as a minister (1975–76), another Race Relations Act was passed, strengthening the 1969 legislation.

However, in contrast to his 1960s term as Home Secretary when his prime task was 'the opening of the windows of freedom', this time Roy saw his top priority 'as the maintenance of the proper authority of the state'.[35] The main threat was from IRA terrorism, which persisted throughout his second period in office. In September 1974 came the Guildford bombing, when two pubs, much used by army personnel, were blown up and five people were killed and many injured. In November followed the horrific explosions that wrecked two Birmingham pubs packed with young people, causing twenty-four deaths and injuring two hundred.

This second tragedy persuaded Jenkins to produce emergency legislation, the so-called Prevention of Terrorism (Temporary Provisions) Act, which was rushed through Parliament in eighteen hours and is still on the statute book today. This made the IRA an illegal organisation, empowered the police to detain terrorist suspects for at least forty-eight hours without charge, introduced tighter physical controls at the points of entry from both the northern and southern parts of Ireland, and, more controversially, enabled the Home Secretary, by a system of orders, to exclude from Great Britain potential terrorists from both the Republic and from Northern Ireland. At the special Cabinet called to approve these measures Jenkins met with considerable opposition to the exclusion orders, despite having Wilson's support, and had to hint at resignation to get his way. Afterwards, he noted that Crosland and Healey were 'cooly unhelpful',[36] an indication of Jenkins' isolation from his two former associates.

During this second term in government, Roy, although an active Home Secretary, was a somewhat detatched member of the government, mainly because he was unimpressed by the government's performance. He was unconvinced by Denis Healey's economic statement on 22 July 1974 which temporarily reduced the rate of inflation by decreasing VAT from ten to eight per cent and gave further subsidies to rates, rents and food. Following the July measures, Healey claimed that the three month rate of inflation was 8.4 per cent at an annualised rate, a claim which, as inflation steadily rose, was repeatedly thrown back at him by the Conservatives. Jenkins thought that Healey's approach was frivolous: 'like throwing stones at a potential avalanche, a dangerous pursuit'.[37]

On 26 July, Jenkins made a widely reported speech at

Haverfordwest, warning about Labour's shift to the left. Roy had told the Prime Minister about the speech at a friendly meeting he had with Wilson on 13 July. Wilson had wanted Jenkins to scotch the idea of a coalition. Jenkins agreed but said he would have to cover other points, including the need for a Labour government to respect the rule of law, to accept the mixed economy, and to remain a member of NATO. Jenkins' later comment was revealing about his state of mind: 'It could, I suppose, be argued that I was merely pontificating platitudes, but at a time when Benn was threatening most of industry, when Foot was running before the trade unions as well as bringing unilateralism into the heart of government, when half the Cabinet was in favour of coming out of Europe, and when even Crosland was putting the Clay Cross councillors above the law, they were not so platitudinous.'[38] The Clay Cross councillors, who had defied the Conservative government's law requiring local councils to increase rents, were threatened with automatic disqualification as well as £6000 fines. To considerable press criticism, Crosland introduced a general amnesty on disqualification, though the fines remained. Barbara Castle's comment when seeing Roy on television was, 'That has cost us the election.'[39] At a Cabinet sub-committee, Tony Benn overheard Tony Crosland ask Ted Short what he thought of the speech. 'Bloody awful,' barked Ted. 'I agree,' Tony Crosland replied, 'And if I'd had any doubt about it Tony Benn's glee would have convinced me.'[40] According to Jenkins, Crosland briefed the press against him, so bad were their relations.

On 30 July, Barbara Castle, who had had a close partnership in the 1960s with Roy when he was Chancellor and she First Secretary, had a private talk with him about the speech. According to her diary, Barbara said, 'Of course the press is waiting to egg you on: you are their mouthpiece for Europe and they are using you. But your friends ought to know better. They are driving you into a course that can only ruin your political career.' Jenkins replied, red in the face with sudden emotion, 'What makes you think I care about my political career? All that matters to me is what is happening in the world, which I think is heading for disaster.'[41] Looked at from the short-term perspective of the Labour Party about to fight a General Election, Jenkins' speech was clearly unhelpful. But, if the issue about what was happening to the Labour Party was becoming a matter of concern to a significant and electorally important body of moderate, uncommitted opinion as well as to the right wing of the PLP, then it was entirely understandable that Roy should wish to raise it. During the summer recess in Italy, Jenkins decided that he had no regrets about his Haverfordwest speech and reflected for the first time that 'the only way through the miasma might be outside the world of traditional two-party politics'.[42]

The period leading up to and immediately after the referendum of 1975 was the most productive of Harold Wilson's lacklustre 1970s government. Preparing for the referendum gave a direction to an otherwise directionless government, while the result of the referendum provided an impetus that enabled Wilson to curb the influence of the left, and for Healey to establish a more effective counter-inflation policy. The referendum campaign also threw a lifeline to Roy Jenkins.

It became clear soon after the October election of 1974 that Wilson and Callaghan intended the so-called renegotiation of the United Kingdom's terms of entry into the European Community, to which Labour had committed itself in opposition, to be successful. A key moment was the speech to the November party conference by Helmut Schmidt, who had become German Chancellor. Schmidt spoke brilliantly in flawless English. Barbara Castle, a fervent anti-marketeer, wrote in her diary on 30 November: 'It was a joy to hear how skilfully he dodged all the pitfalls and how cleverly he played all those emotions in the audience which were most likely to be favourable to him.' He appealed to delegates, who had just been listening to a sour debate about the so-called Shrewsbury Two (two building workers imprisoned for violence on the picket lines), to remember that Labour's sister parties on the continent wanted the United Kingdom to remain in the Community.

Schmidt, whom Benn called a German version of Denis Healey, received a standing ovation; he followed his speech up with successful talks with Wilson at Chequers as well as helping arrange a bilateral meeting between the British Prime Minister and the new French President, Valéry Giscard d'Estaing, in Paris the following month. In March 1975, following the Dublin EC summit meeting, Wilson and Callaghan announced that renegotiations had been a success, especially highlighting the way in which the controversial and costly UK contribution to the Community budget would now be related to gross national product.

Wilson, backed by his Foreign Secretary, then put the result of the negotiations and a recommendation to stay in, to a two-day Cabinet, which endorsed the terms by sixteen votes to seven. Jenkins, Healey and Crosland were this time united on the European issue. Denis, Roy noted, made the most effective positive case.[43] Tony Crosland described himself as an agnostic who was now convinced that there were strong arguments for staying in. Diplomatically Jenkins, who spoke late in the proceedings, said he had been wrong to underestimate the scope for improving the terms.[44]

There was also a big parliamentary majority in favour, though the PLP split marginally against remaining in (145 to 137). A special party conference on 26 April voted by nearly two to one against the terms negotiated by its own government, though, under pressure from Wilson, its impact was blunted by a prior agreement by the NEC that the party as such should not campaign. As a means of his keeping his Cabinet together, the Prime Minister decided that dissenting Cabinet ministers, including Tony Benn, Michael Foot, Peter Shore and Barbara Castle, should be free to campaign against the government's recommendations; in the same way, party members would have the right to differ from the conference decision.

Jenkins, who had decided to throw himself into the referendum campaign, was confident of victory. In the late 1960s and early 1970s, the polls had shown a consistent though shallowly based majority against entry. However, when the referendum faced voters with the need to give a real answer to the question 'Do you think that the United Kingdom should stay in the European Community?' opinion shifted. The highly uncertain economic and political background was certainly a factor. Christopher Soames, former ambassador in Paris and now senior British Commissioner was quoted as saying, 'This is no time for Britain to be considering leaving a Christmas club, let alone the Common Market.'[45]

The pro-European campaign was in a much stronger position than the anti-campaign, not only financially but more importantly because most of the acceptable faces in British public life were gathered together on the pro side. Roy became the president of the umbrella body, Britain in Europe, (BIE) with Willy Whitelaw, Reginald Maudling and Edward Heath, whom Margaret Thatcher had recently replaced as Tory leader. Heath and Thatcher were the Conservative

vice presidents, Jo Grimond and Jeremy Thorpe their Liberal counterparts. Significantly, a Harris poll taken at the beginning of the
campaign tested public reaction to twenty-two leading political figures
who were involved in it. Each of the fourteen names from the 'yes'
campaign drew a positive response. Six out of the eight antis, especially Enoch Powell, Tony Benn and Ian Paisley, elicited a negative
reaction.[46]

For Jenkins, the referendum was a personal triumph. He wrote in
his memoirs: 'It is a perverse but indisputable fact that the event I most
enjoyed during 1974–76 . . . was the one for which I had striven most
officiously, even to the point of resignation, which may have cost me
the Prime Ministership, to prevent taking place.'[47] As leader of the
pro-European coalition, Roy became involved in a series of morning
press conferences with politicians of other parties; in BIE and the
Labour Campaign for Europe meetings up and down the country, in
the specially made propaganda films; and in a number of key television
debates.

During the campaign he had two clashes with Tony Benn, who
had emerged as the main standard bearer of the 'no' campaign. To
Wilson's anger, Roy dismissed Benn's specious claim that entry had
already cost half a million jobs with the remark that he found it
increasingly difficult to take Benn seriously as an economic minister.
Then, in the last week of the campaign, Jenkins met his fellow
Cabinet minister in an unprecedented forty-five minute *Panorama*
programme that was watched by an estimated nine million people.
This time both the men were polite to each other. Jennifer Jenkins felt
that her husband had let Benn get away with too much. But it made
no difference to the result. At 5.15 p.m. on the Friday following referendum day on Thursday 5 June, Jenkins called his last press
conference, flanked by Willie Whitelaw, Jo Grimond and Vic Feather,
representing the TUC, to celebrate a smashing two to one victory for
the 'yes' campaign on a fifty-eight per cent turn-out. Roy said that the
result far exceeded pro-European expectations, referred to a 'day of
jubilation' and recalled that it was the thirty-first anniversary of D-
Day, 6 June 1944.

The British people had voted to stay in partly for economic reasons
(they felt that their economic wellbeing was more likely to be secure
inside rather than outside) and partly for political reasons. Voters often

said that they were voting for their children's or grandchildren's sake. It is simply not true to say that the sovereignty issue was never debated – it was raised by both sides. In answer to the antis charge about loss of sovereignty, the 'yes' campaign document, whose final draft was written by Jenkins, argued that 'so much of the argument about sovereignty is a false one'. Sovereignty was not a dry as dust issue but something that had to be tested in the real world. Staying in would give us greater influence: voting to leave would mean that we would have no say over crucial decisions: 'We should be clinging to the shadow of British sovereignty while its substance flies out of the window.'[48]

If the referendum result was a victory for Jenkins, it was in some ways a vindication of Harold Wilson's strategy. Pro-Europeans could argue that Wilson's behaviour in opposition had helped create the situation in which a referendum had become necessary. But, in government, he had skilfully used the referendum 'to keep his party in power and in one piece and Britain in Europe'.[49] During the referendum, he remained aloof from the official 'yes' campaign, intervening towards the end with a few well-publicised speeches; mixing his metaphors, he argued that Britain would not keep its world influence 'by taking our bat home and sinking into an offshore mentality'.[50] Callaghan made his contribution in similar fashion, though Healey made only one significant intervention, in order to refute Benn's claim about the impact of entry on jobs.

Crosland compaigned more vigorously. Telling Bill Rodgers that he had made a mistake four years before, he made a number of speeches for the Labour Campaign for Europe.[51] At the opening press conference of LCE, he said that 'to withdraw now would create in this country a mood of poor man's inchoate chauvinism, reviving old dreams of Empire and special relationships that have had such disastrous effects on British policy-making since 1945'. When he complained to Dick Leonard that his speeches received little coverage, his former PPS replied, 'The campaign has been carefully calculated as a means of putting Roy back into the political race, and at each and every press conference, several Jenkinsites . . . are there in the back row to brief the press.'[52] Even though he was no longer the front-runner to succeed Wilson, Jenkins still had the support of a devoted band of MPs who, like the author, admired his principled stand on Europe, his style and his charm.

Jenkinsites may have tried to use the referendum to boost Roy's chances of leading the Labour Party. But its effect on Roy was to make him less enthusiastic about leading it. When he met Wilson on 19 March to inform the Prime Minister that he intended to lead the 'yes' campaign, Callaghan, who was also present (Callaghan made himself so indispensable to Wilson that he was often present at crucial meetings), warned Jenkins that leading a cross-party organisation would undoubtedly do him harm in the party. Roy replied, 'For a long time, you and I have taken different views both about how important the party is and about what one does in it, so I don't think we will gain anything by arguing that at this stage.'[53] In 1975, Jenkins found himself increasingly alienated both from the party and from the Labour government which, with considerable justice, he believed was failing to deal effectively either with inflation or with the demands of the unions. If Wilson's fears that Jenkins was about to form a coalition with left-wing Tories were greatly exaggerated, it was undoubtedly true that Roy had found working with moderate Tories and Liberals on the European issue 'a considerable liberation of the spirit' and that his 'heart had been much more in those large Britain in Europe meetings than in any Labour Party gathering for some time past'. As he said to the celebratory Britain in Europe dinner, they had all had an excursion away from their domestic hearths and their humdrum lives 'were never going to be quite the same again'.[54]

Roy Jenkins wrote that the second half of 1975 was 'anticlimatic'.[55] It may have been an anticlimax for him but for the government as a whole it marked a step forward. On 10 June, Wilson moved Tony Benn from Industry to Energy, which effectively muzzled the new darling of the left, at least for a time. Barbara Castle, who was irritated by Benn's populism, called it 'the cleverest move that Harold could make'.[56] More important, the Chancellor of the Exchequer at last began to get a grip on economic policy.

It was about time too. Healey had allowed the economy to get alarmingly out of balance. In 1974, the UK had run up a record current account deficit, amounting to more than five per cent of GDP. The public sector borrowing requirement was forecast to rise to over £10 billion. Inflation was rising to Latin American levels. Action had to be taken speedily if a sterling crisis was to be avoided. His April Budget, which increased both direct and indirect taxes, was mildly deflationary. In May Healey proposed a £3 billion package of cuts and higher charges, which the Cabinet, led by Tony Crosland, as always the defender of public spending, decided to defer until July, though Crosland had himself warned local authorities that 'the party's over'.

The most immediate issue for Healey was to halt the appalling wage–price spiral. The prime cause of accelerating inflation was now the rapid increase in wages. Wage settlements were already running at over twenty per cent and there was talk of claims of up to forty per cent. The so-called Social Contract with the unions had not only failed; it was itself highly inflationary. Denis Healey realised that if he was to save the economy from hyper-inflation and a run on the pound, he had to persuade the Cabinet and the unions to accept an incomes policy. On 20 June he told an all-day Cabinet meeting on economic strategy at Chequers, 'We must have a credible policy by the end of July'.[57]

Edmund Dell, Paymaster General and effectively Healey's number two at the Treasury, wrote: 'Only the most heroic efforts by Healey brought the unions to recognise the dangers of hyper-inflation and to accept their responsibility in the matter.'[58] With the assistance of Jack Jones, General Secretary of the Transport Workers, he persuaded the TUC to agree to a flat rate limit of £6 per week, with zero increases for those earning above £8500. In the first instance, the policy was to be a voluntary one, though it was backed by the government's threat to legislate immediately against employers who broke the policy. On 11 July, Wilson announced the change of direction in a White Paper, *The Attack on Inflation*, to the House of Commons but it was Healey, with the help of Jack Jones, who had saved the government. At last, it had a policy that assisted rather than undermined the struggle against rising prices. Inflation fell from 26.9 per cent in August 1975 to 12.9 per cent in July 1976. For his success on the economic front, Healey had to pay a political price; in September the left voted him off the National Executive of the Labour Party.

On 16 March 1976, Harold Wilson told his astonished Cabinet that he was resigning as Prime Minister and party leader. His exit, on or about his sixtieth birthday, had been planned ever since the October 1974 election. There is no evidence for later theories that Wilson was being hounded by the Secret Service or being blackmailed into resignation. His biographer concluded, after examining the evidence, that there was no need for any explanation 'other than the waning of the appetite for a physically and mentally exhausting office of a Prime Minister who had held it for a very long time'.[59]

He kept his departure a closely guarded secret, though the Cabinet Minister, Harold Lever, and his personal lawyer, Lord Goodman, were in the know. Wilson had told Denis Healey in 1972 that if Labour won, he did not intend to serve another full term as Prime Minister, while, in December 1975, Harold Lever had informed Healey that he thought Wilson would soon announce his retirement. Roy Jenkins received a similar though more precise message from Arnold Goodman, who took him aside at a Boxing Day party given by Ann Fleming to tell him that the Prime Minister was probably going to resign on his birthday. Significantly, the first of the potential candidates to whom Wilson spoke personally about his intentions was Jim Callaghan when they were passengers together in the Prime Minister's ministerial car on the way to the 10 p.m. vote on the night of Wilson's birthday on 16 March. Like Healey, Callaghan had already been tipped off by Harold Lever about Wilson's impending resignation and, despite being nearly four years older than Wilson, had decided to run.

Most Labour MPs, whose votes decided the issue, expected Callaghan to win. It was not so much his wide ministerial experience. Though his posts included the Treasury, the Home Office and the Foreign Office, his record in office was open to criticism. Denis Healey, who was an admirer of Callaghan as Prime Minister, commented that he was 'not particularly distinguished as Chancellor, as Home Secretary (except over Northern Ireland) or even as Foreign Secretary'.[60] Callaghan's great advantage as leader was his acceptability to Labour MPs and the party as a whole. Tony Crosland's former PPS, Dick Leonard, remarked that the Callaghanites were not a distinctive grouping at all but rather made up 'of the least imaginative members of the PLP plus those with a sharp eye for the main chance'.[61] But Leonard's harsh verdict misses the point that, in the febrile state of the Labour Party in spring 1976, Callaghan was the natural unifying candidate, 'more so than either Foot on the left or Jenkins on the pro-market right, more personally approachable than Healey and with more weight than Crosland.'[62]

Roy Jenkins had already by chance arranged a meeting of his

supporters to be held immediately after Cabinet; the consensus was that the odds had moved against Roy, but that 'victory remained a possibility'. Callaghan, Foot and Jenkins were nominated almost immediately after the PLP had agreed the electoral arrangements. The question was who else would enter the field. Tony Benn threw his hat in the ring 'to fight on the issues', and Crosland after some hesitation, decided to stand. His handful of supporters bluntly told Tony that he was very unlikely to get through the first ballot. Crosland ignored this discouraging advice: 'Pride was involved: could he stand back and seem to acknowledge that others who had put their names on the sheet were better than he?'[63] He described himself on television as a radical moderate who would draw support from the 'common ground that unites left and right'.[64]

Denis Healey delayed making his decision. The week before he had a noisy public row with left-wing Tribunite MPs. These MPs had abstained in the debate on the Public Expenditure White Paper which proposed £3 billion cuts by 1978–79. The abstention led to a government defeat and, in the confidence vote that followed next day, Denis Healey had torn a strip off them in his winding-up speech. In the lobbies, fierce words were exchanged between the Chancellor and his critics. The Chief Secretary, Joel Barnett, told Healey that his aggressive behaviour had offended a number of moderate backbenchers who felt that a Prime Minister would need to handle the left with greater subtlety than he had shown. However, Crosland's candidature, combined with pressure from his Treasury colleagues and also a distaste for appearing to run away, finally persuaded Healey to stand.

The key issue of the first ballot was to decide which candidate of the centre-right – Callaghan or Jenkins – would take on Michael Foot in the second or third ballot. In this context, the fact that both Healey and Crosland were standing hurt Jenkins more than Callaghan. Roy had a hard core of about forty to fifty devoted pro-Europeans, led by Bill Rodgers, which he had to expand if he was to equal or surpass Callaghan. The candidatures of Healey and Crosland took out of play votes that might otherwise have gone to him on the first ballot. What was even more serious for the Jenkins cause was that between fifteen and twenty pro-European MPs who would have voted for him four years before now went to Callaghan. They included Roy Hattersley, future deputy leader, John Smith, future leader, Cledwyn

Hughes, the chairman of the PLP, and Ernest Armstrong, future Deputy Speaker.

Ernest Armstrong, MP for North-West Durham, who had admired Roy for many years, told him that 'the party was in such a fragile state that it needed Callaghan's more mollifying bedside manner'.[65] The reason Roy Hattersley gave for not voting for Jenkins was ideological. Roy Jenkins had made a somewhat hyperbolic speech in Anglesey in which he claimed that the level of public spending compatible with a pluralistic democracy was about to be reached in the United Kingdom. Hattersley, who was (and is) very much an intellectual disciple of Crosland, gave this as his reason for not voting for Jenkins, though he also told Crosland that he was supporting Callaghan for fear of splitting the vote and letting Foot in.

If Jenkins' campaign was in trouble, Crosland's and Healey's never got off the ground. Crosland had a small team, including Gordon Oakes, a junior minister at the DOE, Peter Hardy, his PPS, Bruce Douglas-Mann, a bright centrist MP, and Bruce Grocott, a Tribunite who later became Tony Blair's PPS. George Cunningham, an independent-minded Labour MP, told Tony that he would be voting for him and added, 'Mind you, if the press knew the motley collection of screwballs and crackpots who make up your basic support, you'd be finished for good.'[66] Crosland conspicuously failed to get any backing from pro-European Labour MPs. In short, he had alienated his old friends without building up an alternative power base inside the party.

Healey's level of support was not much more impressive than Crosland's. He was a 'loner', who, unlike Callaghan or Jenkins, had not bothered to build up a network of allies in the PLP. In the 1976 campaign, he depended almost entirely on his Treasury team, Edmund Dell, Joel Barnett, Bob Sheldon, Denzil Davies, and on one present and one former PPS, Harry Lambourn and Barry Jones. Harold Lever, who respected the Chancellor and did not want to see him humiliated, also voted for him.

When the first ballot was announced to the PLP on Thursday 25 March, Foot topped the poll with ninety, Callaghan was next with eighty-four, Jenkins had fifty-six, Benn thirty-seven, Healey thirty, Crosland seventeen. As he had come bottom, Crosland was automatically eliminated and Benn also announced that he was withdrawing his name from the second ballot. As soon as the party meeting was over, Jenkins' key workers met in their candidate's room to be told that he too had decided to withdraw. With two exceptions, they accepted his decision. His campaign manager, Bill Rodgers, had predicted that Roy would get at least sixty-eight votes. With Callaghan so obviously ahead, fifty-six was unlikely to be enough as a base to fight on, even if he was able to pick up a good proportion of the Crosland and Healey votes. Jenkins wrote later: 'The country, I thought, needed a new Prime Minister quickly, and not the long drawn-out agony of a third or even a fourth, slow round, and from fifty-six votes that Prime Minister was not going to be me.'[67]

When David Owen told Barbara Castle that Jenkins was withdrawing, she was staggered and commented in her diary: 'This further display of political daintiness proves conclusively what I have always known: that Jenkins will never lead the Labour Party. I bet Denis stays in the ring despite his derisory thirty votes. But then, he's a pugilist, not a patrician.'[68] Although Healey only got another eight votes on the second ballot, he fought on in part to make a point for the future, not only about himself but also about Jenkins.

It was certainly the case that in 1976 Roy Jenkins' desire to lead the Labour Party was weaker than it had been in the 1960s or early 1970s. He was ambivalent about it, otherwise he would either not have made his Anglesey speech about public spending or at least he would have toned it down. He certainly would have been more assiduous in mending fences, especially after Lord Goodman's Boxing Day news. There was an additional factor of which his supporters were not aware.

Before his resignation, Wilson had offered Roy the first refusal of the presidency of the Commission, which both the German Chancellor, Helmut Schmidt, and the French President, Valéry Giscard d'Estaing, wanted him to accept. After first rejecting the offer out of hand, he subsequently asked for more time to consider it. As he wrote in the introduction to his *European Diary*, it would be an opportunity to do something new and in which he believed 'much more than in the economic policy of Mr Healey, the trade union policy of Mr Foot or even the foreign policy of Mr Callaghan'.[69] It was perhaps not just his defeat but the possibility (unknown to his friends) that he might leave British politics that accounted for the quotation to his supporters of General Robert E. Lee's message to the Confederate Army in the American Civil War and for the elegiac tone of voice with which Roy read it, especially the last line: 'With an increasing admiration of your courtesy and devotion to your country and a grateful remembrance of your kind and generous consideration for myself, I bid you all an affectionate farewell.'[70]

In the third and final ballot, Callaghan beat Foot by 176 to 137 – a comfortable victory. The composition of the PLP in the 1974–79 Parliament ensured that, in most circumstances, whoever was the standard bearer of the centre-right in the final ballot would win. In this context, it is intriguing to note that the combined Jenkins/Healey/Crosland first ballot vote came to 103, nineteen votes more than Callaghan's 84. But, in contrast to what happened in the 1994 leadership election when Brown stood down for Blair, there was never any prospect in 1976 of two of them standing down for the third.

Crosland had firmly rejected Jenkins' overtures back in 1971, while relations between Healey and Jenkins were distinctly cool. Denis resented Roy's Anglesey speech about public spending, especially as he was struggling to bring it under control and because he knew that Roy's warnings were not only based on the most unfavourable definition of public spending but, more importantly, were likely to worry, though for different reasons, both the markets and the unions. Jenkins, for his part, was angry with Healey for his protests about the speech and for his failure in September 1975 to support the then Labour Cabinet minister, Reg Prentice, who was under threat of deselection, at a public meeting in his constituency. A revealing conversation took place at that time between the two men that contained the following exchange: 'I don't want to be a politician like you, Roy,' said Denis. 'You are not concerned with the centres of power.' 'What about your centres of belief, Denis?' replied Roy. The good working relationship of the 1960s had degenerated into mutual recrimination. As to the relationship between Crosland and Healey, Crosland was increasingly the main opposition to Healey in Cabinet. When Wilson stood down, Tony discussed the leadership issue with Healey's campaign manager, Joel Barnett, but never spoke to Healey himself who, in any case, took his own decision about standing.

There were clear differences of approach between the three men. Jenkins was the believer in Europe, concerned about the inadequacy of the government and about the drift to the left in the party. Healey was the tough pragmatist, now intent on getting the country out of the mess for which his decisions (or lack of them) in 1974 had been in part responsible. Crosland was the government's leading revisionist thinker and Keynesian intellectual who thought he could bring together right and left. All three could make plausible cases for their candidatures. Jenkins had been waiting eight years for the opportunity. It was his misfortune that it occurred four years too late. It came a little too early for Healey, despite his pivotal position as Chancellor and his confidence in his ability to do the job of Prime Minister. Arguably, however, if neither Jenkins nor Crosland had stood, Healey, without the stigma of Europe, might have had the best chance of the three of winning. Though he knew that his middle-ranking position in the Cabinet counted against him, Crosland was driven to stand by vanity, stubbornness and a kind of recklessness. If Jenkins and Healey stood, why shouldn't he? In the end ego not logic determined the decisions of all three.

Of course, even if two out of Crosland, Healey and Jenkins had stood down, there is no guarantee that their combined vote could have been transferred to the one candidate. There were certainly many Labour MPs on the centre-right, probably the majority, who wondered why on earth the three men, who, despite everything, still had more in common than separated them, could not get together and sort things out. But there were others who only emphasised the differences. A number of pro-European Jenkinsites still had not forgotten the behaviour of Crosland and Healey over Europe in 1971 and 1972, while Croslandites charged Jenkins not only of not being a real socialist but, even worse, a 'crypto-coalitionist'. Supporters of Healey claimed that Jenkins was now too divisive and Crosland not decisive enough to be elected as leader of the Labour Party, in contrast to their candidate.

In one way, these divisions between three men, who had been and in many ways still were natural allies, only highlighted what a formidable candidate for the leadership Jim Callaghan was, given the divided nature of the Labour Party in the 1970s and the existence of a strong left wing. His age was more an advantage than a disadvantage. Indeed, many observers believed that, even if only one of the three had been running against him, he would have still carried the day. However, undoubtedly the intense rivalry between the three most prominent revisionist modernisers in the party made it absolutely certain that the least challenging candidate of the centre-right was the one who became leader of the party and Prime Minister.

Yet, after Wilson's tired performance during the end of his term in office, the arrival of Callaghan was like a breath of fresh air. His bluff, no-nonsense approach, after the evasions of the Wilson era, seemed just what the country needed. His remark to an aide after entering No 10 gives the flavour of the man: 'There are many cleverer people than me in the Labour Party, but they're there and I'm here.'[71] Healey, somebody who everybody, including himself, recognised as being clever, wrote about Callaghan: 'When Wilson's resignation offered him the unexpected opportunity, Callaghan pursued it with resolution. Once Prime Minister, he had no ambition except to serve his country well. The political skills he had perfected in his unregenerate days were just what his office needed.'[72] Jenkins noted: 'I regarded Jim Callaghan as a bit of a bully. I did not greatly mind for I thought that after the very easygoing regime of Wilson's final days a bit of bullying might do the government no harm.'[73]

Callaghan acted decisively in the making of his Cabinet. Michael Foot, representing the left, and with his links to the trade unions, became Leader of the House and effectively Deputy Prime Minister. Denis Healey remained as Chancellor of Exchequer, by 1976 increasingly formidable in the post. The surprise appointment was Tony Crosland who was made Foreign Secretary.

Roy Jenkins had expected to be offered the Foreign Office, though, if the offer had been made, he might still have opted for the presidency of the Commission, which had first been suggested by Wilson. Instead, when he first saw Callaghan on the morning of 6 April, the new Prime Minister made it clear that the Foreign Office was not to go to Jenkins (curiously he did not say to whom the job was to go), though the Home Office was available and there might be the prospect of the Exchequer in the Autumn.

The story behind the blackballing of Jenkins was that Foot had insisted to Callaghan that the left did not want Jenkins as Foreign Secretary, while, in his memoirs, Callaghan wrote that, though Jenkins was well qualified, 'every action he would have taken as Foreign Secretary would have been regarded with deep suspicion by the anti-marketeers on our benches'.[74] Callaghan, in any case, much preferred

Crosland, who was his personal friend, to Jenkins, who had been his rival for nearly a decade. The new Prime Minister may also have calculated that, by closing off the options for Jenkins in this country and by renewing the European presidency offer, he would rid himself of a Cabinet minister who might prove a disruptive force, though Callaghan was punctilious enough to point out to Jenkins that his succession was open – he would not remain long in the job – and that having been in Brussels, it would be difficult to get back into a Labour seat. When Callaghan made these points again to Jenkins in July, Roy gave the significant reply that he did not want a future in British politics in their existing shape.

Was Jenkins right to leave for Brussels and was it sensible of the Labour Party to let him go? First, Roy was genuinely attracted by the prospect of being the UK's first (and, until now, only) President of the Commission. He saw it as an important job that would give him, as a convinced European, the opportunity to help lead the re-launch of the European Community after a stagnant period following the oil crisis. Secondly, he was thoroughly fed up with the Labour Party, as his remark to Callaghan showed. Bill Rodgers took the view that Jenkins was right to go: 'He had no great taste for narrow party politics or the messiness of internal party warfare. If the Labour Party was fast becoming ungovernable, Roy, as a potential leader, was clearly out of time.'[75] Callaghan put much the same point in a blunter way when he told Rodgers that Roy lacked the will to fight.

On the other hand, many MPs wanted Jenkins to stay because they thought that Labour could ill afford to lose a politician of his ability and integrity. Denis Healey, who had a high opinion of Roy's capacities, told Callaghan that he ought to make Jenkins Foreign Secretary and another old Balliol colleague, Edward Heath – his political opponent, but fellow pro-European – believed that Jenkins was wrong to have chosen Brussels. There is no evidence, however, that Tony Crosland lifted a finger to stop his old friend leaving. Certainly, for both Roy Jenkins and the Labour Party, his departure for the European Commission represented a parting of the ways that was later to have a significant impact on British politics.

As a Labour politician, Jenkins had been a brilliant Home Secretary, a good Chancellor and a competent Home Secretary the second time around. His courage had kept the European cause alive inside the

party at a difficult time. Like Nye Bevan, he had the capacity to attract
and maintain the loyalty of a devoted band of adherents. But his attitude to his party was far removed from the romantic view of Tony
Crosland or even the more pragmatic attitude of Denis Healey. Roy's
party roots were impeccable but he was extremely fastidious about his
use of them. A former Labour colleague said of him, 'If Roy had played
the Welsh Valley card, he would have been unstoppable.'[76] He was
comfortable with Gaitskell's and Wilson's meritocratic, modernising
party of the 1960s, but found the corporatist, leftwards leaning party of
the 1970s increasingly distasteful. Above all, despite his deserved reputation for ambition, he had, in the final analysis, an ambivalent view
of power. His close colleague, Shirley Williams, said that 'he became
more ambivalent about the leadership, the nearer he got to it'.[77] There
was a part of himself that he was not prepared to sacrifice for its pursuit.

11

The IMF Crisis and the
Death of Crosland

The new Prime Minister, James Callaghan, recorded his first conversation with his Chancellor, Denis Healey. 'I was shocked when he told me how much had been spent by the Bank of England to support the sterling exchange rate since 1 January 1976. Denis added that we might need to make an approach to the IMF during the summer to replace the reserves we had spent.'[1]

It was an early warning that 1976 was to be a year dominated by the weakness of sterling and by the government's request for a loan from the IMF. The IMF crisis, as it came to be known, shook the Labour government to its foundations and called into question the postwar consensus over economic policy. It was also the occasion of a long drawn-out struggle between the two leading contenders for the succession to Callaghan between Denis Healey, the pragmatic realist, and Tony Crosland, the revisionist intellectual.

In 1976, the most critical time for his Chancellorship, Healey, who was in his fifty-ninth year, was at the height of his powers. He needed to be, because he was under the most intense pressure from the markets, the IMF, foreign governments – especially the United States – from the Cabinet, his parliamentary and party colleagues, and from his trade union allies. Only his intellectual ability, endurance and sheer force of personality and will enabled him to survive the crisis.

By 1976, Healey had become increasingly confident of his judgement as Chancellor. Learning to run the economy in a new world of floating exchange rates, he had lost faith in the Keynesian orthodoxy of demand management that many of his advisors and officials espoused. In his autobiography, he wrote: 'I abandoned Keynesianism in 1975 . . . his theories had two important weaknesses . . . They ignored the economic impact of social institutions, particularly the trade unions. And they ignored the outside world.'[2] Healey had experienced at first hand the enormous power of financial markets to influence exchange rates and he came to understand the brutal reality that economies in substantial deficit, like the UK's, were liable to be punished by the markets. He said in his 1975 Budget speech, 'By relying unduly on borrowing we would run the risk of being forced to accept political and economic conditions imposed by the will of others.'[3] In economics, as in the rest of his politics, he developed into an eclectic pragmatist who believed, above all, in the importance of judgement based on the ascertainable facts of any given situation. In many ways, Healey was the first modern British Chancellor.

Denis now dominated the Treasury almost as much as he had the Ministry of Defence. At first, he had been uncertain of his opinions, and Treasury mandarins were less than impressed with the first year of his Chancellorship. But Healey grew in stature and, as his second-in-command at the Treasury, Edmund Dell, wrote later, he came 'to be admired for the excitement he generated and feared for his penetration of official work less than first class'.[4] Officials came to respect his intellectual stamina and his ability to preside over long, difficult and crowded meetings without flagging. As Chancellor, he sat on more Cabinet committees than any other minister, as well as taking the chair at the most important. He also had weekly meetings with Callaghan. The so-called Social Contract and, above all, its development into an incomes policy brought him into close contact with the most prominent trade union leaders, including Jack Jones and Hugh Scanlon. He used to meet them over dinner in the eighteenth century Soane Room at No 11 Downing Street; Scanlon insisted on a fish course of goujons de sole. Denis's style on these occasions was to combine earthy banter with hard bargaining, an approach that trade unionists appreciated.

As Chancellor, Healey worked harder and longer hours than even at the Ministry of Defence. The work was nearly all intellectually demanding and often strained him to the limit. He admitted to going to bed usually 'dog-tired'.[5] Inevitably the strain took its toll. He looked bulkier and his complexion became more florid. He suffered frequently from colds and flu, had trouble with his teeth and endured a painful attack of shingles.

Unlike Roy Jenkins, he did not find distraction in social life. His solace was his family; at weekends, he escaped with Edna to their country cottage at Withyham, where he worked hard in his garden. In 1975 the Healeys sold their Highgate house and bought a large family house, designed by a pupil of Lutyens and situated on the Sussex downs near Alfriston. It had four acres of garden and rough grass, commanded sweeping views down to the sea, and rapidly became their 'earthly paradise' and bolt-hole. It also provided space for Denis's grand piano and his substantial library. Despite the pressure, Denis was still Denis. He pulled silly faces at his children and played practical jokes on their friends. Those who rang his private number might sometimes, to their surprise, be answered in fractured English by someone who claimed to be from the local Chinese laundry. It was, of course, Denis Healey playing the fool.

The new Foreign Secretary, Tony Crosland, would much rather have been Chancellor. He had desperately wanted the Chancellorship when Jenkins got the job in 1967; he had asked for the shadow post when Wilson made Healey shadow Chancellor in 1972; and in Cabinet he had spent the last two years building himself up as the alternative Chancellor. Apart from his contacts with socialists abroad, he knew little about foreign affairs. And he always disliked doing something he had not thought through first. On the other hand, the Foreign Office was one of the three top jobs in government and, according to the briefing from No 10, there was the prospect of a switch between Healey and Crosland within the next eighteen months. No wonder that a fortnight after finishing a derisory bottom in the leadership election he felt able to send a message back to his wife, waiting at Lansdowne Road for the news about the new Prime Minister's appointments, saying he was feeling 'fairly cheerful' and would be home for lunch. Apart from anything else, he had got the position that his old friend and rival Roy Jenkins had coveted and was now, with Healey, one of the two crown princes most likely to succeed to Callaghan's throne, with Roy relegated to continental exile.

The Tony Crosland who, in his fifty-eighth year, had been appointed Foreign Secretary was a very different person from the intellectual in his late thirties who had written *The Future of Socialism*. For one thing, he looked much older, with bags under his eyes and the slower movements of someone approaching his sixties. With his high blood pressure, he no longer had quite the energy or creative drive of his younger days. He was, however, a far more serious politician and a much more contented man.

Tony's life had been transformed by his marriage to Susan. His wife, his stepchildren and his home in Lansdowne Road provided him with a haven from his stressful life. His Permanent Secretary at the Department of Environment, Sir Ian Bancroft, highlighted what mattered to Crosland: 'His interest in politics, international, national, party. His immense preoccupation with family; it was never overtly mentioned, it was just evident. Grimsby. Football and all that. His writing. What he showed not the slightest interest in was social life; he'd been through that.' During a visit to Central America in 1975, he asked his private secretary after a party given in his honour what he would most like at that moment. His private secretary was noncommittal; Tony was quite certain: 'I'd like to be instantly home with my wife.'[6]

In 1975, the Croslands took out a second mortgage and bought Adderbury, a converted mill three miles south of Banbury, for £45,000. It had a brook at the bottom of the garden, which ran riot over half an acre. It became their pride and joy and refuge from London, Whitehall and Westminster. Crosland even suggested to his wife that they spend their August together in their new country house. This was a radical proposal, because in August Tony usually went alone to France or Italy for three weeks, while Susan saw her family and friends in the United States; they called it 'recharging batteries'. 'Think I like Adderbury best of all in the winter,' decided Tony, 'gives an even greater sense of our being alone together.'[7]

Crosland's predecessor at the Foreign Office, Jim Callaghan, came to the job with experience. He had been shadow Foreign Secretary and his work as Chancellor had also given him a good background.

Crosland brought with him his devoted diary secretary, Maggie Turner, from the Department of Environment and his political advisor, David Lipsey. Otherwise, as his friend Bill McCarthy put it, he 'was dropped from the skies into the FO'.[8] As always when entering a new department, Tony was unwilling to commit himself until he had mastered his brief. Officials were taken aback when he said, 'I don't understand it yet, so I don't want to be committed yet.' Private office rarely succeeded in getting him to take home more than one red box. Officials wanted decisions on a daily basis. Crosland wanted to read himself into the job.

Tony was especially irritated by having to meet foreign ambassadors. 'It's footling to waste time like this when I ought to be learning. What's the point when I don't know what to say to him or understand what he's saying to me.'[9] He worked out a compromise with his Permanent Secretary, Sir Michael Palliser, whereby, as far as possible, he met all the ambassadors together at one big reception. The new Foreign Secretary hated the protocol that came with the job, especially the dress code expected of him. Jim Callaghan was furious when Crosland refused to wear morning dress when he joined the Prime Minister and the Home Secretary as well as generals and admirals in full dress uniform at Victoria Station to meet the French President, Valéry Giscard d'Estaing, at the start of his June state visit. After frantic messages between No 10 and the Foreign Office, Tony issued a statement: 'Except in the case of an invitation from the Sovereign to dine in her own home, I consider it wholly inappropriate that Labour Ministers should have to go to Moss Bros and hire this unnatural uniform.'[10]

In Cabinet, Crosland was at first reticent. When foreign affairs came up at Callaghan's first Cabinet, Crosland said 'Nil'. Tony Benn commented: 'His idea of being clever is to pretend there is nothing that should be brought to the Cabinet.'[11] Benn had missed the point. Crosland was not going to speak until he was ready. Dr Henry Kissinger found that out when he met the new British Foreign Secretary at RAF Waddington near his constituency in Lincolnshire. Kissinger, then at the zenith of his prestige as US Secretary of State, was on his way to Africa to establish a new policy for southern Africa, including a settlement of the intractable problem of Rhodesia, and naturally wished to meet Crosland. Tony's instinct was to delay an encounter with the formidable Kissinger until he was better briefed on Rhodesia and he proposed to use his normal Grimsby weekend as an excuse. His officials refused to permit this ploy, so Crosland suggested that Kissinger should fly to the Lincolnshire RAF station to have breakfast with him. Kissinger, though intrigued by Tony's audacity, was somewhat surprised when the Foreign Secretary appeared more interested in securing a promise that US shipyards would not sell gunboats to Iceland to strengthen their hand in the 'cod war' than in Rhodesia, though he asked the US Secretary of State some intelligent questions about the issue. When Crosland returned to Lansdowne Road, he said to Susan, 'I like Kissinger. He's just like all these New York Jewish intellectuals.' Kissinger's reaction was more guarded: 'At our first meeting . . . I realised he could master the subject. I didn't know if he wanted to.'[12]

On 9 June, Tony Benn had lunch with his former Oxford tutor in his huge room (which had the unfortunate effect of dwarfing its occupants) in the Foreign Office: 'He had his jacket off and was in his blue-and-white striped shirt with his shoes off, his specs on his nose and a cigar. For him, informality is a sort of substitute for radicalism . . . He is enjoying it enormously, though he says it is a bore having to go abroad so much.'[13] Crosland, accompanied by his wife, had already fulfilled one overseas engagement originally earmarked for his predecessor. In early May, they arrived in China at a time of considerable political uncertainty. Mao had died, the Gang of Four were in temporary power, and Deng was for the moment in disgrace. Susan, who had been with Tony to Russia when he was at the Board of Trade, was more impressed by the visit than Tony. 'It seemed better than Russia. I used to hate the way our convoy of government cars was driven through Moscow at eighty miles an hour, horns blaring . . . In China our cars crept along quietly. In fact, at rush hour I wondered whether we'd be engulfed by the sea of bicycles . . . The Chinese seemed more content.' Tony, the democratic socialist individualist, disagreed sharply: 'China was far more horrifying than Russia. How could you have been other than appalled by the lack of any privacy from the regime, the total lack of dissent?' In his own summary of his reaction to China, he put on the plus side participation, equality between the sexes, the determination to combat privilege and bureaucratic remoteness. But he found the totalitarian means repulsive:

'Total political control of every activity; total indoctrination from childhood onwards; the attempt at thought control . . . Can they really change human nature?'[14]

In early July, the Croslands went on another official trip, this time accompanying the Queen and Prince Philip on the royal visit to the United States for the bicentennial celebrations. They flew to Bermuda where the royal party boarded the *Britannia*. On the three-day journey (part of it in a force nine gale) to Philadelphia where the visit was to begin, Tony read his briefs and urgent telegrams, while Susan caught up on her correspondence. On the royal visit itself, Susan commented that she had never experienced anything so 'arduous'. The heat was intense, the walkabouts extensive, the banquets interminable. Susan, who had caught a chill while sunbathing on *Britannia*, passed out at the banquet given by the Queen for President Ford at the British Embassy in Washington and broke her jaw. Only the Queen, who went on to Canada following her US visit, showed no trace of wear and tear.

As the weeks went by, Crosland gradually began to warm to his new post. His first test was the so-called 'cod war' with Iceland. As MP for Grimsby, one of the country's leading fishing ports, this was always going to be a tricky problem for him. The fishing dispute between Iceland and the UK had dragged on for two years, embittering relations between the two countries as well as endangering the lives of British fishermen (including those from Grimsby) whose fishing lines were cut by Icelandic gunboats. But Crosland realised that, whatever the cost to his position as constituency MP, it was essential that the quarrel, which was threatening to damage the unity of NATO, should be ended as quickly as possible. At an EC Council meeting in Copenhagen in June, he accepted a settlement proposed by the Danish Foreign Minister that was favourable to Iceland. Crosland subsequently defended the deal resolutely in Parliament and in Grimsby, which, acording to his Permanent Secretary at the Foreign Office, Sir Michael Palliser, 'redounded greatly to his credit'.[15]

The big issue of Crosland's ten months as Foreign Secretary was, however, Rhodesia. Since Ian Smith, the white Prime Minister of Rhodesia, had declared unilateral independence in 1974, all British attempts to negotiate with him to establish majority rule, followed by independence, had failed, frustrated by South African support for minority white rule. The new element was Henry Kissinger's search for a settlement, backed by US power. Crosland welcomed Kissinger's support for the principle of majority rule but, like the Foreign Office, was convinced that a lasting settlement would not be possible without the endorsement of the black 'front-line' states of Botswana, Tanzania, Zambia, Mozambique and Angola.

In July a Cabinet Committee produced a paper that backed the Kissinger initiative but insisted that any plan should get support from the front-line states. When Rhodesia came before full Cabinet on 23 September, sceptical voices, including Denis Healey's, were raised about the Kissinger plan for a white-dominated interim Council of State, proceeding to majority rule within two years. Tony Benn asked how the UK could avoid legitimising the Smith regime in the interim.[16] Jim Callaghan summed up the sense of the meeting by appointing a group of ministers, including Crosland, Healey and Foot, to express their doubts on behalf of the Cabinet to Kissinger who was flying into London that night.

Within a couple of days, Ian Smith had backtracked on his initial acceptance of the Kissinger plan, while the front-line presidents began to denounce the terms on offer. At the Labour conference the following week, Tony tried to rescue the situation by announcing the convening of a conference on Rhodesia to be held in Geneva. The Geneva talks opened on 28 September and were adjourned seven weeks later, never to be reconvened. A few weeks earlier, Tony had said to his wife, 'What worries me about Henry is his tendency to do things impressionistically without keeping in mind what one party has in fact agreed to.'[17] However, it was not so much Kissinger's diplomatic mistakes that led to the failure of his initiative but the fact that the pressures, both internal and external, on Smith were not yet great enough to persuade him to settle. As Sir Michael Palliser wrote later, Crosland and his Labour successor, David Owen, worked hard at the Rhodesia problem.[18] But, as the underlying conditions for a settlement were not yet in place, they could make little headway; it fell to the next Conservative Foreign Secretary, Lord Carrington, to preside over the successful Lancaster House conference, which established majority rule.

The IMF crisis, which was to lead to such an intense struggle between Healey and Crosland, began with a loss of confidence in sterling.

Healey later blamed the run on the pound on mistakes by the Bank of England. On 4 March 1976, it sold sterling. According to Healey, this intervention by the Bank convinced the markets that the UK authorities were attempting to bring about a depreciation of the currency, so naturally holders of sterling wanted to sell.[19] The Bank's subsequent account differed from Healey's; their version was that they sold sterling on 4 March not to engineer a devaluation but to prevent a rise in the exchange rate and to strengthen already depleted reserves.[20]

But the key factor in the strong market reaction was not so much what the Bank did but the announcement by the Nigerians on 9 March that they had diversified their foreign exchange holdings out of sterling. It was this news, followed by the government's defeat the following day on its Public Expenditure White Paper, that caused the markets to reconsider the value of sterling. In the circumstances it was not irrational to sell sterling, given the level of the UK current account deficit, the continued high inflation, and the government's apparent lack of will and authority. Sterling began to weaken and, despite extensive intervention by the Bank, reported at one time to be running at a rate of up to $500 million a day, nothing seemed to stop its decline.

For the next nine months, Healey tried, in vain, to do enough to satisfy the currency markets that the British economy was back under control. The run on sterling made it even more essential to negotiate a second year of incomes policy to bring UK inflation in line with international levels. A key element of his April 1976 Budget was his tax–pay proposal. Healey offered to increase income tax reliefs in two stages, the first of £370 million unconditionally, the second £1000 million conditional on union agreement to limit wage increases to an average of three per cent. This offer may have represented a further increase in union power, but, to Healey, that was an acceptable price to pay to secure union agreement to an extension of incomes policy.

On 5 May, the Chancellor was able to announce to the Commons that the trade unions had agreed to limit wage increases to five per cent, with a minimum of £2.50 and a top figure of £4. Though this was a significant achievement which helped bring down inflation, the markets noted that Healey had been forced to concede a higher limit than his original Budget position. In the Budget itself, the Chancellor also announced that the public sector borrowing requirement (PSBR)

for 1975–76 had exceeded his target of a year earlier and that his estimate for 1976–77 was that the PSBR would rise to £12 billion. Yet, to
the market's disappointment, Healey did not announce further cuts in
public spending to reduce the PSBR.

Joel Barnett, Chief Secretary from 1974 to 1979, later wrote that
the Labour government 'planned far too high a level of public expenditure, in the expectation of levels of growth that, in the event, never
materalised'.[21] As a consequence of public sector pay rises and
increases in subsidies and transfer payments as well as of a stagnant
economy, the share of public expenditure increased sharply from 40.5
per cent of GDP in 1973–74 to 45.4 per cent in 1974–75.[22] Although
Healey had reined back planned public spending increases in the 1976
Public Expenditure White Paper by £3 billion by 1978–79, this was
not enough to satisfy the markets, especially with the Treasury forecast
of a rising PSBR. Healey initially hoped to resist making further public
spending cuts. When he met the Canadian High Commissioner on 21
May, he pooh-poohed his suggestion for more cuts in public expenditure.[23] His reluctance was understandable given the difficulties he had
in December 1975 persuading the Cabinet to agree to cuts; the
trouble that the 1976 Public Expenditure White Paper had caused in
the Parliamentary Labour Party, especially amongst the Tribune
Group; and the continuing need for the support of the trade unions,
especially those representing public sector workers, for incomes policy.

Instead Healey announced to the Commons on 7 June that the
Bank of England had negotiated a three-month stand-by credit,
(which would be used to support the pound) of $5.3 billion, of which
about $2 billion was to come from the United States and the rest
from other central banks. Healey obviously hoped that the June stand-
by would bolster international confidence in sterling, which had
touched a new low of $1.70, without the need for further major cuts in
public spending.[24] He told the House: 'This is not a situation in which
any responsible British government could allow themselves to be
pushed into hasty and ill-considered changes of policy on public
spending.'

However, the markets were less impressed by the negotiation of
the stand-by credit than by the fact that it had proved necessary and
would soon have to be repaid. The United States had insisted, as a
condition of their contribution, that the stand-by credit could be

renewed only once, making 9 December 1976 the final date for repayment. Callaghan and Healey had been forced to agree that if the British government could not repay the stand-by by that date, then it would have to go to the IMF for a longer-term credit.

Leo Pliatzky, Permanent Secretary in charge of public spending, commented later: 'There were some on both sides of the Atlantic who wanted the UK to have to go to the Fund . . . so that we would come under the financial discipline of the IMF's terms . . . William Simon . . . was said to regard the British nation as on a par with the insolvent municipality of New York City.'[25] Healey's comment on William Simon was that 'he was far to the right of Genghis Khan and was totally devoted to the freedom of the financial markets'.[26] The problem for the Chancellor was that borrowers cannot be choosers. The only way for the Labour government to avoid having to go to the IMF was themselves to carry out further public expenditure cuts which were essential according to Ed Yeo, the American Under Secretary to the Treasury, to 'get your people back on the reservation'.[27] The heat was now turned on public spending.

Callaghan reluctantly accepted Healey's advice that a further round of cuts was necessary to hold the currency. At the end of June, Tony Crosland told his wife, 'Callaghan and Healey are skilfully and unscrupulously preparing the ground. By leaking the desire and intention, they are going to bounce Cabinet.'[28] In fact, there were seven Cabinet meetings on public spending in July, a dress rehearsal for the even more numerous and dramatic Cabinet meetings over the IMF package in November and December. At the opening meeting, Denis Healey introduced a paper calling for cuts. According to Tony Benn, the Chancellor stressed the issue of confidence, though he argued too that the cuts were needed to make room for exports. Michael Foot and Tony Benn were against them, but Roy Jenkins, who remained in the Cabinet until leaving in September to prepare for his departure to Brussels, backed the Prime Minister and the Chancellor with the prophetic words: 'It would be fatal if we drifted through into the autumn with the possibility of a sterling crisis and panic action.'[29] Callaghan summed up by saying that there was a majority for the cuts.

Crosland, who had been away on the royal visit to the United States, came back in time for the second part of the public expenditure meetings in the middle of July and spoke strongly against the Healey package. For the author of *The Future of Socialism*, public expenditure was an essential, if not always effective, means to the achievement of greater equality. As a spending minister in the Labour government of the 1960s and 1970s, he had argued powerfully for increases in spending on education and housing. As a committed Keynesian and the most qualified economist in the Cabinet, he also regarded the economic case for public spending cuts as highly dubious. He asked the Chancellor how resources could be under strain when unemployment was high and increasing. When Tony met Callaghan alone, the Prime Minister candidly admitted that the cuts were being made to restore confidence in the pound. 'So we relapse into total economic orthodoxy,' replied the Foreign Secretary.[30] In Cabinet, Crosland infuriated the Prime Minister when he supported his successor at the Department of Environment, Peter Shore, in challenging the Chancellor's proposed transport cuts. Callaghan then asked Crosland what he would give up from the Foreign Office in place of the transport cuts. Tony coolly responded that he would do the same as Callaghan would have done at the Foreign Office three months ago. When most of the Cabinet laughed, the Prime Minister was roused to reply that, unlike Crosland, he at least supported the Chancellor 'as I have always done'.[31]

However, despite the seven meetings, the Cabinet was unwilling to go beyond cuts of just under £1 billion in 1977–78, together with a £1 billion surcharge on the Employers' National Insurance Contribution. This reduced the PSBR in 1977–78 to no more than £9 billion. The Chancellor told the Commons on 22 July: 'It remains my considered judgement that there is no call for major action in the current financial year.'[32] However, the markets were unimpressed by the July package. Edmund Dell, who, as Secretary of State for Trade, was now a member of the Cabinet, wrote: 'It is possible that if the government had, in July, made a £2 billion cut in public expenditure . . . the market might have been satisfied that enough had been done. As it was, the July public expenditure exercise seems simply to have provided conclusive evidence that there just was no way of persuading this government to come to its senses.'[33] Gavyn Davies, then a member of the No 10 policy unit, put it more graphically. 'The markets wanted blood, and that didn't look like blood. We didn't understand that in No 10 at the time, we didn't know what they wanted was a humiliation . . . trying to avoid the humiliation was a waste of time.'[34]

During August, sterling held steady at about $1.77. During his fort-night in France, Crosland gloomily considered the consequences of the July exercise in his private commonplace book:

a. Demoralisation of decent rank and file.
b. Strain on TU loyalty.
c. Breeding of illiterate and reactionary attitude to public expenditure.
d. Now no sense of direction and no priorities; only pragmatism, empiricism, safety first, £ supreme.
e. Unemployment, even if politically more workable = grave loss of welfare, security, choice: very high price to be paid for deflation and negative growth.[35]

Meanwhile, as Crosland ruminated, the Chancellor and his wife were enjoying wonderful August weather in the highlands of Scotland. At Ullapool on the west coast, Denis's sleep was interrupted by a series of calls from the Treasury and the Bank of England to inform him that sterling was under pressure again. He agreed that they could spend up to $150 million on intervention. Fortunately this was a minor flurry, so the Healeys were able to go on to spend a few days at the Edinburgh Festival, where they went to operas and plays and afterwards met the performers. It was lucky for Healey that he was able to enjoy his holi-day because over the next few months he was to be under the most intense pressure of his life.

On 1 September, the Federal Reserve in New York confirmed that up to 30 June, the UK had withdrawn about $1.1 billion from the $5.3 billion stand-by agreement, thus strengthening market suspicion that the British would soon have to go to the IMF. On the 9th the pound weakened further against the dollar, following the threat of a national seamen's strike. The Chancellor raised the minimum lending rate by 1.5 per cent to thirteen per cent on 10 September. But Healey warned the Economic Strategy Committee that a sterling crisis was about to break and that the government would have to apply to the IMF for a further loan.

On Monday 27 September, the first day of the Labour Party con-ference at Blackpool, sterling was in free fall, dropping 3 cents to

below $1.70. Healey wrote in his diary: 'Beautiful day, sterling going
down.'[36] It dropped a further 4.5 cents on the Tuesday. Denis was at
London airport with the Governor of the Bank of England, about to
leave for a Commonwealth finance ministers' conference at Hong
Kong followed by a meeting of the IMF at Manila at which the British
application for a loan would be considered. Hearing about sterling's
dive, the Chancellor put off his trip and drove back to the Treasury
where, in consultation with the Prime Minister, he decided to
announce that the UK was making a formal application to the IMF for
support amounting to $3.9 billion, the largest sum ever requested of
the organisation. The news about the IMF application, which was
published on the 29th, proved enough to calm the markets for the
time being.

In his memoirs, Healey admitted that for 'the first and last time in
my life, for about twelve hours I was close to demoralisation'.[36] The
retreat from Heathrow, followed by the IMF application, was, in truth,
close to a public humiliation for the Chancellor. With remarkable
resilience, Denis bounced back.

On Thursday 30 September, at Jim Callaghan's request, he flew up
to Blackpool, to put his case directly to Labour Party delegates. Since
Healey was no longer on the National Executive he was only allowed
a five-minute speech from the floor, a strict interpretation of conference rules that brought discredit on the Labour Party. However, in a
courageous intervention, the Chancellor made the most of the time
available. 'I do not come with a Treasury view,' shouted a red-faced
and tousled Denis to a rumble of booing from left-wing delegates: 'I
come from the battle front . . . I left this morning and I have not had
anything to eat since I left'. A mock-sympathetic response from delegates almost threw him off his stride. But Healey immediately
recovered and went on to denounce the Bennite alternative of a siege
economy which, he said, would be a recipe for a world trade war and
would bring the Tories to power with policies of mass unemployment:
'If you do not want those alternatives, then we have got to stick to the
policy we have got. I am going to negotiate with the IMF on the basis
of our existing policies . . . I mean things we don't like as well as things
we do like. It means sticking to the very painful cuts in public expenditure . . . It means sticking to the pay policy.' Tony Benn called the
speech 'vulgar and abusive'[38] but Edmund Dell's verdict was that, at

last, Healey was in fighting mode. 'He was fighting for the country, for the government, and indeed for his own career.'[39] I was one of those who applauded Healey's speech. At last there was someone who was prepared to tell Conference the facts of life.

Denis Healey needed to be in fighting mode. On 6 October the pound fell again to little over $1.50. The Chancellor was advised by the Governor of the Bank to raise interest rates from thirteen per cent to fifteen per cent, not only to get money supply under control but also to steady the currency. When Denis consulted Callaghan at No 10, the Prime Minister refused his consent. Healey persisted and said he wanted to take the issue to Cabinet that morning. The Prime Minister replied, 'All right, but I will not support you.'[40] Healey continued to insist on going to Cabinet, even though he knew that without the Prime Minister's support, he would inevitably be defeated and be forced to resign. In a grim mood, Healey walked back to his office in No 11 and put a call through to Edmund Dell who was 'the only member of Cabinet on whom I could count'. Before he could explain the situation to Dell, the Prime Minister's Private Secretary, Ken Stowe, put his head around the door and said, 'Excuse me, Chancellor, the Prime Minister has asked me to tell you that he was only testing the strength of your conviction. Of course, he will support you.'[41] It was a curious way for a Prime Minister to behave towards his Chancellor.

Callaghan's speech to the party conference advocating an end to living on 'borrowed time, borrowed money and borrowed ideas' and rejecting the idea that 'you could just spend your way out of recession' had been coolly received.[42] He felt badly bruised. His time as Chancellor had made him sceptical of the Treasury and he was determined not to be bounced either by his Chancellor or by the IMF into policies that he could not carry through Cabinet or the Parliamentary Labour Party. As he told his colleagues, he was intent on avoiding another '1931' when a Labour government had collapsed at a time of economic and financial crisis.

But if he was anxious to preserve the widest possible consensus within his party, he also knew he could not afford to lose his Chancellor, especially at this moment. There was never any real alternative to Healey. Crosland had ruled himself out by his opposition to cuts. Jenkins, who a number of Labour MPs believed would make a better Chancellor than Healey, had by now left the Cabinet to become President of the European Commission. Even if Jenkins could have been persuaded to change his mind about his departure, it remains doubtful whether Callaghan could ever have brought himself to appoint as Chancellor the man who had successfully succeeded him in 1967. The Secretary of State for Trade, Edmund Dell, would have had the support of the markets but not of the Labour movement. In the autumn of 1976, Healey was irreplaceable. Callaghan's view was that 'he could afford to lose the Secretary for Energy or, in extremis, even the Foreign Secretary, but the government would not have survived the resignation of the Chancellor'.[43]

Even so, Healey had to fight to the limit of his strength to bring about a successful resolution to the IMF crisis. The Chancellor was now convinced that there would have to be cuts in public expenditure sufficient to satisfy the IMF and win back market confidence: 'To Healey, the price that had to be paid was unfortunate and should be kept as small as could be negotiated, but it had to be paid.'[44] His main task was to convince the Prime Minister that more cuts were necessary. Callaghan was not yet persuaded. Early in November, Edmund Dell was talking to Denis Healey in the corridor behind the Speaker's Chair in the Commons when Callaghan came up to them and said, 'Tony Crosland tells me it is all a bankers' ramp like 1931. I think I agree with him.' Callaghan then walked into the Chamber before Healey could reply; Denis turned to Dell in near despair and said, 'What can I do now?'[45] The struggle between Healey and Crosland for the Prime Minister's support was intensified.

Callaghan had decided to play it long. On Callaghan's orders, the IMF team, which had arrived in London on 1 November and had suggested public spending cuts of £3 billion for 1977–78 and £4 billion for 1978–79, were kept waiting in Brown's Hotel for almost a fortnight before Treasury officials were allowed to talk to them. Meanwhile, the Prime Minister tried to use his personal contacts to seek help from President Ford in the United States and Chancellor Schmidt in Germany in either circumventing the IMF or mitigating its terms. Harold Lever was sent to Washington to persuade the IMF to soften its stance. Ford was sympathetic but on 4 November he had lost his battle for re-election and became a lame-duck president. It was Washington's collective view that the negotiations should be left to the IMF.

Schmidt made an emotional promise of German support but this did not extend to offering specific loans or putting pressure on the IMF. So Callaghan had no alternative but to negotiate with the IMF.

The Prime Minister now had to get the support of his divided Cabinet for any agreement with the IMF, without suffering major resignations. His strategy was to allow exhaustive discussions, involving nine Cabinet meetings in three weeks. There were four main groups of opinion within the Cabinet.[46] The smallest was that around the Chancellor: it consisted of the Secretary of State for Trade, Edmund Dell, the Minister of Overseas Development, Reg Prentice, and the Chief Secretary, Joel Barnett, who was not yet a member of the Cabinet but attended meetings on public expenditure. There was a second, left-wing group that rejected the IMF terms and advocated the alternative strategy of import and exchange controls and the establishment of a siege economy: this included the Leader of the House, Michael Foot, the Secretary of State for the Environment, Peter Shore, and the Secretary of State for Energy, Tony Benn. The crucial group was the third one of Keynesian dissenters, led by Tony Crosland. It included the Chancellor of the Duchy of Lancaster, Harold Lever, the new Secretary of State for Prices and Consumer Protection, Roy Hattersley, and two former supporters of Roy Jenkins, the Secretary of State for Education, Shirley Williams and the newly appointed Secretary of State for Transport, Bill Rodgers. The fourth group, which included the Home Secretary, Merlyn Rees, owed their position to Callaghan and would follow his lead.

The real battle in Cabinet was between Healey and Crosland, with Callaghan a neutral umpire until at a late stage. On the evening of 18 November the Prime Minister called a private meeting of the two main protagonists, with Edmund Dell and Treasury officials in attendance.[47] Healey explained why it was vital that the negotiation with the IMF should be successful. He had to repay the £1.6 billion already drawn on the stand-by credit by December. He could not repay the debt without IMF assistance. But, unless the PSBR was cut to around £9 billion, there would be no agreement with the IMF and the UK would not be able to borrow abroad. Whatever the theoretical economic arguments, there would have to be cuts in public expenditure, both to secure agreement with IMF and restore confidence in the management of the British economy.

Crosland then put his case against the cuts. In his view, there was no respectable economic argument for the cuts. With 1.25 million unemployed, there was plenty of spare capacity to increase exports. Cuts would mean higher unemployment which would actually increase the PSBR. In any case, Treasury forecasts of the PSBR were unreliable; other forecasts were much lower. The cuts would massacre the industrial strategy and upset the public sector unions. The only argument for the cuts that he accepted was international confidence. But what would happen to confidence, asked Crosland rhetorically, if the government accepted the package but was unable to get it through the Commons?

Healey had some sympathy with the merits of Crosland's argu-ments. He agreed with Tony that enough had probably already been done to bring about a balanced recovery. But nobody could yet be cer-tain about the recovery and, in any case, the markets were sceptical, especially about the level of public expenditure. If the markets had believed that all was in place for a recovery, then the UK would already have been able to borrow the money it needed to finance its deficit and pay its debts unconditionally. It was 'the incredulity of the market' that had forced the UK to the IMF. The choice, according to Healey, was either to negotiate with the IMF or be swept from office. The Prime Minister made no overt commitment to either side and referred the issue to Cabinet.

When the Cabinet met on 23 November, Healey argued for cuts of about £3 billion. Crosland repeated the arguments he had made at the private meeting at No 10 earlier in November. He was, however, pre-pared to agree to a concession of mainly cosmetic cuts of around £1 billion. The government should then say to the IMF, the Americans and the Germans: if you demand any more of us, we shall put up the shutters, wind down our defence commitment and introduce a siege economy. This was an extraordinarily irresponsible statement from a British Foreign Secretary. Crosland was apparently convinced that if the government kept its nerve it could insist on its own terms and limit the cuts to 'window-dressing' to appease the irritating and igno-rant currency dealers. 'Our weakness was our strength, it was a test of nerve and the IMF must give us the loan,' was Benn's summation of Crosland's arguments.

According to Susan Crosland's account, ten out of thirteen who spoke supported the Foreign Secretary's position, and the meeting ended inconclusively, with Callaghan proposing a further meeting: 'As reports of this Cabinet rocketed around Whitehall, the Treasury knew it had suffered a defeat; it still expected to win in the end.'[48] Presumably Healey hoped to win Callaghan round. However, Michael Foot told a meeting of the left-wing alternative strategy group the next day that he thought the Prime Minister was going to come down against his Chancellor and that Healey might resign. Benn commented, 'Of course if he does resign, the pound will go through the floor, even if we get the IMF loan.'[49]

Healey continued to fight his corner in Cabinet. On 25 November, Crosland put forward an import deposit scheme which, he claimed, would not only cut the PSBR but also persuade the IMF to give the loan to the UK. Crosland reported to his wife that the Chancellor had been subdued in repeating his case to Cabinet. But Benn noted that Denis, in his summing-up, bluntly pointed out that so long 'as we lived in an open and a mixed economy, we shall depend on the market judgement to determine our future. If we couldn't persuade our followers that these were the facts we would fail in our leadership and then another party would have to take over.'[50] This was the point which Crosland simply failed to take on board.

Over the next few days, the Crosland camp began to disintegrate. Harold Lever and Shirley Williams were unimpressed by Tony's deposit scheme, which they regarded as protectionist and potentially damaging to the Third World. Bill Rodgers was shocked by Crosland's suggestion made on 23 November that the government should threaten to withdraw troops from Germany. Rodgers told a meeting of the 'Keynesian dissidents' that in Britain's own interest there could be no question of abandoning our NATO obligations and that, if this was all Crosland had to offer, the Foreign Secretary could no longer count on his support.[51] Crosland's arguments had been tested by his own supporters and been found wanting.

Crucially, the Prime Minister had finally made up his mind to declare his support for the Chancellor. At a European Summit at the Hague on 29 and 30 November, Helmut Schmidt made it clear to Callaghan and Crosland that the UK could expect no concrete help from Germany. The British would have to settle with the IMF. On the flight back, Jim Callaghan told his Foreign Secretary that he would be supporting Healey. Callaghan's resolve was reinforced by an early morning meeting on 1 December with Johannes Witteveen, the Dutch managing director of the IMF. Although the meeting was a stormy one, with Callaghan presenting Witteveen with the GATT charter to show him that import controls were permissible, the outlines of a compromise began to emerge. Following the meeting, Callaghan, for the first time, told Healey that he would be prepared to support him in Cabinet.

At Cabinet that same morning, Benn, Shore and Crosland presented their 'alternative' strategies.[52] It was a disastrous meeting for them. Benn, who argued for import and capital controls and the introduction of a siege economy, was systematically demolished by his colleagues. Shore made a more effective case for temporary import controls but, in answer to a question from the Chancellor, had to admit that his proposals also involved cuts in the PSBR. Crosland, who grandly announced that his case was stronger than either Benn's or Shore's, put forward his proposal for sticking to existing policies with a concession of cosmetic cuts. But he had no answer to Healey's pointed question as to what would happen if the IMF refused to accept the Crosland plan. Significantly, a number of other middle-ranking Cabinet ministers who had not so far expressed their views, such as the Northern Ireland Secretary, Roy Mason, the Welsh Secretary, John Morris, and the Defence Secretary, Fred Mulley, were critical of Crosland's strategy because it would neither secure the IMF loan nor restore confidence. Roy Mason praised Healey for 'his courage and imperturbality, his intellectual resilience, his strength and moral fibre'. The wind was clearly blowing Healey's way.

At the decisive Cabinet of 2 December, the Chancellor opened with a bravura performance.[53] He said that the Cabinet the day before had led to a rejection of the alternative strategy and, therefore, the government had to seek agreement with the IMF. The Crosland package was totally unsaleable and would not convince the markets. On the other hand, if the Cabinet accepted his recommendations of cuts in public spending of £1 billion in 1977–78 and £1.5 billion for 1978–79 and if the IMF agreed, then the government would be able to borrow again and market confidence would be restored to the great benefit of the UK economy. The Prime Minister then followed Healey and made it clear that he supported the Chancellor. Foot, whose support Callaghan needed, continued to express his reservations, though the Prime Minister knew that the trade union leader, Jack Jones, was urging Foot and his other left-wing colleagues to accept an IMF agreement.

Crosland then made a speech of capitulation in which he withdrew his opposition to the Chancellor. He thought what Healey was proposing was 'wrong economically and socially, destructive of what he believed in all his life'. But the new factor was the Prime Minister's view. 'The unity of the party depends upon sustaining the Prime Minister and the effect on sterling of rejecting the Prime Minister would be to destroy our capacity. Therefore I support the Prime Minister and the Chancellor.' Peter Shore said it was wrong for Crosland to support something which he knew to be wrong but Roy Hattersley, who had been warned of Crosland's switch, followed the Foreign Secretary in supporting the Prime Minister, though 'with apprehension and no conviction'.

Bill Rodgers was for realism. 'We have no bargaining power left; we must accept it.' Benn said that there was 'an eerie parallel with 1931'. Callaghan, who fiercely rejected the parallel, summed up by saying that the overwhelming majority of the Cabinet agreed with the Chancellor's proposals for cuts and that an agreement should be sought with the IMF. It was all over bar the shouting, though it took a further three meetings of the Cabinet to agree the details. Healey settled with the IMF, after threatening Witteveen with a General Election on the issue of the IMF versus the people. On 14 December, the agreement with the IMF in the form of a letter of intent was discussed by the Cabinet and on the 15th the Chancellor announced the package to a subdued House of Commons. The terms agreed with the IMF were for public expenditure cuts of £1.5 billion in 1977–78 and £2 billion in 1978–79 which, according to Treasury forecasts, would bring the PSBR down to £8.7 billion in 1977–78 and £8.6 billion in 1978–79. In addition, the government committed itself for the first time to money supply targets and 'a continuing and substantial reduction over the next few years in the share of resources required for the public sector'.

The IMF agreement was, in the end, a considerable achievement for Jim Callaghan in that he kept the Cabinet together throughout the lengthy negotiations and meetings without resignations. Healey wrote later: 'The consummate skill with which he handled the Cabinet was an object lesson for all prime ministers.'[54] But Healey's contribution was the greater. While Callaghan prevaricated, Healey, with little support from his colleagues except Edmund Dell, and also with a divided Treasury behind him, not only persuaded the Cabinet but comprehensively won the intellectual argument. According to Dell, 'Throughout the long debate in Cabinet . . . Healey remained determined, eloquent and persuasive. He allowed no argument to pass unanswered.'[55]

Roy Hattersley's memoirs contained a delightful vignette of Healey noisily cutting articles from the morning's newspapers with a razor blade, while he listened to his Cabinet colleagues.[56] When Tony Benn said that the alternative strategy could be introduced without a massive cut in public spending, Denis was able triumphantly to produce a couple of column inches which he had just pruned from the letters page of *The Times*. This letter authoritatively stated that Benn's plans would have to be accompanied by severe deflation and was signed by none other than Wynne Godley, the main architect of the alternative strategy. Collapse of stout party! After the dark days of the autumn, Healey, drawing on all his reserves of courage and stamina, had fought his way through to a satisfactory conclusion: 'What could have been the nadir of Healey's career became the apogee.'[57]

Susan Crosland wrote that the outcome of the IMF crisis 'was a draw between the Foreign Secretary and the Treasury'.[58] Dell's rejoinder was that her verdict was like that of a cricketer who claimed to be not out because, although he had been bowled middle stump, two stumps were still standing. The reality was that Crosland had been out-argued by Healey and demolished by the facts.[59]

It was true, as Healey himself accepted, that Crosland's arguments that the Treasury forecasts were too pessimistic and the UK economic situation was already under control proved to be correct. The application to the IMF was authorised on the basis of a forecast of a current account deficit of £3 billion in 1977; in fact, in 1977 the current account returned to surplus. The PSBR in 1976–77 proved to be £2 billion below the £10.5 billion forecast by the Treasury. So, at a time when the IMF and the government supposed the PSBR for 1976–77 to be nine per cent of GDP, it had already fallen to six per cent. In other words, the Cabinet could have accepted the IMF's initial terms and not a penny less would have been spent than was in fact spent. Yet even if Crosland was right to suspect that the Treasury forecasts were wrong, neither he or the markets could have known at the time of the IMF negotiations that the cash limits on public spending introduced in 1975 would have such a marked impact on departmental expenditure. And, even if the markets had known, they might still have wanted cuts. Gavyn Davies' comment that 'the markets wanted blood' was just as apposite in December as it was in July.

The key point of the Healey case, to which the Crosland strategy did not and could not provide an answer, was the issue of international confidence. Healey put it with typical bluntness: 'The trouble with theoretical economists is that they don't understand that when you have a deficit you can only finance it by borrowing, and you've got to persuade people that it's worth lending to you, and that they'll get their money back.'[60] What Healey understood and Crosland refused to face up to was that after a number of botched attempts to persuade the markets that the British economy was on the right track, the IMF package simply had to succeed in restoring international confidence. In the conditions of 1976, with the pound having fallen in value by over twenty per cent since March and with a loan to repay in December, Healey was right and Crosland was wrong.

A year later Roy Hattersley, who alone had backed Crosland to the end, said in Cabinet that, after all, it was Healey who had been correct, as the pound strengthened, interest rates and inflation fell, and growth was resumed.[61] Another of the rebels, Peter Shore, admitted: 'In the event, unemployment hardly moved, and the economy began to move forward again fairly shortly afterwards. It didn't have that dramatic deflationary effect which I so feared at the time.'[62] The IMF's seal of good housekeeping, for which Denis Healey had argued so forcefully, had proved to have beneficial economic results.

Even so, there was a general feeling that, in being forced to go to the IMF in the first place, the Labour government had suffered a psychological setback. The Conservatives criticised the Chancellor for his earlier policies which had led to the approach to the IMF, while the Labour left sedulously built up the myth of a right-wing sell-out to the IMF and the bankers. In a deeper way, the IMF crisis also brought into doubt key elements of the postwar consensus – the Keynesian assumption that priority should be given to full employment and the welfare commitment to high levels of public spending.

The supporters of Mrs Thatcher, the newly elected leader of the Conservative Party, concluded that the commitment to full employment should be abandoned and the proportion of resources going to public spending should be drastically reduced. For the next two decades Labour revisionists from Kinnock, Hattersley and Smith to the New Labour leaders, Blair and Brown, tried to find answers to the underlying question posed by the crisis – how far and in what ways did the Labour Party need to change to continue to be a viable social democratic party in a world of floating exchange rates and global markets. Healey had faced up to the issue but Tony Crosland, the revisionist high priest, no longer had the inclination to rethink his position. When his wife asked him, during the Cabinet discussions, whether he still wanted to be Chancellor 'at a time when apparently nothing can be achieved to further Labour aims', Tony replied that he would still like to see if it was possible to do better, however bad the economic situation would be over the next few years.[63] But his underlying pessimism was revealed in his private notebook in which he wrote that almost everything he had said about the July package could be rewritten about the December cuts. For Tony there was the same lack of direction and the same sense of depressing inevitability; in his heart of hearts, he knew that his brand of revisionism as well as his authority had received a severe blow over the IMF crisis. 'It was a bad time to be a Croslandite social democrat, especially if you were Tony Crosland.'[64]

Crosland may have still wanted to become Chancellor of the Exchequer. But he was beginning to enjoy being Foreign Secretary. He told his wife in December that he would like to stay on at the Foreign Office for another eight months. 'I'm now getting on top of it at an increasing rate.' When she reminded him that he used to say that he was not interested in foreign affairs, he admitted that it was 'a silly, childish remark for me to make'. As the Croslands talked together at Christmas over the wood fire at Adderbury, Tony got up from his chair, which was surrounded by Foreign Office briefings and a draft of Philip Williams' biography of Hugh Gaitskell, to pour a second cup of tea and said, 'That's that. I finally understand about all these bloody countries.' Later he added, 'Hope Jim doesn't change his mind and swap Denis and me before August. Now that I'm in my stride I've rather taken to my job.'[65]

Apart from a new initiative over Rhodesia, the Foreign Secretary was preparing himself for the UK's first six-month presidency of the European Community, including brushing up his French, which had been fluent when he was a child of four. He approached the task as a not uncritical pro-European. In an article for *Socialist Commentary* in November he claimed that his earlier position was being vindicated; the economic arguments about British membership were proving inaccurate or irrelevant, while the political case for Britain's membership was even stronger than before. He made a well-received inaugural address to the European Parliament on 12 January 1977, in which he said that British membership of the European Community represented Britain's first permanent peacetime engagement on the continent of Europe since the Reformation. Crosland stressed that progress on enlargement was to be a priority and that he attached importance to the development of procedures for co-ordinating the foreign policies of member states. He had begun to enjoy chairing European meetings. In his diary, the new President of the European Commission, Roy Jenkins, noted that a Political Co-operation meeting was 'well conducted by Crosland'.[66]

In early February Crosland went down to dinner at St Anthony's College, Oxford, where his old friend Raymond Carr was Warden. Afterwards he grumbled to Carr, 'Why have you put me next to a woman who only wants to talk about the EEC? Don't you realise it is killing me?' The Foreign Office car then dropped the Croslands off at Adderbury for the weekend where they celebrated their thirteenth wedding anniversary. On Sunday, after sleeping late, Tony went for a long walk. As he returned, he remarked to Susan, 'This is an ultimate weekend.' Twenty minutes later sitting in his chair working on Rhodesia papers, he said, 'Something has happened. I can't feel my right side.' At first, the doctors thought it was a twenty-four-hour spasm. However, it soon became clear that Crosland had suffered a severe stroke and he was taken to the Radcliffe Infirmary. By 10 p.m. on Sunday evening, he was in a comatose state. By Monday morning it was obvious that he was not going to recover. Tony Crosland died early on the morning of Saturday 19 February 1977, aged fifty-eight, with his wife and two step-daughters at his side.[67] A few days later, his wife scattered his ashes into a stormy sea off his constituency, the port of Grimsby.

Roy Jenkins heard the news of his death in Rome on an inaugural visit to Italy. His relations with Tony had improved markedly since Roy had announced that he was leaving British politics for Brussels. In the previous summer, they had had an amicable lunch together at East Hendred: in their new roles they had found themselves getting on well again. Curiously, it was while Denis Healey, the third of the Oxford triumvirate, was paying a call on Jenkins in Brussels on the Monday, that Roy first heard about Crosland's illness, without realising the seriousness of the stroke. David Owen, then Crosland's deputy and himself a doctor, told Roy on the Wednesday that Tony was as good as dead. On the Saturday Roy awoke at 6.30 a.m. in Rome having had a vivid dream about Tony, who said in an unmistakable clear, calm voice, 'No, I am perfectly all right. I am going to die, but I'm perfectly all right.' Jenkins had a call at about 8.00 a.m. from the BBC, saying that Tony died at almost exactly the same moment as Roy had awoken from his dream. He decided he ought to write an obituary for the *Sunday Times*. He noted that 'the effect of writing about Tony was to bring the immense closeness of our earlier relationship flooding back into my mind.'[68] His *Sunday Times* memoir of Crosland was personal, at times emotional.

In a moving speech in the Commons, Callaghan described Crosland as 'gifted beyond the reach of many of us', a man who combined physical courage, mental toughness and great personal charm. In the *Observer*, Alan Watkins wrote that he had been the outstanding socialist theoretican since the war, a successful minister, an assiduous constituency MP and beneath his brusque exterior a kind and considerate man. Some of his colleagues were less certain about his ministerial qualities. In his autobiography, Jenkins' judgement was that Crosland was not at his best as a minister. That is too harsh a judgement. True, he was a disappointing and disappointed President of the Board of Trade. But Crosland was an outstandingly innovative Education Secretary in the 1960s and a highly competent Environment Secretary in the 1970s. In the view of his Permanent Under Secretary at the Foreign Office, he was a major political figure who might have become an outstanding Foreign Secretary.

Whether or not Crosland would finally have become Chancellor in 1977 had he lived remains an open question. At the end of 1976, Healey told trade union leaders that he expected Crosland to succeed him. However, until the economy recovered, Callaghan would not have risked giving the Chancellorship to Tony and, once it recovered, Denis would have been loath to give his rival any of the credit for turning the economy round. Whether Crosland would have succeeded Callaghan is even more difficult to judge. His problem, as in 1976, might still have been to get enough first-round votes to survive to the final round. Though he was clearly a candidate for the leadership, some doubted that he would have had sufficient ruthlessness to make a good leader. One is on safer ground in saying that Crosland would not have joined the SDP. Indeed, his presence in Labour's ranks as a thinker as well as a leading figure would have surely made the SDP breakaway less likely.

Despite his achievements as a minister, however, his greatest contribution to the Labour Party was as a revisionist intellectual, whose writings and speeches helped shape a generation. It is significant that his ideas remain of interest to New Labour's leaders. The new Clause IV of the party constitution, put into place by Tony Blair, is a revisionist tract; while Gordon Brown has stressed the need to translate Crosland's notion of equality into today's context.[69] Even if many of Crosland's assumptions and policy prescriptions are no longer valid, his way of looking at things, especially the distinction he drew between ends and means and his insistence that social democracy must constantly be revised, continues to be of relevance in the twenty-first century.

12

The Death of Labourism and Healey's Defeat

With the death of Crosland and Jenkins in continental exile, Healey was left in command of the field. The success of the IMF package in restoring international confidence in the British economy ought to have given the Labour government a real chance of victory at the following election, a victory that would have made Denis Healey, as the architect of economic recovery, the odds-on favourite to succeed Jim Callaghan as party leader and Prime Minister.

1977 was Denis Healey's *annus mirabilis* as Chancellor of the Exchequer. After the agreement with the IMF, suddenly all the indicators began to move in the right direction. The pound, which had sunk to as low as $1.50 during the crisis, increased in value by the end of the year to more than $1.90, even causing the Treasury to worry about the strength of sterling. Interest rates fell sharply from fifteen per cent in October 1976 to five per cent the following October. For the first time for five years the current account, now benefiting from North Sea oil, moved into balance. Inflation continued to decline and, by the beginning of 1978, it had fallen to just under ten per cent. The rise in unemployment, which had increased by 500,000 in 1975 and 170,000 in 1976, slowed to only 100,000 in 1977 and in 1978 the number of jobless actually started to decline. By then, Healey was able to claim that inflation and unemployment were falling at the same time and growth had recovered to over three per cent.

At the end of 1977 the UK agreed not to draw on its full entitlement with the IMF. When Denis Healey attended the IMF annual meeting in October 1977, the British correspondents described him as 'walking on water'. The leading American financial monthly *Institutional Investor* produced a cover story that put him first among the six best finance ministers of the day. Even the Labour Party conference, which had treated him so cruelly in 1976, gave him a standing ovation in 1977.[1]

The political situation also began to turn in Labour's favour. Soon after Jim Callaghan became Prime Minister, by-elections were lost and his government had become a minority one. In February 1977, its ability to get major legislation through the Commons was thrown into doubt by its defeat by twenty-nine votes over guillotining the Devolution Bill. On 17 March, the government, in order to avoid defeat, was forced into an inglorious abstention at the end of a debate on public spending. Mrs Thatcher immediately put down a 'no-confidence' motion. However, on the evening of 21 March, Callaghan met the new leader of the Liberals, David Steel. They agreed on a Lib-Lab pact, which was put to an emergency meeting of the Cabinet. It proposed the setting-up of a joint consultative committee under Michael Foot; regular meetings between the Chancellor and the Liberal economic spokesman, John Pardoe; a Bill for direct elections to the European Parliament with a free vote on the voting system; and progress on devolution. In return, the Liberals would sustain the government in Parliament.

The Prime Minister told his Cabinet colleagues that there was no alternative to the pact, as otherwise the vote of confidence would be lost and the government would be forced to hold an election. Foot and Healey gave their strong backing to the agreement, Denis saying that a deal with the Liberals was preferable than having to rely on 'Nats and nutters' (referring to the Welsh Nationalists and the Ulster Unionists). Benn was firmly opposed on the grounds that an arrangement with the Liberals was a parliamentary coalition but the Cabinet endorsed the pact by twenty votes to four and, as over the IMF agreement, neither Benn nor anybody else resigned. The motion of confidence of 23 March was then won by 322 votes to 298, with all thirteen Liberals voting for the government and three Ulster Unionists abstaining. The Labour government had, in effect, bought itself a new lease of life, with the prospect of holding the election at a more favourable time.

For the next sixteen months, the Labour government, boosted by improving economic performance and the Lib-Lab arrangement, appeared in charge of events. Labour began to eat into the Tory lead in the polls and the Prime Minister's popularity soared. Apart from the Prime Minister himself, Healey was the administration's outstanding figure, dominating the Cabinet and Parliament by the power of his personality.

Sometimes, Denis's forcefulness led to conflict. Healey did not get on with the Liberal economic spokesman, John Pardoe. Healey's comment was that Pardoe 'was robust and intelligent enough, but sometimes I felt he was simply Denis Healey with no redeeming features. More than once Joel Barnett had to pick up the pieces after we had sent the crockery flying.'[2] Joel Barnett related how Pardoe walked out of a meeting at the end of 1977 because he disliked the way in which the Chancellor rubbished the Liberal proposal on cutting income tax. Barnett then suggested to David Steel that they should be present at future meetings between Healey and Pardoe, 'if only to hold the coats'.[3] In a more serious though ultimately abortive exercise, Healey clashed with Benn over how the proceeds of North Sea oil, which by 1985 would be adding five per cent to GNP and twelve per cent to government revenues, should be spent. The Treasury argued that North Sea oil should be used to swell government revenues to repay debts, to cut taxes and to encourage overseas investment. Benn wanted a special fund to direct investment into nationalised industries, the social infrastructure and energy resources. When the paper came before Cabinet in February 1978, an overwhelming majority supported Healey in his view that the oil money should be absorbed into general revenue, though it could be used for special purposes, which might include capital investment as well as debt redemption and tax cuts.

Healey's new authority as Chancellor of the Exchequer was enhanced when he was elected chairman of the IMF's Interim Committee in the autumn of 1977. He persuaded the IMF to agree to subsidise interest rates for Third-World countries whose economies had suffered as the result of the slow-down in the world economy, as well as to increase their Special Drawing rights. Denis was approached several times during 1978 to see if he would be prepared to succeed

Johannes Witteveen when he retired as managing director of the IMF the following year. But Healey did not want to be an international civil servant, and, in any case, had reasonable grounds to hope that he would become leader of the Labour Party and Prime Minister when Callaghan stepped down.

Roy Jenkins, meanwhile, was going through a depressing first few months as President of the Commission. For most of 1976, once he had made up his mind to go to Brussels, he had been in an optimistic frame of mind. He was pleased to be leaving British politics and was exhilarated by the prospect of being in a position to move things forward in the European Community. He spent time choosing his staff, brushing up his French and visiting the governments of the member states. The latter was partly in order to discuss the appointment of the individual Commissioners. It was over the nomination of the German Commissioners that he received his first setback, failing, despite Helmut Schmidt's initial support, to get the relatively lightweight existing German Commissioners replaced.[4] The harsh reality that being President of the Commission was not like being a minister in a national government began to dawn on him. At least as a Labour minister Jenkins could pull the levers of power in the expectation that something would happen. As President, outside the narrow fields of agriculture and coal and steel, nothing happened unless he could persuade the majority of members to support the course of action that he proposed.

In Jenkins' view, his first six months in Brussels were not a success. He felt that he had no clear objective and that, even if he had one, he was not well qualified to achieve it. At the end of 1977, he wrote in his diary: 'Certainly my mood for the greater part [of 1977] . . . was such that I would not have made the decision to go to Brussels had I been able to see things in advance. The job is more difficult to get hold of and less rewarding than I thought. Also in many ways I am not particularly well suited to do it, lacking patience, perhaps at times resilience, certainly linguistic facility.'[5]

One reason for his depression was that by his insistence on attending the summit meeting in London of the leaders of the industrial world (now known as the G7), he had earned the displeasure of one of his original backers, Valéry Giscard d'Estaing. The smaller member states believed very strongly that the President of the Commission should be present at these gatherings. In order to establish his credibility as the new president, Jenkins felt he had to attend. Giscard, who had launched the G8 idea as an intimate forum, wanted to limit the numbers. He also argued that Jenkins was not eligible as he was not leader of a sovereign government. With the help of Schmidt, a compromise was reached whereby Roy attended half the 1977 summit; at later summits he was allowed to participate fully. But this victory was achieved at the cost of a long-term deterioration in his relations with Giscard, as the following conversation in French between Jenkins and Giscard at the Elysée Palace recorded in Roy's diary illustrates: 'Ah, Mr Jenkins, I hear that you speak French well now – I think it was the King of Spain who told me,' said Giscard. 'That's strange,' replied Jenkins, 'because the King of Spain and I always speak in English.'

Roy was also upset by a critical article in the *Economist*, widely read in Brussels, on the first six months of his presidency. And the weather, always an important factor in the state of Roy's morale, was appalling. In June there were seventeen consecutive days in which the sun never appeared from behind the clouds. Fortunately, at a picnic in the Forêt de Soignes in July, Jennifer Jenkins, always firm in a crisis, told him to pull himself together and, instead of moaning, prepare an initiative that would help revive the Community. Roy decided to restate the goal, already foreshadowed in the 1970 Werner report, of monetary union. After preparing the Commission and discussing the project at a Foreign Ministers' weekend, he launched it in a Jean Monnet lecture in Florence on 27 October 1977, arguing that the era of extreme currency fluctuations, which had set in with the end of the Bretton Woods system in 1971, had coincided with a worsening of Europe's relative economic performance and calling for the creation of 'a zone of monetary stability' in Europe.

As Jenkins had already found out, he needed the support of major national players if any action was to follow his Florence speech. Fortunately, after initial coolness, Helmut Schmidt, who was disturbed by the adverse effect on the German economy of the decline of the dollar, decided to take over Jenkins' idea and make it his own. Schmidt first raised his plan privately with the other heads of government at the Copenhagen European Council in April 1978 and unveiled it publicly at Bremen in July. Under the European Monetary

System (EMS), which was set up in March 1979, the Exchange Rate Mechanism (ERM) established fixed but adjustable exchange rates, and required the central banks to intervene in the currency markets to keep fluctuations within narrow bands, with the deutschmark acting as the anchor. Characteristically, the United Kingdom declined to become a full member, standing aloof from the ERM. Callaghan, who had good relations with both Schmidt and Giscard, understood some of the arguments for involvement but was concerned about the possible deflationary consequences of being tied in at too high a rate, as well as about hostile reaction in his divided Cabinet and in the Labour Party.[6]

According to Denis Healey, his response to Schmidt's and Jenkins' monetary initiative was at first 'fairly agnostic until I realised, from long discussions with Manfred Lahnstein and others, how it was likely to work in practice; then I turned against it'.[7] Lahnstein, who was head of the German finance ministry, supported the ERM because it would cap the value of the DM against other European countries, giving the German economy a competitive edge over its neighbours. Healey advised the Cabinet that the UK should stay out of the ERM, though it should participate in a general (though undefined) way in the EMS. Roy Jenkins' *European Diary* has a number of references to Healey's forceful interventions in debates at the Council of Economic and Finance Ministers (ECOFIN) in the autumn of 1978 about the details of the ERM. However, the British position fell apart when Healey was asked whether the British were actually going to join the ERM. Jenkins commented, 'Franco-German hegemony, even when as constructively exercised as it was that autumn, breeds a certain impatience and makes other countries flicker their eyes towards the possibility of a British lead, particularly when Britain is represented by as powerful a personality as Denis Healey. But when only negative points are forthcoming the eyes quickly flicker away.'[8]

Throughout his political career, Denis Healey had always been 'agnostic', when not downright sceptical, about European initiatives. He had been against the UK joining the Coal and Steel Community in 1950; he had been against UK membership of the Common Market in the 1960s, though he supported a membership bid after de Gaulle resigned in 1969; in opposition in the early '70's, after initial dithering, he voted against joining on Conservative terms; and then, at the time of the 1975 referendum, he decided in favour of staying in. His arguments against the ERM were, as one would expect from Healey, cogent ones. It is also uncertain whether the Labour government could have carried British membership of the ERM through the Parliamentary Labour Party, at least before the election. However, in contrast to the UK's experience in the 1980s, the ERM delivered greater exchange rate and interest stability to its members, as well as closer convergence of its economies. Typically the UK joined late in 1990, 'at the wrong time, for the wrong reasons and at the wrong rate',[9] and two years later left again in humiliation. In 1993, the ERM itself was shaken to its foundations by the impact of German unification. However, it is doubtful if the single European currency would have gone ahead at the end of the 1990s without the experience of both the successes and failures of its predecessor, the European Exchange Rate Mechanism, which Roy Jenkins had done much to bring about.

If the sixteen months following the IMF agreement were the best of times for the Callaghan government, the 'winter of discontent' of 1978–79 was, by a long way, the worst of times. Yet, only a few months earlier, in July 1978, Labour had appeared to stand a good chance of winning a General Election, if one was called in the autumn. Inflation, which had reached twenty-seven per cent in 1975, was down to eight per cent by mid summer 1978. Steady growth had been resumed and unemployment was falling. Living standards were rising again, while the less well-off had been protected by increases in benefits. Jim Callaghan had a big advantage over Mrs Thatcher in the public opinion polls and the Tory overall lead was down to low single figures; indeed, by the autumn, Labour was running ahead of the Tories in some polls.

There was a general expectation that there would be an election in the autumn of 1978. David Steel said in July that the Liberals would withdraw from the Lib-Lab pact when the new session began in November, so the government could no longer guarantee getting its legislation through Parliament. There was also a growing problem over the so far remarkably successful incomes policy. Callaghan had recommended to Cabinet a five per cent pay norm for 1978–79 on the reasonable grounds that five per cent was the highest figure consistent with continuing to bring inflation down. However, the government's main trade union allies, Hugh Scanlon of the Engineers and Jack Jones of the Transport Workers had both retired, with Jack Jones suffering the humiliation of being defeated on pay policy at his farewell trade union conference. The prospects of continuing TUC support were looking decidedly gloomy. If the government was to carry through a new, tougher round of incomes policy, it needed a fresh mandate.

However, after much deliberation at his farm over August and having teased the TUC conference in early September by singing them an old musical hall song 'There was I waiting at the church', the Prime Minister announced to an astonished nation, including most of his Cabinet, that he had decided to delay the election. William Rodgers, the Transport Secretary, presciently told Callaghan's senior policy advisor, Bernard Donoghue, following the Cabinet meeting at which the Prime Minister informed his colleagues of his decision, that 'that was the most disastrous Cabinet of this government'.[10] Significantly, Rodgers' opinion was shared by all the younger members of the Cabinet.

Callaghan's main reason for hanging on was that he was not certain of victory (his best guess was another hung Parliament) and he hoped that things might have improved by the spring. Healey wrote that the Prime Minister was 'sick to death of the continual compromises required for our survival as a minority government; I think he would rather have lost than be condemned to a repetition of the previous three years'. In Denis's view, there was also an element of hubris (which led on, as in a Greek tragedy, to the nemesis of the 'winter of discontent') in Callaghan believing that the government could make a five per cent norm stick without at least trade union acquiescence.[11] According to Edmund Dell, Healey recommended an autumn election.[12] If so, he did not do so very strongly. On 18 August, the Callaghans had invited themselves to tea at the Healeys' country house at Alfriston, a few miles from Jim Callaghan's Sussex farm. When Jim Callaghan told Healey about his preference for a spring election, Denis fatally hedged his bets, though he warned that the improvement in living standards would slow down over the winter.[13] As to the decision about the five per cent norm, the Chancellor backed the Prime Minister, though Denis had been warned by the TGWU officer in his region during a visit to his Leeds constituency that it would be impossible to operate another year of tight incomes policy. Healey admitted afterwards that if the government had agreed on a formula such as 'single figures', it would have achieved a better outcome and almost certainly have avoided the 'winter of discontent'.

The 'winter of discontent' was indeed a disaster, which still remains in the memory of those who lived through it. The trade union revolt against incomes policy gathered pace. Following a major strike at Ford, there were strikes threatened in December by oil tanker drivers, road haulage workers, local authority manual workers, British Leyland production workers and by water and sewage workers. The Prime Minister's senior policy advisor's comment was apposite: 'There was a curious, feverish madness infecting industrial relations and in some cases unions actually went on strike before their pay claims had been submitted.'[14] The government was rapidly loosing control of events, with the Prime Minister seeming out of touch. Callaghan returned from a summit in Guadeloupe on 10 January and unwisely gave a press conference at London airport, during which he was famously misquoted by the *Sun* newspaper as saying, 'Crisis? What crisis?'

Above all, the strikes in the public service, which began in late January, were extremely damaging both to the government and to the reputation of the trade unions. Sick patients went unattended, hospitals were picketed, and schools were closed. The remark of the leader of the London ambulancemen, who were refusing to answer 999 calls, was a gift to Mrs Thatcher and to the enemies of trade unionism: 'If it means lives must be lost, that is how it must be.'[15] The television images of the rubbish in the streets, the piles of unwashed hospital sheets and, most upsetting of all, the dead left unburied removed at a stroke what had been Labour's most potent electoral card in the 1970s – its claim to be able to work with the unions. In those bitter winter months, Labour's authority as an actual and potential government and, until then, its most relevant governing idea were fatally exposed. Jim Callaghan, the politician who had prided himself on his relations with trade union leaders, had been decisively rejected by trade unionists. He privately told Healey he was so disenchanted with the behaviour of the unions that he was contemplating legislation to control them. Healey, only half-jokingly, threatened to 'do a Callaghan' on him, a reference to Callaghan's behaviour over *In Place of Strife*.[16]

The stuffing went out of the government. The Prime Minister, now almost a Lear-like figure, was despairing, appearing to have no idea what to do next. Afterwards, he confided to his principal private secretary, Kenneth Stowe, 'I let the country down.'[17] The five per cent norm was tacitly abandoned and on 14 February an agreement was cobbled together with the TUC, which too late talked about guidelines for the orderly conduct of industrial disputes and the need for bringing down inflation to five per cent over three years. Callaghan wrote formally to Healey asking him to chair a group of ministers to flesh out the agreement with the TUC, including a new commitment on pay comparability in the public sector.

However, the voters had ceased listening, because they no longer believed that the unions could deliver their members. On 28 March Parliament put the government out of its misery when it was defeated by one vote on a confidence motion tabled by Margaret Thatcher, following the government's failure to win a referendum on Scottish devolution by the requisite forty per cent of the Scottish voters and the subsequent desertion of Labour by the minority parties. A number of Cabinet ministers, including Michael Foot and Denis Healey, believed that if Callaghan had been prepared to offer more inducements to the minority parties the government might have struggled on until the autumn. But Callaghan had had enough manoeuvring; in Healey's view, he was 'exhausted and dispirited' and wanted to get the election over.[18]

Although the Labour leader fought a dignified, almost elegiac campaign, the result was never in doubt. The collapse of the Labour government's authority during the 'winter of discontent' gave the Conservatives a decisive victory, with seventy-one seats more than Labour and an overall majority of forty-four. Labour's share of the vote was 36.9 per cent, its lowest since 1931, with many working-class voters, including a third of trade unionists, deserting to the Tories. There was a feeling that Labour had suffered more than just a one-off political defeat. Towards the end of the campaign, Callaghan remarked to his senior policy advisor, 'You know there are times, perhaps once every thirty years, when there is a sea-change in politics . . . I suspect there is now such a sea-change – and it is for Mrs Thatcher.'[19] With considerable help from the Labour Party, the Tories were to be in power for the next eighteen years.

*

For Denis Healey, the Labour Party's defeat in 1979 was a big personal setback. If Labour had won, Healey would almost certainly have succeeded Callaghan as leader and Prime Minister. In opposition, with the party deeply divided, his prospects were less certain. His best chance would have been if Callaghan had resigned immediately after the election, before the left was able to gather its forces and while Labour was still recognisably a party interested in power. However, Callaghan decided to stay on for a while as leader, ostensibly in order to use his authority to keep the party on an even keel, and, as he told Healey in a somewhat misleading cricketing metaphor, 'to take the shine off the ball' for Denis, his chosen successor.[20] This was a disastrous misjudgement because by the time he decided to resign after the 1980 Labour conference, the Left was in full cry and the odds on a Healey victory had lengthened considerably. As Healey sharply but accurately put it, 'Jim's last eighteen months as leader not only took the shine off the ball, but ripped away the leather as well.'[21]

For the moment Healey was almost relieved to be out of office, so exhausted was he after his five-year stint at the Treasury. He recharged his batteries by putting together a delightful photographic memoir, *Healey's Eye*, published in 1981. In the summer of 1979 he took advantage of visits to Japan and Greece to increase his collection of colour slides. However, his powerful mind soon turned back to Labour's appalling defeat. In the Sarah Barker Memorial Lecture that he delivered on 8 September, a couple of months before Roy Jenkins made his much more widely publicised Dimbleby Lecture, Healey set out his vision of social democracy.

He was clear that, with Mrs Thatcher adopting liberal market policies, Labour needed to do a Bad Godesberg (like the German Social Democrats in 1959) and adopt the social market approach. Denis quoted with approval the example of Austria, a favourite Healey model: 'Austria came to terms with its political and economic disadvantages after the war, jettisoned those parts of its Marxist ideological inheritance which were obviously no longer relevant, and turned a country which in the interwar years had been suffering from an ex-imperial hangover into a model welfare state, without sacrificing any of its cultural attractions in the process.'[22]

He warned party activists against believing their views necessarily represented those of Labour voters and tried to show how his hard-won experience as Chancellor was still relevant to Labour's economic policies. A future Labour government would have to continue to combine management of demand with control of the money supply and reduction of unit costs. Healey could offer no New Jerusalem, 'simply a country with stable prices, jobs for those who want them and help for those who need it', objectives familiar to New Labour. He ended with the moving and relevant words of Leszek Kolakowski, the Polish philosopher and historian:

> The trouble with the social democratic idea is that it does not stock and does not sell any of the exciting commodities which various totalitarianism movements – Communist, Fascist, or Leftist – offer dream-hungry youth . . . It has no prescription for the total salvation of mankind . . . It requires, in addition to a number of basic values, hard knowledge and rational calculation . . . It is an obstinate will to erode by inches the conditions which produce avoidable suffering, oppression, hunger, wars, racial and national hatred, insatiable greed and vindictive envy.[23]

Healey's Sarah Barker Memorial Lecture was an eloquent social democratic text that showed that the self-styled arch-pragmatist did after all have a vision. Critics might say that it did not discuss the unions, which had played such a large part in Labour's defeat. As Healey wrote later, 'The Labour Party's financial and constitutional links with the unions made it difficult for us to draw too much attention to their role in our defeat.' The other problem was that Healey was waiting in the wings and did not want to frighten off the unions or indeed his fellow Labour MPs before a leadership election. So the Sarah Barker speech was a one-off. For most of 1980, Healey kept his head down and his mouth shut, hoping to take over from Callaghan as quietly and smoothly as possible. It was a mistaken strategy.

It allowed Tony Benn to make all the running inside the Labour Party. Benn was then at the height of his powers – charming, witty, and eloquent. Indeed, in terms of eloquence if not content, he was at that time (with the possible exception of Shirley Williams) the best all-round communicator in the Labour Party: good on TV, able to command both Parliament and Conference and fill halls with big audiences, as he travelled up and down the country preaching his version of left-wing socialism. His energy was almost demonic, as his diaries for the period from Labour's defeat in May 1979 to the narrow failure of his deputy leadership bid in October 1981 testify.

The Bennite cocktail was a heady brew, part economic and part constitutional. He had put together all the left-wing nostrums of the last decade – import controls, public ownership, planning agreements, workers' control and withdrawal from the Common Market – and called it 'the Alternative Strategy'. To this superficially plausible, if wrong-headed, economic programme, Benn added the notion of 'internal party democracy'. In a breathtaking leap for a minister who had served throughout the Wilson and Callaghan administrations, he accused those governments of ignoring conference and manifesto commitments and argued that to prevent this happening again the Labour leadership and members of Parliament needed to be made more accountable. Hence the case for giving the extra-parliamentary party (the trade unions and constituency parties) a predominant say in electing the leadership; for giving constituency parties the mandatory right to reselect members of Parliament; and for taking control of the manifesto away from the leadership and giving it to the National Executive – the three demands of the Campaign for Labour Party Democracy (CLPD), a grass-roots organisation established to make the Labour Party more accountable.

The Bennite agenda appealed not only to the hard left and Trotskyite fringe groups (which, following the abandonment of the proscribed list in 1972, had grown more influential within the party) but also to idealistic younger members drawn from the new salariat of teachers, local government employees and social workers who felt that Labour governments had failed and were looking for something different. At the 1979 party conference that followed Labour's defeat, speaker after speaker, including the party's general secretary, Ron Hayward, accused the leadership and Labour MPs of betrayal; both mandatory reselection and the principle of exclusive NEC control over the manifesto were won. The wind was with the Bennites and Callaghan seemed powerless to stop them.

It was against this background of Labour convulsion as well as of an ideological Thatcherite government that a siren voice from the continent made itself heard. In November 1979, Roy Jenkins was invited to give the Dimbleby Lecture. As President of the European Commission, he was expected to speak about European issues but he decided to talk on British politics under the title of 'Home Thoughts from Abroad'.

The last part of Jenkins' presidency had been dominated and to some extent undermined by the British budgetary question or what the new Conservative Prime Minister, Mrs Thatcher, called 'my money'. Because of the pattern of its trade, the UK paid more on average in import levies and custom duties to the EC, while, because of the huge preponderance of agriculture in EC expenditure, it received little back. Jenkins believed that it was essential for the UK's long-term relations with the EC for a fair solution to be found but was dismayed by Mrs Thatcher's strident negotiating tactics which needlessly upset the other members of the EU. Their annoyance with the UK also had the effect of making it less likely that Jenkins, as a UK national, would be given the chance of staying on for a second term as President, though even if the offer had been made, Jenkins probably would not have accepted – his interest had now firmly switched back to British politics. Not yet sixty, he told friends, 'My adrenalin is flowing again. The sap is rising in my old bones.'[24]

The question for Roy was what kind of politics it was to be. He had left for Brussels at the end of 1976 disillusioned by the Labour Party and what had happened to it since had not made him any more enthusiastic. Meanwhile his European experience, particularly of the Federal Republic, had attracted him strongly towards the continental power-sharing model. Though he still remained nominally a member of the Labour Party (the Jenkins paid by banker's order), he had not voted at the 1979 election, while his wife had voted Liberal. However, his relations with Callaghan, who twice offered him a peerage and once the governorship of Hong Kong, remained cordial, while a few months after he had delivered the Dimbleby Lecture he received a warm message from Denis Healey through Shirley Williams at a lunch with Roy in Brussels in early 1980.

Denis, who, according to Shirley, was confidently expecting to become leader of the Labour Party in the autumn, wanted Jenkins to come back to the Commons with a view to becoming Foreign Secretary under Healey's premiership. This was an indication of the high regard which Healey continued to have for Jenkins' abilities, but

Roy was unattracted by the offer. One of the reasons given in his autobiography was revealing. 'I did not feel that I could bear dealing with foreign affairs under Healey, which was a subject about which, apart from Europe, he genuinely knew more than I did. As he could not resist lecturing everybody (or at least me) on every subject under the sun, including the few subjects about which he knows less, I thought that the double inferiority would be intolerable.'[25] Ever since their Oxford days, Jenkins had always resented Healey's brand of one-upmanship and too often allowed it to affect their personal relationship. Healey wrote about Jenkins: 'Above all, he was never satisfied with second place in any field. He always wanted to be top. I believe this explains much in his career after his poor showing in the election for the Labour Party leadership in 1976.'[26] No doubt Jenkins had a certain Whig grandeur, accentuated by his experience of the European Commission presidency. It was at about this time that even friends took to calling him 'Le Roi Jean Quinze'. But a more potent consideration was that Roy and Denis simply rubbed each other up the wrong way, an instinctive reaction that both their wives thought foolish.

It would, however, be wrong to attribute Jenkins' post-Brussels political venture purely to his unwillingness to serve under Healey, even though it was clearly a factor. Roy genuinely believed that a new political approach was needed; what was required was 'not to slog through an unending war of attrition, stubbornly and conventionally defending as much of the old citadel as you can hold, but to break out and mount a battle of movement on new and higher ground'. Healey would have agreed with much of Jenkins' analysis, as set out in the Dimbleby Lecture: 'We need the innovating stimulus of the free-market economy without either the unacceptable brutality of its untrammelled distribution of rewards or its indifference to unemployment. This is by no means an impossible combination. It works well in a number of countries.' Jenkins continued: 'The state must know its place which must be an important but far from omnipotent one . . . You want the class system to fade away without being replaced either by an aggressive and intolerant proletarianism or by the dominance of the brash and selfish values of a "get rich quick" society.' All this was the stuff of continental social democracy, which both Jenkins and Healey admired.

The difference between Jenkins and Healey was that Jenkins no longer believed that these objectives could be achieved within the Labour Party. Jenkins condemned 'the constricting rigidity – almost the tyranny of the present party system'. Without actually advocating the creation of a new party, he called for the 'strengthening of the radical centre' to provide both more continuity and more effective political change. He spoke up strongly for proportional representation and for honest coalitions between parties. The conventional wisdom was that parties which split were slaughtered at the polls. But, in a typically erudite Shakespearean allusion, Jenkins claimed that he believed the electorate could tell 'a hawk from a handsaw' and if it saw 'a new grouping with cohesion and relevant policies it might be more attracted by this new reality than by old labels which had become increasingly irrelevant'. A few months later in June 1980, while he was still President of the European Commission, Jenkins was more specific in a parliamentary press gallery speech, calling for a break out from the out-of-date 'mould' in which the politics of left and centre were frozen. With a characteristic flourish, he used the metaphor of an 'experimental plane' to describe his project for a new political party. It could well crash but it might 'soar into the sky', carrying with it 'great and more untapped reserves of political energy and commitment'.

To propose a new political party was a remarkably bold move for a politician who had been born into the Labour Party and, until then, had spent all his life in it. It is doubtful whether he would have seriously considered it without the interlude on the continent which taking up the presidency had given him. Going to Brussels had enabled him to break his old Labour ties without a major wrench. It had also given him the perspective to sort out his political direction. All the same, a public declaration in favour of his 'experimental plane' risked public humiliation. The *Spectator* of 14 June 1980 described Jenkins as 'a fat, flabby and nearly-extinct bird endeavouring to fly but lacking the muscle and momentum to take flight. Mr Jenkins might soar: he is altogether more likely to crash.'[27]

If Jenkins' project was to get off the ground, it needed the support of as many right-wing Labour MPs as possible, especially the three former Cabinet ministers, Shirley Williams, Bill Rodgers and David Owen, who were amongst the brightest and best of the next generation of potential Labour leaders. Dick Taverne, the former MP and one of Jenkins' closest advisors, put it bluntly: 'Unless he (Jenkins) got leading parliamentarians it wasn't likely to be a very successful break . . . He looked like a fat cat from Brussels and wasn't ideally qualified to start a new sort of popular movement.'[28] Before his Dimbleby Lecture, Jenkins had talked to David Steel, the leader of the Liberals who was on the social democratic wing of his party, and agreed with Steel that, rather than Jenkins and his friends joining the Liberals, the creation of a new party would be more likely to strengthen the centre of British politics because it would attract potential Labour defectors. However, at that stage, the three former Labour Cabinet ministers were extremely cautious about what would, after all, be a momentous step for them.

Whereas Roy Jenkins had already virtually burned his Labour Party boats, Bill Rodgers and David Owen were still in the Labour shadow Cabinet, while Shirley Williams, although she had lost her seat at the 1979 election, remained a leading member of Labour's National Executive. Despite being extremely concerned about the victories of the left, they still had not yet given up on the Labour Party. After the Dimbleby Lecture, David Owen said, 'We will not be tempted by siren voices from outside, from those who have given up the fight from within,' while a few months later Shirley Williams, although she was increasingly worried by the influence of the hard left, especially Militant, declared that a centre party would have 'no roots, no principle, no philosophy, and no values'. In November 1979, Bill Rodgers, the right's political organiser par excellence, had warned in a speech at Abertillery that the Labour Party had 'a year – not much longer – in which to save itself' but, as a politician with strong Labour Party loyalties, he still hoped desperately that the battle inside the party would be won.

In a sense, Jenkins and Healey were in a competition for the support of Williams, Rodgers and Owen – the 'Gang of Three', as they came to be known. Healey's handicap, and his biggest failure, was that he did not understand, until it was too late, how desperate the Gang of Three were feeling and how close they were becoming to leaving the party. Healey's dilemma was that in order to be elected leader of the PLP he had also to court the votes of some twenty or thirty MPs who were not strongly aligned to left or right and who basically wanted a quiet life. Yet in the longer term losing Labour MPs from the party, especially those of the quality of the Gang of Three, was a far greater threat to Healey's position in the party and to Labour's future.

As the Bennites swept all before them during 1980, the right, especially David Owen, belatedly threw themselves into the fight-back. 'We must not be afraid,' said Owen at a meeting at Newcastle-upon-Tyne in January, 'to challenge openly authoritarianism, dogma or the threat posed by the élitism of the activists . . . we have not challenged vigorously enough those who are contemptuous of consensus and scornful of compromise.'[29] In a meeting organised by the Campaign for Labour Victory, the right-wing grass-roots organisation, he called for 'ten years' hard slog'. But his treatment at a special one-day Labour Party conference in May, held to launch an anti-EEC, pro-unilateralist policy statement entitled *Peace, Jobs and Freedom*, when he was hounded down as he bravely put the case against unilateralism, drawing on his experience as Foreign Secretary, changed his mind about the viability of the Labour Party.

After hearing that the left proposed reopening the issue of British membership of the EEC, Owen got together for the first time with Rodgers and Williams and they issued a firm statement in June about their position. 'Is this decision endlessly to be reopened? Are the old divisions to be stirred up again and again? There are some of us who will not accept a choice between Socialism and Europe. We will choose them both.' In August, the Gang of Three, as they came then to be known, wrote a broader and sharper 'open letter', published in the *Guardian* and the *Daily Mirror*, which spoke up for parliamentary democracy, the mixed economy, British membership of the EEC and NATO; attacked left-wing dishonesty, escapism and anti-democratic tendencies; and concluded with a threat. Although they believed that the best option was to fight for a democratic socialist Labour Party, they specifically said that if the Labour Party 'abandons its democratic and internationalist principles, the argument may grow for a new democratic socialist party to establish itself as a party of conscience and reform committed to those principles'. The prospect of a split was, for the first time, out in the open.

The Gang of Three had been dismayed by the weakness of the Callaghan leadership, especially over the left's constitutional agenda. If today the idea of reselection and extending the franchise for the election of a leader beyond purely MPs, provided it is on the basis of one person, one vote, appears non-controversial, at the time it was clear to most Labour MPs that the Bennite proposals were as much motivated by the left's drive for power as by democratic considerations. The so-called Rank and File Mobilising Committee, a Bennite hard-left umbrella organisation that included the Trotskyite Militant Tendency, made it clear that their 'game plan' was to pack constituency General Management Committees in order to replace right-wing MPs by left-wing ones, while the purpose of the electoral college idea of MPs, unions and constituency parties was to stop Healey, if possible by electing Benn and if not by an interim figure such as Michael Foot.

It was against the background of left-wing intransigence that the disastrous Commission of Inquiry, the brainchild of David Basnett, General Secretary of the General and Municipal Workers, was held. Basnett, at that time the most prominent trade union leader, was a decent, honourable man who hoped that by getting the contestants together he could broker an honourable compromise. But the left-wing majority proceeded to rig the membership of the Commission by appointing seven left wingers to represent itself, while allowing the PLP only two representatives, Jim Callaghan and Michael Foot. The five representing the trade unions were more balanced politically; but the overall figures gave the left a built-in majority, in Benn's estimate, of ten to four.[30] Denis Healey, who was not a member of the Commission, protested against the rigged membership but his pleas were ignored.[31]

At the final meeting of the Commission at Bishop's Stortford in June, Callaghan, despite pleas from the shadow Cabinet and the PLP to hold firm, weakly accepted a compromise proposal of an electoral college, with fifty per cent for the PLP, twenty-five per cent for the unions, twenty per cent for the constituencies, and five per cent for the socialist societies. This led to a furious row in the shadow Cabinet, with Callaghan being accused by Owen, Rodgers and Hattersley of 'selling out'; while at a PLP meeting at the end of June, speaker after speaker denounced the Bishop's Stortford compromise. Both right and left rejected its electoral college formula, the right because it conceded the principle and the left because the PLP had been given too large a share of the electoral college vote. The Callaghan leadership was fatally wounded.

The fall-out over Bishop's Stortford also badly damaged Denis

Healey. Healey was angry with Callaghan for compromising the PLP's position but, when urged by David Owen either to insist on Callaghan's resignation or at least to publicly lead the PLP's opposition to Bishop's Stortford, he refused to speak out. He kept quiet for fear of upsetting Callaghan, whom he felt still might be able to influence the result of a leadership election, and also of offending trade union leaders whose support he would need to turn the party around. He assured Bill Rodgers that he had 'told Jim to toughen up' but there was no evidence of this.[32] Healey himself later wrote that 'it was Bishop's Stortford which caused the conception of the Social Democratic Party, although its birth took place, appropriately enough, nine months later'. Denis later justified his silence by arguing in a contradictory way that, if the Bishop's Stortford compromise had been accepted by Conference, it might have kept the party together.[33]

In September, just before Conference, Healey had a meeting with the Gang of Three, which he badly mishandled. At last aware of the danger of a split, he correctly predicted that, given the first-past-the-post electoral system, a new centre party was unlikely to establish itself as a serious competitor to the Labour Party. He also said that the moderates, working with the unions, had a good chance of winning a majority on the NEC but that it was bound to take several years, a prediction which also proved accurate. The Gang of Three were less impressed by his predictions than by his complacent attitude. One of them reported him as saying, 'The Labour Party wasn't in much of a mess: the trade unions could sort it out in any case; and it didn't matter about policy, because you could say what you like in opposition and then put it right in government. The main thing was to be in power. It was a typical Healey performance. I got very angry with him.'[34] One of Healey's journalist friends commented that Denis had 'an unshakeable faith in the proposition that it would all be right on the night',[35] which was not the message that the despairing trio wanted to hear. After their long meeting with Healey, the Gang of Three had little confidence that he would be the fighting leader along the lines of Gaitskell, which they believed that Labour now needed.

The next event and another nail in Labour's coffin was the Blackpool party conference which began on 29 September 1980. For Benn, the 1980 conference represented the zenith of his influence inside the Labour Party. He seemed to be everywhere, addressing innumerable fringe meetings to rapturous applause and electrifying the main conference hall by his platform speeches. In an extraordinary blast of demagoguery, Benn wound up Monday's economic debate by promising three Bills as soon as the next Labour government took power – the first, an Industry Act to nationalise industries, to control capital and to introduce industrial democracy 'within days'; the second to restore all powers from Brussels to Westminster 'within weeks'; the third to create an immediate thousand peers, to be followed by the abolition of the House of Lords. Conference delegates roared their approval but many of his parliamentary colleagues thought he had literally taken leave of his senses. At a Campaign for Labour Victory fringe meeting, Shirley Williams, who had served in Labour Cabinets with Benn, repeated his three legislative commitments. She went on: 'And all this would be done in a couple of weeks. I wonder why Tony was so unambitious. After all, it took God only six days to make the world.'

The right, however, suffered defeat after defeat that week, including withdrawal from the European Community without a referendum and the removal of all nuclear bases, British as well as American, from the United Kingdom. David Owen and Bill Rodgers both made coura- geous speeches from the floor but were hissed and booed for their pains. In a reversal of the vote the previous year, the right succeeded in keeping control of the manifesto away from the NEC. But the other constitutional proposals were lost. Mandatory reselection was ratified. The principle of an electoral college was carried, though after consid- erable confusion following the rejection of all the specific voting proportions. The issue of mechanics was postponed to a special con- ference in January. If it was a heady triumph for the left-wing delegates who flooded the conference, it was a horrendous experience for the beleaguered right, especially the Gang of Three, who were on the brink of leaving the party. The distinguished political columnist, Peter Jenkins of the *Guardian*, summed up their desperation when he wrote: 'My nightmare of the week is that political liberty is now at threat in Britain, for I cannot feel confident that it would long survive the coming to power of the people who have taken hold of the Labour Party.'[36]

A few days after Conference, on 15 October, Callaghan resigned, thus ensuring that the resulting leadership election would be under the old rules. I noted in my diary that day: 'I see Jim Callaghan waving a last farewell to the cameramen. He was a good Prime Minister but he mistimed the election and then stayed on too long afterwards.'[37] Trying to make up for lost time, Denis Healey, the only candidate of the centre-right, immediately announced his candidature. Peter Shore, shadow Foreign Secretary, who fancied his chances of victory, and John Silkin, the former Agriculture Minister who, like Shore, was passionately anti-Common Market, also put their hats in the ring. A surprise late entry was Michael Foot. He was persuaded to stand by Neil Kinnock, newly appointed by Jim Callaghan to the front bench as shadow Education Secretary; by Clive Jenkins, the shrewdly manipulative leader of the white collar union, ASTMS; and by his adoring wife, Jill Craigie, in order both to 'stop Healey' and to unite the Labour Party. The GMWU General Secretary, David Basnett, unwisely allowed himself to be pressured by some of his trade union colleagues, led by Clive Jenkins, into backing Foot's candidature, at least as a caretaker candidate until the new leadership rules had been decided at the January special conference. Tony Benn, still fresh from his conference victories, decided not to stand on the grounds that after the vote at Blackpool a purely parliamentary election was illegitimate; he would, in any case, have been trounced.

In normal circumstances Healey would have won. With his experience as Defence Secretary and Chancellor he was by far the best equipped of the candidates to be Prime Minister. Michael Foot had many qualities but the ability to lead the country was not one of them. In October 1980, Healey was comfortably the most popular politician in the country with Foot scarcely registering in the polls. But these were not normal times. Even if the leadership election was being decided under the old rules, the Blackpool conference had changed everything. It was true that Healey suffered from obvious disadvantages as candidate. He was a loner, without a network of political friends like Jenkins (though a campaign team, which included ex-Cabinet ministers Roy Hattersley and Eric Varley, as well as Healey stalwarts, such as his former PPS Barry Jones, was quickly assembled). There were also MPs who had been offended at some time or other by Healey's well-known abrasiveness. But these handicaps were minor compared with two competing post-Blackpool pressures with which Denis had to contend.

The first was from demoralised and alienated right wingers, a number of whom were considering leaving the party. They wanted Denis to act as their champion, to speak out clearly against what had happened at Blackpool. Healey brusquely refused, at least until he was elected, though he said he would lead the PLP's fight on the workings of reselection and on making the electoral college as democratic as possible. In contrast to the other candidates, Denis mistakenly declined to contribute a *Guardian* article setting out his personal credo. And when he met the officers of the right-wing Manifesto group, Denis's reply to the question: 'Why should we vote for you?' was said to have been: 'You have nowhere else to go.'[38] He was about to be proved wrong.

The main reason for Healey's caution was that he was trying to persuade a nervous bunch of uncommitted MPs, many of whom were under attack in their constituencies, to vote for him. An indication of the pressure MPs were under is that, even in my normally solidly moderate northern constituency party, a local Rank and File Mobilising Committee minority grouping (under Militant control) unsuccessfully tried to mandate me to vote for Foot, though I was working for Healey. After Blackpool, some MPs were desperately worried about their reselection prospects. They were also concerned that even if Healey won he would be immediately challenged under the new rules by Tony Benn, thus unleashing a fresh period of instability and disruption. The election of Michael Foot, they hoped, would solve their reselection problems. In this sense, as Roy Hattersley put it, 'Michael Foot was the candidate of the quiet life,'[39] though, once elected, Foot comprehensively failed to deliver.

Healey led on the first ballot with 112 votes to Michael Foot's eighty-three, with thirty-eight for Silkin and thirty-two for Shore. This was about ten votes short of the Healey camp's private predictions, so it was clear that the run-off was going to be close. Even so, Foot's narrow victory by 139 votes to 129 for Healey on 10 November was an almost unbelievable result to many of Healey's supporters. How could a man so eminently qualified to be leader and Prime Minister be beaten by someone so obviously inferior? Afterwards it was revealed that certainly five and probably more potential defectors had voted for Foot in order to make a split more likely – enough at least to produce a tie[40] – while at least a dozen uncommitted MPs succumbed to constituency pressure and went for Foot to save their skins (though some lost their seats at the subsequent election). Faced with a critical test in the last purely parliamentary leadership election, the PLP lost their collective nerve and voted for a prolonged spell in opposition.

A Healey leadership is one of the great might-have-beens of Labour Party history. It would certainly have prevented an SDP breakaway. Even if Mrs Thatcher had still won in 1983, it would have been by a much narrower margin, leaving Labour well placed both to modernise itself and then to stage a political comeback at least one, if not two elections before it finally took place in 1997. Yet Healey himself, because of his poor tactics following Labour's defeat in 1979 and especially after Bishop's Stortford, must take some of the blame for Foot's victory and for the SDP breakaway.

13

Labour's Civil War and the SDP Split

The defeat of Healey greatly strengthened Jenkins' position. Yet Roy had still to sit and wait, like a patient angler, for the Gang of Three to make up their minds about whether to leave Labour and join him in the setting up of a new party. Although Jenkins was closer to Shirley Williams and especially to Bill Rodgers, it was David Owen, with his impetuous and headstrong nature, who moved furthest and fastest.

Jenkins had a first meeting with him at the Owens' Buttermere home on 31 August, followed by a second on 19 October. By the third, which took place at East Hendred on 29 November after Foot's election as leader, Owen told Jenkins that he had decided to leave the Labour Party and that he believed that Shirley Williams would come as well though he was less sure about Bill Rodgers. He wanted the new party to be firmly social democratic and not a centre party, and Shirley not Roy to be its leader. Owen insisted that it was Jenkins who would be joining the Gang of Three rather than the other way round. According to Owen's account, he also raised with Jenkins the issue of choosing the new leader by a vote of the party membership on the basis of 'one member, one vote'.[1] During 1980, mainly as a response to the Bennite constitutional proposals, Owen and Williams had come round to support full party democracy for the leadership, though Rodgers still preferred to confine the vote to MPs. For Owen, it now became a point of principle, one of the reasons he gave for refusing to stand for the shadow Cabinet and for leaving the Labour Party.

If it was David Owen who made the running, it was Shirley Williams who was the key figure in any Labour breakaway. Popular both within the Labour Party and with the voters, she had a charm and warmth almost unique in politics. She was a success as a Labour Cabinet minister, but she was notoriously unpunctual and had a reputation for indecisiveness, at least about her own future. Jenkins, who had a number of meetings with her throughout 1980, commented that he never came away from an encounter with her 'without being encouraged, bewitched and inspirited, yet also totally mystified about what she was going to do next'.[2] On 28 November, the day before Jenkins' East Hendred meeting with Owen, she had told her constituency party at Stevenage (where she had been unexpectedly defeated at the 1979 election) that she was not prepared to stand as their candidate at the next election because she could not 'honestly expound and defend' the policies agreed at the October conference. Yet she remained a member of the National Executive Committee and, only a few days before the Wembley conference, told a lunch meeting of her three ex-PPSs that, though a breakaway party would come into being, she had not yet finally made up her mind to join. At this lunch, she asked, 'Is it possible to bring the party round?' John Cartwright replied, 'No,' Bob Mitchell said, 'Probably, no,' and I said, 'It will take time.'[3]

Bill Rodgers was both the closest to Roy Jenkins in personal terms and at the same time the most reluctant of the three to leave the Labour Party. He had the strongest emotional ties of the Gang of Three and a number of his most intimate associates were urging him to stay and fight. Unlike Owen, he stood for the shadow Cabinet in November 1980 and had come a respectable eighth out of twelve. However, despite being warned, Michael Foot seemed blissfully unaware of the imminent threat of a breakaway and foolishly failed to offer him a portfolio commensurate with his status. Rodgers, understandably, came to the conclusion that Foot was totally unsuited to be a party leader and, while in bed with a bad back over the Christmas recess, eventually decided that 'leaving the Labour Party was the only course open to me consistent with what my life in politics had been'.[4] He rang up Roy Jenkins and Shirley Williams and broke the news to them that he would join. A few days later, on the eve of the Wembley conference, Rodgers told a traumatic meeting at his home with three officers of the Manifesto Group, Ken Weetch, his former PPS, George Robertson (now Secretary General of NATO) and myself, that he was leaving the party. Bill, upset by the parting, not only upbraided me but also threatened to put up a candidate against Ken Weetch, who had narrowly won his marginal Ipswich seat in 1979. Weetch, who was very shocked, exclaimed, 'I cannot believe this is happening.'[5]

Once the Gang of Three had decided on leaving Labour and on joining with Jenkins in a 'Gang of Four' to set up a new party, the shambolic Wembley conference held on 24 January to decide the mechanics of an electoral college provided a tailor-made pretext for the break. At Wembley Owen made a good speech in favour of electing the leader by 'one member, one vote' but, as he confidently expected, the motion was decisively rejected. Then by a bizarre combination of right-wing incompetence (the AUEW abstained on the key vote) and fast left-wing footwork, the conference voted for an electoral college formula (forty per cent for the unions, thirty per cent for the PLP and thirty per cent for the constituencies) which the majority did not want. The Wembley conference, with its television images of trade union barons manipulating votes, did the Labour Party maximum damage and provided the ideal launch pad for the five hundred word statement issued by the Gang of Four the following day. The so-called Limehouse Declaration began: 'The calamitous outcome of the Labour Party Wembley conference demands a new start in politics.'

The Limehouse Declaration, named after the district of the East End of London where David Owen lived, was, for the most part, an unexceptional revisionist document which nearly all German Social Democrats, most Labour right-wingers of the time and indeed the vast majority of Tony Blair's New Labour Party today would have no trouble in supporting. It specifically rejected 'the politics of an inert centre purely representing the lowest common denominator between two extremes'. Its purpose was 'to rally all those who are committed to the values, principles and policies of social democracy'. It called for 'an open, classless and more equal society' and the need for Britain 'to recover its self-confidence and be outward-looking rather than isolationist, xenophobic or neutralist'. It wanted 'to eliminate poverty and promote greater equality without stifling enterprise or imposing bureaucracy from the centre'. It supported 'more, not less, radical change in our society, but with a greater stability of direction'; it backed a healthy public sector and a healthy private sector 'without frequent frontier changes'.

The dynamite was not in the Limehouse Declaration's principles or policies. It was rather in its politics. The call for the setting up of a Council for Social Democracy was clearly a staging post on a journey out of the Labour Party. If there was any doubt about their message, the last two sentences made the position of the Gang of Four obvious: 'We recognise that for those people who have given much of their lives to the Labour Party the choice that lies ahead will be deeply painful. But we believe that the need for a realignment of British politics must now be faced.'

How far did the Limehouse Declaration represent Jenkins' views? Reflecting later conflicts, David Owen stressed in his autobiography that the Declaration was 'not a rallying cry for the new centre party with which Roy had been associated since the Dimbleby Lecture' and accused Jenkins of signing up under false pretences: 'He had not abandoned his concept of a centre party linked to the Liberals; if we wanted to call ourselves social democrats, talk about socialism and even join the Socialist International he would go along with that, biding his time until we were out of the Labour Party and had burnt our boats and then push the Liberal link.'[6] Jenkins firmly rejected the charge of false pretences. He not only signed the Declaration but wrote the first draft. He had made it clear from the time of the Dimbleby Lecture onwards that he was seeking to strengthen the 'radical centre' and he believed that the most effective way that this could be achieved was by setting up a new party that would work in alliance with the Liberals. At that time, he had no plans for promoting a merger with the Liberal Party. He also believed that the other three had endorsed the alliance idea when they had agreed to call for a realignment of British politics.

Jenkins, however, was strongly of the view that the new party had to appeal to those who had never been Labour voters as well as those who had and that, though it should be radical, it should not 'cling to the imprecise and musty "socialist label"'. While prepared to accept the term 'social democrat', Jenkins had stopped using the word 'socialist' for some years; as Roy pointed out, Owen himself removed mentions of 'socialist' from the second edition of his book *Face The Future*.[7] Bill Rodgers' judgement was that when it came to decisions on policy, Jenkins generally agreed with Rodgers and Williams but that he 'was much less committed to an identifiable political philosophy'. Rodgers described Roy 'as a tolerant liberal, believing that the best guarantee of good government was that it should be entrusted to intelligent, wise and generous men and women who by instinct would make the right decisions'.[8] Probably the best way to place Roy Jenkins at the beginning of 1981 was that he was a liberal social democrat by tradition and instinct but extremely sceptical about the conventions of party politics. He hoped that the SDP would be a non-ideological 'anti-party party' which would unite behind it a broad swathe of opinion that was 'liberal and internationalist, concerned with conscience and reform'.[9]

The publication of the Limehouse Declaration and the setting up of the Council of Social Democracy created an almost irresistible momentum. Thousands of messages of support as well as donations poured in in response to an advertisement in the *Guardian*. The launch of the new party, to be called the Social Democratic Party (SDP), was brought forward to 26 March. The launch, masterminded by the former Labour MP Mike Thomas, was a highly professional media 'spectacular'.[10] About five hundred members of the press and media attended the press conference at the Connaught Rooms, where the Gang of Four, seated in strict alphabetic order, fielded questions with growing confidence. Jenkins said that the SDP offered a new political approach: 'We want to get away from the politics of outdated dogmatism and class confrontation . . . to release the energies of the people.'

The creation of the first new national party since 1900 aroused great enthusiasm. It was a wonderful time to start a new political party. During 1981 the Conservative government, faced by both rising inflation and rising unemployment, became increasingly unpopular, with Mrs Thatcher herself the least well-regarded Prime Minister since polling began. Labour, led by the manifestly incompetent Michael Foot and wracked throughout much of 1981 by a divisive deputy leadership election, slipped from forty-six per cent in January's Gallup poll to twenty-three per cent by the end of the year, the biggest fall ever by any party in any one year. Following the SDP launch, the SDP and Liberals combined moved into second place and, after the party conference season, went top with fifty per cent of the poll. A third party surge on this scale and duration had never been seen before. Jenkins' 'experimental plane' had apparently transformed itself into a mighty rocket.

A key part of the SDP's initial strategy was to persuade Labour MPs to join it. Thirteen MPs left the Labour Party to become founder members of the SDP; fifteen more came over during 1981 or at the beginning of 1982. The departure of twenty-eight Labour MPs was the biggest breakaway from any party for nearly a century and helped give the new party momentum. A few went over to the SDP because they were in trouble over reselection. The majority were motivated by despair about their old party and their hopes for the new one they were joining. Obviously their departure weakened the right inside the Labour Party. Yet, crucially, the twenty-eight defectors represented only just over a third of the members of the centre-right Manifesto Group and under a quarter of the 129 members of the PLP who had voted for Denis Healey in the second ballot of the leadership election.

For a variety of reasons the majority of moderate Labour MPs, most of whom shared almost identical political views with those MPs who left the party, stayed. For some, leaving the party to which they were attached both by tradition and sentiment was simply unthinkable. Roy Hattersley's reaction following the disastrous Wembley conference was typical: 'If the ship sank, I would go down with it.'[11] Others felt an overriding loyalty not so much to the national Labour Party but to their local constituency parties who had backed them through thick and thin; leaving would have been kicking them in the teeth. Another factor was the assessment that different MPs made about Labour's prospects. If the defectors were pessimistic, many of those that stayed thought that with time the Labour Party could be brought to its senses. We believed that 'staying and fighting' was a viable option. Those who had European links, such as myself, doubted whether the SDP could or would become a genuine social democratic party on the continental model. We also drew on continental experience to make the obvious point that, in those countries where the left was split, the right was almost always in power.[12]

If the right was to maintain its position and begin the fight-back inside the Labour Party the crucial figure was Denis Healey. Peter

Jenkins, the *Guardian* columnist, who at that time was close to Healey, claimed that after the Wembley conference and the SDP breakaway, Denis had very seriously considered putting himself at the head of the new party.[13] Healey had made clear in the Sarah Barker Memorial Lecture that Labour needed 'to do a Bad Godesberg' and modernise its approach. If he had joined the new party, the breakaway from Labour would have been much larger and the SDP would have won over the most popular politician in the country to their ranks. However, whether the Gang of Four, especially Jenkins, would have accepted Healey as their leader is another matter.

But if Healey saw the attraction of the new party as a means of achieving what Labour revisionists had failed to deliver inside the Labour Party, his loyalty to the party, especially in Leeds, and to its working-class and trade-union roots held him back. His knowledge of international politics also made him sceptical about the long term prospects for the breakaway party, though he was only too well aware of the short- and medium-term damage that the SDP could do to Labour. Healey had another option. Following his leadership defeat he could have decided to leave politics altogether. In early April 1981 Denis was officially approached in Bonn to see if he would accept nomination as Secretary General of NATO but he turned it down because he saw it as his duty to stay and fight for the future of the Labour Party.

He certainly had a fight on his hands. On April Fool's Day Denis was speaking in Hamburg when he heard the news that Tony Benn was challenging him for the deputy leadership. Healey had been elected deputy leader by acclamation of the PLP immediately following his defeat by Michael Foot. Now Benn announced his candidature at the bizarre time of 3.30 a.m., ostensibly to try out the new electoral rules but in reality to consolidate the hard-left gains and to try and replace Healey, whom many of Benn's associates regarded as beatable, as a first step to toppling Foot.

Imagine Healey's predicament. Here he was having to fight with all his might for a position that he did not really want, as deputy to a man whom he knew was not cut out to be leader of the Labour Party. While Benn was on a high, Healey described the six months of elec-tioneering 'as the busiest and least agreeable of his life'.[14] On top of his duties in Parliament, (he was shadow Foreign Secretary as well as deputy leader) in the shadow Cabinet and on the NEC of the party, he now had to travel the length and breadth of the country speaking to constituency and trade union meetings and giving daily radio and television interviews. His public rallies were sometimes disrupted by groups of Trotskyites and other extremists whom Benn, to his discredit, did nothing to discourage or condemn. Yet Healey ploughed doggedly on, determined to prevent Benn becoming deputy leader. With justification, he believed that the result of a Benn victory would turn the trickle of defections to the SDP into an avalanche and the Labour Party would find it virtually impossible to recover.

Denis retained his good humour. Here is a contemporary account by his research assistant, Richard Heller, of Healey in his office:

> Some heavy steps in the corridor. The door crashes open. Some hummed vaudeville music on a rising beat: 'Yah, dah-de-dah-dah-DAH.' Arms flung aloft to greet the applause for the star . . . The man moves to his desk.
>
> 'I was brilliant on TV last night.'
>
> 'You were rude and omniscient as usual.'
>
> 'I called Howe a sado-monetarist . . . What have I got today? Lunch for the King of G and PM questions. Then I want to dictate to Harriet [his devoted secretary]. Then I've got this new ambassador. The Foreign Affairs team. Then I've got to see Bugalugs.'
>
> 'Bugalugs?'
>
> 'Francis Pym' [the Conservative Foreign Secretary].
>
> He peers intently at the next entry in his diary. 'It says Dracula.' I look at my own diary. 'That's Dr Acola, Chairman-in-exile of the National Liberation Front.'[15]

If his leadership campaign had been a disaster, Healey was at his most impressive when he had his back to the wall during the deputy leadership. He did not talk much about constitutional matters, though he stressed the importance of one-person, one-vote in the constituency parties and of trade unions consulting their members before they decided whom to support. He made authoritative speeches and wrote articles about a wide range of policy issues including employment, economic and industrial policy, foreign affairs, the north–south divide, disarmament and arms control. He did not attack frontally the new party position on unilateralism and withdrawal from the Common Market but he conspicuously failed to endorse them.

He criticised the left for its intolerance and sectarianism and deplored the assault on the authority and integrity of Labour MPs. In a swipe at Benn, he declared, 'I believe that we must be honest with our movement and with the electorate as a whole by rejecting the easy answer, the instant solution and the temptation to promise more than we can help perform.' He compared the approach of the democratic socialist to that of a gardener: 'You have to respect the nature of the soil. You must know that certain plants will grow in certain places and not in others. And you've got to be prepared for a plague of rabbits to eat them all up before they grow.' Above all, he put with dignity and courage the unfashionable case for a broadly based Labour Party, in touch with the concerns of the voters and prepared to take on the responsibilities of government: 'For us to spend our time chopping logic about detailed issues of the constitution when we ought to be trying to lead the world to peace and lead our own people to full employment and low inflation is a cop-out.'

Instantly recognisable by his bulky frame, florid complexion and, of course, his bushy eyebrows, he would be warmly welcomed on his journey round the country. Shamelessly trading on the impersonation of him by the television performer, Mike Yarwood, Healey would go into a comic routine that gave great pleasure to all those he met. To his campaign team, he revealed aspects of his personality which those who thought of him only as an arrogant bully had never seen. Returning on the train from meetings, he would nurse a gin and tonic and apply his formidable mind to books, photography, travel, marriage and children, as well as politics and international relations. I wrote at the time: 'I am struck not only by the breadth of his interests but also by his lack of resentment over his leadership defeat. For Denis, there is far more to life than personal ambition.'[16]

Meeting the evening before the count (to take place on the Sunday of party conference), Healey and his campaign managers agreed that the contest for the deputy leadership was too close to call. The outcome turned on three votes. The first was that of the National Union of Public Employees, which had carried out a full consultation of its branches. This showed a majority for Healey, though until its pro-Benn leadership announced that it would vote for Healey, there was some doubt as to how its vote would actually be cast. The Transport and General Workers' Union's regional soundings also revealed a big pro-Healey majority which, to its great shame, the executive decided to ignore. On the first ballot it voted for John Silkin, the 'soft left' candidate who had been persuaded to run by Michael Foot. On the second ballot, the TGWU delegation decided on the floor of the conference to vote for Benn, which left the overall result too close to call. In the end, the deputy leadership was decided by a handful of left-wing MPs led by the future leader, Neil Kinnock, who preferred to abstain rather than vote for Benn. Healey was ahead by 50.426 per cent to Benn's 49.574 per cent. Denis had won by an eyebrow – or four-fifths of one per cent.

That evening, I wrote in my diary, 'By beating Benn, however narrowly, Denis Healey has saved the Labour Party.'[17] This instant judgement looked wildly over-optimistic in late 1981, as Labour, discredited by the glaring disunity and the gross trade union manipulation displayed during the deputy leadership election, plummeted in the polls and the SDP went from strength to strength. Kinnock's remark about Benn: 'He's created the SDP single-handed,' was apposite.[18] Yet, though it took another sixteen years and four General Elections before Labour got back to power, Healey's victory was nevertheless a turning point. Benn, who subsequently lost his seat at the 1983 election, was stopped in his tracks. The hard left's stranglehold on the National Executive was broken. And, despite the subsequent defection of a dozen more Labour MPs to the SDP, the size of the breakaway was effectively limited by Healey's victory. If Healey had been defeated by Benn, at least thirty or forty more MPs might either have joined the SDP or, as in my case, have left politics altogether.[19] Labour might indeed have found it difficult to survive a haemorrhage of such proportions. In that sense, Healey's deputy leadership victory in 1981 did save the Labour Party. It also dished Jenkins.

While Denis Healey was contesting Labour's deputy leadership election with considerable courage and tenacity, Roy Jenkins was risking his political credibility and that of the SDP in a gambler's throw at the Warrington by-election. In May 1981, Sir Tom Williams, the Labour MP for Warrington, resigned to become a circuit judge. On the face of it, Warrington, a solid working-class Lancashire constituency, was very unpromising ground for the SDP. In 1979, Labour had got sixty-two per cent of the vote, the Liberals a derisory nine per cent. Yet the SDP had no choice but to contest the seat. If it did not fight Warrington, its pretensions as a national party would immediately be exposed. On the other hand, if it did badly there, the 'experimental plane' might crash ignominiously into the ground.

The obvious candidate, with all her charismatic appeal, was Shirley Williams. She had the added advantage of being a Catholic in a constituency with a sizeable Catholic majority. An early private poll commissioned by the party showed that Shirley would attract more votes from both Labour and Conservatives than Roy Jenkins.[20] But, for both personal and political reasons, she declined to stand. David Owen described this as 'the worst decision Shirley has ever made in politics'.[21] Certainly, it cost her the leadership of the SDP, if she had ever wanted it.

Although just as doubtful as Shirley Williams about Warrington, Roy Jenkins knew that her decision not to stand left him with no alternative but to put his own hat in the ring, even though a bad result would almost certainly finish his political comeback. On 8 June, he announced his candidature and three days later he was adopted by a meeting of SDP members in the town and then endorsed by the Liberals, who had decided to give Jenkins a free run. Putting employment and a break-out from the old political system at the top of his agenda, he reminded the meeting that 'the idea that I have served my political life in rolling pastures or leafy suburban avenues, which some papers seem to suggest, is ludicrous. I have represented one of the most industrial seats in Birmingham for twenty-seven years and I believe I had happy relations with them.'[22]

The image of Roy Jenkins, which even the best broadsheets uncritically accepted, was that of a claret-drinking, Euro-fanatic élitist, quite unable to mingle with ordinary people. The reality was different. Jenkins could be shy on first encounter and his style and manner of speaking was both more reserved and more convoluted than, say, Shirley Williams'. But he was a highly experienced politician whose charm, courtesy and honesty could win over people from all walks of life. Even David Owen, not Jenkins' most friendly critic, admitted that he fought a spirited campaign at Warrington.

After a quiet start, Roy got into his stride. Though later at Hillhead and elsewhere, the SDP held highly successful public meetings, at Warrington the battle was fought mainly on the doorstep. As Jenkins wrote later, 'We canvassed the town, almost all made up of small ter-raced or semi-detached houses and practically no tenements, with the intensity of carpet-bombing.'[23] The voters of Warrington seemed to like having such a distinguished statesman so anxious to meet them, especially when he was supported by Shirley Williams, Bill Rodgers and David Owen, as well as David Steel, Jo Grimond, and Cyril Smith for the Liberals. Bill Rodgers developed a remarkable technique on a portable microphone, acting as a one-man Greek chorus on the pass-ing scene and treating politics as entertainment: 'And now Roy Jenkins is speaking to a lady in a bright green dress and very fetching it is – just outside Harrison's the greengrocers, where they have some excellent cauliflowers on sale for only 41p.'[24] As the carnival atmos-phere invaded the town, Roy increasingly looked as though he was enjoying himself and his smile became broader. By the Monday before polling, SDP canvassers were getting a warm response and, on polling day itself, Jenkins and his supporters were greeted by a chorus of toot-ing motorhorns wherever they went.

Even so, Jenkins did not expect to get much more than thirty per cent of the vote, and to finish a long way behind Doug Hoyle, the Labour candidate who was then a left-wing trade unionist. The result exceeded his expectations. Roy Jenkins achieved 42.5 per cent of the poll, more than quadruple the 1979 Liberal vote, and reduced Labour's 1979 majority from 10,274 to a highly marginal 1759. On BBC tele-vision the election pundit, Robert McKenzie, called Warrington 'the most sensational by-election result of the century', while the *Guardian* declared that 'there has been no time when a fundamental change in the pattern of British politics looked more likely to come than it does this morning'.[25]

After the declaration, in response to what Jenkins called a 'sour and truculent' speech from Hoyle, Roy cast aside his notes and pointed out that Hoyle had just got the worst Labour result in Warrington for fifty years and that, though it was Jenkins' first election defeat since 1945, it was also 'by far the greatest victory in which I have ever par-ticipated'.[26] As Jenkins' battle wagon toured the streets of Warrington the next morning thanking his supporters to the accompaniment of blasts from the film *Chariots of Fire* and Copland's *Fanfare for the Common Man*, it was already clear that the SDP's prospects had been transformed and that Roy Jenkins, by his courageous and daring campaign, had made himself the new party's leading figure. Jim Callaghan, who had never much rated Jenkins' fighting qualities, said later that his opinion of Roy went up sharply after the Warrington by-election.[27] Robin Oakley wrote in the *Daily Mail*: 'Never again will they be able to say that the only thing he is capable of fighting for is a corner table in a good restaurant.'

For the next few months, the new party went from strength to strength. In September, the Liberal assembly, which Jenkins, Williams, and Rodgers, though not David Owen, attended, endorsed the idea of an electoral pact with the SDP. The SDP's first conference, a 'rolling' one that went by train from London to Perth, then to Bradford and back to Central Hall, Westminster, was a great success. In October, the Liberals won the Croydon North-West by-election and on 26 November Shirley Williams sensationally turned a nineteen thousand Conservative majority at Crosby into an Alliance majority of over five thousand. By December, fifty-one per cent of Gallup's respondents said that they would vote for the SDP or Liberal parties at the next General Election. There was heady talk of an Alliance government, perhaps with Roy Jenkins as its Prime Minister, always provided he could find a seat in Parliament.

Then, on 2 January 1982, the death of Sir Thomas Galbraith, a former Conservative junior minister, caused a by-election at Glasgow Hillhead. But though Hillhead was one of the SDP's target seats, Jenkins had no Scottish connections. Even so, his advisors, especially the Labour MP, Bob Maclennan, urged him to fight the seat. For Roy, there was much at stake. Another good second place would not do. This time he had to win. In fact, despite being in Scotland, Hillhead was a good prospect for Jenkins. It was a socially mixed constituency of working-class neighbourhoods along the Clyde with some far more prosperous wards higher up. Hillhead, which could claim to be the best-educated constituency in the United Kingdom, also had a large professional middle class of doctors, university lecturers and teachers who were likely to be susceptible to the charms of both the SDP and Roy Jenkins. Even so Jenkins, after first persuading the Liberals to stand aside, had to fight desperately hard to win the seat. In early 1982, the

Alliance started to decline in the opinion polls. It was a long, ten-week campaign, mostly in poor weather. A poll in the *Observer* on 14 March, only eleven days before polling day, showed Jenkins trailing badly in third place, with Labour in the lead. Roy needed to draw on all his reserves of resilience and determination to keep going. *The Times* columnist Frank Johnson described Jenkins' unusual canvassing technique: 'When working the shopping-centre pavements, Mr Jenkins, once he had trained his woman in his sights, would approach her, and engage her in fatuously polite conversation, bowing slightly from the waist, and sometimes making a graceful gesture as if to raise his hat to her, a considerable trick considering he was not wearing a hat at the time.'[28]

However, in contrast to Warrington, Jenkins' Hillhead campaign was mainly based on public meetings. According to the historians of the SDP, it resembled, 'a noisy lecture series or one of Gladstone's earliest campaigns in the nineteenth century'.[29] At the end, Jenkins calculated that up to twenty-five per cent of the electorate had come to one of his meetings. The high point came a week before the poll, when the Gang of Four spoke at the meeting in a secondary school and then immediately to another huge moonlight meeting made up of those who had been waiting outside. By polling day three opinion polls showed Jenkins in the lead and he won by just over two thousand from the Conservative candidate, with Labour third. It was a good result, though he got only 33.5 per cent of the poll, nine points below Warrington. At the age of sixty-one, Jenkins had returned to the Commons with a strong claim to the SDP's leadership.

Roy Jenkins had hoped that he would be elected leader of the SDP without a contest but David Owen had other ideas. Owen had tried to persuade Shirley Williams to stand because he thought that she was more likely to beat Roy but when she declined he put his own hat in the ring. The chief difference between the two candidates, apart from age, temperament and personal rivalry, was their attitude to the Liberal Party. Unlike Owen, Jenkins got on with Liberals. He also saw a close alliance as the most effective means available for breaking the political mould speedily. By contrast, Owen was suspicious of the Liberals and stressed the need for the SDP to keep their distance from them. 'We gain strength and respect, as Liberals and Social Democrats, from being seen as two parties, working together while retaining an appeal to a broader spectrum of the electorate,' said Owen in his personal statement.[30]

In a one-member, one-vote election, Jenkins won quite comfortably with 55.7 per cent, though Owen ran a very good second and could claim to be the moral victor. But Owen, with his impatience and frustrated ambition, proved to be a bad loser and, according to Rodgers, went into a 'prolonged sulk'.[31] The factional rift between Jenkinsites and Owenites that so marred the SDP's later years took shape during this election and the SDP became a less happy party than before.

For reasons mainly out of the SDP's control and despite the Hillhead triumph, the national position of the Alliance began to weaken. Even before the Falklands War, economic recovery had boosted Conservative support, mainly at the expense of the Alliance parties. After the Falklands, Mrs Thatcher unashamedly cashed in on the victory of British troops: 'We have ceased to be a nation in retreat. We have instead a new-found confidence . . . that confidence comes from the rediscovery of ourselves, and grows with the recovery of our self respect,' she proclaimed.[32] In May 1982, the Tories, who had been so unpopular, went ahead in the polls and never lost their lead in that Parliament, while Labour, without looking remotely like a potential governing party, had at least stabilised its position somewhat after Healey's narrow victory in the deputy leadership election. As he put it in his autobiography, after Hillhead the path grew steeper for both the SDP and Jenkins himself.

Jenkins did not prove as energetic or dynamic a leader of the Social Democrats as his Warrington and Hillhead performances seemed to suggest. Maybe he was already suffering from the thyroid condition that was first diagnosed in 1984. As the Alliance parties' popularity waned and they failed to repeat during the rest of 1982 their by-election success of 1981, Roy seemed incapable of seizing the political initiative. He was unable to establish his authority either in the House of Commons or at his party's headquarters at Cowley Street. Although his political reputation in the late 1960s and early 1970s had been founded on his performances at the Commons dispatch box, he found himself at sea in the more hostile atmosphere of the 1980s. Speaking from the Opposition front bench below the gangway, he was constantly heckled from close quarters by the Labour MP, Dennis Skinner, and his band of left-wing guerrillas. Simon Hoggart, then of the *Observer*, mocked his wrist-rolling oratorical gestures by saying that he looked 'like some medieval baron exerting his *droit de seigneur*, cupping the breast of an innocent young peasant girl.'

Unlike Owen, who performed brilliantly, he had little to say about the Falklands War and failed to make an impact after the war was over. Even his television style, instead of being sharp and direct like Owen's, was lengthy and ponderous, inappropriate for the short interview. A hostile judgement was that 'Roy Jenkins was not at all suited by either aptitude or temperament to be the leader of a struggling new party,' while Harold Lever, an old Labour ally of Jenkins, is said to have remarked, 'Roy would make an admirable Prime Minister if only he could somehow be dropped into Downing Street by helicopter.'[33] Even Bill Rodgers, who considered Roy as 'his elder brother in politics', was disappointed by his lack of drive.[34] Viewed from the Labour benches, I found Jenkins curiously diminished.

As deputy leader of the Labour Party, Denis Healey was having an almost equally frustrating time as Roy Jenkins. His main problem was the inadequacy of Michael Foot's leadership. Although Healey's victory in the deputy leadership election had prevented Labour from disintegrating, the party still had as its leader somebody who was wholly unfitted for the job and who had quickly become a major electoral liability. As Foot's loyal deputy, Healey found himself 'compelled to agree with Michael in public on all issues at all times'.[35]

In private, Denis tried to persuade Foot to modify his policy positions, especially on defence. In September 1981, Foot and Healey flew to Moscow, where Denis argued strongly for the so-called zero option, whereby the Soviet Union would dismantle all its SS-20 intermediate missiles in return for NATO not deploying Cruise or Pershing. Despite his firm line with the Russians, the danger for Healey was that by accompanying Foot to Moscow (significantly Foot never went to the United States) his political opponents could claim that Denis was lending his authority as a former Defence Secretary to unilateralism, especially when he suggested scrapping Polaris in return for an equivalent number of Russian missiles. Curiously enough, over the Falklands it was Foot who was the more bellicose and Healey who voiced reservations about British action to win back the islands. One internal Labour Party issue on which progress began to be made under

Foot was in dealing with the Trotskyite Militants inside the Labour Party. Having gained control of the NEC, Foot and Healey instigated a new inquiry into the grouping and in 1983 the five members of the *Militant* newspaper's editorial board were expelled. However, most voters continued to see Labour as divided, too dominated by extremists, with unpopular policies, above all over unilateralism, and led by a weak leader.

As the Labour Party slid in the poll during 1982 many MPs, including some who had voted for Foot, began openly to talk about replacing him with Denis Healey. The Bermondsey by-election of February 1983, when the Liberal candidate, Simon Hughes, triumphed over a left-wing candidate, Peter Tatchell, and turned a Labour majority of nearly twelve thousand into a Liberal majority of over nine thousand not only gave a much-needed fillip to the Alliance parties but led to renewed calls inside the Labour Party for Foot's resignation. As Foot's deputy, Denis Healey was in a tricky position. He could not campaign to replace Foot as leader and, unless Foot himself decided to step down, it was hard to see how he could be forced to go. The key moment was the Darlington by-election that followed a few weeks later.

At Darlington Labour was defending a highly marginal seat. The first poll, published just after Bermondsey, put the Alliance in the lead with Labour coming a poor third. But the SDP had chosen a weak candidate who, although a popular presenter on Tyne-Tees television, was incapable of getting his head round political issues. With union support, the north-east Labour party, led by moderate local MPs, organised a highly effective campaign behind their candidate, Ossie O'Brien, a respected County Durham teacher. Labour managed to double their 1979 majority, with the Tories a good second and the SDP pushed into third place. After the triumph of Bermondsey, Darlington was a disaster for the Alliance and for the SDP in particular. The irony was that Labour's Darlington victory, organised in the main by centre-right supporters of Denis Healey, also had the effect of saving Michael Foot's leadership, thus guaranteeing the party's disastrous defeat at the coming General Election.

The real victor of Darlington was Mrs Thatcher, who, after good local election results in May, called a June election. Given Labour's unelectability it was always clear that the Conservatives would win the 1983 election. The real battle was for second place, a struggle in which the two remaining Labour revisionists of the 1950s and 1960s, Jenkins and Healey, fought on opposite sides.

The Labour Party fought an appalling election campaign, managing to lose eight points during the campaign itself. Michael Foot, marooned on top of a battle bus, looked increasingly beleaguered. The election manifesto, sardonically described by the shadow Environment Secretary, Gerald Kaufman, as 'the longest suicide note in history', was a ragbag of Labour promises. It was pro-nationalisation, anti-EEC, and semi-unilateralist. To accommodate Denis Healey and the shadow Cabinet majority, the defence section was deliberately ambiguous; it was in favour of getting rid of British nuclear weapons, but a Labour government was committed to a bilateral agreement with the Soviet Union to eliminate an equivalent number of Russian nuclear weapons. It was, however, silent, on what would happen if Russia did not agree. When Denis was asked on a radio phone-in if he would be in favour of keeping Polaris if Russia refused a deal, he replied, 'that seems sensible'. Then Jim Callaghan spoke out strongly in favour of Labour's traditional multilateral position. The split on defence was out in the open, as was Foot's widely unpopular support for unilateralism. Healey tried to rescue a flagging campaign but at the end of one exhausting day he accused Mrs Thatcher of glorying 'in slaughter' over the Falklands and had to apologise. It was not Denis's finest hour.

The Alliance parties fought a better and more coherent campaign than Labour but they too had difficulties over leadership. Just before the election was called, it was announced that Roy Jenkins was to be the Alliance Prime Minister designate, while David Steel would be the leader of the Alliance campaign. The problem was that Steel was more popular with the voters than Jenkins and, as the Alliance remained flat in the polls, pressure grew within the Liberal Party to get Jenkins to step down and make Steel the Alliance leader.

Matters came to ahead at a council of war between the SDP and Liberal leaders at Ettrick Bridge, David Steel's home in the Borders, on Sunday 29 May. The historians of the SDP described it as 'one of the more bizarre episodes in recent British political history, with more than faint echoes of the second act of Macbeth'.[36] At the meeting Steel tried to bounce Jenkins into standing down as Prime Minister designate and to agree to Steel being declared the Alliance's undisputed leader. Rodgers and Williams spoke strongly against Steel's attempted political assassination mainly because, at this stage of the campaign, it would be counterproductive. Owen remained ominously silent. In the end the Liberals dropped their proposal, though it was agreed that David Steel would take a higher profile for the remainder of the campaign.

On 9 June 1983, Mrs Thatcher won a triumphant victory, with the Tory overall majority going up from 43 to 141 seats, although the Tory share of the vote declined slightly compared to 1979. The outstanding feature of the 1983 election was the collapse of the Labour vote, which fell by over nine percentage points to 27.6 per cent – the sharpest fall by any party since the war and the lowest Labour share of the poll since 1918. In 1983 Labour was driven back to its bedrock support in its heartlands of the north of England, Scotland, and Wales, in the big cities and amongst the unskilled workers. The affluent, skilled and home-owning working class deserted Labour in droves. The Alliance parties gained 25.4 per cent of the popular vote, only two per cent behind Labour and the best third-party performance since the 1920s. Yet they won only twenty-three seats and only five SDP members, including Roy Jenkins and David Owen, were elected. Two members of the Gang of Four, Shirley Williams and Bill Rodgers, both lost their seats. Healey's victory in the deputy leadership election in 1981 and the massive handicap of the first-past-the-post electoral system had prevented the breakthrough for which Jenkins had so fervently hoped.

Immediately following the election both Denis Healey and Roy Jenkins fell on their swords. On the Sunday after the election Clive Jenkins, the trade union leader who had played such a prominent part in persuading Michael Foot to run for leadership, announced at his union conference that Foot was standing down and that his union had nominated Neil Kinnock. Clive Jenkins' intervention forced Healey's hand. In any case Denis was aware that, especially after Foot's feeble leadership, the party was likely to prefer somebody younger. Denis, therefore, decided not to run for leader or deputy and supported Roy Hattersley in the ensuing leadership election in which Kinnock won an overwhelming victory.

On the Monday Roy Jenkins issued a press statement that he was resigning from the SPD leadership. On the Saturday before, David Owen, trying his hand, like David Steel, at political assassination, had threatened to force a leadership election in July. Jenkins would have preferred to stay on until autumn but, following Owen's ultimatum, he told a meeting of the Gang of Four held at East Hendred on the Monday morning that he would resign forthwith. Shirley Williams was dismayed but, given Owen's insistence on an immediate handover, Roy had little alternative. It was better for him to go at once rather than wait to be defeated in a leadership election by a younger, more vigorous man.

1983 was the end of the road for both Jenkins and Healey at the very top of British politics, though they remained as influential and respected figures. After the election they both had to resign, partly because of their age (Roy was in his sixty-third and Denis in his sixty-sixth year) but mainly because they had failed. The major blame for Labour's disastrous 1983 performance lay with Michael Foot for his poor leadership and Tony Benn for his irresponsible and destructive behaviour between 1979 and 1982, but Healey had to share some of the responsibility for defeat, above all for his slow response in 1980 to the danger of a breakaway by the Gang of Three, though he could take consolation from his narrow victory in the 1981 deputy leadership election which enabled the party to survive the SDP challenge.

For nearly a year after the formation of the SDP, it seemed a possibility that the 'experimental plane', first floated by Jenkins in his parliamentary press gallery speech in June 1980, might be the means for 'breaking the mould' of British politics. But, although the Alliance performance in 1983 was the best third-party result for fifty years, the reality was that the two allied parties did not make the breakthrough, while Jenkins himself did not prove to be the vigorous campaigning leader which his initial efforts at Warrington and Hillhead had promised.

There was a deeper way in which Healey and Jenkins failed. The split in the Labour Party and the SDP breakaway, to which they had both, in various ways, contributed, led to a dispersal and weakening of the social democratic ideas in which they still believed, despite their differing views and styles. Healey blamed the SDP for Mrs Thatcher's victories and the delay in Labour's recovery.[37] Jenkins argued that without the SDP Labour would never have been dragged back 'from the wilder shores of lunacy and arrogance'.[38] These two contentions are both plausible and are not necessarily mutually exclusive. It is possible, however, that the Labour Party's rejection by the voters in 1983 and 1987 would have taken place even without the SDP and that successive defeats by Mrs Thatcher were the main reason why first Neil Kinnock and then John Smith and, above all, Tony Blair were able to transform Labour into a modern social democratic party. In this sense, democracy produced its own remedy.

All the same, both Jenkins and Healey must take some of the responsibility both for Labour's lurch into unelectability and for its slowness to recover. There is force in the judgement by the shrewd former *Guardian*, *Observer*, and BBC television journalist John Cole, that 'their failure to find a way of working together was a huge factor in giving Mrs Thatcher a free electoral run'.[39] If the two men had been able to co-operate more closely, in the 1970s as well as in the early 1980s, then it is likely that the revisionist, modernising social democratic tendency, both inside the Labour Party and in politics more generally, would have been a good deal more successful than it proved at that time to be.

14

Vigorous Old Age

Denis Healey sometimes used to tease his ambitious younger colleague, Roy Hattersley, that he came of tough, long-lived stock and would be around in politics for a long time to come. When Healey resigned from the deputy leadership in 1983 he was already an old-age pensioner and it would have been understandable if he had retired quietly to Sussex. Yet, even after he left Labour's front bench in 1987 and then the Commons in 1992, he remained astonishingly active well into his eighties, enjoying his status as a celebrity, giving his views on defence, international affairs and the economy, lecturing, writing books, including a splendid autobiography, and cultivating his extensive cultural and intellectual interests.

For Roy Jenkins the last thirteen years of the twentieth century were almost as illustrious and productive a time as the earlier years when he had been a successful Labour Cabinet minister. After a frustrating period in the Commons from 1983 to 1987, he was chosen to be the leader of the Liberal Democrats in the Lords in 1988, a post that he held for ten years. He was elected Chancellor of Oxford University in 1987. The quality of his literary output remained extremely high and included a distinguished autobiography, as well as highly acclaimed lives of two former Prime Ministers, Gladstone and Churchill. Fifteen years after leaving Labour to set up a new party, he became an unofficial mentor to the new Labour leader, Tony Blair, and in 1997, at the Prime Minister's request, he chaired the Independent Commission on the Voting System.

In some ways, Denis Healey's last years as shadow Foreign Secretary were a kind of Indian summer. The new leader, Neil Kinnock, asked Denis, who had come top in the shadow Cabinet elections, to stay on as Foreign Affairs spokesman, presumably because he felt that Healey's heavyweight presence would lend credibility to his untried leadership. Healey agreed, though he had been invited by Arnold Weinstock to become chairman of GEC. For the first time in his parliamentary career, Healey, using wit as well as argument, was able to dominate the Commons. His speech in the debate on the Conservative government's decision in 1984 that members of GCHQ should no longer be allowed to be members of trade unions was a tour de force. 'The Foreign Secretary,' he said, 'is not the real villain in this case; he is the fall guy . . . who is the Mephistopheles behind this shabby Faust? The handling of this decision by . . . the great she-elephant, she-who-must-be-obeyed, the Catherine the Great of Finchley . . . the Prime Minister herself has drawn sympathetic trade unionists into open revolt. Her pig-headed bigotry has prevented her closest colleagues . . . from offering and accepting a compromise'. He went on with words with which many Conservative MPs agreed: 'The Right Honourable lady, for whom I have great personal affection, has formidable qualities – a powerful intelligence and great courage – but those qualities can turn into horrendous vices, unless they are moderated by colleagues who have more experience, understanding and sensitivity.'[1]

As well as being outstanding in the Commons, Healey was much in demand at Labour Party events. Even Tony Benn, who had lost his seat at Bristol in the 1983 General Election, asked Denis to come and speak for him at the 1984 Chesterfield by-election. At the by-election meeting, Denis began by referring to his friendship with the former MP, Eric Varley, who had left politics for business and then went to say, 'And as for Tony, he and I for many years have been inseparable – like Torvill and Dean.'[2] While Denis was speaking, the trade union banner on the wall behind him slid slowly to the floor, as if in sympathy at his predicament, an incident that was faithfully captured on television. Late in life, Denis Healey was enjoying a new role as a popular comic character, who waggled his famous bushy eyebrows, made funny faces, played the piano or even broke into song.

However, it was not the opportunity for clowning that persuaded Healey to remain on the front bench. It was partly the possibility, however remote, of fulfilling his greatest ambition of becoming Foreign Secretary. More immediately relevant was the sheer interest of foreign affairs, especially in the middle 1980s. This was the crucial period when the crisis in superpower relations of the early 1980s (caused first by the Russian invasion of Afghanistan and then by the election of Ronald Reagan as United States President, committed to a massive arms build up), was transformed by the ascent to power in the Soviet Union of Mikhail Gorbachev who, by a remarkable combination of courage and skill, then proceeded to dismantle the Cold War.

Healey, who as a young man had seen the Iron Curtain descend on Eastern Europe, was fascinated. He visited the Soviet Union five times following the death of Andropov in February 1984 and had twelve hours of conversation with Gorbachev in all, beginning with the Russian's ground-breaking visit to London in December 1984 before he assumed power. At his initial meetings in London, Healey was bowled over by Gorbachev's personal charm and intellectual flexibility: 'I had never before met such humanity and frankness in a Soviet leader, and not often in Western leaders either.'[3] Denis wondered how such a nice man could have risen to the top in the Soviet system and whether he would be able to survive as leader: he noted, however, Gromyko's observation that, though Gorbachev might have a nice smile, he had 'steel teeth'.

In 1986, Healey acted as deputy leader of a British parliamentary delegation to Russia, led by Willie Whitelaw, Mrs Thatcher's Deputy Prime Minister. Healey remarked that, in acting as second fiddle to Whitelaw, with whom he had excellent relations, he felt 'rather like a gentleman's gentleman'; an MP who was also a member of the delegation said that Healey's formidable command of defence issues was appreciated by all, including Willie Whitelaw.[4] They had a three-hour interview with Gorbachev in the Kremlin who, in contrast to his predecessor, answered their questions with astonishing openness and fluency. He went on to outline his plans for international detente and the modernisation of Russia.

The thaw in superpower relationships might have been expected to have benefited the Labour Opposition rather than the Conservative government. However, Mrs Thatcher, who had previously been dubbed the Iron Lady because of her fervent anti-Communism and strong support of President Reagan, decided that she could 'do business' with Gorbachev. Like Reagan, she became a convert to detente and, to a lesser extent, to negotiated multilateral disarmament, though she was deeply alarmed when, before the 1986 Reykjavik Summit broke down on the issue of Star Wars, Reagan and Gorbachev had appeared to agree to the complete elimination of nuclear weapons. She was concerned about what this would mean for European defence in general and for the British nuclear deterrent in particular.

Neil Kinnock had no such doubts. He was then a convinced unilateralist, who told the 1986 Blackpool conference that nuclear retaliation by the United States on Britain's behalf was immoral and that a Labour government would call for the removal of all American nuclear bases in the UK, as well as unilaterally decommissioning Polaris, the British nuclear deterrent, and cancelling the Trident replacement programme. In an unprecedented move during the Blackpool conference, the American ambassador bluntly stated that if there was a Labour government the United States would have to think carefully about whether or not it was advantageous to continue to maintain bases in Great Britain at all. In American eyes, Labour's unilateralism was a threat to NATO.

Kinnock's uncompromising unilateralism placed Healey in an uncomfortable position. Denis had for years argued for a NATO defence strategy that was less dependent on nuclear weapons and he was delighted by the agreement reached between the superpowers to get rid of intermediate range nuclear weapons. On the other hand, he believed that, so long as the Soviet Union had nuclear weapons, there had to be a countervailing NATO nuclear deterrent. He was also well aware that Labour's proposal to get rid of Polaris unilaterally was extremely unpopular with the voters. He tried, with only limited success, to get Neil Kinnock to modify his position. The Labour leader was prepared to accept that Cruise missiles should be considered as part of the deal on intermediate nuclear weapons but he was not prepared to buy Healey's deterrence argument. Healey wrote that Labour party policy 'remained an uneasy amalgam between dogmatic unilateralism and a commitment to support the alliance while seeking multilateral disarmament'.[5]

Just before the 1987 election, Kinnock unwisely decided on a trip to the United States, which was to include a meeting with President Reagan. To lend the visit credibility he asked Healey to accompany him. The meeting with Reagan, who was a great admirer of Mrs Thatcher, was perfunctory, lasting less than half an hour. As Kinnock and Healey entered the Oval Office, Reagan thrust out his hand and said to Healey, 'Nice to meet you, Mr Ambassador.' The contrast with Mrs Thatcher's triumphantly successful trip to Moscow, when Gorbachev treated her as an international star, was only too obvious.

Despite an energetic campaign by Neil Kinnock, Labour was decisively defeated at the 1987 election. The Conservatives, with 42.3 per cent of the vote, won a massive majority of 101 seats. Neil Kinnock had restored unity and dignity to the Labour Party, especially by his decisive action over Militant. But Labour still finished eleven percentage points behind the Tories, though comfortably beating the Alliance parties for second place. Polls indicated that defence alone cost the party over one million voters,[6] while a margin of two to one thought that the Tories were more likely to deliver higher living standards than Labour.[7]

Healey played a prominent role in Labour's campaign, including a part in Hugh Hudson's celebrated political broadcast when Denis said that Kinnock, like Gorbachev, had steel teeth to go with his nice smile. Denis himself caused a stir when he walked out of a television discussion at the end of the campaign, when he was asked about a hip operation which Edna had had done privately two years before. With characteristic decency, Kinnock stood by his shadow Foreign Secretary, pointedly asking Edna to join him on the platform in the final party rally at Leeds Town Hall. After the election, Denis Healey, now in his seventieth year, understandably decided to return to the back benches and two years later announced that he was standing down as an MP at the next election. He had helped save the Labour Party in 1981 and added lustre to Neil Kinnock's inexperienced leadership by agreeing to serve as shadow Foreign Secretary. But the old revisionist was well aware that, without radical reforms in policy and overall approach, Labour would not be able to make a credible bid for power. After the 1987 election, Kinnock began the process of change, which ten years later was to carry Blair and New Labour to power.

The 1983–87 Parliament was an unhappy one for Jenkins. Between mid-April 1984 and July 1986, he was not fully fit. In mid-April 1984, he was diagnosed as suffering from a thyroid condition, which responded to rest and drugs. Six months later he had a sudden operation on his prostate which was unsuccessful. Further operations followed and it was not until a final one in July 1986 that he fully recovered. Although he carried on with his parliamentary and constituency duties he was, on his own admission, functioning at 'about two-thirds power'.[8] Even so, he made major speeches, wrote short biographies of President Truman and Stanley Baldwin, published a volume of his speeches (which was edited by Clive Lindley and entitled *Partnership of Principle*) and began editing his *European Diary*, his account of his European Commission presidency.

It was during this Parliament that his relations with David Owen turned sour. Although he already had reservations about Owen, especially after the way in which he had been so ruthlessly deposed, Jenkins publicly endorsed Owen's leadership at the 1983 SDP conference: 'I assumed and greatly welcomed his uncontested election. I congratulate David and wish him well. A large part of our future is now bound up in him.' Between 1983 and 1987, Owen's public performance, especially in Parliament, was breathtaking. Although there were only a handful of SDP members Owen, by sheer force of character and energy, succeeded in keeping himself and his party in the limelight. He was not usually a great speech-maker but, by his sharp interventions in the Commons and by his incisive television appearances, he forced the media to take notice of what he said. Under his leadership, the SDP won two by-elections, at Portsmouth in 1984 and Greenwich in 1987, and the Alliance parties went into the 1987 election breathing down Labour's neck.

Yet, beneath the surface, there were increasing strains and divisions not just between David Owen and the leader of the Liberal Party, David Steel, but between Owen, on the one hand, and Jenkins, Williams and Rodgers on the other. It was partly a question of Owen's abrasive personality. He could be charming to older politicians or younger acolytes. With his equals he was all too frequently rude, moody and suspicious. In a stormy conversation that took place in the smoking room of the House of Commons in June 1986 during the defence row, Jenkins bluntly told Owen that he ought to ask himself why he sooner or later quarrelled with everyone with whom he was politically closely associated.[9] In private conversation Jenkins likened Owen to the Javanese upas tree, which poisons all life around it. Healey's comment about Owen, who had been one of his junior ministers when he was Secretary of State for Defence was even more acerbic: 'The good fairy gave the young doctor almost everything: thick dark locks, matinée idol features, a lightning intelligence; the bad fairy also made him a shit.' Not for nothing was he known in Alliance circles as Dr Death.

There was also a key difference of principle between Jenkins and Owen. Owen was desperate to preserve the separate identity of the Social Democrats and to block a merger with the Liberals, whom, according to Jenkins, he regarded as 'a disorderly group of bearded vegetarian pacifists'.[10] Hence his vehement opposition to any proposal such as the joint selection of candidates or a single leader for the Alliance which might lead to a Liberal takeover. Jenkins liked the Liberals, though Owen claimed that the only Liberals whom Roy knew were either called Bonham Carter or Grimond. After 1983 Jenkins, while not calling for a premature merger, saw it as inevitable at some time in the future. His message, to which Owen strongly objected, was 'do not set a limit to the march of the Alliance'. Jenkins was also concerned that David Owen was taking the SDP too close to Mrs Thatcher, whom Owen much admired. In a speech in mid-1986, Roy declared that the SDP was and must continue to be opposed to Thatcherism.

It was the old Achilles heel of the Labour Party, defence, that brought these tensions out in the open, nearly split the Alliance in two, and led indirectly to the destruction of the SDP, amid bitterness and mutual recrimination. Defence was a tricky issue for the Alliance, because the Liberal Party contained a sizeable unilateralist minority, while the SDP was, in contrast, firmly multilateralist, with Owen himself taking a hard line on the retention of the British deterrent. Owen and Steel had, therefore, decided to set up a Joint Commission on Defence, on which there was a handpicked anti-unilateralist majority, including Bill Rodgers, the former Labour scourge of the CND.

Suddenly, before the Commission had published its conclusions, Owen, on the basis of an inaccurate report in the *Scotsman* that it had come out against a replacement for Polaris, angrily denounced the Commission's efforts as 'fudging and mudging' and reaffirmed his commitment to a continuing British nuclear deterrent.

Owen's over-reaction outraged the other founders of the SDP. Jenkins said that there was 'a danger of theatre taking over from valour: Custer's last stand should not be a nightly event.'[11] It also upset the Liberals and led to an anti-nuclear motion being narrowly passed at their assembly, in part as a reaction to Owen, which was very damaging to the Alliance's standing in the polls. Although Steel and Owen patched up their row and the Alliance produced an agreed defence policy on Owen's terms, this damage was lasting, especially inside the SDP. Jenkins, Williams and Rodgers had all become convinced, more or less independently, that Owen had become impossible to work with and that after the election the Alliance would have to be put on a new basis, preferably through a merger.

Despite their underlying tensions, the post-Greenwich by-election surge in their fortunes gave the Alliance parties fresh heart for the election. Their campaign, however, failed to catch fire. In part it was because the two Alliance leaders, Owen and Steel, had different answers to the question of whether they would prefer a Conservative or Labour government. In response to a question from Robin Day, Owen admitted that he found Labour's position on defence unacceptable, while Steel later hinted that, if there was a hung Parliament, he would find it impossible to work with Mrs Thatcher. A more fundamental reason for the Alliance's failure was the underlying strength of the Tory position and Kinnock's energetic campaign, which helped firm up the Labour vote. In contrast to 1983, the Alliance lost support during the campaign and finished a disappointing third, with twenty-three per cent of the vote.

Jenkins had gone into the election hoping to hold Hillhead, which he much enjoyed representing in Parliament. But during the campaign he met too many voters who had decided to switch from the SDP to the Labour candidate (partly because of Owen's leaning towards the Conservatives) and on election night he was defeated by over three thousand votes by the Labour left-winger, George Galloway. Jenkins' long career in the House of Commons was over.

Following the Alliance's electoral failure the SDP rapidly disintegrated. On the day after the poll, Owen declared his implacable opposition to a merger, while on the Sunday Jenkins announced his support for a single party, as did David Steel. The lines were drawn for an unseemly battle for the soul of the SDP, all too reminiscent of Labour in 1981. In a ballot of party members announced on 6 August, the SDP voted by almost sixty to forty to merge with the Liberals. This was not, however, the end of the story, as Owen, although he would have had a good chance of leading the merged party, refused to accept the verdict of the ballot and proceeded to set up a new SDP. The Owenite party contested by-elections in mutually damaging competition with the merged party (which came to be known as the Liberal Democrats) until the Bootle by-election in May 1990, when the SDP candidate finished seventh out of eight and polled less than Screaming Lord Sutch, the Monster Raving Loony Party candidate. Even Owen got the message.

The journalist, Peter Jenkins, wrote Owen's political obituary: 'The virtuoso one-man band performer, which in the last Parliament made him the most impressive politician in the country after Margaret Thatcher, has degenerated in a display of megalomania,' while the comment of the SDP's historians was that 'David Owen began as Napoleon and ended up as Baron Munchausen.'[12] The SDP adventure, which Roy Jenkins had launched with such high hopes, ended first in a bitterly contested merger and, then in its Owenite version, in ignominy and farce.

After 1987 Healey and Jenkins both pursued different versions of elder statesmanship with panache and style; Jenkins was the more dignified, Healey the more populist. Both used the House of Lords as a platform. Jenkins was the more serious House of Lords figure. After becoming a life peer in 1987 he was chosen as the new merged party's first leader in the Lords, a part that he held for a decade. Even so, he did not take the upper house entirely seriously. It was important, he wrote, not to succumb to its cosseting charm, but 'treat its mixture of archaic pageantry and Puginesque extravagance of decor with a touch of polite mockery'.[13] Denis Healey was even more relaxed in his attitude to the Lords. He had stayed on in the Commons until the 1992 election, after which he too was made a life peer. He made the occasional speech in the Lords on defence and international affairs or economic issues. Otherwise, he found the House of Lords' facilities useful when he wanted a meeting place or to look up a reference.

In March 1987, just before his defeat at Hillhead, Jenkins had been elected Chancellor of Oxford University following the death of Harold Macmillan. In a keenly contested election, Jenkins defeated two Conservative candidates, the former Prime Minister Edward Heath, and the distinguished historian Robert Blake. In contrast to the Vice Chancellor of Oxford, who is the most important figure in the University's administration, the Chancellor of Oxford, who is not paid a salary, has few formal powers. However, the Chancellor is Oxford's prestigious figurehead, with the right to be consulted about issues and to represent the University to the wider world. In an era in which major fundraising has become increasingly important, the Chancellor is also expected to meet possible benefactors and address alumni over most of the world. Jenkins much enjoyed the Chancellorship, which took up over a quarter of his time.

Healey did not occupy or wish to occupy any position comparable to Jenkins' Chancellorship of Oxford. But he was frequently invited as a lecturer and speaker to corporate and institutional conferences for which he was lucratively paid. And, especially in the late 1980s and early 1990s, he was often on television and radio, not only as a defence, international affairs and economics pundit but also as a celebrity. He appeared live on comedy programmes such as *Spitting Image*, and was a guest of entertainers like Morecambe and Wise, Barry Humphries and Victoria Wood. To those who complained of his frivolity, he argued that politics should not be seen as 'a bitter abstract thing' and a politician should be more than 'an old bellows full of angry wind'.

Denis Healey's retirement from front line politics also gave him the time to pursue his wide intellectual and cultural interests. In his autobiography he confessed that 'even my family would not have been sufficient to reconcile me to a life in politics if I had not also been able to refresh myself with music, poetry, painting'.[14] He was now able to indulge his passion for photography, to listen to music, to read even more widely about poetry and painting, and reflect on what he had learnt from books. In 1992, he published a moving anthology of the writings which had influenced his life, called *My Secret Planet*: Emily Dickinson, Virginia Woolf and W. B. Yeats were among his particular favourites. Edward Pearce wrote in the *New Statesman*, 'Circulate *My Secret Planet* to the entire fourteen-year-old nation, and the next generation will grasp not one man's hinterland, but the purpose of books.' His autobiography *The Time of My Life*, published in 1989, was not only a popular success (selling over 170,000 copies), but widely acclaimed as one of the outstanding political autobiographies of the time, while, a year later, he published a collection of his earlier political writings and speeches, with the arresting title of *When Shrimps Learn to Whistle*. In 2002 a second volume of his photographs was published entitled *Healey's World* – a beautifully produced collection of images of his extensive trips abroad. His wife Edna, in a late flowering, also wrote excellent biographies of Angela Burdett-Coutts and Emma Darwin, as well as histories of Coutts' Bank and of Buckingham Palace.

Healey, together with his wife Edna, spends much of his time at his lovely Sussex home high up in the Downs. Surrounded by his library of sixteen thousand books, by his CDs and tapes, by his thousand videos, Denis listens to his favourite composers such as Bach, Haydn, Beethoven, and Schubert, and reads his favourite poets, especially Yeats and Emily Dickinson. However, he still spends two hours a day reading and cutting newspapers and journals, as he has for the last fifty years or so, so that he can be fully briefed for the broadcasts that he makes and the articles that he still writes for leading newspapers.

Roy Jenkins also wrote a brilliant autobiography, *A Life at the Centre*, which was published in 1991. The *Economist* described it as 'truly distinguished' and 'a model of what a modern politician's autobiography should be'. In 1995, his outstanding biography of Gladstone, the great nineteenth-century Prime Minister, was launched at No 11 Carlton Gardens, Gladstone's former home. Paddy Ashdown, the Liberal Democrat leader, recorded in his diary that Roy began by playing the only recording of Gladstone's voice: 'I had imagined a deep bass, but it was a rather thin, high-timbred tenor with a strong trace of a Lancashire accent, particularly in the vowels. Extraordinarily eerie.'[15] But Jenkins' greatest literary achievement of all was his outstanding biography of the great twentieth-century Prime Minister, Winston Churchill, which was published in 2001, in Roy's eighty-first year. He ended the book by saying that in the course of writing it he had changed his mind and now believed that Churchill, not Gladstone, was the greater of his two subjects. 'I now put Churchill, with all his idiosyncrasies, his indulgences, his occasional childishness, but also his genius, his tenacity and his persistent ability, right or wrong, success-ful or unsuccessful, to be larger than life, as the greatest human being ever to occupy 10 Downing Street.'[16] In his book, he had triumphantly succeeded in bringing Churchill to life. It was an instant bestseller: over a hundred thousand copies have been sold both in the United Kingdom and the United States.

Roy Jenkins usually wrote at East Hendred rather than at his flat at Kensington Park Gardens. As he grew older, he worked in shorter spurts. During a writing day, he normally started at about 5.30 a.m. and read in bed, occasionally getting up to write about 250 words. He then exercised, sometimes by walking round and round his tennis court, before returning for breakfast and a concentrated perusal of the morning papers. He got to his desk at about 11.30 a.m., corrected what he had written the day before and wrote a further few hundred words. After a late lunch with a bottle of claret he started again at about 3 p.m. and wrote through to pre-dinner drinks, almost always managing to complete a thousand words for the day, an astonishing output for a man of his age.

This is an extract for my diary for Sunday 4 June 2000 when Roy and Jennifer Jenkins came to stay with us in Lincolnshire after a European Movement dinner: 'Roy's energy is phenomenal. He is up early and, by breakfast, has already written 700 words of his *Independent* article. After breakfast, we go to Lincoln Cathedral . . . before driving back for lunch at which Roy drinks liberally. He then retires to my study where he finishes his *Independent* article . . . At about 4.30 p.m., we go to Belton, the splendid seventeenth-century manor house . . . back to tea, more writing by Roy (finishing off his latest Churchill chapter) and dinner at which he drinks more claret. After much talk about Europe, Blair, Crosland and Healey, the Jenkins retire to bed at about 10.30 p.m., as Roy is to do a *Today* programme interview down the line.'

During the 1990s, Jenkins was the more influential politician of the two. Healey enjoyed the role of the outsider, opposing American action against Iraq and American bombing in Bosnia, Serbia and Afghanistan. He also joined David Owen in a campaign against the UK joining the single currency. In contrast, Jenkins was the insider, acting as one of Ashdown's chief counsellors, especially over

Ashdown's developing relations with Tony Blair, the new Labour leader who was elected after John Smith's death in 1994. On the day of Smith's death, Healey openly backed Blair for the leadership. Yet, paradoxically it was to Jenkins, the Labour renegade, to whom Blair turned for advice. Jenkins said about Blair's attitude: 'I think Tony treats me as a sort of father-figure in politics. He comes to me a lot for advice, particularly about how to construct a government.'[17]

Blair had been to lunch at East Hendred even before he became leader. Their relationship blossomed in a series of lunches and dinners during the next few years. Blair found in Roy Jenkins somebody with whom he could talk frankly about politics. He admired his style and his historical perspective. Jenkins warmed to Blair's charm and modesty. Once before the 1997 election Blair said to Jenkins, 'One morning I wake up thinking I've lost the election, I've blown it. The next that I've won and am Prime Minister, but am no good at it.' Jenkins commented, 'I can think of no other Prime Minister or possible Prime Minister who can be so self-deprecating – I find it rather attractive.'[18]

Jenkins was useful to Blair as a discreet channel to the Liberals. As part of his policy of co-operation with them, he made Roy chairman of the Independent Commission on the Voting System.

Jenkins proved a highly effective chairman of the Commission. He quickly mastered the mathematical and political complexities of the proportional systems. He prepared meticulously for the series of public meetings, fortifying himself beforehand with a good lunch and a ration of red wine on the train and then chairing these meetings without forgetting a name or an argument. He wrote much of the report himself and persuaded his Commission colleagues, with one minor note of dissent, to agree to a strengthened system of the alternative vote – AV+. It was not his fault that while it had an overall majority the Labour Party was unlikely to be attracted to any change in the electoral system.

For his part, Jenkins' opinion of Blair depended to a considerable extent on the strength of Blair's support for British involvement in Europe in general and for joining the euro in particular. Both men continued to enjoy seeing each other, especially as their wives, who were both extremely formidable women in their own right (Jennifer Jenkins being a former chairman of the National Trust and Cherie Booth a leading QC), liked each other.

Both Healey and Jenkins held parties to celebrate their eightieth birthdays. Healey's, which was held on 9 September 1997 at the House of Lords, was the more intimate occasion. Jim Callaghan, Prime Minister when Healey was Chancellor, and Edward Heath, Healey's old Balliol colleague, made short speeches of appreciation; Heath said that Healey was 'a great patriot'. In his reply, Healey said how important his friends had been to him. That may have been true in his private life but in politics he was a loner. Jenkins was invited and came. In conversation, Roy commented that he and Denis, like two cats, had always rubbed each other up the wrong way.[19]

Jenkins' eightieth birthday party took place on 7 March 2001 at the Reform Club. It was held a few months after his actual birthday because he had had a heart by-pass operation in the autumn. Not surprisingly, given Jenkins' Whiggish predilections, it was a much grander affair altogether, with nearly a hundred guests and a sit-down dinner for which they paid. The guest list was a roll-call of the liberal establishment. John Grigg, Arthur Schlesinger, the distinguished American historian, and Shirley Williams made the speeches. John Grigg referred to Jenkins' phenomenal energy. Despite recovering from his heart operation, he had written over 80,000 words between November 2000 and February 2001 in order to finish his Churchill biography. Shirley Williams paid tribute to Jenkins's humanity and gift for friendship. In his reply, Jenkins said that he now no longer minded not having been Prime Minister.

Both Jenkins and Healey had the ability and the experience to have made good Prime Ministers. Significantly two ex-Prime Ministers, Edward Heath and Jim Callaghan, agreed that Roy and Denis could have done the job well.[20] Sadly, a combination of circumstance, misjudgement, and a failure to work together (and with Crosland) kept them out of No 10.

Conclusion

By the 1980s, revisionist social democracy of the 1950s' Gaitskellite vintage, under whose banner Crosland, Jenkins and Healey, in their different ways and styles, had marched, was threadbare. Mrs Thatcher, leader of the Conservatives, was left in command of the field.

The reasons for the failure of the revisionist project inside the Labour Party are complex. Its best chance of a breakthrough came under the Wilson administrations of the 1960s when Jenkins was in the ascendant, Healey and Crosland were powerful ministers and Wilson himself was a convert to the modernisation idea. But after the 1970 defeat, which was a crucial turning point, both the left and the unions became more powerful. Tony Benn was the most charismatic and energetic leader of the left since Nye Bevan and his ability to put the revisionists on the defensive grew during the 1970s. With the defeat of *In Place of Strife* and the successful assault on the Conservative Industrial Relations Act, the unions' political clout also increased substantially which made governing, especially for a Labour administration, more difficult.

Denis Healey attempted to develop a more corporatist model of social democracy with some success, especially in overcoming the IMF crisis. Healey's model took account of recent developments, especially the impact of global markets. But this version, and with it the

Callaghan government, was fatally undermined by the so-called 'winter of discontent' of 1978–79. Denis' defeat by Michael Foot in the 1980 leadership election was the last straw. In 1981 Roy Jenkins, together with the Gang of Three, made a bold but unsuccessful attempt at a social democratic breakout when they set up the Social Democratic Party in alliance with the Liberals. But Jenkins' dramatic 'cavalry charge' ended in defeat at the 1983 election, when the Alliance parties failed to overcome the virtually insuperable handicap of the first-past-the-post electoral system.

In the 1980s, Mrs Thatcher was very much in the ascendant. She triumphed over a divided Opposition in both the 1983 and 1987 elections. Equally important, the Tory leader set the political agenda, putting forward ideas and policies that effectively challenged the postwar settlement, including a substantial reduction in the role of the state, a decrease in union power, and a commitment to market forces and private enterprise. It was already clear by the mid-1980s that the version of social democracy espoused by Crosland, Healey and Jenkins was badly in need of revision and that a new radical thrust would be required if the Labour Party were ever to return to power.[1]

How far did the undoubted rivalry between the three leading revisionists contribute to the decisive defeat of social democracy in the 1980s? An underlying thesis of this book is that it was an important factor. Rivalry is, of course, endemic in politics, as elsewhere. The ambitions of supremely talented, strong-willed politicians inevitably collide. The real question is to what extent it is possible to combine healthy and natural ambition with constructive co-operation in shared objectives.

Today the relationship between the Labour Prime Minister, Tony Blair, and his Chancellor, Gordon Brown, is subjected to continued and fevered analysis by political commentators and journalists.[2] There is undoubtedly a strong element of rivalry between these two men and their entourages, which adds tension to the most powerful partnership in British politics. This tension between them is increased by their shared knowledge that Brown wants to succeed Blair as Prime Minister. Yet the remarkable fact about their relationship, which began when they were first elected as young MPs in 1983, is that it survived the election of Blair as Labour's leader in 1994, with Brown standing down in Blair's favour. It then went on to become the linch-pin of the New Labour government, first elected in 1997 and then re-elected by a landslide in 2001. As James Naughtie has perceptively written, 'It was their bonded, concentrated power at the centre of government that allowed an administration of more or less completely inexperienced ministers to manage the first term in a way that pro-duced the second big majority.'[3]

Blair asked Jenkins on a number of occasions about how his rela-tions with Crosland deteriorated after Jenkins had become Chancellor of the Exchequer in 1967.[4] He could also have inquired of Jenkins and Healey why they did not work together more effectively.

If the three men had been able to combine better in the late 1960s, then Jenkins might have been able to replace Wilson as Prime Minister and Labour would probably have won the 1970 election. The row over Europe, which led to the resignation of Roy as the party leader in 1972 and permanently damaged their relationship, could have been avoided if the three had agreed on a joint approach to the European issue. The 1976 leadership election might well have had a different outcome if they had been able to unite behind a single can-didate. If one of the three revisionists had been elected as leader in the late 1960s or in 1976, then Labour's fortunes might have been very different. And if Jenkins and Crosland in the 1970s, and Jenkins and Healey in the 1970s and in the 1980s had been able to sink their divisions, then the situation inside the Labour Party might not have deteriorated so alarmingly and the SDP split might never have occurred. By definition, one can never be sure about the might-have-beens of political history. But my judgement as a close observer of and minor participant in these events is that greater co-operation between them would have made a crucial difference, not only to their own careers, but also to the social democratic position inside the Labour Party and to the fate of Labour itself.

But the three men did not work together. When Jenkins became Chancellor in 1967, Crosland and, to a lesser extent, Healey resented the rise of the man who had been their junior at Oxford. In the 1970s Tony and Denis believed that Roy was wrong to put the European issue above party. In 1976 they did not see why Jenkins, who had severely damaged his chances by resigning the deputy leadership in 1972, should be allowed a clear run in the leadership election, and, in any case, they thought that their own abilities and seniority entitled them to a shot at becoming leader. Jenkins, who by this time distrusted Healey, had no intention of standing down in his favour; and did not believe Crosland was decisive enough to be leader. After Jenkins left British politics for the presidency of the European Commission, Crosland, who became Callaghan's Foreign Secretary, consistently opposed Healey's economic policies in Cabinet, especially during the IMF crisis and, right up until his tragic death, wanted to replace Denis as Chancellor.

Healey's view of Jenkins was that he always desired to be top in politics and that his departure for Brussels and subsequent return to launch the SDP was, to a considerable extent, explained by his thwarted ambition. In 1980 Roy turned down out of hand Denis's offer, admittedly only made at second hand, of a return to British politics as a Labour MP, with the prospect of being Healey's Foreign Secretary. He disliked what he considered to be Denis's patronising manner, and despised his sometimes brutal pragmatism. He did not, in any case, believe that Healey was capable of turning the Labour Party round. One is on safe ground in saying that if Hugh Gaitskell had been alive, he would surely have been amazed to find two of his closest revisionist allies of the 1950s fighting the 1983 election in different parties and would have been disturbed at how little political influence the social democratic revisionists seemed to have in the Thatcherite world of the 1980s.

Yet, despite the failure of the Gaitskellite revisionists, it is remarkable how much the New Labour project of the 1990s has drawn on their ideas and themes. Of course, the world of the twenty-first century is very different from that of the 1960s and 1970s. The power of government has been considerably diminished by the growth of globalism. Corporatist policies have far less relevance today. Social change, especially the decline of class, has transformed the political landscape. And after the long years of Conservative rule and after four election defeats, the new leadership was in a much stronger position than the revisionists had ever been to impose their views on their party.

From the start, whatever the talk about the 'third way', it was clear that Tony Blair was intent on modernising social democracy. Rethinking the party's strategy and policies in the light of changing circumstances was pure revisionism. Revisionism was, after all, not so much a doctrine as a radical cast of mind, a critical way of evaluating events, in order to develop policies that take account of change. Crosland used to quote with approval Joseph Conrad's *Typhoon*: 'Always facing it, Captain McWhirr, that's the way to get through.'[5] New Labour leaders, like the Gaitskellite revisionists before them, were facing up to change.

They were also doing it in a thoroughly revisionist way by attempting to keep ends and means separate. One of the key points about *The Future of Socialism* was the distinction that Crosland made between ends and means. Moral values were the ends which were constant; by contrast, means which might be thought suitable in one generation could become wholly irrelevant in the next and were, therefore, dispensable. Hence the Croslandite argument for defining socialism in terms of greater equality rather than of nationalisation.

As a way of symbolising Labour's new approach, Blair decided to complete the work begun by Gaitskell and rewrite Clause IV of the party constitution.[6] This was a bold but successful move, from which both his predecessors, Kinnock and Smith, had shrunk. Significantly, Blair's new Clause IV made no mention of nationalisation and little of policies. It was expressed primarily in terms of values. The new clause declared that 'by the strength of our common endeavour we achieve more than we achieve alone, so as to create for each of us the means to realise our true potential and for all of us a community in which power, wealth and opportunity are in the hands of the many not the few.' Blair's comment was that with the revision of Clause IV, 'the Labour Party has reclaimed its basic values.'[7] The revised Clause IV was, in this sense, a classic revisionist document because it recognised a clear distinction between ends and means, between values and policies.

As well as learning from the mistakes of the three great modernisers of the previous generation, New Labour can also draw inspiration from their achievements. Tony Crosland was the revisionist intellectual whose path-breaking *Future of Socialism* is still of relevance today. He was also an outstanding innovative Secretary of State for Education who launched the first serious effort to provide good secondary education for the seventy-five per cent of children who failed to get into grammar schools.

As Home Secretary in the 1960s, Roy Jenkins encouraged a raft of liberal reforms, which made the United Kingdom a far more civilised society than it had been before. He was also a successful Chancellor of the Exchequer. In the 1970s his courageous and principled support for British membership of the European Community at the cost of his own career helped ensure that membership became a reality. Jenkins was the first British President of the European Commission and helped launch the process which led to the European single currency.

Denis Healey was an outstanding Defence Secretary whose reforms produced a realistic defence policy, suitable for a medium-sized power. In the 1970s he was arguably Labour's first modern Chancellor who learned on the job to grapple with the impact of global markets. In 1981, he helped save the Labour Party by beating Tony Benn in the deputy leadership election.

Crosland, Jenkins and Healey were inspiring figures, major politicians whose careers helped shape not only the Labour Party but British politics and society as well. In many ways they had more lasting impact than the Labour Prime Ministers of the period, Wilson and Callaghan. They were big men, larger-than-life personalities who could light up a room or gathering by their presence. And their extensive 'hinterlands' serve as a valuable reminder to the present generation of politicians that there is more to human affairs than politics.

A Note on Sources

Both Denis Healey's *The Time of My Life* (Michael Joseph, 1989) and Roy Jenkins' *A Life at the Centre* (Macmillan, 1991) are outstanding autobiographies. For Healey, I have also drawn on Edward Pearce's comprehensive biography, *Denis Healey* (Little, Brown 2002), which I was fortunate to read in proof, as well as on his essay on Healey in *The Lost Leaders* (Little, Brown, 1997). John Campbell wrote a useful interim biography of Jenkins, *Roy Jenkins* (Weidenfeld & Nicolson, 1983). I have also had extensive interviews with both Healey and Jenkins.

Susan Crosland's classic personal memoir, *Tony Crosland* (Cape, 1982) has now been supplemented by Kevin Jefferys' *Anthony Crosland* (Richard Cohen, 1999). I have also consulted the Crosland Papers in the British Library of Political and Economic Science (BLPES) at the London School of Economics. Both *The Socialist Agenda*, edited by David Lipsey and Dick Leonard (Cape, 1981) and *Crosland and New Labour*, edited by Dick Leonard (Palgrave Macmillan, 1999) contain valuable material.

For the 1950s, there are two excellent biographies of Gaitskell – Philip Williams' *Hugh Gaitskell* (Cape, 1979) and Brian Briavati's *Hugh Gaitskell* (Richard Cohen, 1996). Gaitskell's diaries from 1945–56, edited by Philip Williams (Cape, 1983), and the second volume of Michael Foot's *Aneurin Bevan* (Davis-Poynter, 1973) are worth consulting.

The Wilson governments of the 1960s are extensively covered in the Tony Benn, Barbara Castle and Dick Crossman diaries. Harold Wilson gave his own account in *The Labour Government 1964–1970* (Weidenfeld & Nicolson, 1971), while Ben Pimlott has written a brilliant biography of Harold Wilson (HarperCollins, 1992). There is useful information in Peter Hennessy's *The Prime Minister* (Allen Lane, 2000), as well as in material deposited in the Public Record Office.

The 1970s feature in the Benn and Castle diaries and in James Callaghan's autobiography, *Time and Chance* (Collins, 1987), while Kenneth O. Morgan has written an authoritative life of Callaghan (Oxford University Press, 1997). There is a stimulating history of the 1970s by Phillip Whitehead – *The Writing on the Wall* (Michael Joseph, 1985); and Bernard Donoghue has given his account of life in No 10 under Wilson and Callaghan in *Prime Minister* (Cape, 1987). For economic policy and the IMF crisis, Edmund Dell's two splendid works – *The Chancellors* (HarperCollins, 1991) and *Hard Pounding* (OUP, 1991) – are essential reading, as is Joel Barnett's *Inside the Treasury* (Andre Deutsch, 1982).

For the fall of the Labour government and the creation of the SDP, there are a number of informative memoirs, including Roy Hattersley's *Who Goes Home?* (Little, Brown, 1995), Bill Rodgers' *Fourth Among Equals* (Politico's, 2000), and David Owen's *Time to Declare* (Michael Joseph, 1991). The definitive history of the SDP is by Ivor Crewe and Anthony King (OUP, 1995).

As first an observer and then a minor player in these events from 1960 onwards, I have drawn on my own memories and judgements, and from 1980, on my diaries. I have also been able to interview nearly fifty participants, most of whom are mentioned by name in the Acknowledgements. Other sources quoted are to be found in the Notes.

Notes

Introduction

1 Denis Healey, *The Time of My Life*, Michael Joseph, 1989, p. 457.
2 Roy Jenkins, *A Life at the Centre*, Macmillan, 1991, p. 30.
3 Ibid., p. 617.
4 Interview with Denis Healey.
5 Healey, *The Time of My Life*, p. 329.
6 Ibid., p. 329.
7 Paddy Ashdown *The Ashdown Diaries, Vol. 1: 1988–1997*, Allen Lane, 2000, p. 130. My thanks to Paddy Ashdown for pointing out this reference.
8 Roy Jenkins, *A Life at the Centre*, p. 217.
9 Healey, *The Time of My Life*, p. 329.

Chapter 1: Provenance

1 Susan Crosland, *Tony Crosland*, Jonathan Cape, 1982, p. 4.
2 'Essays' in Anthony Crosland Papers (ACP), at the London School of Economics, 1/7.
3 Healey, *The Time of My Life*, p. 2.
4 Ibid., p. 19.
5 Edward Heath, *The Course of My Life*, Hodder & Stoughton, 1999, p. 47.
  Kevin Jefferys, *Anthony Crosland*, Richard Cohen Books, 1999, p. 10.
6 Jenkins, *A Life at the Centre*, p. 66.
7 Interview with Hugh Brace.
8 Leo Abse, *Private Member*, MacDonald, 1973, pp. 34–6.
9 Jenkins, *A Life at the Centre*, pp. 8–9.

Chapter 2: Oxford on the Eve

1 Healey, *The Time of My Life*, p. 34.
2 Jenkins, *A Life at the Centre*, p. 25.
3 A. J. P. Taylor, *English History, 1914–45*, Oxford, 1965, p. 308.
4 Peter Hennessy, *Never Again*, Vintage, 1993, p. 161.
5 Taylor, *English History*, p. 308.
6 Woodrow Wyatt, *Confessions of an Optimist*, Collins, 1985, p. 59.
7 Healey, *My Secret Planet*, Penguin, 1992, p. 37.

8   Heath, *The Course of My Life*, p. 24.
9   Jenkins, *A Life at the Centre*, p. 32.
10 Richard Hillary, *The Last Enemy*, Pimlico, 1997.
11 Jefferys, *Anthony Crosland*, p. 7.
12 Woodrow Wyatt, *Confessions of an Optimist*, p. 179.
13 Taylor, *English History*, p. 260.
14 Jenkins, *A Life at the Centre*, p. 30.
15 Anthony Crosland Papers (ACP), 9/1.
16 Healey, *The Time of My Life*, p. 36.
17 The account of the 1938 Oxford by-election is drawn from Drusilla Scott, *A. D. Lindsay*, Basil Blackwell, Oxford, 1971 and Patrick Gordon Walker, *Political Diaries 1932–1971*, The Historian's Press, 1991.
18 Gordon Walker, *Political Diaries*, p. 88.
19 Jenkins, *A Life at the Centre*, p. 27.
20 Heath, *The Course of My Life*, p. 60.
21 Healey, *The Time of My Life*, pp. 41–3.
22 Ibid., p. 44.
23 Ibid., p. 46.
24 Tony Crosland to Jessie Crosland, ACP 3/21.
25 Jenkins, *A Life at the Centre*, p. 26.
26 Ibid., p. 40.
27 Interview with Edmund Dell.
28 Crosland, *Tony Crosland*, p. 383.
29 *The Labour Party and the War*, ACP 2/18,

Chapter 3: Wartime
1   Healey, *The Time of My Life*, p. 47.
2   Tony Crosland's diary, 22 June 1944, ACP, 24 June 1944, 3/2.
3   Jenkins, *A Life at the Centre*, p. 51.
4   Ibid., p. 54.
5   Paul Kennedy, *The Rise and Fall of the Great Powers*, Unwin Hyman, 1988, p. 341.
6   Crosland to Williams, August 1940, ACP 3/26.
7   Crosland to Williams, December 1940, ACP 3/26.
8   Crosland to Williams, ACP 3/26.
9   John Keegan, *The Second World War*, Pimlico, 1997, p. 140.
10 Crosland to Williams, July 1942, ACP 3/26.
11 Jenkins, *A Life at the Centre*, p. 46.
12 Ibid., p. 47.
13 Crosland to Williams, undated, ACP 3/26.
14 Crosland to Williams, September 1942, quoted in Crosland, *Tony Crosland*, p. 20.
15 Healey, *The Time of My Life*, p. 56.
16 Keegan, *The Second World War*, p. 305.
17 Crosland's diary, 31 January 1944, ACP 3/1.
18 Healey, *The Time of My Life*, pp. 57–8.
19 Crosland's diary, 4 October 1943, ACP, 3/1
20 Ibid., 3 December 1943.
21 Ibid., 8 December 1943.
22 Ibid., 9 December 1943.
23 Ibid., 17 December 1943.
24 Ibid., 31 January 1944.
25 Healey, *The Time of My Life*, p. 60.

26 Crosland's diary, 30 August 1944.
27 Healey, *The Time of My Life*, p. 59.
28 Ibid., p. 61.
29 Robert Harris, *Enigma*, Arrow, 1995, p. 39.
30 Crosland to Williams, 12 February 1944, ACP 3/26, quoted in Kevin Jefferys, *Anthony Crosland*, p. 27.
31 Ronald Levin, *Ultra Goes to War*, Hutchinson, 1978, p. 183.
32 F. H. Hinsley and Alan Stripp, *Codebreakers*, Oxford University Press, 1993, pp. 1–13 and Keegan, *The Second World War*, pp. 418–23.
33 Levin, *Ultra Goes to War*, p. 112.
34 Jenkins, *A Life at the Centre*, p. 53.
35 Ibid., p. 54.
36 Healey, *The Time of My Life*, p. 63.
37 Crosland's diary, 11 March 1945, ACP.
38 Healey, *The Time of My Life*, p. 64.
39 Crosland, *Tony Crosland*, p. 36.
40 Crosland's diary, 8 May 1944, ACP, 3/1.
41 Ibid., 29 May 1944, ACP, 3/1.
42 Healey. *The Time of My Life*, p. 53.
43 Ibid., p. 69.
44 Ibid., p. 66.
45 Jenkins to Crosland, 28 November 1944, ACP, 9/1.

Chapter 4: Into Parliament
1 Healey, *The Time of My Life*, p. 67.
2 Jenkins, *A Life at the Centre*, p. 56.
3 Crosland to Williams, 4 November 1945, ACP 3/26.
4 Jenkins, *A Life at the Centre*, p. 56.
5 Crosland to Williams, 8 August 1945, ACP 3/26.
6 Crosland to Williams, 9 September 1945, ACP 3/27.
7 Crosland to Williams,12 March 1945, ACP, 3/26.
8 Healey, *The Time of My Life*, p. 71.
9 George Brown, *In My Way*, Penguin 1972, p.235.
10 Alan Bullock, *Ernest Bevin*, Heinemann, 1983, p. 69.
11 *Cards on the Table*, Labour Party, May 1947.
12 'Keep Left' *New Statesman*, May 1947, p. 38.
13 Healey, *The Time of My Life*, p. 102.
14 Bullock, *Ernest Bevin*, pp. 543–6.
15 Roy Jenkins, *Mr Attlee*, Heinemann, 1948, p. 44; R. H. S. Crossman, *The Charm* ? Hamish Hamilton, 1958, pp. 69–74.
16 Jenkins, *A Life at the Centre*, p. 68.
17 Ibid., p. 69.
18 Roy Jenkins *DNB*, 1971–1980, entry for Crosland, p. 193.
19 Interview with Ian Little; Jefferys, *Anthony Crosland*, p ?
20 John Vaisey, *In Breach of Promise*, Weidenfeld & Nicolson, 1983, p. 82.
21 Crosland's diary, 4 September 1949, ACP 16/1.
22 Interview with Tony Benn.
23 Crosland, *Tony Crosland*, p. 43.
24 William Rodgers, *Daily Telegraph*, 5 June 1983.
25 Quoted in Ben Pimlott, *Hugh Dalton*, Cape, 1985, p. 6 ?
26 Quoted in Pimlott, *Hugh Dalton*, p. 424.

27 Nicholas Davenport, *Memoirs of a City Radical*, Weidenfeld & Nicolson, 1974, p. 171.
28 Quoted in Pimlott, *Hugh Dalton*, p. 589.
29 Dalton to Crosland, 29 September 1948, ACP.
30 Quoted in Jefferys, *Anthony Crosland*, pp. 33–4.
31 Crosland, *Tony Crosland*, p. 50.
32 Dalton to Crosland, 8 April 1950, ACP.
33 *Hansard*, 19 April 1950, cols 181–6.
34 Quoted in Jefferys, *Anthony Crosland*, p. 31.
35 Hennessy, *Never Again*, p. 410.
36 Healey, *The Time of My Life*, pp. 128–9.
37 Edwin Plowden, *An Industrialist in the Treasury*, André Deutsch, 1989, p. 72.
38 Jean Monnet, *Memoirs*, Collins, 1978, p. 293.
39 Dean Acheson, *Present at the Creation*, Macmillan, 1970, p. 385.
40 Healey, *The Time of My Life*, pp. 116–17.
41 Edmund Dell, *The Schuman Plan and the British Abdication of Leadership in Europe*, Clarendon Press, 1995, pp. 140–214.
42 Ben Pimlott, *Hugh Dalton*, Cape, 1985, p. 382.
43 Hugh Dalton, *High Tide and After*, Muller, 1962, p. 331; Healey, *The Time of My Life*, p. 118.
44 Crosland, *Tony Crosland*, p. 54.
45 Ibid., pp. 55–6.
46 Ibid., p. 57.
47 Quoted in Jefferys, *Anthony Crosland*, p. 41.

Chapter 5: Opposition and *The Future of Socialism*

1   Pimlott, *Hugh Dalton*, p. 606.
2   Healey, *The Time of My Life*, p. 56.
3   Jenkins, *A Life at the Centre*, p. 93.
4   Ibid., p. 88.
5   Richard Crossman's diaries, 29 March 1955, quoted in Anthony Howard, *Crossman*, Pimlico, 1991, p. 159.
6   Jenkins, *A Life at the Centre*, p. 103.
7   *Hansard*, 14 May 1952, cols 1497–1505.
8   Healey, *The Time of My Life*, p. 150.
9   Ibid., pp. 151–2.
10 Ibid., p. 152.
11 Ibid., p. 133.
12 Ibid., p. 139.
13 Ibid., p. 133.
14 Quoted in Jefferys, *Anthony Crosland*, p. 50.
15 Crosland, *Tony Crosland*, p. 65.
16 Roy Hattersley, *Who Goes Home?*, Little, Brown, 1995, p. 188.
17 Bill Rodgers, *Fourth Among Equals*, Politico's, 2000, p. 48.
18 Wyatt, *Confessions of an Optimist*, Collins, 1985, p. 179.
19 *New Fabian Essays*, Turnstable Press, 1952, p. 2.
20 Ibid., pp. 61–2.
21 Quoted in Jefferys, *Anthony Crosland*, p. 48.
22 Jenkins, *A Life at the Centre*, p. 89.
23 Lord Donaldson in *The Socialist Agenda*, ed. David Lipsey and Dick Leonard, Cape, 1981, pp. 15–16.
24 Crosland, *Tony Crosland*, p. 63.
25 Healey, *The Time of My Life*, pp. 122–3.

26 Jenkins, *A Life at the Centre*, p. 101.
27 C. A. R. Crosland, *The Future of Socialism*, Cape, 1956, p. 249.
28 Ibid., p. 12.
29 Ibid., pp. 75–6.
30 Ibid., pp. 100–3.
31 Ibid., p. 113.
32 Ibid., p. 518.
33 Ibid., p. 524.
34 Ibid., p. 515.
35 Ibid., p. 60.
36 Jefferys, *Anthony Crosland*, pp. 60–1.
37 Crossman to Crosland, 23 October 1956, ACP 13/10.
38 Quoted in David Reisman, *Anthony Crosland: The Mixed Economy*, Macmillan Press, 1997, p. 119.

Chapter 6: Hugh Gaitskell's Supporters

1 Brian Briavati, *Hugh Gaitskell*, Richard Cohen, 1996, p. 419.
2 Philip Williams, *Hugh Gaitskell*, Cape, 1979, p. 787.
3 Michael Foot, *Aneurin Bevan*, vol. 2, Davis-Poynter, 1973, p. 497.
4 Williams, *Hugh Gaitskell*, p. 371.
5 *Hansard*, 27–31 October 1955, col. 408.
6 Quoted in Williams, *Hugh Gaitskell*, p. 363.
7 Ibid., p. 375.
8 Jenkins, *A Life at the Centre*, p. 109.
9 Ibid., p. 148.
10 Ibid., p. 109.
11 Wyatt, *Confessions of an Optimist*, p. 225.
12 *New Statesman*, 12 March 1960.
13 Crosland, *Tony Crosland*, p. 113.
14 Ibid., p. 88.
15 Healey, *The Time of My Life*, p. 154.
16 Ibid., p. 154.
17 Interview with Julia McNeal.
18 *The Diary of Hugh Gaitskell*, ed. Philip Williams, Cape 1983, pp. 444, 457.
19 Healey, *The Time of My Life*, p. 169.
20 *The Diary of Hugh Gaitskell*, ed. Williams, p. 567.
21 *Hansard*, 2 August 1956, col. 1617 and cols 1624–6.
22 *The Diary of Hugh Gaitskell*, ed. Williams, pp. 574–5.
23 Williams, *Hugh Gaitskell*, pp. 429–30.
24 *The Diary of Hugh Gaitskell*, ed. Williams, p. 621.
25 The author first became a Labour supporter after reading Gaitskell's speeches, while a national service officer in the Coldstream Guards at the time of Suez.
26 Michael Foot, *Aneurin Bevan*, p. 516.
27 Quoted in Williams, *Hugh Gaitskell*, p. 437.
28 *Hansard*, 30 October 1956, col. 1291.
29 Healey, *The Time of My Life*, p. 169.
30 Ibid., p. 328.
31 Roy Jenkins, *The Labour Case*, Penguin, 1959, pp. 11, 146.
32 Rodgers, *Fourth Among Equals*, p. 48.
33 Briavati, *Hugh Gaitskell*, p. 304.
34 This account is based on Jefferys, *Anthony Crosland*, pp. 64–5.

35 Crossman's diaries, 11 July 1958, pp. 64–5.
36 Tony Benn, *The Years of Hope*, Arrow Books, 1995, p. 237.
37 Crosland, *Tony Crosland*, pp. 83–7.
38 *The Politics of Education*, ed. Maurice Kogan, Penguin, 1971, p. 14.
39 Benn, *The Years of Hope*, p. 312.
40 Crosland, *Tony Crosland*, p. 92.
41 Briavati, *Hugh Gaitskell*, p. 332.
42 Crosland, *Tony Crosland*, p. 93.
43 Williams, *Hugh Gaitskell*, p. 560.
44 Healey, *The Time of My Life*, p. 159; John Campbell, *Roy Jenkins*, p. 71.
45 Williams, *Hugh Gaitskell*, p. 580.
46 Crosland, *Tony Crosland*, pp. 96–7.
47 Patrick Gordon Walker, *Political Diaries*, The Historian's Press, 1991, pp. 259–60.
48 Rodgers, *Fourth Among Equals*, p. 54.
49 Williams, *Hugh Gaitskell*, pp. 610–12.
50 Ibid., p. 613.
51 Crosland, *Tony Crosland*, p. 103.
52 Williams, *Hugh Gaitskell*, p. 725.
53 Ibid., p. 702.
54 Ibid., p. 708.
55 C. A. R. Crosland, *The Conservative Enemy*, Cape, 1962, p. 127.
56 Jenkins, *A Life at the Centre*, p. 145.
57 Williams, *Hugh Gaitskell*, pp. 734–5.
58 Ibid., p. 736.
59 Healey, *The Time of My Life*, pp. 211–12.
60 Jenkins, *A Life at the Centre*, p. 147.
61 Rodgers, *Fourth Among Equals*, p. 71.
62 Crosland, *Tony Crosland*, p. 236.

Chapter 7: Harold Wilson's Ministers
1 Rodgers, *Fourth Among Equals*, p. 71.
2 Jenkins, *A Life at the Centre*, p. 148.
3 Crosland, *Tony Crosland*, pp. 115–16.
4 Ben Pimlott, *Harold Wilson*, p. 256.
5 Ibid., p. 260.
6 Crosland, *Tony Crosland*, p. 116.
7 Healey, *The Time of My Life*, p. 297.
8 Information supplied by Denis Healey.
9 Rodgers, *Fourth Among Equals*, p. 74.
10 Gordon Walker, *Political Diaries*, p. 279.
11 Jenkins, *A Life at the Centre*, p. 149.
12 Ibid., p. 150.
13 Tony Benn's diary, 10 May 1963.
14 Crosland, *Tony Crosland*, p. 117.
15 Jefferys, *Anthony Crosland*, p. 92.
16 The author heard Denis Healey speak with gusto at an open-air meeting in Salisbury market place in the run-up to the 1964 election.
17 Quoted in Pimlott, *Harold Wilson*, p. 327.
18 Healey, *The Time of My Life*, p. 253.
19 Healey, *The Time of My Life*, p. 251.
20 Crosland, *Tony Crosland*, p. 126.

21 Jenkins, *A Life at the Centre*, p. 157.
22 Crosland, *Tony Crosland*, p. 130.
23 Healey, *The Time of My Life*, p. 331.
24 Ibid., p. 253.
25 Ibid., p. 258.
26 Peter Hennessy, *The Prime Minister*, Allen Lane, 2000, p. 290.
27 Healey, *The Time of My Life*, p. 302.
28 Ibid., p. 279.
29 Jenkins, *A Life at the Centre*, p. 162.
30 *Hansard*, 5 November 1964, col. 513.
31 *Hansard*, 9 February 1965, cols 228, 241, 328.
32 *Hansard*, 13 April 1965, cols 1282–92; 'Government defeat TSR-2 censure by 26 votes', *The Times*, 14 April 1965.
33 Crosland, *Tony Crosland*, pp. 130–1.
34 Ibid., p. 131.
35 Harold Wilson, *The Labour Government, 1964–1970*, Weidenfeld & Nicolson 1971, p. 66.
36 Crossman's diaries, 22 January 1965, p. 136.
37 Ibid., p. 136.
38 *The Politics of Education*, ed. Maurice Kogan, Penguin, 1971, p. 154.
39 Crosland, *Tony Crosland*, p. 144.
40 Christopher Price in *Crosland and New Labour*, ed. Dick Leonard, Macmillan, 1999, p. 74.
41 I found that the eleven plus was an important doorstep issue in the 1964 election.
42 For example, *Early Learning*, Report of the Central Advisory Council for Education, HMSO 1955; J. E. Floud, A. H. Halsey and F. M. Martin, *Social Class and Educational Opportunity*, 1956; P. E. Vernon, ed., *Secondary School Selection*, 1957; J. W. B. Douglas, *The Home and The School*, 1964.
43 Price in *Crosland and New Labour*, p. 74; interview with Christopher Price.
44 Quoted in Jefferys, *Anthony Crosland*, p. 106.
45 See, for example, *Black Paper 1975*, J. M. Dent Ltd, 1975.
46 Crosland, *Tony Crosland*, p. 148.
47 Ibid., p. 150.
48 *The Politics of Education*, ed. Kogan, p. 94.
49 Quoted in Jefferys, *Anthony Crosland*, p. 110.
50 Jenkins, *A Life at the Centre*, pp. 176–7.
51 Sir Robin Day, *But with Respect*, Weidenfeld & Nicolson, 1993, p. 60.
52 Roy Jenkins, *Essays and Speeches*, ed. Anthony Lestor, Collins, 1967, p. 244.
53 Pimlott, *Harold Wilson*, p. 487.
54 Wilson, *The Labour Government*, p. 297.
55 *Hansard*, 31 October 1966, cols 156–6.
56 Healey, *The Time of My Life*, p. 326.
57 Neil Cameron, *In the Midst of Things*, Hodder & Stoughton, 1968, p. 149.
58 Quoted in Edward Pearce, *The Lost Leaders*, Little, Brown, 1997, p. 178; interview with Roy Hattersley.
59 Hennessy, *The Prime Minister*, p. 289.
60 Healey, *The Time of My Life*, p. 327.
61 Crosland, *Tony Crosland*, p. 152.
62 Crossman's diaries, 18 April 1965, p. 204.
63 Barbara Castle's diaries, 27 July 1965, p. 27.
64 Crossman's diaries, 3 August 1965, p. 300.
65 Ibid., 18 April 1965, p. 203.
66 Crosland, *Tony Crosland*, p. 174.

67 Crossman's diaries, 18 July 1966, p. 574.
68 Pimlott, *Harold Wilson*, pp. 424–5.
69 Jenkins, *Life at the Centre*, p. 195.
70 Edmund Dell, *The Chancellors*, p. 348.
71 Crosland, *Tony Crosland*, p. 189.
72 Ibid., p. 187.
73 Jenkins, *A Life at the Centre*, p. 218.
74 Crossman's diaries, 8 June 1967, p. 373.
75 Jenkins, *A Life at the Centre*, p. 217.
76 Edward Pearce, *Denis Healey*, Little, Brown, 2002, p. 341.

Chapter 8: The Ascendancy of Jenkins

1 Dell, *The Chancellors*, p. 347.
2 Jenkins, *A Life at the Centre*, p. 220.
3 Castle's diaries, 20 November 1967.
4 Jenkins, *A Life at the Centre*, p. 226, Castle's diaries, 21 November 1967, Crossman's diaries, 16 April 1968, p. 784.
5 Crosland, *Tony Crosland*, p. 165: interview with Dick Taverne.
6 Day, *But with Respect*, p. 54.
7 Crossman's diaries, 12 April 1968, pp. 778–9; John Campbell, *Roy Jenkins*, Weidenfeld & Nicolson, 1983, pp.116–17
8 Dell, *The Chancellors*, p. 355.
9 Jenkins, *A Life at the Centre*, pp. 220–2, 230.
10 *Hansard*, 5 December 1967, col. 1199.
11 Jenkins, *A Life at the Centre*, p. 222.
12 James Callaghan, *Times and Chance*, Collins, 1987, p. 221.
13 Jenkins, *A Life at the Centre*, p. 230.
14 Crossman's diaries, 12 January, p. 646; Public Record Office (PRO), Cabinet Records (CAB), 128/43, 12 January 1968.
15 Crosland, *Tony Crosland*, p. 194.
16 Ibid., p. 195.
17 Jenkins, *A Life at the Centre*, p. 228.
18 Callaghan, *Time and Chance*, p. 221.
19 Tony Benn's diaries, 1968–72, 12 January 1968, p. 15.
20 Crossman's diaries, 6 February 1968, p. 665.
21 Jenkins, *A Life at the Centre*, p. 222.
22 Healey, *The Time of My Life*, p. 335.
23 Quoted in Pimlott, *Harold Wilson*, p. 481; Alec Cairncross, *The Wilson Years*, The Historian's Press, p. 246.
24 Jenkins, *A Life at the Centre*, p. 228.
25 Ibid., p. 232.
26 Crossman's diaries, 17 March 1968, p. 719.
27 Benn's diaries, 14 March 1968, p. 46.
28 Dell, *The Chancellors*, p. 357.
29 Crossman's diaries, 19 March 1968, p. 724.
30 Pimlott, *Harold Wilson*, p. 503.
31 Interview with Dick Taverne.
32 Rodgers, *Fourth Among Equals*, p. 114; interview with Bill Rodgers.
33 David Owen, *Time to Declare*, Michael Joseph, 1991, p. 105.
34 Quoted in Jefferys, *Anthony Crosland*, p. 119.
35 Jenkins, *A Life at the Centre*, p. 197.

36 Rodgers, *Fourth Among Equals*, p. 115.
37 Jenkins, *A Life at the Centre*, p. 257.
38 Crossman's diaries, 27 November 1967, p. 595.
39 Jenkins, *A Life at the Centre*, p. 257.
40 Rodgers, *Fourth Among Equals*, p. 114; interview with Bill Rodgers.
41 Patrick Gordon Walker's diaries, 4 July 1968, p. 323; Healey, *The Time of My Life*, p. 329.
42 Jenkins, *A Life at the Centre*, p. 258.
43 Ibid., p. 249.
44 Ibid., p. 261.
45 Castle's diaries, 23 October 1968, p. 269; Crossman's diaries, 5 September 1968, p. 180.
46 Jenkins, *A Life at the Centre*, p. 265.
47 Healey, *The Time of My Life*, pp. 340–1.
48 Jenkins, *A Life at the Centre*, p. 278.
49 Ibid., p. 285; the author was impressed by the authority of Jenkins' conference speech.
50 Report of the Royal Commission on Trade Unions and Employers' Associations, para. 475.
51 Pimlott, *Harold Wilson*, p. 528.
52 Callaghan, *Time and Chance*, p. 274.
53 Jenkins, *A Life at the Centre*, p. 288.
54 Ibid., p. 287.
55 Crosland, *Tony Crosland*, p. 203.
56 Crossman's diaries, 24 June 1969, p. 535.
57 Healey, *The Time of My Life*, p. 347; PRO, Prime Minister's Office Records (PREM), 13/2724, Healey to Wilson, 14 January 1969.
58 PRO, PREM, note of a meeting of the Management Committee, 9 June 1969.
59 Jenkins, *A Life at the Centre*, pp. 288–9.
60 Rodgers, *Fourth Among Equals*, p. 114.
61 Jenkins, *A Life at the Centre*, pp. 289–90.
62 Crossman's diaries, 2 July 1969, p. 545.
63 Quoted in Jefferys, *Anthony Crosland*, p. 40; Crosland, *Tony Crosland*, p. 206. For the background to this see PRO, PREM 13/2598.
64 Pimlott, *Harold Wilson*, p. 546.
65 David Butler and Michael Pinto-Duschinsay, *The British General Election of 1970*, Macmillan, 1971, p. 121.
66 Jenkins, *A Life at the Centre*, p. 291.
67 Crossman's diaries, 8 March 1970, p. 847.
68 Jenkins, *A Life at the Centre*, p. 295.
69 Crossman's diaries, 8 March 1970, p. 158.
70 Jenkins, *A Life at the Centre*, p. 296.
71 Quoted in Pimlott, *Harold Wilson*, p. 553.
72 Ibid., p. 555.
73 Butler and Pinto-Duschinsay, *The British General Election of 1970*, p. 158.
74 Ibid., pp. 315–16.
75 Ibid., p. 167.
76 Jenkins, *A Life at the Centre*, pp. 299–300.
77 Ibid., p. 302.
78 Benn's diaries, 19 June 1970, p. 293.
79 Crosland, *Tony Crosland*, p. 210.
80 Jenkins, *A Life at the Centre*, p. 302.
81 Marcia Williams, *Inside Number 10*, Weidenfeld & Nicolson, 1972, p. 10.
82 Crossman's diaries, 19 June 1970, p. 949.

83 Healey, *The Time of My Life*, p. 345.
84 Pimlott, *Harold Wilson*, p. 564.
85 Dell, *The Chancellors*, p. 367.
86 Jenkins, *A Life at the Centre*, p. 302.

Chapter 9: The Spectre of Europe
 1 Pimlott, *Harold Wilson*, p. 568.
 2 Jenkins, *A Life at the Centre*, p. 307.
 3 Healey, *The Time of My Life*, p. 347; BBC TV programme 'Yesterday's Men',
 4 Jefferys, *Anthony Crosland*, p. 146; Crosland, *Tony Crosland*, p. 211; 'Yesterday's Men'.
 5 Jefferys, *Anthony Crosland*, pp. 146–7.
 6 Jenkins, *A Life at the Centre*, p. 310.
 7 Healey, *The Time of My Life*, p. 358.
 8 Crosland, *Tony Crosland*, p. 210.
 9 'A Social Democratic Britain' by Anthony Crosland in *Socialism Now*, ed. Dick Leonard, Jonathan Cape, 1974, pp. 71–95.
10 Quoted in Jefferys, *Anthony Crosland*, p. 151.
11 David Marquand, *The Progressive Dilemma*, William Heinemann, 1991, pp. 174–5.
12 Crosland, *Tony Crosland*, pp. 216–17.
13 Hugo Young, *This Blessed Plot*, Macmillan, 1998, pp. 223–4.
14 Jenkins, *A Life at the Centre*, p. 316.
15 Pimlott, *Harold Wilson*, p. 585.
16 Ibid., p. 581.
17 Kenneth O. Morgan, *Callaghan*, Oxford University Press, 1997, p. 395.
18 The *Daily Mirror*, 26 May 1971.
19 Healey, *The Time of My Life*, p. 359.
20 Crosland, *The Conservative Enemy*, p. 8.
21 Jenkins, *A Life at the Centre*, p. 318.
22 Ms notes by Crosland, May 1971, ACP 9/9, quoted in Jefferys, *Anthony Crosland*, p. 154.
23 Jenkins, *A Life at the Centre*, pp. 319–20.
24 Ibid., p. 320.
25 Crosland, *Tony Crosland*, p. 219.
26 'The speech that was never delivered', early July, ACP 4/9.
27 Crosland, *Tony Crosland*, p. 220.
28 Quoted in Jefferys, *Anthony Crosland*, pp. 155–6; ms note by Crosland on 1963 Club, 20 July 1971, ACP 4/9.
29 Crosland, *Tony Crosland*, p. 222.
30 *The Times*, 21 July 1971.
31 Pimlott, *Harold Wilson*, p. 585–6; Jenkins, *A Life at the Centre*, p. 320.
32 Healey, *The Time of My Life*, p. 360.
33 Interviews with John Horam and Philip Whitehead.
34 Jenkins, *A Life at the Centre*, p. 322.
35 Benn's diaries, 19 July 1971, p. 358; *The Times*, 20 July 1971.
36 Jenkins, *A Life at the Centre*, p. 323.
37 Benn's diaries, 19 July 1971, p. 358.
38 Pimlott, *Harold Wilson*, p. 587.
39 Jenkins, *A Life at the Centre*, p. 324.
40 Crosland, *Tony Crosland*, p. 221.
41 Jenkins, *A Life at the Centre*, p. 329.
42 Rodgers, *Fourth Among Equals*, p. 130; *Hansard*, 21–28 October 1971.
43 Crosland, *Tony Crosland*, p. 224.

44 Ibid., p. 225.

45 Ibid., p. 229; ms note by Crosland, 18 November 1971, ACP.

46 Benn's diaries, 26 July, p. 362.

47 Philip Whitehead, *The Writing on the Wall*, Michael Joseph, 1985, p. 66.

48 Healey, *The Time of My Life*, p. 329.

49 Ibid., p. 360.

50 Jenkins, *A Life at the Centre*, p. 332.

51 Ibid., p. 338.

52 Rodgers, *Fourth Among Equals*, p. 131.

53 Jenkins, *A Life at the Centre*, p. 338.

54 Benn's diaries, 11 November 1970, p. 316.

55 Jenkins, *A Life at the Centre*, pp. 341–4; Benn's diaries, 29 March 1972, pp. 420–1.

56 Benn's diaries, 5 November 1970, pp. 313–14.

57 Quoted in Pimlott, *Harold Wilson*, p. 592.

58 Roy Jenkins, *What Matters Now*, Fontana, 1972, p. 22.

59 Jenkins, *A Life at the Centre*, pp. 341–2.

60 Benn's diaries, 29 March 1971, p. 420.

61 Ibid., 10 April 1971, p. 422.

62 Jenkins, *A Life at the Centre*, p. 345.

63 Owen, *Time to Declare*, p. 194.

64 Pimlott, *Harold Wilson*, p. 595.

65 Crosland, *Tony Crosland*, pp. 239–40.

66 Healey, *The Time of My Life*, p. 367.

67 Ibid., p. 368.

68 Jenkins, *A Life at the Centre*, p. 352.

69 Press statement by Crosland, quoted in Jefferys, *Anthony Crosland*, p. 165.

70 Crosland, *Tony Crosland*, p. 244.

71 Jenkins, *A Life at the Centre*, p. 353.

Chapter 10: Return to Office and the 1976 Leadership Election

1 Benn's diaries, 16 May 1973, pp. 34–5; Jefferys, *Anthony Crosland*, p. 168.

2 Benn's diaries, 30 May 1973, pp. 42–3.

3 Whitehead, *The Writing on the Wall*, p. 122.

4 Benn's diaries, 26 September 1973, p. 61; Jefferys, *Anthony Crosland*, p. 167.

5 Healey, *The Time of My Life*, p. 346.

6 Benn's diaries, 12 June 1973, p. 46.

7 Healey, *The Time of My Life*, p. 368.

8 Crosland, *Tony Crosland*, p. 233.

9 Ibid., pp. 250–3.

10 I was elected at Chester-le-Street with a much reduced majority, with the Liberal in second place.

11 Quoted in Jefferys, *Anthony Crosland*, p. 168; Williams to Crosland, 6 February 1973, ACP 12/4.

12 Jenkins, *A Life at the Centre*, p. 351.

13 Rodgers, *Fourth Among Equals*, pp. 136–7.

14 In the author's twenty-eight years in the Commons, only Sir Geoffrey Howe's 1990 resignation speech was comparable for power and impact.

15 Owen, *Time to Declare*, p. 213.

16 Healey, *The Time of My Life*, p. 370.

17 Jenkins, *A Life at the Centre*, p. 365.

18 Ibid., pp. 368–72.

19 Rodgers, *Fourth Among Equals*, p. 139.

20 Callaghan, *Time and Chance*, p. 294.

21 Joel Barnett, *Inside the Treasury*, André Deutsch, 1982, p. 49.

22 Healey, *The Time of My Life*, p. 392.

23 Dell, *The Chancellors*, p. 401.

24 Ibid., p. 407.

25 Humphrey Cole, 'Environment Secretary' in *Crosland and New Labour*, ed. Dick Leonard, Macmillan, 1999, p. 88.

26 Quoted in Jefferys, *Anthony Crosland*, p. 176; notebook, Easter 1974, ACP 16/8.

27 August 1974, ACP 16/8.

28 Joel Barnett, *Inside the Treasury*, p. 47; Benn's diaries, 2 August 1979, p. 212.

29 Anthony Crosland, *Socialism Now*, Cape, 1974, p. 43.

30 Ibid., p. 44.

31 Benn's diaries, 10 March 1974, p. 118.

32 Review in *New Society*, 4 April 1975, quoted in Jefferys, *Anthony Crosland*, p. 174.

33 Giles Radice, 'Revisionism Re-visited', *Socialist Commentary*, May 1974.

34 Jenkins, *A Life at the Centre*, p. 374.

35 Ibid., p. 376.

36 Ibid., p. 396.

37 Ibid., p. 387.

38 Ibid., p. 388.

39 Castle's diaries, 29 July 1975, p. 156.

40 Benn's diaries, 29 July 1975, p. 208.

41 Castle's diaries, 30 July 1975, p. 159.

42 Jenkins, *A Life at the Centre*, p. 388.

43 Ibid., p. 403.

44 Benn's diaries, 18 March, pp. 347, 349.

45 Young, *This Blessed Plot*, p. 289.

46 Ibid., p. 291.

47 Jenkins, *A Life at the Centre*, p. 399.

48 Quoted in Young, *This Blessed Plot*, p. 293; a respected local councillor told the author that he was personally against the Common Market but had voted 'yes' for his grandchildren.

49 Peter Jenkins in the *Guardian*, 14 March 1975.

50 Quoted in Pimlott, *Harold Wilson*, p. 659.

51 Rodgers, *Fourth Among Equals*, p. 154.

52 Crosland, *Tony Crosland*, pp. 292–3.

53 Jenkins, *A Life at the Centre*, p. 405.

54 Ibid., p. 424.

55 Ibid., p. 426.

56 Castle's diaries, 9 June 1975, p. 410.

57 Ibid., 20 June 1975, p. 426.

58 Dell, *The Chancellors*, p. 417.

59 Pimlott, *Harold Wilson*, p. 652.

60 Healey, *The Time of My Life*, p. 448.

61 Morgan, *Callaghan*, p. 475.

62 Jenkins, *A Life at the Centre*, p. 434.

63 Crosland, *Tony Crosland*, p. 314.

64 Jefferys, *Anthony Crosland*, p. 189.

65 Jenkins, *A Life at the Centre*, p. 435.

66 Crosland, *Tony Crosland*, p. 318.

67 Jenkins, *A Life at the Centre*, p. 436.

68 Castle's diaries, 25 March 1976, p. 705.
69 Roy Jenkins, *European Diary 1977–1981*, Collins, 1989, pp. 3–4.
70 Jenkins, *A Life at the Centre*, p. 437.
71 Quoted in Hennessy, *The Prime Minister*, p. 379.
72 Healey, *The Time of My Life*, p. 448.
73 Jenkins, *A Life at the Centre*, p. 441.
74 Callaghan, *Time and Change*, p. 399.
75 Rodgers, *Fourth Among Equals*, p. 157.
76 Morgan, *James Callaghan*, p. 477; confirmed by Kenneth Morgan in a letter to the author.
77 Interview with Shirley Williams.

Chapter 11: The IMF Crisis and the Death of Crosland
 1 Callaghan, *Time and Chance*, p. 414.
 2 Healey, *The Time of My Life*, pp. 378–9.
 3 *Hansard*, 15 April 1975, col. 284.
 4 Dell, *The Chancellors*, p. 402.
 5 Healey, *The Time of My Life*, p. 384.
 6 Crosland, *Tony Crosland*, pp. 310, 305.
 7 Ibid., p. 384.
 8 Ibid., p. 324.
 9 Ibid., p. 323.
10 Ibid., p. 340.
11 Benn's diaries, 13 April 1976, pp. 557–8.
12 Crosland, *Tony Crosland*, p. 326.
13 Benn's diaries, 9 June 1976, p. 576.
14 Account of the China visit is drawn from Crosland, *Tony Crosland*, pp. 329–35.
15 Michael Palliser, 'Foreign Secretary', in *Crosland and New Labour*, ed. Dick Leonard, Macmillan, 1999, p. 102; interview with Sir Michael Palliser.
16 Benn's diaries, 23 September 1976, p. 614.
17 Crosland, *Tony Crosland*, p. 363.
18 Palliser, 'Foreign Secretary', p. 102; interview with Palliser.
19 Healey, *The Time of My Life*, pp. 426–7.
20 Dell, *The Chancellors*, p. 423.
21 Barnett, *Inside the Treasury*, p. 32.
22 White Paper on Public Expenditure 1979, Cmnd 7439.
23 Paul Martin, *The London Diaries, 1975–79*, University of Ottawa Press, 1988, pp. 136–9; quoted in Edmund Dell, *A Hard Pounding*, Oxford University Press, 1991, p. 218.
24 *Hansard*, 7 June 1976, col. 915.
25 Leo Pliatzky, *Getting and Spending*, Basil Blackwell, 1982, p. 152.
26 Healey, *The Time of My Life*, p. 419.
27 Whitehead, *The Writing on the Wall*, p. 185.
28 Crosland, *Tony Crosland*, p. 342.
29 Benn's diaries, 6 July 1970, pp. 591–2.
30 Crosland, *Tony Crosland*, p. 343.
31 Ibid., p. 353.
32 *Hansard*, 22 July 1976, col. 2011.
33 Dell, *The Chancellors*, p. 426; interview with Edmund Dell.
34 Whitehead, *The Writing on the Wall*, p. 187; interview with Gavyn Davies.
35 Notebook, August 1876, ACP 16/8.
36 Healey's diary, quoted in Edward Pearce, *Denis Healey*, Little, Brown, 2002, p. 469.
37 Healey, *The Time of My Life*, p. 429.

38 Benn's diaries, 30 September 1976, p. 616.
39 Dell, *The Chancellors*, p. 428.
40 Healey, *The Time of My Life*, p. 430.
41 Ibid., p. 431.
42 Morgan, *Callaghan*, p. 537.
43 Callaghan, *Time and Chance*, p. 435.
44 Dell, *A Hard Pounding*, p. 253.
45 Ibid., p. 251.
46 Bernard Donoghue, *Prime Minister*, Cape, 1987, pp. 89–91.
47 Dell, *A Hard Pounding*, pp. 256–8.
48 Crosland, *Tony Crosland*, pp. 377–8; Benn's diaries, 23 November 1976, pp. 653–5.
49 Benn's diaries, 24 November 1976, p. 656.
50 Crosland, *Tony Crosland*, p. 379; Benn's diaries, 25 November 1976, p. 659.
51 Rodgers, *Fourth Among Equals*, p. 165.
52 Benn's diaries, 1 December 1976, pp. 661–9.
53 Benn's diaries, 2 December 1976, pp. 670–9.
54 Healey, *The Time of My Life*, p. 431.
55 Dell, *The Chancellors*, p. 434.
56 Roy Hattersley, *Who Goes Home?*, p. 174.
57 Dell, *The Chancellors*, p. 430.
58 Crosland, *Tony Crosland*, p. 382.
59 Dell, *A Hard Pounding*, p. 271; interview with Dell.
60 Whitehead, *The Writing on the Wall*, pp. 196–7.
61 Dell, *A Hard Pounding*, pp. 285–6.
62 Whitehead, *The Writing on the Wall*, p. 22.
63 Crosland, *Tony Crosland*, p. 383.
64 Quoted in Jefferys, *Anthony Crosland*, p. 215; Tony Wright in *Crosland and New Labour*, ed. Leonard, p. 199.
65 Crosland, *Tony Crosland*, pp. 382, 385–6.
66 Jenkins, *European Diary*, p. 41.
67 Crosland, *Tony Crosland*, pp. 391–402.
68 Jenkins, *European Diary*, 19 February, pp. 49–50.
69 Gordon Brown in *Crosland and New Labour*, ed. Leonard, p. 35.

Chapter 12: The Death of Labourism and Healey's Defeat
 1 Healey, *Time of My Life*, p. 432.
 2 Ibid., p. 403.
 3 Barnett, *Inside the Treasury*, p. 143.
 4 Jenkins, *A Life at the Centre*, pp. 451–3.
 5 Jenkins, *European Diary*, pp. 193, 194.
 6 Callaghan, *Time and Chance*, p. 493.
 7 Healey, *The Time of My Life*, p. 439.
 8 Jenkins, *A Life at the Centre*, p. 483.
 9 Giles Radice, *Hansard*, 15 October 1990, col. 937.
10 Donoghue, *Prime Minister*, p. 163.
11 Healey, *The Time of My Life*, p. 462.
12 Dell, *The Chancellors*, p. 447.
13 Callaghan, *Time and Chance*, pp. 516–7; Healey, *Time of My Life*, pp. 461–2.
14 Donoghue, *Prime Minister*, p. 171.
15 Whitehead, *The Writing on the Wall*, p. 283.
16 Healey, *The Time of My Life*, p. 398.

17 Morgan, *Callaghan*, p. 665; the author remembers being called in to Jim Callaghan's office in the House of Commons at about that time to discuss the public service disputes and finding the Prime Minister in a depressed state.

18 Healey, *Time of My Life*, p. 463.

19 Donoghue, *Prime Minister*, p. 191.

20 Morgan, *Callaghan*, p. 703.

21 Healey, *Time of My Life*, p. 466.

22 Ibid., p. 467.

23 Sarah Barker Memorial Lecture, 8 September 1979; Peter Jenkins, *Mrs Thatcher's Revolution*, Jonathan Cape, 1987, pp. 141–2.

24 Jenkins, *Mrs Thatcher's Revolution*, p. 138.

25 Jenkins, *A Life at the Centre*, pp. 523–4.

26 Healey, *The Time of My Life*, p. 329.

27 Quoted in John Campbell, *Roy Jenkins*, Macmillan, 1983, p. 206.

28 Whitehead, *The Writing on the Wall*, p. 352.

29 Quoted in Ivor Crewe and Anthony King, *SDP*, Oxford University Press, 1995, p. 35.

30 Benn's diaries, 24 October 1979, p. 551.

31 Benn's diaries, 27 November 1979, p. 559.

32 Owen, *Time to Declare*, p. 441; Morgan, *Callaghan*, p. 771.

33 Healey, *The Time of My Life*, pp. 474–8.

34 Quoted in Crewe and King, *SDP*, p. 74.

35 Jenkins, *Mrs Thatcher's Revolution*, p. 143.

36 Ibid., p. 118.

37 The author's diary, 15 October 1980.

38 Quoted in Crewe and King, *SDP*, p. 74.

39 Hattersley, *Who Goes Home?*, p. 225.

40 Crewe and King, *SDP*, p. 75.

Chapter 13: Labour's Civil War and the SDP Split

1 Owen, *Time to Declare*, pp. 464–5.

2 Jenkins, *A Life at the Centre*, p. 523.

3 The author's diary, 19 January 1981.

4 Rodgers, *Fourth Among Equals*, p. 205.

5 Author's diary, 22 January 1981; Rodgers, *Fourth Among Equals*, p. 208.

6 Owen, *Time to Declare*, pp. 482, 483.

7 Jenkins, *A Life at the Centre*, p. 535.

8 Rodgers, *Fourth Among Equals*, p. 207.

9 Jenkins, *A Life at the Centre*, p. 548.

10 Crewe and King, *SDP*, pp. 101–3.

11 Hattersley, *Who Goes Home?*, p. 229.

12 The author made a number of these arguments for staying and fighting in two articles, 'Why the Labour Party Must not Split', the *Guardian* 12 January 1981 and 'Labour is still the most effective vehicle for Change', the *Guardian*, 14 December 1981.

13 Jenkins, *Mrs Thatcher's Revolution*, p. 140.

14 Healey, *The Time of My Life*, p. 481.

15 The *Observer*, 21 May 1983, quoted in Pearce, *Denis Healey*, pp. 566–7.

16 Radice, 'Heroes and Villains', the *Independent*, 2 December 1989.

17 The author's diary, 27 September 1981.

18 Whitehead, *The Writing on the Wall*, p. 405.

19 Both Philip Whitehead, then Labour MP for Derby North, and the author told Crewe and King that they would have left politics if Benn had won the deputy leadership election:

Crewe and King, *SDP*, p. 108.

20 Ibid., p. 136.

21 Owen, *Time to Declare*, p. 520.

22 Roy Jenkins, *Partnership of Principle*, Secker & Warburg, 1985, p. 51.

23 Jenkins, *A Life at the Centre*, p. 542.

24 Rodgers, *Fourth Among Equals*, p. 216.

25 Quoted in Crewe and King, *SDP*, p. 155.

26 Jenkins, *A Life at the Centre*, p. 544.

27 Interview with James Callaghan.

28 *House of Cards*, ed. Simon Hoggart, Elm Tree Books, 1988, p. 80.

29 Crewe and King *SDP*, p. 155.

30 Owen, *Time to Declare*, p. 553.

31 Rodgers, *Fourth Among Equals*, p. 232.

32 Jenkins, *Mrs Thatcher's Revolution*, p. 164.

33 Crewe and King, *SDP*, p. 163.

34 Rodgers, *Fourth Among Equals*, p. 232.

35 Healey, *The Time of My Life*, p. 481.

36 Crewe and King, *SDP*, p. 204.

37 Healey, *The Time of My Life*, p. 480.

38 Jenkins, *A Life at the Centre*, pp. 603–4.

39 John Cole, *As It Seemed to Me*, Phoenix, 1996, p. 248.

Chapter 14: Vigorous Old Age
1 *Hansard*, 27 February 1984, col. 42.

2 Healey, *The Time of My Life*, p. 507; Benn's diaries, 27 February 1984, p. 337.

3 Healey, *The Time of My Life*, pp. 524–5.

4 Ibid., p. 528; interview with Lord Temple Morris.

5 Healey, *The Time of My Life*, p. 533.

6 Peter Kellner, the *Independent*, 13 June 1987.

7 Ivor Crewe, the *Guardian*, 16 June 1987.

8 Jenkins, *A Life at the Centre*, p. 583.

9 Ibid., p. 591; see Owen, *Time to Declare*, p. 654 for Owen's account of the row.

10 Jenkins, *A Life at the Centre*, p. 587.

11 The *Observer*, 15 June 1986, quoted in Crewe and King, *SDP*, p. 347.

12 *Anatomy of Decline*, ed. Brian Brivati and Richard Cockett, Cassell, 1995, p. 148; Crewe and King, *SDP*, p. 451.

13 Jenkins, *A Life at the Centre*, p. 617.

14 Healey, *The Time of My Life*, p. 566.

15 Ashdown, *The Ashdown Diaries, 1985–1997*, p. 345.

16 Roy Jenkins, *Churchill*, Macmillan, 2001, p. 912.

17 Ashdown, *The Ashdown Diaries*, p. 346.

18 Ibid., p. 440.

19 Conversation with the author.

20 Interviews with Edward Heath and James Callaghan.

Conclusion
1 Giles Radice, *Labour's Path to Power: the New Revisionism*, Macmillan, 1989.

2 For example Andrew Rawnsley, *Servants of the People*, Hamish Hamilton, 2000, and James Naughtie, *The Rivals*, Fourth Estate, 2001.

3 Naughtie, *The Rivals*, p. 283.

4 Quoted by David Lipsey, 'Revisionists Revise', in *Crosland and New Labour*, ed. Dick

US envelope sizes

Description	Size (inches)
#6 1/4	3 1/2 × 6
#6 1/2	3 1/2 × 6 1/4
#6 3/4	3 5/8 × 6 1/2
#7	3 3/4 × 6 3/4
Check Size	3 5/8 × 8 5/8
#9	3 7/8 × 8 7/8
#10	4 1/8 × 9 1/2
#14	5 × 11 1/2

Letter	216 × 356	8 1/2 × 14
Legal	216 × 356	8 1/2 × 14
Ledger / Tabloid	279 × 432	11 × 17

C4 size envelopes hold an A4 sheet unfolded

162mm

C5 size envelopes hold an A4 sheet folded once or an A5 sheet unfolded

229mm

DL size envelopes hold an A4 sheet folded twice or an A5 sheet folded once

110mm
220mm

1 oz	=	28.3495 g
1 g	=	0.03527 oz
1 lb	=	453.59 g
1 g	=	0.002204 lb
1 kg	=	2.2046 lb
1 t	=	1016.0469 kg
1 kg	=	0.000984 t
1 UK gal	=	4.546 litre
1 litre	=	0.2199 UK gal

1 in^3	=	16.387 cm^3
1 cm^3	=	0.06102 in^3
1 ft^3	=	0.02831 m^3
1 m^3	=	35.3147 ft^3
1 yd^3	=	0.76455 m^3
1 m^3	=	1.30795 yd^3
1 US gal	=	3.7854 litre
1 litre	=	0.2642 US gal
1 US gal	=	0.8327 UK gal

1 in^2	=	6.4516 cm^2
1 cm^2	=	0.155 in^2
1 ft^2	=	0.0929 m^2
1 m^2	=	10.7639 ft^2
1 miles^2	=	2.5899 km^2
1 km^2	=	0.3861 miles^2
1 acres	=	0.4046 ha
1 ha	=	2.471 acres

Temperature

0°F	32°F	212°F
-18°C	0°C	100°C

$$F = {}^9/_5 C + 32 \qquad C = {}^5/_9 (F-32)$$

A2
420 × 594mm
16 1/2 × 23 3/8

A3
297 × 420mm
11 3/4 × 16 1/2

A4
210 × 297mm
8 1/4 × 11 3/4

A5
148 × 210mm
5 7/8 × 8 1/4

A6
105 ×
148mm
4 1/8 × 5 7/8

Conversion tables

1 in	=	2.54 cm
1 cm	=	0.3937 in
1 ft	=	0.3048 m
1 m	=	3.2808 ft
1 yd	=	0.9144 m
1 m	=	1.0936 yd
1 mile	=	1.6093 km
1 km	=	0.6213 mile

Speed

MPH	30	40	50	60	70	80	Km = 8/5 m
KPH	48	64	80	96	112	128	M = 5/8 Km

D A John Dickinson product

www.BlacknRed.com

saaangregory21@hotmail.com

fredfunkyfox@yahoo.co.uk

clarkson61@wanadoo.co.uk

Personal Information

Black n' Red

If this book is found please contact

Name	Dates of use

Guide to book contents

Important contact details

bingo@mr-bingo.co.uk

whiheya@bpplaw.co.uk

benjamin.dodds@durham.ac.uk

beth.atkins@educationconnections.co.uk

kristen.holt@gmail.com

mjewitt@brookeffing.com

aaxpse@nottingham.ac.uk

Useful Information

Black n' Red

World time zones

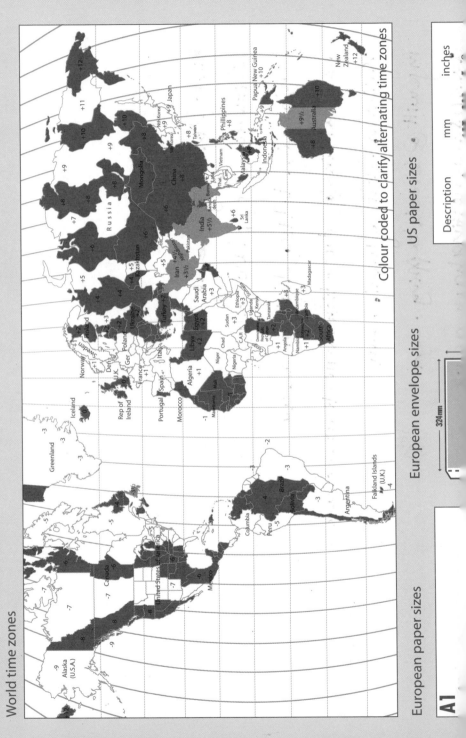

Colour coded to clarify/alternating time zones

European paper sizes

European envelope sizes

US paper sizes

324mm

Description	mm	inches

A1

Leonard, Macmillan, 1999, p. 15.

5 A number of Labour MPs, including the author, had been urging a revision of Clause IV (iv). See *Labour's Path to Power*, p. 14, and 'Southern Discomfort', Fabian Society, 1992, p. 19.

6 Tony Blair, 'My Vision for Britain', in *What Needs to Change*, ed. Giles Radice, HarperCollins, 1996, p. 6.

Index

Heath, Edward
Balliol College, Oxford 21–2
Britain in Europe 229–30
candidate for Chancellor of Oxford
University 324
coalition with Liberals 219
European Community 190, 192, 195–6,
199–200, 202
General Elections
(1970) 182
(1974 February) 218–19
government incomes policy 221
Jenkins 14, 146–7, 241
maiden speech on Europe 76
miners 218
opposition to 193–4, 198
Oxford Union 26
Suez Crisis 104
trade unions 213
Heinemann publishers 66, 81
Heller, Richard 301
Henderson, Sir Nicholas 22
Heseltine, Michael 216
Hillary, Richard, *The Last Enemy* 23
Hitler, Adolf 18–19
Czechoslovakia 19–20, 27
defeat of 53
facing defeat 51
Munich Agreement 27
Poland (1 September 1939) 28–9
Russia (June 1941) 37
Hogg, Quintin 27
Hoggart, Simon, *Observer* 309
Holland, Stuart 212–13
Hong Kong 136, 283
Houghton, Douglas 175, 201, 205
House of Lords, abolition of 290
Housing Finance Act 215, 223
Howard, Anthony 129
Howard, George 21
Howard, Professor Michael 147
Howell, Denis 116
Hoyle, Doug 305
Hudson, Hugh 319
Hughes, Cledwyn 162, 235–6
Hughes, Simon 310
Humphries, Barry 324
Hungary 63, 103–6
Hutton, Graham, *Spectator* 95

Iceland, cod-war 248–9
IMF 243
agreement 263–4, 276
annual meeting (October 1977) 271
crisis 243–5, 243–69, 250–69, 329, 332
negotiations 265
package 270–1

Washington meeting 172
In Place of Strife 173–8, 184–5, 191, 213,
278, 329
incomes policy 244, 276
Independent Commission on the Voting
System 316, 327
Indonesia, frontier war in Borneo 148
Industrial Board 173
Industrial and Commercial Finance
Corporation (ICFC) 60–1
Industrial Relations Act 213, 329
Industry Act 290
Industry White Paper 223
Institute of Strategic Studies 118
IRA 226
Iron Curtain 317
Israel, Suez Crisis 104
Italy
armistice (8 September 1943) 42
campaign 40–53
General Election (1948) 65
King of 42
Socialists 65, 73

Japan, surrender 59
Jay, Douglas 23, 80, 91
Campaign for Democratic Socialism
116
Forward 113
Gaitskell 100
General Election (1959) 112
The Times letter 103
Jebb, Gladwyn 65
Jenkins, Arthur 13–16, 20, 25, 30, 48, 54,
67
Jenkins, Charles 83, 157
Jenkins, Clive 291, 312
Jenkins, Cynthia 83
Jenkins, Edward 83, 131–2, 157
Jenkins, Hattie 14, 25, 83
Jenkins, Jennifer 31–2, 39, 60–1, 124, 140,
200
Benn 230
Cherie Blair 327
Frognal Gardens 112
General Election (1970) 182–3
Jenkins, Peter
Guardian 290, 299–300
Owen's political obituary 323
Jenkins, Roy 1, 73, 76
Alliance 306, 321, 323
Prime Minister designate 306, 322
allies 220
ambition to become Labour MP 33,
54–5
American Embassy job 39
Anglesey speech 236–8